P9-DBP-572

Featuring

Realemon and *Eagle Brand*

IF IT'S BORDEN, IT'S GOT TO BE GOOD! – not just a slogan but a commitment to quality that we live by. The Borden Company has a rich heritage of bringing quality food products to the Canadian consumer and our dedication to quality is carried throughout the recipes we develop. We are proud to present this collection of our "Best Recipes" featuring the best from Realemon Lemon Juice and Eagle Brand Sweetened Condensed Milk.

Realemon brand lemon juice is a trusted Borden brand. It is a wonderfully versatile ingredient – adding real lemon zing to everything from appetizers and fresh salads to hearty main dishes, beverages and desserts.

Eagle Brand Sweetened Condensed Milk has been the classic dessert-maker for over 125 years. Its creamy – rich goodness is the key ingredient in the best candies, custards, cookies, ice creams, cheesecakes and pies. Eagle Brand recipes provide the perfect dessert choice for every occasion.

Each of the over 140 recipes contained in this collection has been carefully researched, developed and tested by the Borden Kitchens' home economists to assure you great taste and convenient preparation. We hope you will find Borden "Best Recipes" a valuable source of new ideas and traditional favourites to delight your family and friends.

Good cooking!

The Borden Company, Ltd.

Pictured on the cover:	*Baked Apricot Chicken*
	Vegetables with Blender Hollandaise Sauce
	Creamy Baked Cheesecake with Peach Melba Topping
	White Sangria
Recipe development:	Borden Kitchens – Annie Watts Cloncs, Director
	Veda Rose, Senior Home Economist
	Charlene Sneed, Senior Home Economist
	Dale & Colnett Ltd. – Sharon Dale and Joan Colnett.
Photography and coordination:	Glenn Peterson, Steve McHugh,
	Robert Wigington, Gordon Meinecke,
	Mallard Marketing Associates, Inc.

Editing and production: Les Éditions de la Chenelière inc.
    Design: Norman Lavoie

Copyright © 1989 by The Borden Company, Ltd.

ISBN 2-89310-026-0

Legal Deposit: 3rd quarter 1989
Bibliothèque nationale du Québec
National Library of Canada

Printed in Canada

CONTENTS

APPETIZERS

GUACAMOLE

2   ripe medium avocados, seeded, peeled
2   Tbsp. (30 mL) REALEMON Lemon Juice or
       REALIME Lime Juice
1   Tbsp. (15 mL) finely-chopped onion
1   tsp. (5 mL) seasoned salt
1/4 tsp. (1 mL) hot pepper sauce
1/4 tsp. (1 mL) garlic powder
     Tortilla chips

In medium bowl, mash avocados. Add Realemon, onion, salt, pepper sauce and garlic powder; mix well. Chill thoroughly to blend flavours. Garnish as desired. Serve with tortilla chips. Cover leftovers; refrigerate. Makes about 11/2 cups (375 mL).

Variations: Add 1 or more of the following: cooked crumbled bacon, coarsely-chopped water chestnuts, chopped tomato or chopped chilies.

Pictured at left: on plate – Teriyaki Wing Dings and Teriyaki Scallop roll-ups; in bowl – Guacamole.

TERIYAKI WING DINGS

1/3	cup (75 mL) REALEMON Lemon Juice
1/4	cup (50 mL) ketchup
1/4	cup (50 mL) soya sauce
1/4	cup (50 mL) vegetable oil
2	Tbsp. (30 mL) packed brown sugar
1/4	tsp. (1 mL) garlic powder
1/4	tsp. (1 mL) pepper
3	lbs. (750 g) chicken wings, cut at joints, wing tips removed

In medium bowl, combine Realemon, ketchup, soya sauce, oil, sugar, garlic powder and pepper; mix well. Place chicken pieces in shallow baking dish; pour marinade over. Cover; refrigerate overnight, turning occasionally. Preheat oven to 375°F (190°C). Arrange chicken on rack in foil-lined shallow baking pan. Bake 40 to 45 min., basting occasionally with marinade. Cover leftovers; refrigerate. Makes about 3 dozen appetizers.

TERIYAKI SCALLOP ROLL-UPS

1/3	cup (75 mL) REALIME Lime Juice
1/4	cup (50 mL) soya sauce
1/4	cup (50 mL) vegetable oil
1	Tbsp. (15 mL) packed brown sugar
2	cloves garlic, crushed, chopped
1/2	tsp. (2 mL) pepper
12	large scallops, cut in half
24	fresh pea pods
12	water chestnuts, cut in half
12	slices bacon, partially cooked, cut in half crosswise

In small bowl, combine Realime, soya sauce, oil, sugar, garlic and pepper; mix well. Wrap 1 scallop half, 1 pea pod and 1 water chestnut half in each bacon slice; secure with wooden pick. Place in shallow baking dish; pour marinade over. Cover; refrigerate 4 hours or overnight, turning occasionally. Preheat oven to 450°F (230°C). Place roll-ups on rack in foil-lined shallow baking pan; bake 6 min. Turn; continue baking 6 min. or until bacon is crisp. Serve hot. Cover leftovers; refrigerate. Makes about 2 dozen appetizers.

SWEET 'N' SOUR MEATBALLS

11/2	lbs. (750 g) lean ground beef
1	can (10 ozs./284 mL) water chestnuts, drained, chopped
2	eggs
1/3	cup (75 mL) dry bread crumbs
4	tsp. (20 mL) chicken bouillon mix
1	Tbsp. (15 mL) Worcestershire sauce
	Vegetable oil
1	cup (250 mL) water
1/2	cup (125 mL) packed brown sugar
1/2	cup (125 mL) REALEMON Lemon Juice
1/4	cup (50 mL) ketchup
2	Tbsp. (30 mL) corn starch
1/4	tsp. (1 mL) salt
1	large green pepper, cut into squares
	Chopped parsley (optional)

In large bowl, combine meat, water chestnuts, eggs, bread crumbs, bouillon mix and Worcestershire sauce; mix well. Shape into 11/4-inch (3 cm) balls. In large frypan, brown meatballs in hot oil, a few at a time. Remove from pan; pour off fat. In frypan, combine water, sugar, Realemon, ketchup, corn starch and salt; mix well. Over medium heat, cook and stir until mixture boils and thickens. Reduce heat. Add meatballs; simmer, uncovered, 10 min. Add green pepper; heat through. Garnish with parsley if desired. Cover leftovers; refrigerate. Makes about 5 dozen appetizers.

WARM HERB CHEESE SPREAD

3   *pkgs. (125 g* each*) cream cheese, softened*
2   *Tbsp. (30 mL) milk*
2   *Tbsp. (30 mL) REALEMON Lemon Juice*
1/4   *tsp. (1 mL)* each *dried basil, oregano, marjoram* and *thyme leaves*
     Pinch garlic powder
     Assorted crackers or *raw vegetables*

Preheat oven to 350°F (180°C). In small mixer bowl, beat cream cheese just until smooth. Gradually beat in milk, then Realemon. Stir in basil, oregano, marjoram, thyme and garlic powder. Pour into 2-cup (500 mL) casserole. Cover with foil; bake 10 min. or until hot. Garnish as desired. Serve warm as a spread for crackers or with raw vegetables for dipping. Cover leftovers; refrigerate. Makes about 2 cups (500 mL).

Microwave: Prepare cheese mixture as above. Turn into 3-cup (750 mL) microwave-safe bowl. Cover loosely with wax paper. Microwave at MEDIUM (50%) 4 to 5 min. or until hot. Stir well before serving. Proceed as above.

RUMAKI

1/4	cup (50 mL) REALEMON Lemon Juice
1/4	cup (50 mL) soya sauce
1/4	cup (50 mL) vegetable oil
3	Tbsp. (45 mL) ketchup
2	cloves garlic, crushed, chopped
1/2	tsp. (2 mL) pepper
12	chicken livers, cut in half (about 1/2 lb./ 250g)
12	water chestnuts, cut in half
12	slices bacon, cut in half crosswise
	Brown sugar

In small bowl, combine Realemon, soya sauce, oil, ketchup, garlic and pepper; mix well. Wrap 1 liver half and 1 water chestnut half in each bacon slice; secure with wooden pick. Place in shallow baking dish; pour marinade over. Cover; refrigerate 4 hours or overnight, turning occasionally. Preheat oven to 450°F (230°C). Roll rumaki in brown sugar; place on rack in foil-lined shallow baking pan. Bake 10 min. Turn; continue baking 15 min. or until bacon is crisp. Serve hot. Cover leftovers; refrigerate. Makes 2 dozen appetizers.

SALADS AND DRESSINGS

TROPICAL CHICKEN SALAD

4   cups (1 L) cubed cooked chicken or turkey
2   large oranges, peeled, sectioned, drained
11/2 cups (375 mL) cut-up fresh pineapple, drained
1   cup (250 mL) seedless green grape halves
1   cup (250 mL) sliced celery
3/4 cup (175 mL) mayonnaise or salad dressing
3 to 4 Tbsp. (45 to 60 mL) REALEMON Lemon Juice
1/2 tsp. (2 mL) ground ginger
1/2 tsp. (2 mL) salt
1/2 to 3/4 cup (125 to 175 mL) cashews
    Lettuce leaves or hollowed-out pineapple shells

In large bowl, combine chicken, orange sections, pineapple, grapes and celery; chill. In small bowl, combine mayonnaise, Realemon, ginger and salt; chill. Just before serving, combine chicken mixture, dressing and nuts. Serve on lettuce leaves or in hollowed-out pineapple shells. Cover leftovers; refrigerate. Makes 4 to 6 servings.

Pictured at left: Marinated Confetti Coleslaw, Sweet Onion Dressing and Tropical Chicken Salad.

SWEET ONION SALAD DRESSING

(Pictured on previous page.)

1	cup (250 mL) vegetable oil
1/2	cup (125 mL) sugar
1/3	cup (75 mL) REALEMON Lemon Juice
1/3	cup (75 mL) ketchup
1	small onion, cut up
1	Tbsp. (15 mL) Worcestershire sauce

In blender or food processor, combine oil, sugar, Realemon, ketchup, onion and Worcestershire sauce; cover and blend until smooth. Chill to blend flavours. Cover leftovers; refrigerate. Makes about 2 cups (500 mL).

MARINATED CONFETTI COLESLAW

(Pictured on previous page.)

5	cups (1.25 L) coarsely-shredded cabbage
1	firm large tomato, seeded, diced
1/2	cup (125 mL) chopped green pepper
1/3	cup (75 mL) sliced green onions
1/2	cup REALEMON Lemon Juice
1/3	cup (75 mL) vegetable oil
1/4	cup (50 mL) sugar
1	tsp. (5 mL) salt
1/2	tsp. (2 mL) dry mustard

In medium bowl, combine cabbage, tomato, pepper and onions. In small saucepan, combine Realemon, oil, sugar, salt and mustard; bring to boil. Pour over vegetables. Cover; chill 4 hours or overnight to blend flavours. Drain before serving. Cover leftovers; refrigerate. Makes 6 to 8 servings.

CALIFORNIA CAESAR SALAD

1/2	cup (125 mL) vegetable oil
1/3	cup (75 mL) REALEMON Lemon Juice
1	egg, beaten *
2	cloves garlic, crushed, chopped
2	medium heads romaine lettuce, torn into bite-size pieces (about 8 cups/ 2 L)
2	medium tomatoes, seeded, diced
1	ripe avocado, seeded, peeled, sliced
1/3	cup (75 mL) grated Parmesan cheese
1/4	cup (50 mL) sliced green onions
1	cup (250 mL) garlic croutons
1/4	cup (50 mL) cooked crumbled bacon or imitation bacon bits

In 2-cup (500 mL) jar with tight-fitting lid or cruet, combine oil, Realemon, egg and garlic; shake well. Chill to blend flavours. Just before serving, in large salad bowl combine romaine, tomatoes, avocado, cheese, onions, croutons and bacon. Toss with dressing. Cover leftovers; refrigerate. Makes 6 servings.

* Use only clean, uncracked egg.

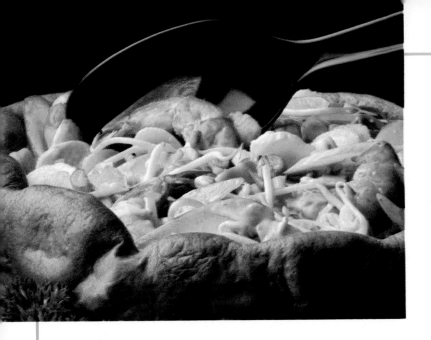

CHUNKY BLUE CHEESE SALAD DRESSING

1	*cup (250 mL) crumbled blue cheese, divided*
1	*pkg. (125 g) cream cheese, softened*
1/2	*cup (125 mL) vegetable oil*
3	*Tbsp. (45 mL) REALEMON Lemon Juice*
2	*tsp. (10 mL) sugar*

In small mixer bowl, beat 1/2 cup (125 mL) of the blue cheese and cream cheese until smooth; gradually beat in oil, then Realemon. Stir in sugar and remaining blue cheese. Chill to blend flavours. Cover leftovers; refrigerate. Makes about 12/3 cups (400 mL).

CREAMY RUSSIAN SALAD DRESSING

1	*cup (250 mL) mayonnaise* or *salad dressing*
1/3	*cup (75 mL) chili sauce*
1/4	*cup (50 mL) sliced green onions*
1/4	*cup (50 mL) REALEMON Lemon Juice*
2	*tsp. (10 mL) sugar*

In small bowl, combine mayonnaise, chili sauce, green onions, Realemon and sugar. Chill to blend flavours. Cover leftovers; refrigerate. Makes about 12/3 cups (400 mL).

ORIENTAL SHRIMP SALAD
WITH PUFF BOWL

3/4 cup (175 mL) mayonnaise or salad dressing
1/4 cup (50 mL) REALEMON Lemon Juice
1 Tbsp. (15 mL) prepared horseradish
1/4 to 1/2 tsp. (1 to 2 mL) garlic salt
1 lb. (500 g) small raw shrimp, peeled, deveined, cooked
4 ozs. (125 g) fresh pea pods*
1 can (10 ozs./284 mL) sliced water chestnuts, drained
1 cup (250 mL) sliced fresh mushrooms
1 cup (250 mL) diagonally-sliced celery
1 cup (250 mL) fresh bean sprouts
1/4 cup (50 mL) sliced green onions
Puff Bowl or lettuce leaves

In large bowl, combine mayonnaise, Realemon, horseradish and garlic salt. Add shrimp, pea pods, water chestnuts, mushrooms, celery, bean sprouts and green onions; mix well. Cover; chill to blend flavours. Just before serving, spoon into Puff Bowl or lettuce leaves. Cover leftovers; refrigerate. Makes 6 servings.

* Or substitute 1 pkg. (170 g) frozen pea pods, thawed.

PUFF BOWL

2 eggs
1/2 cup (125 mL) all
        purpose flour

1/2 cup (125 mL) milk
1/4 tsp. (1 mL) salt
2 Tbsp. (30 mL) butter, melted

Preheat oven to 425°F (220°C). In small mixer bowl, beat eggs until frothy. Gradually beat in flour; beat until smooth. Add milk, salt and butter; mix well. Pour into well-greased 9-inch (23 cm) pie plate. Bake 15 min. Reduce oven temperature to 350°F (180°C); continue baking 10 to 15 min. or until browned. Cool.

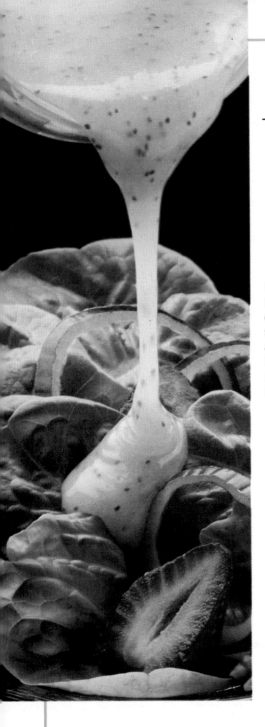

CELERY SEED SALAD DRESSING

1/4	cup (50 mL) sugar
1/4	cup (50 mL) REALEMON Lemon Juice
2	tsp. (10 mL) cider vinegar
1	tsp. (5 mL) dry mustard
1/2	tsp. (2 mL) salt
1/2	cup (125 mL) vegetable oil
1	tsp. (5 mL) celery seed or poppy seed

In blender container combine sugar, Realemon, vinegar, mustard and salt; cover and blend until smooth. On low speed, continue blending, slowly adding oil. Stir in celery seed. Chill to blend flavours. Cover leftovers; refrigerate. Makes about 1 cup (250 mL).

CHICKEN SALAD SUPREME

1	cup (250 mL) mayonnaise or salad dressing
1/4	cup (50 mL) REALIME Lime Juice
1	tsp. (5 mL) salt
1/4	tsp. (1 mL) ground nutmeg
4	cups (1 L) cubed cooked chicken or turkey
1	can (10 ozs./284 mL) mandarin orange segments, drained
1	cup (250 mL) seedless green grape halves
3/4	cup (175 mL) chopped celery
1/2	cup (125 mL) slivered almonds, toasted
	Lettuce leaves

In large bowl, combine mayonnaise, Realime, salt and nutmeg. Add chicken, orange segments, grapes, celery and almonds; mix well. Chill. Serve on lettuce leaves. Cover leftovers; refrigerate. Makes 4 to 6 servings.

MAGIC MAYONNAISE

1   can EAGLE BRAND Sweetened Condensed Milk
1/2 cup (125 mL) vinegar
1/2 cup (125 mL) vegetable oil
1   tsp. (5 mL) dry mustard
1   tsp. (5 mL) salt
    Pinch cayenne pepper
1   egg *

In small mixer bowl, combine Eagle Brand, vinegar, oil, mustard, salt, pepper and egg. Beat until mixture thickens, about 2 min. Chill to blend flavours. Cover leftovers; refrigerate. Makes about 2 1/2 cups (625 mL).

* Use only clean, uncracked egg.

DIETER'S MOCK MAYONNAISE

1   cup (250 mL) low fat cottage cheese
2   Tbsp. (30 mL) REALEMON Lemon Juice
2   egg yolks *
    Pinch cayenne pepper
1/4 tsp. (1 mL) prepared mustard
1/4 tsp. (1 mL) onion powder
    Salt

In blender container, blend cottage cheese until smooth. Add Realemon, egg yolks, pepper, mustard and onion powder. Cover and blend until smooth. Add salt to taste. Chill to blend flavours. Cover leftovers; refrigerate. Makes about 1 cup (250 mL).

* Use only clean, uncracked eggs.

MARINATED ORIENTAL BEEF SALAD

1	*flank steak (about 1 lb./ 500 g)*
1/3	*cup (75 mL) REALEMON Lemon Juice*
1/4	*cup (50 mL) ketchup*
1/4	*cup (50 mL) vegetable oil*
1	*Tbsp. (15 mL) packed brown sugar*
1/4	*tsp. (1 mL) garlic powder*
1/4	*tsp. (1 mL) ground ginger*
1/4	*tsp. (1 mL) pepper*
2	*cups (500 mL) sliced fresh mushrooms*
1	*can (10 ozs./ 284 mL) sliced water chestnuts, drained*
1	*medium sweet onion, sliced, separated into rings*
4	*ozs. (125 g) fresh pea pods **
	Lettuce leaves
	Tomato wedges

Broil meat 5 min. on each side or to desired doneness; slice diagonally into thin strips. In large bowl combine Realemon, ketchup, oil, sugar, garlic powder, ginger and pepper; mix well. Add meat, mushrooms, water chestnuts and onion; mix well. Cover; refrigerate 8 hours or overnight, stirring occasionally. Before serving, add pea pods. Serve on lettuce leaves; garnish with tomato. Cover leftovers; refrigerate. Makes 4 servings.

* Or substitute 1 pkg. (170 g) frozen pea pods, thawed.

VERSATILE LEMON SALAD DRESSING

1/2	cup (125 mL) REALEMON Lemon Juice
1/2	cup (125 mL) vegetable oil
1/3	cup (75 mL) white or red wine
2	Tbsp. (30 mL) grated Parmesan cheese
2	tsp. (10 mL) sugar
1	tsp. (5 mL) Worcestershire sauce
3/4	tsp. (4 mL) garlic salt
1/2	tsp. (2 mL) pepper
1/2	tsp. (2 mL) dried thyme leaves, crushed

In 2-cup (500 mL) jar with tight-fitting lid or cruet, combine Realemon, oil, wine, cheese, sugar, Worcestershire sauce, garlic salt, pepper and thyme; shake well. Chill to blend flavours. Use as salad dressing or marinade. Cover leftovers; refrigerate. Makes about 11/3 cups (325 mL).

To use as marinade: In shallow baking dish, pour dressing over chicken parts, salmon, haddock or other firm-fleshed fish; marinate several hours or overnight. Bake, grill or broil to desired doneness.

VEGETABLE PASTA SALAD

3	cups (750 mL) spiral-shaped pasta
1/2	cup (125 mL) vegetable oil
1/3	cup (75 mL) REALEMON Lemon Juice
2	Tbsp. (30 mL) grated Parmesan cheese
2	Tbsp. (30 mL) water
1	pkg. (42 g) dry Italian salad dressing mix
11/2	cups (375 mL) sliced zucchini
2	small tomatoes, seeded, diced
1	cup (250 mL) shredded carrots
1	cup (250 mL) sliced fresh mushrooms

Cook pasta according to package directions; drain. In 2-cup (500 mL) jar with tight-fitting lid or cruet, combine oil, Realemon, cheese, water and salad dressing mix; shake well. In large bowl, combine **hot** pasta, dressing, zucchini, tomatoes, carrots and mushrooms. Chill 4-6 hours or overnight. Cover leftovers; refrigerate. Makes 8 to 10 servings.

JELLIED CHERRY WALDORF SALAD

2	cups (500 mL) boiling water
2	pkg. (85 g) cherry jelly powder
1	cup (250 mL) cold water
1/4	cup (50 mL) REALEMON Lemon Juice
1 1/2	cups (375 mL) chopped apples
1	cup (250 mL) chopped celery
1/2	cup (125 mL) chopped walnuts or *pecans*
	Lettuce leaves
	Apple slices (optional)
	Celery leaves (optional)

In medium bowl, pour boiling water over jelly powder; stir until dissolved. Add cold water and Realemon; chill until partially set. Fold in apples, celery and nuts. Pour into lightly-oiled 6-cup (1.5 L) mold or 9-inch (2.5 L) square baking pan. Chill until set, 4 to 6 hours or overnight. Unmold and serve on lettuce leaves. Garnish with apple and celery leaves if desired. Cover leftovers; refrigerate. Makes 8 to 10 servings.

BEVERAGES

LEMONADE

Sugar
REALEMON Lemon Juice
Cold Water

To make about:
1 cup/250 mL
- 2   *Tbsp. (30 mL) sugar*
- 2   *Tbsp. (30 mL) REALEMON*
- 3/4   *cup (175 mL) cold water*

4 cups/1 L
- 1/2   *cup (125 mL) sugar*
- 1/2   *cup (125 mL) REALEMON*
- 3 1/4   *cups (800 mL) cold water*

16 cups/4 L
- 2   *cups (500 mL) sugar*
- 2   *cups (500 mL) REALEMON*
- 12   *cups (3 L) cold water*

32 cups/8 L
- 4   *cups (1 L) sugar*
- 4   *cups (1 L) REALEMON*
- 26   *cups (6.5 L) cold water*

Minted Lemonade: Stir 2 to 3 drops peppermint extract into 4 cups (1 L) lemonade.

Pink Lemonade: Stir 1 to 2 tsp. (5 to 10 mL) grenadine syrup *or* 1 or 2 drops red food colour into 4 cups (1 L) lemonade.

Slushy Lemonade: In blender container, combine 1/2 cup (125 mL) Realemon and 1/2 cup (125 mL) sugar with 1 cup (250 mL) water; add ice to make 4 cups (1L). Cover and blend until smooth. Serve immediately. Makes about 4 cups (1 L).

Sparkling Lemonade: Substitute club soda for cold water.

HOMEMADE IRISH CREAM LIQUEUR

1	can EAGLE BRAND Sweetened Condensed Milk
1 to 11/2	cups (250 to 375 mL) Irish whiskey
1	cup (250 mL) table cream
3	eggs*
1	Tbsp. (15 mL) chocolate syrup
1/2	tsp. (2 mL) coconut extract (optional)

In blender container, combine Eagle Brand, whiskey, cream, eggs, syrup and coconut extract if desired. Cover and blend until smooth. Serve over ice. Store, tightly covered, in refrigerator up to 1 month. Stir before serving. Makes about 4 cups (1 L).

Mixer Method: In large mixer bowl, beat eggs; beat in remaining ingredients until smooth and well blended. Proceed as above.

* Use only clean, uncracked eggs.

HOMEMADE CREAM LIQUEUR

1 can *EAGLE BRAND Sweetened Condensed Milk*
1 1/4 cups (300 mL) flavoured liqueur (almond, coffee, orange or mint)
1 cup (250 mL) table cream
4 eggs*

In blender container, combine Eagle Brand, liqueur, cream and eggs. Cover and blend until smooth. Serve over ice and garnish if desired. Store, tightly covered, in refrigerator up to 1 month. Stir before serving. Makes about 4 cups (1 L).

Mixer Method: In large mixer bowl, beat eggs; beat in remaining ingredients until smooth and well blended. Proceed as above.

* Use only clean, uncracked eggs.

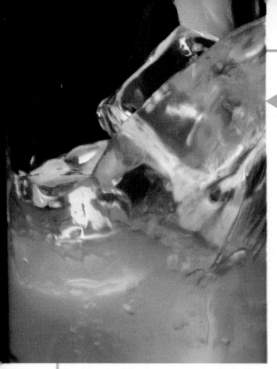

LEMONY ICED TEA

**6   cups (1.5 L) brewed tea,
        chilled
1/2   cup (125 mL) REALEMON
        Lemon Juice
3/4   cup (175 mL) sugar
        Ice**

In pitcher, combine tea, Realemon and sugar; stir until sugar dissolves. Chill; serve over ice. Makes about 7 cups (1.75 L).

MULLED CIDER

**2   quarts (2 L) apple cider
3/4 to 1 cup (175 to 250 mL) REALEMON Lemon Juice
1   cup (250 mL) packed brown sugar
8   whole cloves
2   cinnamon sticks
3/4   cup (175 mL) light rum (optional)
        Additional cinnamon sticks (optional)**

In large saucepan, combine cider, Realemon, sugar, cloves and 2 cinnamon sticks; bring to a boil. Reduce heat; simmer, uncovered, 10 min. to blend flavours. Remove spices; add rum just before serving if desired. Serve hot with cinnamon sticks if desired. Makes about 8 cups (2 L).

Microwave: In deep 4-quart (4 L) microwave-safe bowl, combine ingredients as above. Cover loosely with wax paper. Microwave at HIGH (100%) 13 to 14 min. or until heated through. Proceed as above.

Note: Can be served cold.

ORANGE PINEAPPLE PUNCH

1 can *(48 ozs/1.36 L) pineapple juice, chilled*
1 1/2 *cups (375 mL) light rum (optional)*
1 can *EAGLE BRAND Sweetened Condensed Milk*
1 can *(178 mL) frozen orange juice concentrate, thawed*
2 *bottles (750 mL* each*) ginger ale, chilled*
   Orange sherbet
   Orange slices
   Mint leaves

In large punch bowl, combine pineapple juice, rum if desired, Eagle Brand and orange juice concentrate. Just before serving gradually add ginger ale. Top with scoops of sherbet, orange slices and mint. Makes about 16 cups (4 L).

STRAWBERRY DAIQUIRIS

2   *pkgs. (425 g each) frozen strawberries in syrup, thawed*
1/2   *cup (125 mL) light rum*
1/3   *cup (75 mL) REALIME Lime Juice*
1/4   *cup (50 mL) icing sugar*
2   *cups (500 mL) ice cubes*
    Fresh strawberries (optional)

In blender container, combine strawberries, rum, Realime and sugar. Cover and blend well. Gradually add ice, blending until smooth. Garnish with strawberries if desired. Makes about 4 cups (1 L).

FROSTY PITCHER MARGARITAS

2   *bottles (225 mL each) REALIME Lime Juice, chilled*
    Salt
1   *cup (250 mL) icing sugar*
4   *cups (1 L) crushed ice*
1 1/2 *cups (375 mL) tequila*
3/4   *cup triple sec or other orange-flavoured liqueur*

In saucer, dip rims of cocktail glasses in 1 Tbsp. (15 mL) Realime then dip in salt; set aside. In blender container, combine remaining Realime with sugar. Cover and blend well. Add ice; blend until slushy. Pour into 2-quart (2 L) pitcher; stir in tequila and liqueur. Serve in prepared glasses. Makes about 7 cups (1.75 L).

PARTY MAI TAIS

3   cups *(750 mL) pineapple
       juice, chilled*
1   cup *(250 mL) light rum*
1   can *(178 mL) frozen orange
       juice concentrate, thawed*
1/2   cup *(125 mL) REALEMON
       Lemon Juice*
       Ice
       Orange slices (optional)
       Maraschino cherries (optional)

In pitcher, combine pineapple juice,
rum, orange juice concentrate and
Realemon; stir well. Serve over ice;
garnish with orange slices and
cherries if desired. Makes about
5 cups (1.25 L).

PARTY DAIQUIRIS

2   *bottles (225 mL each)*
       REALIME Lime Juice,
       chilled
1   *cup (250 mL) sugar*
2   *cups (500 mL) cold water*
2   *cups (500 mL) light rum*
       Crushed ice or *ice cubes*

In 2-quart (2 L) pitcher, combine
Realime and sugar; stir until sugar
dissolves. Stir in water and rum. Add
ice. Makes about 6 cups (1.5 L).

RED SANGRIA

3/4   *cup (175 mL) sugar*
3/4   *cup (175 mL) orange juice,*
       chilled
1/3   *cup (75 mL) REALEMON
       Lemon Juice*
1/3   *cup (75 mL) REALIME Lime
       Juice*
2   *bottles (750 mL each)*
       medium-dry red wine,
       chilled
       Orange, peach or *plum slices*
       Ice

In pitcher, combine sugar, orange
juice, Realemon and Realime; stir until
sugar dissolves. Just before serving,
add wine, fruit and ice. Makes about
8 cups (2 L).

SPARKLING HARVEST CIDER

2   quarts (2 L) apple cider, chilled
1   cup (250 mL) REALEMON Lemon Juice
1/2 cup (125 mL) sugar
1   bottle (750 mL) ginger ale, chilled
    Apple slices (optional)
    Cinnamon sticks (optional)
    Ice

In punch bowl, combine cider, Realemon and sugar; stir until sugar dissolves. Just before serving add ginger ale. Garnish with apple slices and cinnamon sticks if desired. Serve over ice. Makes about 12 cups (3 L).

LEMON-LIME SLUSH

2   cups (500 mL) water
2/3 cup (150 mL) sugar
1/3 cup (75 mL) REALEMON Lemon Juice
1/3 cup (75 mL) REALIME Lime Juice
1 to 1 1/2 cups (250 to 375 mL) light rum
1   bottle (750 mL) lemon-lime carbonated beverage

In large bowl, combine water, sugar, Realemon and Realime; stir until sugar dissolves. Add rum and carbonated beverage. Freeze. About 1 hour before serving, remove from freezer; when mixture is slushy, spoon into cocktail glasses. Garnish as desired. Makes about 7 cups (1.75 L).

STRAWBERRY LEMONADE

4 *cups (1 L) fresh strawberries, cleaned, hulled*
3/4 *cup (175 mL) REALEMON Lemon Juice*
3/4 to 1 *cup (175 to 250 mL) sugar*
1 *bottle (750 mL) club soda, chilled*
Ice
Additional fresh strawberries (optional)
Mint leaves (optional)

In blender container, combine strawberries and Realemon. Cover and blend until smooth. In pitcher, combine strawberry mixture and sugar; stir until sugar dissolves. Add club soda. Serve over ice; garnish with strawberries and mint if desired. Makes about 8 cups (2 L).

STRAWBERRY WATERMELON SLUSH

   2   *cups (500 mL) cubed watermelon*
   2   *cups (500 mL) fresh strawberries, cleaned, hulled*
1/2   *cup (125 mL) sugar*
1/3   *cup (75 mL) REALEMON Lemon Juice*
   2   *cups (500 mL) ice cubes*
      Mint leaves (optional)
      Additional watermelon chunks (optional)
      Additional strawberries (optional)

In blender container, combine watermelon, strawberries, sugar and Realemon. Cover and blend well. Gradually add ice, blending until smooth. Garnish with mint, watermelon and strawberries if desired. Makes about 5 cups (1.25 L).

WHITE SANGRIA

1/2 to 3/4 *cup (125 to 175 mL) sugar*
 1/2   *cup (125 mL) REALEMON Lemon Juice*
 1/4   *cup (50 mL) REALIME Lime Juice*
  1   *bottle (750 mL) sauterne, chilled*
 1/4   *cup (50 mL) orange-flavoured liqueur*
  1   *bottle (750 mL) club soda, chilled*
    Orange, plum *or* ***nectarine slices, green grapes*** *or* ***other fresh fruit***
    Ice

In pitcher, combine sugar, Realemon and Realime; stir until sugar dissolves. Add sauterne and orange-flavoured liqueur. Just before serving, add club soda, fruit and ice. Makes 8 cups (2 L).

FISH AND SEAFOOD

QUICK TARTAR SAUCE

3/4   **cup (175 mL) mayonnaise** or **salad dressing**
2   **Tbsp. (30 mL) pickle relish, drained**
1   **Tbsp. (15 mL) chopped green onion**
1   **Tbsp. (15 mL) REALEMON Lemon Juice**

In small bowl, combine mayonnaise, relish, onion and Realemon; mix well. Chill to blend flavours. Cover leftovers; refrigerate. Makes about 1 cup (250 mL).

TANGY COCKTAIL SAUCE

3/4   **cup (175 mL) chili sauce** or **ketchup**
3   **Tbsp. (45 mL) REALEMON Lemon Juice**
1/2   **tsp. (2 mL) prepared horseradish**
1/2   **tsp. (2 mL) Worcestershire sauce**

In small bowl, combine chili sauce, Realemon, horseradish and Worcestershire sauce; mix well. Chill to blend flavours. Cover leftovers; refrigerate. Makes about 1 cup (250 mL).

Pictured at left: Quick Tartar Sauce, Tangy Cocktail Sauce and Savory Lemon Butter.

SAVORY LEMON BUTTER

(Pictured on previous page.)

1/2 **cup (125 mL) butter, softened**
3 **Tbsp. (45 mL) REALEMON Lemon Juice**
Pinch salt

In small mixer bowl, cream butter. Gradually beat in Realemon and salt. Chill to blend flavours. Serve on fish or vegetables. Cover leftovers; refrigerate. Makes about 1/2 cup (125 mL).

Variations

Lemon Parsley Butter: Add 1 Tbsp. (15 mL) chopped fresh parsley.

Lemon Herb Butter: Add 1 tsp. (5 mL) dried oregano leaves **or** dill weed.

Lemon Garlic Butter: Omit salt. Add 1/4 tsp. (1 mL) garlic salt.

GRILLED FISH IN FOIL

1 **lb. (500 g) fish fillets, fresh** or **frozen, thawed**
2 **Tbsp. (30 mL) butter**
1/4 **cup (50 mL) REALEMON Lemon Juice**
1 **Tbsp. (15 mL) chopped fresh parsley**
1 **tsp. (5 mL) dried dill weed**
1/2 **tsp. (2 mL) salt**
1/4 **tsp. (1 mL) pepper**
Paprika
1 **medium onion, sliced**

On 4 large, buttered squares of heavy-duty foil, place equal amounts of fish. In small saucepan, melt butter; add Realemon, parsley, dill weed, salt and pepper. Pour equal amounts over fish. Sprinkle with paprika; top with onion slices. Fold foil around fish; crimp edges to seal. Grill 5 to 7 min. on each side or until fish flakes with fork. Cover leftovers; refrigerate. Makes 4 servings.

LEMON HERBED SALMON STEAKS

1/4   cup (50 mL) butter, melted
1/4   cup (50 mL) REALEMON Lemon Juice
1/4   cup (50 mL) sliced green onions
2   Tbsp. (30 mL) water
1/2   tsp. (2 mL) garlic salt
1/4 to 1/2 tsp. (1 to 2 mL) dried dill weed
2 or 4 salmon steaks (about 1 lb/ 500 g) fresh or frozen, thawed

In shallow baking dish, combine butter, Realemon, onions, water, salt and dill weed. Add fish; marinate 1 hour. Bake fish in marinade in preheated 350°F (180°C) oven 15 to 20 min. or until fish flakes with fork. Garnish as desired. Cover leftovers; refrigerate. Makes 2 to 4 servings.

Microwave: Prepare fish as above. Cover with vented plastic wrap. Microwave at HIGH (100%) 5 to 7 min. or until fish flakes with fork. Serve as above.

Preheat oven to 350°F (180°C). In large bowl combine salmon, bread crumbs, eggs, onion, butter, Realemon, salt and dill weed; mix well. In greased shallow baking dish, shape into loaf. Bake 35 to 40 min. or until done. Let stand 5 min. Slice and serve with Lemony Dill Sauce; garnish as desired. Cover leftovers; refrigerate. Makes 4 to 6 servings.

LEMONY DILL SAUCE

1/3	**cup (75 mL) butter**
3/4	**cup (175 mL) mayonnaise** or **salad dressing**
1	**egg**
1/4	**cup (50 mL) REALEMON Lemon Juice**
2	**Tbsp. (30 mL) water**
1	**Tbsp. (15 mL) sugar**
1	**tsp. (5 mL) chicken bouillon mix**
1/4	**tsp. (1 mL) dried dill weed**

In small saucepan, melt butter. Add mayonnaise, egg, Realemon, water, sugar, bouillon mix and dill weed; mix well. Over low heat, cook and stir until thickened (do not boil). Cover leftovers; refrigerate. Makes about 11/2 cups (375 mL).

DILLY SALMON LOAF WITH LEMONY DILL SAUCE

1	**can (151/2 ozs./439 g) salmon, drained, flaked**
2	**cups (500 mL) fresh bread crumbs**
2	**eggs, beaten**
1/4	**cup (50 mL) finely-chopped onion**
3	**Tbsp. (45 mL) butter, melted**
2	**Tbsp. (30 mL) REALEMON Lemon Juice**
1/2	**tsp. (2 mL) salt**
1/4	**tsp. (1 mL) dried dill weed Lemony Dill Sauce**

SWEET AND SOUR SHRIMP

1	lb. (500 g) medium raw shrimp, peeled, deveined
1	can (19 ozs./ 540 mL) pineapple chunks, drained, reserving juice
3/4	cup (175 mL) cold water
1/3	cup (75 mL) REALEMON Lemon Juice
1/3	cup (75 mL) packed brown sugar
3	Tbsp. (45 mL) corn starch
3	Tbsp. (45 mL) soya sauce
	Pinch ground ginger
1	can (10 ozs./ 284 mL) sliced water chestnuts, drained
1	green pepper, cut in chunks
	Hot cooked rice

In large frypan, combine reserved pineapple juice, water, Realemon, sugar, corn starch, soya sauce and ginger. Over medium heat, cook and stir until mixture boils and thickens. Add shrimp; cook 3 min. Add water chestnuts, green pepper and pineapple chunks; heat through. Serve with rice. Cover leftovers; refrigerate. Makes 4 servings.

LINGUINE TUNA SALAD

1/4	of 900 g pkg. linguine, broken in half
1/3	cup (75 mL) REALEMON Lemon Juice
1/3	cup (75 mL) vegetable oil
2 1/2	tsp. (12 mL) sugar
1 1/2	tsp. (7 mL) Italian seasoning
1 1/2	tsp. (7 mL) seasoned salt
2	cans (6.5 ozs. / 184 g each) tuna, drained, flaked
2	cups (500 mL) frozen green peas, thawed
2	firm medium tomatoes, chopped
1/4	cup (50 mL) chopped green onions
	Lettuce leaves

Cook linguine according to package directions; drain. In 2-cup (500 mL) jar with tight-fitting lid or cruet, combine Realemon, oil, sugar, Italian seasoning and salt. Shake well. In large bowl, combine hot linguine, dressing, tuna, peas, tomatoes and onions. Cover; chill 2 to 3 hours. Serve on lettuce; garnish as desired. Cover leftovers; refrigerate. Makes 6 servings.

STIR-FRIED SCALLOPS AND VEGETABLES

1	lb. (500 g) scallops, fresh or frozen, thawed
1/4	cup (50 mL) REALEMON Lemon Juice
1	cup (250 mL) thinly-sliced carrots
3	cloves garlic, crushed, chopped
1/3	cup (75 mL) butter
2	cups (500 mL) sliced fresh mushrooms
3/4	tsp. (4 mL) dried thyme leaves
2	tsp. (10 mL) corn starch
1/2	tsp. (2 mL) salt
1/4	cup (50 mL) diagonally-sliced green onions
4	ozs. (125 g) fresh pea pods, blanched*
2	Tbsp. (30 mL) dry sherry
	Hot cooked rice

In shallow dish marinate scallops in Realemon for 30 min., stirring occasionally. In large frypan, over high heat, cook carrots and garlic in butter until tender-crisp, about 3 min. Add mushrooms and thyme; cook and stir about 5 min. Stir corn starch and salt into scallop mixture; add to vegetables. Cook and stir until scallops are opaque, about 4 min. Stir in onions, pea pods and sherry. Remove from heat. Serve immediately with hot cooked rice. Cover leftovers; refrigerate. Makes 4 servings.

* Or substitute 1 pkg. (170 g) frozen pea pods, thawed.

MEATS AND POULTRY

SOYA MARINADE

1/2 cup (125 mL) REALEMON Lemon Juice
1/2 cup (125 mL) soya sauce
1/2 cup (125 mL) vegetable oil
3 Tbsp. (45 mL) ketchup
3 to 4 cloves garlic, crushed, chopped
1/4 tsp. (1 mL) pepper

In small bowl, combine Realemon, soya sauce, oil, ketchup, garlic and pepper. Pour over meat or poultry. Refrigerate 6 hours or overnight, turning occasionally. Remove meat from marinade; grill or broil as desired, basting frequently with marinade. Makes about 1 1/2 cups (375 mL).

TERIYAKI MARINADE

1/3 cup (75 mL) REALEMON Lemon Juice
1/4 cup (50 mL) soya sauce
1/4 cup (50 mL) vegetable oil
3 Tbsp. (45 mL) chili sauce
2 cloves garlic, crushed, chopped
1/2 tsp. (2 mL) ground ginger
1/4 tsp. (1 mL) pepper

In small bowl, combine Realemon, soya sauce, oil, chili sauce, garlic, ginger and pepper. Pour over meat or poultry. Refrigerate 6 hours or overnight, turning occasionally. Remove meat from marinade; grill or broil as desired, basting frequently with marinade. Makes about 1 cup (250 mL).

LIME KABOBS POLYNESIAN

1/2   **cup (125 mL) REALIME Lime Juice**
1/2   **cup (125 mL) vegetable oil**
3   **Tbsp. (45 mL) sugar**
1   **Tbsp. (15 mL) chili sauce**
1/2 to 1 tsp. (2 to 5 mL) curry powder
1/4   **tsp. (1 mL) garlic powder**
1   **sirloin steak, about 1 inch (2.5 cm) thick, cut into cubes**
        (about 1 1/2 lbs./ 750 g)
1   **cup (250 mL) drained pineapple chunks**
1   **large green pepper, cut into bite-size pieces**
2   **medium onions, quartered, separated into bite-size pieces**
2   **cups (500 mL) fresh whole mushrooms**
1   **cup (250 mL) cherry tomatoes**
        Hot cooked rice

In 2-cup (500 mL) jar with tight-fitting lid or cruet, combine Realime, oil, sugar, chili sauce, curry powder and garlic powder; shake well. In large shallow baking dish, pour marinade over meat. Cover; refrigerate 6 hours or overnight, stirring occasionally. Remove meat from marinade; skewer with pineapple and vegetables. Grill or broil as desired, basting frequently with marinade. Serve with rice. Cover leftovers; refrigerate. Makes 6 servings.

LAMB CHOPS WITH LEMONY APPLE GLAZE

1/2   **cup (125 mL) apple jelly**
1/4   **cup (50 mL) REALEMON Lemon Juice**
1/4   **cup (50 mL) steak sauce**
    Salt and pepper
8   **loin lamb chops, 1 inch (2.5 cm) thick**

In small saucepan, melt jelly; stir in Realemon and steak sauce. Heat through. Add salt and pepper to taste. Grill or broil lamb chops as desired, basting frequently with sauce. Makes 4 servings.

HURRY-UP HAM GLAZE

1   **cup (250 mL) packed brown sugar**
1/4   **cup (50 mL) REALEMON Lemon Juice**
1/4   **cup (50 mL) honey**
1   **tsp. (5 mL) dry mustard**

In small saucepan, combine sugar, Realemon, honey and mustard; bring to boil. Use to baste ham frequently during last 30 min. of baking. Makes about 1 cup (250 mL), enough to glaze a large ham.

Microwave: In 1-quart (1 L) glass measure, combine sugar, Realemon, honey and mustard. Microwave, uncovered, at HIGH (100%) 2 1/2 to 3 min. or until mixture comes to a boil, stirring every min. Proceed as above.

BAKED APRICOT CHICKEN

1   cup (250 mL) apricot or peach jam
1/4 cup (50 mL) REALEMON Lemon Juice
2   tsp. (10 mL) soya sauce
1/2 tsp. (2 mL) salt
1   broiler-fryer chicken (about 3 lbs./ 1.5 kg), cut up
1   cup (250 mL) dry bread crumbs
1/4 cup (50 mL) butter, melted

Preheat oven to 350°F (180°C). In shallow dish, combine jam, Realemon, soya sauce and salt. Coat chicken with jam mixture; roll in bread crumbs. Set aside remaining jam mixture. In greased 13 x 9-inch (3 L) baking dish, arrange chicken; drizzle with butter. Bake, uncovered, 1 hour or until tender. Heat remaining jam mixture; serve with chicken. Cover leftovers; refrigerate. Makes 4 to 6 servings.

SIMPLE SAUERBRATEN

2   medium onions, sliced
2   medium carrots, pared, sliced
2   bay leaves
1   tsp. (5 mL) peppercorns
2 1/2 cups (625 mL) water
1   cup (250 mL) REALEMON Lemon Juice
1   rolled beef rump roast (about 4 lbs./2 kg)
2   Tbsp. (30 mL) vegetable oil
1/2 cup (125 mL) gingersnap cookie crumbs

In large saucepan, combine onions, carrots, bay leaves, peppercorns, water and Realemon; heat. Place meat in large bowl; pour hot marinade over meat. Cover; refrigerate 1 to 3 days, turning meat occasionally. Reserving marinade, remove meat and pat dry. In Dutch oven, brown meat in hot oil. Add marinade; cover and simmer 2 hours or until meat is tender. Remove meat; keep warm. Strain marinade, reserving 2 1/2 cups (625 mL) liquid. In medium saucepan, combine reserved liquid and cookie crumbs; cook and stir mixture until it boils and thickens. Serve with meat. Cover leftovers; refrigerate. Makes 8 to 10 servings.

BEER MARINATED STEAK

1	*large onion, thinly sliced*
2	*cloves garlic, crushed*
1/2	*cup (125 mL) vegetable oil, divided*
1	*cup (250 mL) beer*
1/2	*cup (125 mL) REALEMON Lemon Juice*
2	*Tbsp. (30 mL) packed brown sugar*
2	*Tbsp. (30 mL) Worcestershire sauce*
1	*flank steak (about 1 1/2 lbs./ 750 g), scored*

In medium frypan, cook onion and garlic in 1/4 cup (50 mL) of the oil until tender; remove from heat. Add beer, Realemon, remaining oil, sugar and Worcestershire sauce. Place meat in shallow baking dish; pour marinade over. Cover; refrigerate 6 hours or overnight, turning occasionally. Remove meat from marinade; grill or broil as desired, basting frequently with marinade. Makes 6 servings.

SWEET AND SOUR PORK CHOPS

6	**centre-cut pork chops (about 1_{3/4} lbs./ 875 g)**
	Vegetable oil
1	**cup (250 mL) thinly-sliced carrots**
1/2	**cup (125 mL) REALEMON Lemon Juice**
3	**Tbsp. (45 mL) corn starch**
1/2	**cup (125 mL) packed brown sugar**
1/4	**cup (50 mL) chopped onion**
1	**Tbsp. (15 mL) soya sauce**
1	**tsp. (5 mL) chicken bouillon mix**
1	**can (19 ozs./ 540 mL) pineapple chunks, drained, reserving juice**
	Green pepper rings
	Hot cooked rice

Preheat oven to 350°F (180°C). In large frypan, brown chops in oil. Remove chops from frypan; drain fat from pan. Place chops and carrots in 2-quart (2 L) shallow baking dish. In same frypan combine Realemon and corn starch; mix well. Add sugar, onion, soya sauce, bouillon mix and reserved pineapple juice; cook and stir until mixture boils and thickens. Pour sauce over chops. Cover; bake 1 hour or until tender. Add pineapple; cover and bake 10 min. longer. Garnish with green pepper; serve with rice. Cover leftovers; refrigerate. Makes 6 servings.

ZESTY BARBECUED RIBS

6   *lbs. (3 kg) spareribs, cut in serving-size pieces*
     Water
2   *cups (500 mL) ketchup*
1/2 *cup (125 mL) REALEMON Lemon Juice*
1/2 *cup (125 mL) packed brown sugar*
1   *Tbsp. (15 mL) prepared mustard*
1/2 *cup (125 mL) finely-chopped onion*
1/4 *cup (50 mL) butter*
1/4 *cup (50 mL) Worcestershire sauce*
1   *clove garlic, crushed*
1/4 *tsp. (1 mL) salt*
     Few drops hot pepper sauce

In large pan, cook ribs in boiling water 45 to 60 min. or until tender. In medium saucepan, combine ketchup, Realemon, sugar, mustard, onion, butter, Worcestershire sauce, garlic, salt and hot pepper sauce; simmer, uncovered, 20 min., stirring occasionally. Grill or broil ribs as desired, turning and basting frequently with sauce. Cover leftovers; refrigerate. Makes 6 to 8 servings.

CHICKEN PICCATA

1/4	cup (50 mL) all purpose flour
1	tsp. (5 mL) salt
1/4	tsp. (1 mL) pepper
6	boneless chicken breast halves, skinned
1/4	cup (50 mL) butter
1/4	cup (50 mL) REALEMON Lemon Juice
2	cups (500 mL) sliced fresh mushrooms
	Hot cooked rice
	Chopped parsley

In paper or plastic bag, combine flour, salt and pepper. Add chicken, a few pieces at a time; shake to coat. In large frypan brown chicken in butter on both sides until golden brown. Add Realemon and mushrooms. Reduce heat; cover and simmer 20 min. or until tender. Serve over rice; garnish with parsley. Cover leftovers; refrigerate. Makes 6 servings.

CHICKEN AND GREEN PEPPERS

1	**container (900 g) frozen fried chicken pieces, thawed**
3	**cups (750 mL) water, divided**
1/4	**cup (50 mL) packed brown sugar**
1/4	**cup (50 mL) REALEMON Lemon Juice**
4	**tsp. (20 mL) chicken bouillon mix**
2	**Tbsp. (30 mL) soya sauce**
11/2 tsp.	**(7 mL) garlic powder**
1 to 11/2 tsp.	**(5 to 7 mL) ground ginger**
3	**Tbsp. (45 mL) corn starch**
2	**medium green peppers, cut in strips**
1	**cup (250 mL) diagonally-sliced celery**
1	**large onion, sliced**
	Hot cooked rice

In medium saucepan, combine 21/2 cups (625 mL) of the water, sugar, Realemon, bouillon mix, soya sauce, garlic powder and ginger; cook and stir until bouillon dissolves. Mix corn starch with remaining water; stir into bouillon mixture. Over medium heat, cook and stir until mixture boils and thickens. In large frypan, arrange chicken, green pepper, celery and onion; pour sauce over. Cover; cook 15 min. or until vegetables are tender-crisp. Serve with rice. Cover leftovers; refrigerate. Makes 4 servings.

LEMON CHICKEN

1 1/4 *lbs. (625 g) boneless chicken breasts, skinned, cut into bite-size pieces*
1   *egg, slightly beaten*
3   *Tbsp. (45 mL) corn starch, divided*
2   *Tbsp. (30 mL) soya sauce*
1/2 *cup (125 mL) sugar*
2   *tsp. (10 mL) chicken bouillon mix*
1/2 *tsp. (2 mL) garlic powder*
1   *cup (250 mL) water*
1/2 *cup (125 mL) REALEMON Lemon Juice*
2   *Tbsp. (30 mL) ketchup*
    Additional corn starch
    Vegetable oil
    Shredded lettuce or *hot cooked rice*

In medium bowl, combine egg, 1 Tbsp. (15 mL) of the corn starch and soya sauce; mix well. Add chicken, stirring to coat; marinate 10 min. In medium saucepan, combine remaining 2 Tbsp. (30 mL) corn starch, sugar, bouillon mix and garlic powder. Gradually add water, Realemon and ketchup; mix well. Over medium heat, cook and stir until mixture boils and thickens. Keep sauce warm. Drain chicken; coat with additional corn starch. In large frypan, heat 1/2-inch (12 mm) oil; cook chicken, a few pieces at a time, until golden and tender. Arrange chicken on shredded lettuce; pour warm sauce over chicken. Garnish as desired. Serve immediately. Cover leftovers; refrigerate. Makes 4 servings.

BARBECUE MARINADE

1/2 *cup (125 mL) prepared barbeque sauce*
1/4 *cup (50 mL) vegetable oil*
1/4 *cup (50 mL) REALEMON Lemon Juice*
1   *Tbsp. (15 mL) packed brown sugar*

In small bowl, combine ingredients. Pour over meat or poultry. Refrigerate 6 hours or overnight, turning occasionally. Remove meat from marinade; grill or broil as desired, basting frequently with marinade. Makes about 1 cup (250 mL).

BARBECUE HAM SANDWICHES

1	**cup (250 mL) ketchup**
3	**Tbsp. (45 mL) REALEMON Lemon Juice**
1/4	**cup (50 mL) chopped onion**
1/4	**cup (50 mL) packed brown sugar**
2	**Tbsp. (30 mL) Worcestershire sauce**
1	**tsp. (5 mL) prepared mustard**
1	**lb. (500 g) thinly-sliced ham**
	Hamburger buns or crusty rolls

In small saucepan, combine all ingredients except ham and buns. Simmer uncovered 5 min. Add ham; heat through. Serve on buns. Refrigerate leftovers. Makes 6 to 8 sandwiches.

Microwave: In 2-quart (2 L) round microwave-safe baking dish, combine ingredients as above. Cover with wax paper; microwave at HIGH (100%) 3 min. Stir in ham; re-cover with wax paper and microwave at HIGH (100%) 3 to 4 min. or until hot. Serve as above.

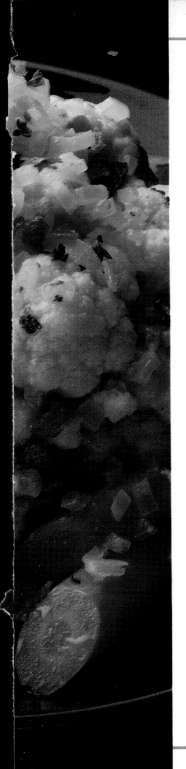

VEGETABLES

SAVORY LEMON VEGETABLES

1	lb. (500 g) carrots, pared, sliced
1	medium head cauliflower, core removed
6	slices bacon
1	cup (250 mL) finely-chopped onion
1/2	cup (125 mL) REALEMON Lemon Juice
1/2	cup (125 mL) water
4	tsp. (20 mL) sugar
1	tsp. (5 mL) salt
1	tsp. (5 mL) dried thyme leaves
	Chopped parsley

Cook carrots and cauliflower until tender; drain. Meanwhile, in large frypan, cook bacon until crisp; drain, reserving 1/4 cup (50 mL) drippings. Crumble bacon; set aside. Cook onion in reserved drippings until tender. Add Realemon, water, sugar, salt and thyme; bring to a boil. Arrange vegetables in serving dish; pour sauce over. Garnish with reserved bacon and parsley. Makes 8 servings.

BLENDER HOLLANDAISE SAUCE

 2 **egg yolks***
1 to 2 **Tbsp. (15 to 30 mL) REALEMON Lemon Juice**
   Pinch salt
1/2 **cup (125 mL)** hot **melted butter**

In blender container, combine egg yolks, Realemon and salt. Cover and blend at high speed; slowly pour in butter, blending until thick, about 30 sec. Serve immediately. Cover leftovers; refrigerate. Makes about 3/4 cup (175 mL).

Variations: Add 1 tsp. (5 mL) dried dill weed, tarragon, basil or mint.

* Use only clean, uncracked eggs.

ALMONDINE BUTTER SAUCE

1/2 **cup (125 mL) sliced almonds**
1/3 **cup (75 mL) butter**
1/4 **cup (50 mL) REALEMON Lemon Juice**

In small frypan, over medium heat, cook almonds in butter until golden; remove from heat. Stir in Realemon. Serve warm over cooked vegetables or fish. Makes about 2/3 cup (150 mL).

LEMONY CREAM DIP

1/4   cup (50 mL) REALEMON Lemon Juice
2   egg yolks
1/4   cup (50 mL) butter
1 to 2 tsp. (5 to 10 mL) chicken bouillon mix
       Pinch cayenne pepper
1   cup (250 mL) sour cream, at room temperature
       Assorted raw vegetables for dipping

In small saucepan, combine Realemon and egg yolks; add butter, bouillon mix and pepper. Over low heat, cook and stir until thickened and bouillon dissolves. Slowly stir in sour cream. Cool. Chill. Serve as a dip for raw vegetables. Makes about 11/2 cups (375 mL).

Microwave: In 1-quart (1 L) glass measure, microwave butter at HIGH (100%) 30 sec. or until melted. Stir in Realemon and egg yolks; mix well. Add bouillon mix and pepper. Microwave at MEDIUM-HIGH (70%) 11/2 to 2 min. or until thick, stirring every 30 sec. Proceed as above.

Note: Sauce can be served hot on cooked vegetables.

LEMON PARSLEY POTATOES

2   lbs. (1 kg) small new potatoes
1/2   cup (125 mL) butter
1/4   cup (50 mL) REALEMON Lemon Juice
1   Tbsp. (15 mL) chicken bouillon mix
1   Tbsp. (15 mL) chopped parsley or chives
1/2   tsp. (2 mL) hot pepper sauce (optional)

Cook potatoes until tender; drain. In small saucepan, melt butter; add Realemon, bouillon mix, parsley and hot pepper sauce if desired. Heat until bouillon dissolves. Pour over hot potatoes, stirring to coat. Makes 6 to 8 servings.

Microwave: In 2-cup (500 mL) glass measure, microwave butter at HIGH (100%) 30 sec. or until melted. Add Realemon, bouillon mix, parsley and hot pepper sauce, if desired. Microwave, uncovered, at HIGH (100 %) 11/2 to 2 min. or until bouillon is dissolved, stirring after 1 min. Proceed as above.

ITALIAN VEGETABLE SALAD

1	cup (250 mL) vegetable oil
2/3	cup (150 mL) REALEMON Lemon Juice
1/2	cup (125 mL) water
1/4	cup (50 mL) sugar
2	tsp. (10 mL) salt
1	tsp. (5 mL) dried oregano leaves
1/2	tsp. (2 mL) pepper
1	small head cauliflower, separated into flowerets
4	medium carrots, pared, cut into 2-inch (5 cm) strips
4	stalks celery, cut into 1-inch (2.5 cm) pieces
1/2	cup (125 mL) stuffed olives

In large saucepan, combine oil, Realemon, water, sugar, salt, oregano and pepper; bring to boil. Add cauliflower, carrots and celery; cover and simmer 5 min. Add olives; pour into medium bowl. Cover; chill overnight. Drain before serving. Cover leftovers; refrigerate. Makes 6 to 8 servings.

OVEN GERMAN POTATO SALAD

5	cups (1.25 L) cooked potato slices
	(about 1 1/2 lbs./ 750 g potatoes)
6	slices bacon
2	Tbsp. (30 mL) chopped onion
1/4	cup (50 mL) sugar
1	Tbsp. (15 mL) corn starch
1/2	tsp. (2 mL) dry mustard
1	tsp. (5 mL) salt
1/2	cup (125 mL) water
1/4	cup (50 mL) REALEMON Lemon Juice
1/4	cup (50 mL) cider vinegar
1/4	cup (50 mL) chopped celery

In large frypan, cook bacon until crisp; drain, reserving 3 Tbsp. (45 mL) drippings. Crumble bacon. In 2-quart (2 L) shallow baking dish, combine potatoes, bacon and onion; set aside. In small saucepan, combine sugar, corn starch, mustard and salt. Gradually add reserved drippings, water, Realemon and vinegar; mix well. Over medium heat, cook and stir until mixture boils and thickens; pour over potatoes. Let stand, covered, several hours to blend flavours; stir in celery. Preheat oven to 350°F (180°C). Bake 30 min. or until hot. Makes 4 to 6 servings.

BREADS, CAKES AND CHEESECAKES

GLAZED LEMON NUT BREAD

2	cups (500 mL) all purpose flour
1	tsp. (5 mL) baking powder
1/2	tsp. (2 mL) baking soda
1/4	tsp. (1 mL) salt
1 1/4	cups (300 mL) sugar
1/2	cup (125 mL) butter, softened
3	eggs
1/2	cup (125 mL) REALEMON Lemon Juice
1/2	cup (125 mL) milk
3/4	cup (175 mL) chopped pecans
	Lemon Glaze, divided

Preheat oven to 350°F (180°C). Stir together flour, baking powder, baking soda and salt; set aside. In large mixer bowl beat sugar and butter until fluffy. Add eggs, one at a time, beating well after each addition. Gradually beat in Realemon. Add milk alternately with dry ingredients. Stir in nuts. Turn into greased 9 x 5-inch (1.5 L) loaf pan. Bake 55 to 60 min. or until done. Remove from oven. While in pan, with metal skewer, poke holes in bread about 1 inch (2.5 cm) apart. Slowly pour half the Lemon Glaze over warm bread. Cool 10 min. Remove from pan; pour remaining glaze over bread. Cool completely. Makes 1 loaf.

Lemon Glaze: In small bowl combine 1/3 cup (75 mL) icing sugar and 1/4 cup (50 mL) Realemon Lemon Juice.

LEMON PECAN STICKY ROLLS

1/2	cup (125 mL) granulated sugar
1/2	cup (125 mL) packed brown sugar
1/4	cup (50 mL) butter
1/4	cup (50 mL) REALEMON Lemon Juice
1/2	tsp. (2 mL) ground cinnamon
1/2	cup (125 mL) chopped pecans
2	pkgs. (235 g each) refrigerated crescent rolls

Preheat oven to 375°F (190°C). In small saucepan, combine sugars, butter, Realemon and cinnamon. Bring to a boil; boil 1 min. Reserving 1/4 cup (50 mL) of the Realemon mixture, pour remaining mixture into 9-inch (1.5 L) round layer cake pan. Sprinkle with nuts. On lightly floured surface, separate rolls into 8 rectangles; spread with reserved Realemon mixture. Roll up jelly-roll fashion, beginning with short side; seal edges. Cut in half. Place rolls, cut side down, in prepared pan. Bake 30 to 35 min. or until dark golden brown. Loosen sides. Immediately turn onto serving plate; do not remove pan. Let stand 5 min.; remove pan. Serve warm. Makes 16 rolls.

LEMON TEA MUFFINS

2	cups (500 mL) all purpose flour
2	tsp. (10 mL) baking powder
1/2	tsp. (2 mL) salt
1	cup (250 mL) butter, softened
1	cup (250 mL) granulated sugar
4	eggs, separated
1/2	cup (125 mL) REALEMON Lemon Juice
1/4	cup (50 mL) finely-chopped nuts
2	Tbsp. (30 mL) packed brown sugar
1/4	tsp. (1 mL) ground nutmeg

Preheat oven to 375°F (190°C). Stir together flour, baking powder and salt; set aside. In large mixer bowl, beat butter and granulated sugar until fluffy. Add egg yolks; beat until light. Gradually stir in Realemon alternately with dry ingredients (do not overmix). In small mixer bowl, beat egg whites until stiff but not dry; fold one-third egg whites into Realemon mixture. Fold remaining egg whites into Realemon mixture. Fill paper-lined or greased muffin cups 3/4 full. Combine nuts, brown sugar and nutmeg; sprinkle evenly over muffins. Bake 15 to 20 min. Cool 5 min.; remove from pan. Serve warm. Makes 1 1/2 dozen muffins.

GINGERBREAD LEMON CAKE ROLL

3/4	cup (175 mL) all purpose flour
1/2	tsp. (2 mL) baking powder
1/2	tsp. (2 mL) baking soda
3/4	tsp. (4 mL) ground cinnamon
3/4	tsp. (4 mL) ground ginger
1/4	tsp. (1 mL) ground allspice
1/4	tsp. (1 mL) ground cloves
4	eggs
1/2	cup (125 mL) sugar
1/3	cup (75 mL) molasses
	Icing sugar
	Lemon Cheese Filling

Preheat oven to 375°F (190°C). Stir together flour, baking powder, baking soda, cinnamon, ginger, allspice and cloves; set aside. In large mixer bowl, beat eggs until thick and lemon-coloured; gradually add sugar, beating until very thick. Add molasses; mix well. Stir in dry ingredients. Grease 15 x 10-inch (2 L) jelly roll pan; line with wax paper; grease again. Pour batter into prepared pan. Bake 10 to 12 min. or until cake springs back when lightly touched. Immediately loosen sides; turn onto towel sprinkled with icing sugar. Remove wax paper. Starting at narrow end, roll cake with towel; cool thoroughly. Unroll; spread with chilled Lemon Cheese Filling. Roll up; chill. Sprinkle with icing sugar before serving. Makes one 10-inch (25 cm) roll.

LEMON CHEESE FILLING

3/4	cup (175 mL) sugar
2	Tbsp. (30 mL) corn starch
2/3	cup (150 mL) water
2	egg yolks, beaten
1/4	cup (50 mL) REALEMON Lemon Juice
1	pkg. (125 g) cream cheese, softened
2	Tbsp. (30 mL) butter, softened

In medium saucepan, combine sugar and corn starch. Gradually add water, egg yolks and Realemon; mix well. Over medium heat, cook and stir until mixture boils and thickens; remove from heat. Add cream cheese and butter; beat until smooth. Chill, stirring occasionally. Makes about 12/3 cups (400 mL).

NO-BAKE CHOCOLATE CHEESECAKE

1 1/4   *cups (300 mL) graham wafer crumbs*
1/3   *cup (75 mL) butter, melted*
1   *envelope unflavoured gelatin*
2/3   *cup (150 mL) water*
2   *pkgs. (250 g* each*) cream cheese, softened*
4   *squares (28 g* each*) semi-sweet chocolate, melted, cooled*
1   *can EAGLE BRAND Sweetened Condensed Milk*
1   *tsp. (5 mL) vanilla*
1   *cup (250 mL) whipping cream, whipped*

Combine crumbs and butter; press firmly on bottom of 9-inch (23 cm)
springform pan. In small saucepan, sprinkle gelatin over water; let stand 1 min.
Over low heat, stir until gelatin dissolves; set aside. In large mixer bowl, beat
cream cheese and chocolate until fluffy. Gradually beat in Eagle Brand and vanilla
until smooth. Stir in gelatin mixture. Fold in whipped cream. Pour into prepared
pan. Chill 3 hours or until set. Garnish as desired. Cover leftovers; refrigerate.
Makes one cheesecake.

LEMON BUTTER FROSTING

1/2   **cup (125 mL) butter, softened**
4   **cups (1 L) icing sugar, divided**
1/4   **cup (50 mL) REALEMON Lemon Juice**

In small mixer bowl, beat butter and 1 cup (250 mL) of the sugar until light and fluffy. Gradually beat in Realemon alternately with remaining 3 cups (750 mL) sugar, beating until light and fluffy. Makes about 2 1/4 cups (550 mL) *or* enough to frost one 2-layer cake or 35 cupcakes.

LUSCIOUS BLACK FOREST CHEESECAKE

11/4 **cups (300 mL) graham wafer crumbs**
1/3   **cup (75 mL) butter, melted**
1/4   **cup (50 mL) sugar**
3   **pkgs. (250 g each) cream cheese, softened**
1   **can EAGLE BRAND Sweetened Condensed Milk**
8   **squares (28 g each) semi-sweet chocolate, melted, cooled**
4   **eggs**
2   **tsp. (10 mL) vanilla**
1   **can (19 ozs./540 mL) cherry pie filling, chilled**
      Whipped cream
      Chocolate curls

Preheat oven to 300°F (150°C). Combine crumbs, butter and sugar; press firmly on bottom of 9-inch (23 cm) springform pan. In large mixer bowl, beat cream cheese until fluffy. Gradually beat in Eagle Brand, chocolate, eggs and vanilla until smooth. Pour into prepared pan. Bake 1 hour and 5 min. or until cake springs back when lightly touched. Cool. Chill. Top with cherry pie filling. Garnish with whipped cream and chocolate curls. Cover leftovers; refrigerate. Makes one cheesecake.

FAST 'N' FABULOUS FRUITCAKE

2 1/2 cups (625 mL) all purpose flour
1   tsp. (5 mL) baking soda
2   eggs, slightly beaten
1   jar (750 mL) mincemeat
1   can EAGLE BRAND Sweetened Condensed Milk
2   cups (500 mL) chopped mixed glacé fruit*
1   cup (250 mL) coarsely-chopped walnuts
**   Whole glacé cherries**

Preheat oven to 300°F (150°C). Grease two 9 x 5-inch (1.5 L) loaf pans**. Stir together flour and baking soda; set aside. In large bowl, combine eggs, mincemeat, Eagle Brand, chopped fruit and nuts. Add dry ingredients; mix well. Divide batter between prepared pans. Bake 1 hour and 20 to 25 min. or until done. Cool 15 min. Turn out of pans; cool completely. Garnish with glacé cherries. Wrap well in foil. Store in refrigerator or freezer. Makes two cakes.

* Or substitute 2 cups (500 mL) chopped red and green glacé cherries.

** Or use a 10-inch (3 L) tube or Bundt pan. Bake 1 hour and 50 min. or until done.

BLUEBERRY CUSTARD CAKE

11/2 cups (375 mL) all purpose flour
3/4   cup (175 mL) sugar, divided
1   Tbsp. (15 mL) baking powder
1/2   tsp. (2 mL) salt
2   eggs
2   Tbsp. (30 mL) milk
1   tsp. (5 mL) vanilla
1/4   cup (50 mL) butter, melted
2   cups (500 mL) cleaned, fresh blueberries *
1/2   tsp. (2 mL) ground cinnamon
1   can EAGLE BRAND Sweetened Condensed Milk
1   cup (250 mL) sour cream
1/4   cup (50 mL) REALEMON Lemon Juice
       Additional ground cinnamon

Preheat oven to 400°F (200°C). Stir together flour, 1/2 cup (125 mL) of the sugar, baking powder and salt. In large mixer bowl beat eggs, milk and vanilla. Add flour mixture and butter; beat on low speed until well blended. Spread evenly into greased 9-inch (23 cm) springform pan. Arrange blueberries on batter. Combine remaining 1/4 cup (50 mL) sugar and 1/2 tsp. (2 mL) cinnamon; sprinkle evenly over berries. Bake 30 min. In medium bowl, combine Eagle Brand and sour cream. Stir in Realemon. Remove cake from oven; pour cream mixture over blueberries. Sprinkle with additional cinnamon. Return to oven; bake 10 min. longer or until done. Serve warm or chilled. Makes one cake.

* Or use 1 pkg. (300 g) frozen blueberries.

CREAMY BAKED CHEESECAKE

1	*cup (250 mL) graham wafer crumbs*
1/4	*cup (50 mL) butter, melted*
1/4	*cup (50 mL) sugar*
2	*pkgs. (250 g each) cream cheese, softened*
1	*can EAGLE BRAND Sweetened Condensed Milk*
3	*eggs*
1/4	*cup (50 mL) REALEMON Lemon Juice*
1	*cup (250 mL) sour cream*
	Peach Melba Topping or fresh fruit

Preheat oven to 300°F (150°C). Combine crumbs, butter and sugar; press firmly on bottom of 9-inch (23 cm) springform pan. In large mixer bowl, beat cream cheese until fluffy. Gradually beat in Eagle Brand and eggs until smooth. Stir in Realemon. Pour into prepared pan. Bake 50 to 55 min. or until cake springs back when lightly touched. Cool. Chill. Top with sour cream. Garnish with Peach Melba Topping or fresh fruit. Cover leftovers; refrigerate. Makes one cheesecake.

Peach Melba topping: Reserve 2/3 cup (150 mL) syrup drained from 1 pkg. (425 g) thawed, frozen red raspberries in syrup. In small saucepan, combine reserved syrup, 1/4 cup (50 mL) red currant jelly and 1 Tbsp. (15 mL) corn starch. Over medium heat, cook and stir until mixture boils and thickens. Cool. Stir in raspberries. Drain one can (19 ozs./540 mL) peach slices. Top cake with peach slices and sauce.

AMBROSIA COMPANY CAKE

1   pkg. (about 520 g) yellow or white cake mix
1   can EAGLE BRAND Sweetened Condensed Milk
2   Tbsp. (30 mL) frozen orange juice concentrate, thawed
1   tsp. (5 mL) grated orange rind
1   cup (250 mL) whipping cream, whipped
1/3 cup (75 mL) flaked coconut, toasted
    Additional coconut (optional)
    Orange slices (optional)

Preheat oven to 350°F (180°C). Prepare and bake cake as package directs for 13x 9-inch (3.5 L) pan. Cool thoroughly. While in pan using a table-knife handle, poke holes about 1 inch (2.5 cm) apart in cake halfway through to bottom. Combine Eagle Brand, orange juice concentrate and rind; mix well. Spoon small amounts of mixture into each hole in cake; spread remaining mixture evenly over top. Chill at least 1 hour. To serve, spread whipped cream over cake; garnish with coconut and orange slices if desired. Cover leftovers; refrigerate. Makes one cake.

CHOCOLATE CHIP CHEESECAKE

1 1/2 cups (375 mL) finely-crushed cream-filled chocolate sandwich cookies
     (about 18 cookies)
3   Tbsp. (45 mL) butter, melted
3   pkgs. (250 g each) cream cheese, softened
1   can EAGLE BRAND Sweetened Condensed Milk
3   eggs
2   tsp. (10 mL) vanilla
1   cup (250 mL) mini semi-sweet chocolate chips, divided
1   tsp. (5 mL) flour

Preheat oven to 300°F (150°C). Combine crumbs and butter; press firmly on bottom of 9-inch (23 cm) springform pan. In large mixer bowl, beat cream cheese until fluffy. Gradually beat in Eagle Brand, eggs and vanilla. In small bowl, toss 1/2 cup (125 mL) of the chips with flour to coat; stir into cheese mixture. Pour into prepared pan. Sprinkle remaining chips over top. Bake 1 hour or until cake springs back when lightly touched. Cool. Chill. Garnish if desired. Cover leftovers; refrigerate. Makes one cheesecake.

Note: For best distribution of chips throughout cheesecake, do not oversoften or overbeat cream cheese.

COOKIES AND BARS

CHOCO-COCONUT LAYER BARS

1/3 **cup (75 mL) butter, melted**
3/4 **cup (175 mL) all purpose flour**
1/2 **cup (125 mL) sugar**
2 **Tbsp. (30 mL) unsweetened cocoa powder**
1 **egg**
1 **can EAGLE BRAND Sweetened Condensed Milk, divided**
1 1/3 **cups (325 mL) flaked coconut**
Flavour variations*
1 **pkg. (175 g) semi-sweet chocolate chips**

Preheat oven to 350°F (180°C) *or* 325°F (160°C) for glass dish. In medium mixing bowl, combine butter, flour, sugar, cocoa and egg; mix well. Spread evenly onto lightly-greased 9-inch (2.5 L) square baking pan. In small bowl, combine 3/4 cup (175 mL) Eagle Brand, coconut and desired flavour variation; spread over chocolate layer. Bake 20 min. or until lightly browned around edges. In heavy saucepan, over low heat, melt chips with remaining Eagle Brand. Remove from heat; spread evenly over coconut layer. Cool. Chill thoroughly. Cut into bars. Store loosely covered, at room temperature. Makes 24 bars.

* Flavour Variations

Almond
1 cup (250 mL) chopped slivered almonds
1/2 tsp. (2 mL) almond extract

Mint
1/2 tsp. (2 mL) peppermint extract
4 drops green food colour (optional)

Cherry
1 cup (250 mL) chopped, drained maraschino cherries

TOFFEE BARS

1/2   cup (125 mL) butter, divided
1   cup (250 mL) rolled oats
1/2   cup (125 mL) packed brown sugar
1/2   cup (125 mL) all purpose flour
1/2   cup (125 mL) finely-chopped walnuts
1/4   tsp. (1 mL) baking soda
1   can EAGLE BRAND Sweetened Condensed Milk
2   tsp. (10 mL) vanilla
1   pkg. (175 g) semi-sweet chocolate chips

Preheat oven to 350°F (180°C) or 325°F (160°C) for glass dish. In medium saucepan, melt 6 tbsp. (90 mL) of the butter; stir in oats, sugar, flour, nuts and baking soda. Press firmly onto bottom of greased 13 x 9-inch (3.5 L) baking pan; bake 10 to 15 min. or until lightly browned. In medium saucepan, combine remaining 2 Tbsp. (30 mL) butter and Eagle Brand. Over medium heat, cook and stir until mixture thickens slightly, about 10 min. Remove from heat; stir in vanilla. Pour over crust. Return to oven; bake 10 to 12 min. longer or until golden brown. Remove from oven; immediately sprinkle chips on top. Let stand 1 min.; spread while still warm. Cool to room temperature; chill thoroughly. Cut into bars. Store tightly covered at room temperature. Makes 36 bars.

TRIPLE LAYER BARS

1/2   cup (125 mL) butter
1 1/2 cups (375 mL) graham wafer crumbs
1   pkg. (200 g) flaked coconut
1   can EAGLE BRAND Sweetened Condensed Milk
1   pkg. (350 g) semi-sweet chocolate chips
1/2   cup (125 mL) creamy peanut butter

Preheat oven to 350°F (180°C) or 325°F (160°C) for glass dish. In 13 x 9-inch (3.5 L) baking pan, melt butter in oven. Sprinkle crumbs evenly over butter; mix together and press into pan. Top evenly with coconut then Eagle Brand. Bake 25 min. or until lightly browned. In small saucepan over low heat, melt chips with peanut butter. Spread evenly over hot coconut layer. Cool 30 min.; chill. Cut into bars. Store loosely covered at room temperature. Makes 36 bars.

APPLESAUCE FRUITCAKE BARS

1	can EAGLE BRAND Sweetened Condensed Milk
2	eggs
1/4	cup (50 mL) butter, melted
2	tsp. (10 mL) vanilla
3	cups (750 mL) biscuit baking mix
2	cups (500 mL) canned applesauce
1	cup (250 mL) chopped dates
3/4	cup (175 mL) chopped green glacé cherries
3/4	cup (175 mL) chopped red glacé cherries
3/4	cup (175 mL) chopped nuts
3/4	cup (175 mL) raisins
	Icing sugar

Preheat oven to 325°F (160°C). In large mixer bowl, beat Eagle Brand, eggs, butter and vanilla. Stir in baking mix, applesauce, dates, cherries, nuts and raisins. Spread evenly into well-greased and floured 15 x 10-inch (2 L) jelly roll pan. Bake 35 to 40 min. or until wooden pick inserted in centre comes out clean. Cool thoroughly. Sprinkle with icing sugar; cut into bars. Store tightly covered at room temperature. Makes 48 bars.

MAGIC COOKIE BARS

1/2   **cup (125 mL) butter**
1 1/2 **cups (375 mL) graham wafer crumbs**
1   **can EAGLE BRAND Sweetened Condensed Milk**
1   **cup (250 mL) semi-sweet chocolate chips**
1 1/3 **cups (325 mL) flaked coconut**
1   **cup (250 mL) chopped nuts**

Preheat oven to 350°F (180°C) *or* 325°F (160°C) for glass dish. In 13 x 9-inch (3.5 L) baking pan melt butter in oven. Sprinkle crumbs over butter; mix together and press into pan. Pour Eagle Brand evenly over crumbs. Sprinkle with chips, then coconut and nuts; press down firmly. Bake 25 to 30 min. or until lightly browned. Cool well before cutting. Store loosely covered at room temperature. Makes 24 bars.

COCONUT MACAROONS

3 pkgs. (200 g each) flaked coconut
1 can EAGLE BRAND Sweetened Condensed Milk
2 tsp. (10 mL) vanilla
1½ tsp. (7 mL) almond extract

Preheat oven to 325°F (160°C). In large mixing bowl combine coconut, Eagle Brand, vanilla and almond extract; mix well. Drop by rounded spoonfuls onto well-greased cookie sheets. Bake on middle rack of oven, twelve at a time, 10 to 12 min. or until browned around edges. Cool slightly. Remove to wire racks; cool completely. Store loosely covered at room temperature. Makes about 4 dozen cookies.

Chocolate: Omit almond extract. Add 4 squares (28 g *each*) unsweetened chocolate, melted. Proceed as above.

Chocolate Chip: Omit almond extract. Add 1 cup (250 mL) mini semi-sweet chocolate chips. Proceed as above.

SLICE 'N' BAKE LEMON COOKIES

2 1/4   **cups (550 mL) all purpose flour**
1/4   **tsp. (1 mL) baking soda**
1/2   **cup (125 mL) butter, softened**
1/2   **cup (125 mL) shortening**
1/2   **cup (125 mL) granulated sugar**
1/2   **cup (125 mL) packed brown sugar**
1   **egg**
3   **Tbsp. (45 mL) REALEMON Lemon Juice**
  Egg white, beaten
  Sliced almonds

Stir together flour and baking soda; set aside. In large mixer bowl beat butter, shortening and sugars until fluffy. Add egg; beat well. Gradually add dry ingredients and Realemon; mix well. Chill until firm enough to form into two 10-inch (25 cm) rolls. Wrap well; chill about 1 hour or until firm enough to slice. Preheat oven to 350°F (180°C). Cut rolls into 1/4-inch (6 mm) slices; place 1 inch (2.5 cm) apart on greased cookie sheets. Brush with egg white; top with almonds. Bake 10 to 12 min. or until lightly browned. Makes about 5 dozen cookies.

CRANBERRY CRUMB SQUARES

3/4 cup (175 mL) butter, softened
1/3 cup (75 mL) icing sugar
11/2 cups (375 mL) all purpose flour
1   pkg. (250 g) cream cheese, softened
1   can EAGLE BRAND Sweetened Condensed Milk
1/4 cup (50 mL) REALEMON Lemon Juice
3   Tbsp. (45 mL) packed brown sugar, divided
2   Tbsp. (30 mL) corn starch
1   can (14 ozs./ 398 mL) whole cranberry sauce
1/3 cup (75 mL) all purpose flour
1/4 cup (50 mL) cold butter
3/4 cup (175 mL) chopped walnuts

Preheat oven to 350°F (180°C). Cream together soft butter and icing sugar until fluffy. Gradually stir in 11/2 cups (375 mL) flour. Press onto bottom of 13 x 9-inch (3.5 L) baking pan. Bake about 15 min. or until lightly browned. Reduce oven temperature to 325°F (160°C). In large mixer bowl, beat cream cheese until fluffy. Gradually beat in Eagle Brand until smooth. Stir in Realemon. Pour over prepared crust. In small bowl, combine 1 Tbsp. (15 mL) of the brown sugar and corn starch; mix well. Stir in cranberry sauce. Spoon evenly over cheese mixture. In medium mixing bowl, combine remaining brown sugar and 1/3 cup (75 mL) flour. Cut in cold butter until mixture resembles coarse crumbs. Stir in nuts. Sprinkle evenly over cranberry mixture. Bake 45 to 50 min. or until bubbly and golden. Cool. Serve warm or chilled. Cover leftovers; refrigerate. Makes one pan.

CASHEW PEANUT BUTTER BARS

1	cup (250 mL) all purpose flour
1/4	cup (50 mL) packed brown sugar
1/2	tsp. (2 mL) baking powder
1/4	tsp. (1 mL) baking soda
1/2	cup (125 mL) cold butter, cut into small pieces
3	tsp. (15 mL) vanilla, divided
3	cups (750 mL) miniature marshmallows
1	can EAGLE BRAND Sweetened Condensed Milk
1	cup (250 mL) peanut-butter flavoured chips*
2	cups (500 mL) chow mein noodles
1	cup (250 mL) coarsely-chopped cashews or peanuts

Preheat oven to 350°F (180°C) *or* 325°F (160°C) for glass dish. In medium mixing bowl, combine flour, sugar, baking powder and baking soda. Cut in butter and 1 tsp. (5 mL) of the vanilla until mixture resembles coarse crumbs. Press firmly on bottom of 13 x 9-inch (3.5 L) baking pan. Bake 15 min. or until lightly browned. Top evenly with marshmallows; bake 2 min. longer or until marshmallows begin to puff. Remove from oven; cool thoroughly. In heavy saucepan, over medium heat, combine Eagle Brand and chips; cook and stir until slightly thickened, about 4 to 6 min. Remove from heat; stir in chow mein noodles, nuts and remaining vanilla. Spread evenly over marshmallows. Chill thoroughly. Cut into bars. Store loosely covered at room temperature. Makes 36 bars.

* Or substitute 1/2 cup (125 mL) cream-style peanut butter.

HOLIDAY CITRUS LOGS

3   *cups (750 mL) vanilla wafer crumbs*
13/4 *cups (425 mL) coarsely-chopped dates*
11/2 *cups (375 mL) coarsely-chopped glacé cherries*
1   *cup (250 mL) chopped pecans* or *almonds*
1/4   *cup (50 mL) REALEMON Lemon Juice*
2   *Tbsp. (30 mL) orange-flavoured liqueur*
1   *Tbsp. (15 mL) corn syrup*
     Additional corn syrup, heated
     Additional finely-chopped pecans or *almonds*

In large bowl, combine crumbs, dates, cherries, pecans, Realemon, liqueur and corn syrup. Shape into two 10-inch (25 cm) logs. Brush with heated corn syrup; roll in nuts. Wrap tightly; refrigerate 3 to 4 days to blend flavours. To serve, cut into 1/4-inch (6 mm) slices. Makes two 10-inch (25 cm) logs.

VERSATILE CUT-OUT COOKIES

3 cups (750 mL) all purpose flour
1 Tbsp. (15 mL) baking powder
1/2 tsp. (2 mL) salt
1 can EAGLE BRAND Sweetened Condensed Milk
3/4 cup (175 mL) butter, softened
2 eggs
2 tsp. (10 mL) vanilla or lemon extract
Ready-to-spread frosting

Preheat oven to 350°F (180°C). Combine flour, baking powder and salt; set aside. In large mixer bowl, beat Eagle Brand, butter, eggs and vanilla until well blended. Add dry ingredients; mix well. On floured surface, lightly knead dough to form a smooth ball. Divide into thirds. On well-floured surface, roll out each portion to 1/8-inch (3 mm) thickness. Cut with floured cookie cutter. Place 1 inch (2.5 cm) apart on greased baking sheets. Bake 7 to 9 min. or until lightly browned around edges. Cool thoroughly. Frost and decorate as desired with ready-to-spread frosting. Store loosely covered at room temperature. Makes about 6 1/2 dozen cookies.

Sandwich cookies: Use 2 1/2-inch (7 cm) cookie cutter. Bake as directed. Sandwich 2 cookies together with ready-to-spread frosting. Sprinkle with sugar if desired. Makes about 3 dozen cookies.

GRANOLA BARS

3   *cups (750 mL) rolled oats*
1   *cup (250 mL) chopped nuts*
1   *cup (250 mL) raisins* or *chopped dried fruit*
1   *cup (250 mL) sunflower seeds*
1   *cup (250 mL) semi-sweet chocolate chips (optional)*
1   *can EAGLE BRAND Sweetened Condensed Milk*
1/2 *cup (125 mL) butter, melted*

Preheat oven to 325°F (160°C). Line 15 x 10-inch (2 L) jelly roll pan with foil; grease. In large mixing bowl, combine oats, nuts, raisins, sunflower seeds, chips if desired, Eagle Brand and butter; mix well. Press evenly into prepared pan. Bake 25 to 30 min. or until golden brown. Cool slightly; remove from pan and peel off foil. Cut into bars. Store loosely covered at room temperature. Makes 36 bars.

MILK CHOCOLATE BROWNIES

1	pkg. (300 g) semi-sweet chocolate chips, divided
1/4	cup (50 mL) butter
2	cups (500 mL) biscuit baking mix
1	can EAGLE BRAND Sweetened Condensed Milk
1	egg, beaten
1	tsp. (5 mL) vanilla
1	cup (250 mL) chopped walnuts
	Icing sugar

Preheat oven to 350°F (180°C) or 325°F (160°C) for glass dish. In large saucepan, over low heat, melt 1 cup (250 mL) of the chips with butter; remove from heat. Add baking mix, Eagle Brand, egg and vanilla. Stir in nuts and remaining chips. Turn into well-greased 13 x 9-inch (3.5 L) baking pan. Bake 20 to 25 min. or until brownies begin to pull away from sides of pan. Cool. Sprinkle with icing sugar. Cut into squares. Store tightly covered at room temperature. Makes one pan.

CHEESECAKE BARS

2	cups (500 mL) all purpose flour
11/2	cups (375 mL) packed brown sugar
1	cup (250 mL) cold butter
11/2	cups (375 mL) rolled oats
2	pkgs. (250 g each) cream cheese, softened
1/2	cup (125 mL) granulated sugar
3	eggs
1/4	cup (50 mL) milk
1	tsp. (5 mL) vanilla
1/4	cup (50 mL) REALEMON Lemon Juice

Preheat oven to 350°F (180°C). In bowl, combine flour and brown sugar; cut in butter until crumbly. Stir in oats. Reserving 11/2 cups (375 mL) mixture, press remainder onto bottom of 15 x 10-inch (2 L) jelly roll pan; bake 10 min. In large mixer bowl, beat cream cheese and granulated sugar until fluffy. Add eggs; beat well. Add milk and vanilla, then Realemon; beat well. Pour over crust; sprinkle with reserved mixture. Bake 25 min. longer or until lightly browned. Cool. Cut into bars. Cover leftovers; refrigerate. Makes 40 bars.

GERMAN CHOCOLATE SNACKIN' BARS

4	squares (28 g each) sweet cooking chocolate
1/4	cup (50 mL) butter
1	can EAGLE BRAND Sweetened Condensed Milk, divided
2	eggs, beaten
1/2	cup (125 mL) biscuit baking mix
1	tsp. (5 mL) vanilla
2 2/3	cups (650 mL) flaked coconut
1	cup (250 mL) chopped pecans

Preheat oven to 350°F (180°C) or 325°F (160°C) for glass dish. In medium saucepan, over low heat, melt chocolate with butter. Remove from heat; stir in 1/2 cup (125 mL) Eagle Brand, eggs, baking mix and vanilla. Spread evenly into greased 13 x 9-inch (3.5 L) baking pan. In medium bowl, combine remaining Eagle Brand and coconut. Spoon small amounts evenly over chocolate mixture. Sprinkle nuts over top; press down firmly. Bake 25 min. or until wooden pick inserted near centre comes out clean. Cool thoroughly. Cut into bars. Store loosely covered at room temperature. Makes 36 bars.

85

PIES

REALEMON MERINGUE PIE

9   **inch (23 cm) baked pastry shell**
1 1/3 cups (325 mL) sugar, divided
1/3   **cup (75 mL) corn starch**
1/2   **cup (125 mL) REALEMON Lemon Juice**
4   **eggs, separated**
1 1/2 cups (375 mL) boiling water
2   **Tbsp. (30 mL) butter**
1/4   **tsp. (1 mL) cream of tartar**
    Mint leaves (optional)

Preheat oven to 350°F (180°C). In heavy saucepan, combine 1 cup (250 mL) of the sugar and corn starch; add Realemon. In small bowl, beat egg yolks; add to Realemon mixture. Gradually add water, stirring constantly. Over medium heat, cook and stir until mixture boils and thickens. Remove from heat. Add butter; stir until melted. Pour into prepared pastry shell. In small mixer bowl, beat egg whites with cream of tartar until soft peaks form; gradually add remaining 1/3 cup (75 mL) sugar, beating until stiff but not dry. Spread meringue on top of pie, sealing carefully to edge of shell. Bake 12 to 15 min. or until golden brown. Cool. Chill before serving. Garnish with mint leaves if desired. Cover leftovers; refrigerate. Makes one pie.

HARVEST PUMPKIN PIE

9   *inch (23 cm) unbaked homemade pastry shell**
1   *can (19 ozs./540 mL) pumpkin pie filling*
1   *can EAGLE BRAND Sweetened Condensed Milk*
2   *eggs*
1/2 *tsp. (2 mL) each ground cinnamon, ginger and nutmeg*
    Pastry Cut-Outs (optional)

Preheat oven to 425°F (220°C). In large mixing bowl, combine pie filling, Eagle Brand, eggs, cinnamon, ginger and nutmeg. Pour into prepared pastry shell. Bake 15 min. Reduce oven temperature to 350°F (180°C). Bake an additional 35 to 40 min. or until knife inserted near centre comes out clean. Cool. Garnish with Pastry Cut-Outs if desired. Cover leftovers; refrigerate. Makes one pie.

Pastry Cut-Outs: Cut decorative shapes from pastry trimmings. Brush with a little milk. Bake on ungreased cookie sheet in preheated 400°F (200°C) oven 8 to 10 min. or until lightly browned. Cool.

Topping Variation

Crunchy Almond: In small bowl, combine 1/4 cup (50 mL) packed brown sugar and 2 Tbsp. (30 mL) all purpose flour. Cut in 2 Tbsp. (30 mL) cold butter until mixture resembles coarse crumbs. Stir in 1/2 cup (125 mL) chopped toasted almonds. After 30 min. of baking sprinkle nut mixture evenly over top of pie; bake 10 to 15 min. longer.

* Or substitute a 9-inch (23 cm) frozen deep-dish pie shell, thawed.

FLUFFY GRASSHOPPER PIE

2	cups (500 mL) finely-crushed cream-filled chocolate sandwich cookies (about 20 cookies)
1/4	cup (50 mL) butter, melted
1	pkg. (250 g) cream cheese, softened
1	can EAGLE BRAND Sweetened Condensed Milk
3	Tbsp. (45 mL) REALEMON Lemon Juice
3	Tbsp. (45 mL) green crème de menthe
3	Tbsp. (45 mL) white crème de cacao
1	cup (250 mL) whipping cream, whipped*

Combine crumbs and butter; press firmly on bottom and side of buttered 9-inch (23 cm) pie plate. Chill. In large mixer bowl, beat cream cheese until fluffy; gradually beat in Eagle Brand until smooth. Stir in Realemon and liqueurs. Fold in whipped cream. Chill 20 min. Pour into prepared crust. Chill 4 hours or until set. Garnish as desired. Cover leftovers; refrigerate. Makes one pie.

For Frozen Fluffy Grasshopper Pie, prepare pie as above. Freeze 4 hours or until firm. Wrap leftovers; return to freezer.

* Or substitute 1 container (500 mL) frozen non-dairy whipped topping, thawed.

CHERRY CHEESE PIE

9 inch (23 cm) graham wafer crumb crust or baked pastry shell
1 pkg. (250 g) cream cheese, softened
1 can EAGLE BRAND Sweetened Condensed Milk
1/3 cup (75 mL) REALEMON Lemon Juice
1 tsp. (5 mL) vanilla
1 can (19 ozs./ 540 mL) cherry pie filling, chilled

In large mixer bowl, beat cream cheese until fluffy. Add Eagle Brand; blend thoroughly. Stir in Realemon and vanilla. Pour into prepared crust. Chill 3 hours or until set. Top with desired amount of pie filling before serving. Cover leftovers; refrigerate. Makes one pie.

BANANA SPLIT DESSERT PIZZA

1	can EAGLE BRAND Sweetened Condensed Milk
1/2	cup (125 mL) sour cream
6	Tbsp. (90 mL) REALEMON Lemon Juice, divided
1	tsp. (5 mL) vanilla
1/2	cup (125 mL) butter, softened
1/4	cup (50 mL) packed brown sugar
1	cup (250 mL) all purpose flour
3/4	cup (175 mL) finely-chopped nuts
3	medium bananas, sliced
1	cup (250 mL) canned sliced pineapple, drained and halved
	Maraschino cherries
	Additional nuts
1	square (28 g) semi-sweet chocolate
1	Tbsp. (15 mL) butter

Preheat oven to 375°F (190°C). In medium mixing bowl, combine Eagle Brand, sour cream, 4 Tbsp. (60 mL) of the Realemon and vanilla; mix well. Chill. In large mixer bowl, beat 1/2 cup (125 mL) butter and sugar until fluffy; add flour and 3/4 cup (175 mL) nuts. Mix well. On lightly-greased pizza pan or baking sheet, press dough into 12-inch (30 cm) circle, forming rim around edge. Prick with fork. Bake 10 to 12 min. or until lightly browned. Cool. Arrange 2 of the bananas on prepared crust. Spoon filling evenly over bananas. Dip remaining banana slices in remaining 2 Tbsp. (30 mL) Realemon; arrange on top along with pineapple, cherries and additional nuts. In small saucepan, over low heat, melt chocolate with 1 Tbsp. (15 mL) butter; drizzle over pie. Chill thoroughly. Cover leftovers; refrigerate. Makes 1 dessert pizza.

Note: Crust and filling can be made in advance and kept in refrigerator until ready to assemble.

TROPICAL LIME PIE

2   *cups (500 mL) flaked coconut, toasted **
1/3   *cup (75 mL) butter, melted*
1   *pkg. (250 g) cream cheese, softened*
1   *can EAGLE BRAND Sweetened Condensed Milk*
1/3   *cup (75 mL) REALIME Lime Juice*
     Few drops green food colour (optional)
1   *cup (250 mL) whipping cream, whipped ***

Combine coconut and butter; press firmly on bottom and side of 9-inch (23 cm) pie plate. Chill. In large mixer bowl, beat cream cheese until fluffy. Gradually beat in Eagle Brand then Realime and food colour if desired, until smooth. Fold in whipped cream. Pour into prepared crust. Chill 3 hours or until set. Garnish as desired. Cover leftovers; refrigerate. Makes one pie.

*   See page 132 for instructions for toasting coconut.

** Or substitute 1 container (500 mL) frozen non-dairy whipped topping, thawed.

FRESH FRUIT DESSERT PIZZA

1	can EAGLE BRAND Sweetened Condensed Milk
1/2	cup (125 mL) sour cream
1/4	cup (50 mL) REALEMON Lemon Juice
1	tsp. (5 mL) vanilla
1/2	cup (125 mL) butter, softened
1/4	cup (50 mL) packed brown sugar
1	cup (250 mL) all purpose flour
1/4	cup (50 mL) rolled oats
1/4	cup (50 mL) finely-chopped nuts
	Assorted fresh or canned fruit (strawberries, grapes, kiwi fruit, oranges, pineapple, bananas, etc.)

Preheat oven to 375°F (190°C). In medium mixing bowl, combine Eagle Brand, sour cream, Realemon and vanilla; mix well. Chill. In large mixer bowl, beat butter and sugar until fluffy; add flour, oats and nuts. Mix well. On lightly-greased pizza pan or baking sheet, press dough into 12-inch (30 cm) circle, forming rim around edge. Prick with fork. Bake 10 to 12 min. or until lightly browned. Cool. Pour filling evenly over prepared crust. Arrange fruit on top. Chill before serving. Cover leftovers; refrigerate. Makes one dessert pizza.

FUDGE DELUXE PIE

9	inch (23 cm) baked pastry shell
3	squares (28 g each) semi-sweet chocolate
1	can EAGLE BRAND Sweetened Condensed Milk
1/4	tsp. (1 mL) salt
1/4	cup (50 mL) hot water
1	tsp. (5 mL) vanilla
1	cup (250 mL) whipping cream, whipped*

In heavy saucepan, over medium heat, melt chocolate with Eagle Brand and salt. Cook and stir until very thick and fudgey, 5 to 8 min. Add water; cook and stir until mixture thickens and boils. Immediately remove from heat; stir in vanilla. Cool 15 min. Chill thoroughly, 20 to 30 min.; stir. Fold whipped cream into chocolate mixture. Pour into prepared pastry shell. Chill 3 hours or until set. Garnish as desired. Cover leftovers; refrigerate. Makes one pie.

* Or substitute 1 container (500 mL) frozen non-dairy whipped topping, thawed.

KEY LIME PIE

9	*inch (23 cm) baked pastry shell*
3	*eggs, separated*
1	*can EAGLE BRAND Sweetened Condensed Milk*
1/2	*cup (125 mL) REALIME Lime Juice*
	Few drops green food colour (optional)
1/2	*tsp. (2 mL) cream of tartar*
1/3	*cup (75 mL) sugar*

Preheat oven to 350°F (180°C). In medium bowl beat egg yolks; stir in Eagle Brand, Realime and food colour if desired. Pour into prepared pastry shell. In small mixer bowl, beat egg whites with cream of tartar until foamy; gradually add sugar, beating until stiff but not dry. Spread meringue on top of pie, sealing carefully to edge of shell. Bake 15 min. or until meringue is golden brown. Cool. Chill before serving. Makes one pie.

ALOHA CREAM PIE

2	*cups (500 mL) flaked coconut, toasted **
1/3	*cup (75 mL) butter, melted*
1	*pkg. (250 g) cream cheese, softened*
1	*can EAGLE BRAND Sweetened Condensed Milk*
1	*can (178 mL) frozen orange juice concentrate, thawed*
1	*can (14 ozs./ 398 mL) crushed pineapple, well drained*
1	*cup (250 mL) whipping cream, whipped***

Combine coconut and butter; press firmly onto bottom and side of 9-inch (23 cm) pie plate. Chill. In large mixer bowl, beat cream cheese until fluffy. Gradually beat in Eagle Brand then orange juice concentrate until smooth. Stir in pineapple. Fold in whipped cream. Pour into prepared crust. Chill 6 hours or until set. Garnish as desired. Cover leftovers; refrigerate. Makes one pie.

* See page 132 for instructions for toasting coconut.

** Or substitute 1 container (500 mL) frozen non-dairy whipped topping, thawed.

FUDGEY PECAN PIE

9	inch (23 cm) unbaked pastry shell
2	squares (28 g each) semi-sweet chocolate
1/4	cup (50 mL) butter
1	can EAGLE BRAND Sweetened Condensed Milk
1/2	cup (125 mL) hot water
2	eggs, beaten
1	tsp. (5 mL) vanilla
	Pinch salt
1 1/4	cups (300 mL) pecan halves

Preheat oven to 350°F (180°C). In medium saucepan, over low heat, melt chocolate with butter. Stir in Eagle Brand, hot water and eggs; mix well. Remove from heat; stir in vanilla, salt and pecans. Pour into prepared pastry shell. Bake 40 to 45 min. or until centre is set. Cool slightly. Serve warm or chilled. Garnish as desired. Cover leftovers; refrigerate. Makes one pie.

STREUSEL-TOPPED APPLE CUSTARD PIE

9	inch (23 cm) unbaked pastry shell
4	cups (1 L) pared, cored, sliced apples (about 4 large apples)
1	Tbsp. (15 mL) REALEMON Lemon Juice
2	eggs
1	can EAGLE BRAND Sweetened Condensed Milk
1/4	cup (50 mL) butter, melted
1/2	tsp. (2 mL) ground cinnamon
1/4	tsp. (1 mL) ground nutmeg
1/4	cup (50 mL) chopped nuts
2	Tbsp. (30 mL) packed brown sugar

Preheat oven to 425°F (220°C). Toss apples with Realemon; arrange in prepared pastry shell. In medium bowl, beat eggs; stir in Eagle Brand, butter, cinnamon and nutmeg. Mix well. Pour over apples. In small bowl, combine nuts and sugar; sprinkle over pie. Bake 10 min. Reduce oven temperature to 375°F (190°C); continue baking 40 min. or until golden and set in centre. Cool. Serve warm or chilled. Cover leftovers; refrigerate. Makes one pie.

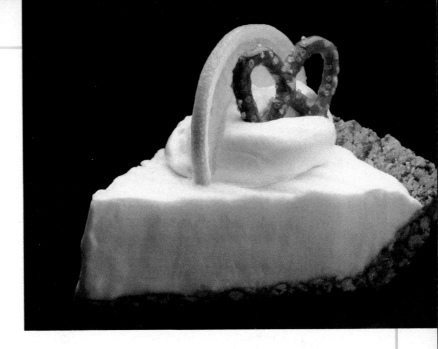

MARGARITA PIE

1 1/4 cups (300 mL) finely-crushed pretzel crumbs
1/2 cup (125 mL) butter, melted
1/4 cup (50 mL) sugar
1 can EAGLE BRAND Sweetened Condensed Milk
1/3 cup (75 mL) REALIME Lime Juice
3 to 4 Tbsp. (45 to 50 mL) tequila
2 Tbsp. (30 mL) triple sec or **other orange-flavoured liqueur**
1 cup (250 mL) whipping cream, whipped *

Combine crumbs, butter and sugar; press on bottom and side of lightly-buttered 9-inch (23 cm) pie plate. Chill. In large mixing bowl, combine Eagle Brand, Realime, tequila and liqueur; mix well. Fold in whipped cream. Pour into prepared crust. Chill 2 hours or until set. Garnish as desired. Cover leftovers; refrigerate. Makes one pie.

Frozen Margarita pie: Prepare pie as above. Freeze 4 hours or until firm. Wrap leftovers; return to freezer.

* Or substitute 1 container (500 mL) frozen non-dairy whipped topping, thawed.

CLASSIC DESSERTS

STRAWBERRIES AND CREAM DESSERT

1   **can EAGLE BRAND Sweetened Condensed Milk**
1 1/2 **cups (375 mL) cold water**
1   **pkg. (4-serving size) vanilla instant pudding mix**
2   **cups (500 mL) whipping cream, whipped**
1   **pkg. (298 g) frozen pound cake, thawed, cubed**
4   **cups (1 L) fresh strawberries, cleaned, hulled, sliced**
1/2 **cup (125 mL) strawberry jam**
     Additional fresh strawberries
     Toasted slivered or **sliced almonds**

In large mixer bowl, combine Eagle Brand and water. Add pudding mix; beat well. Chill until thickened, about 20 min. Fold in whipped cream. Spoon 2 cups (500 mL) of the pudding mixture into 4-quart (4 L) round glass serving bowl; top with half the cake cubes, half the strawberries, half the jam and half the remaining pudding mixture. Repeat layering, ending with pudding mixture. Chill at least 4 hours. Garnish with additional strawberries and almonds. Cover leftovers; refrigerate. Makes 10 to 12 servings.

LUSCIOUS LEMON CREAM

2	eggs
1	cup (250 mL) sugar, divided
1/3	cup (75 mL) REALEMON Lemon Juice
1	Tbsp. (15 mL) corn starch
1/2	cup (125 mL) water
1	tsp. (5 mL) vanilla
1	cup (250 mL) whipping cream, whipped
	Fresh fruit

In small bowl, beat eggs, 1/2 cup (125 mL) of the sugar and Realemon until well combined; set aside. In medium saucepan, combine remaining 1/2 cup (125 mL) sugar and corn starch. Gradually add water; mix well. Over medium heat, cook and stir until mixture boils and thickens; remove from heat. Gradually beat in egg mixture. Over low heat, cook and stir until slightly thickened. Remove from heat; stir in vanilla. Cool. Fold whipped cream into lemon mixture. Chill. Serve with fresh fruit. Cover leftovers; refrigerate. Makes about 3 cups (750 mL).

RASPBERRIES AND CREAM TRIFLE

1   can *EAGLE BRAND Sweetened Condensed Milk*
11/2 cups (375 mL) cold water
1   pkg. (4-serving size) vanilla instant pudding mix
2   cups (500 mL) whipping cream, whipped
1   pkg. (298 g) frozen pound cake, thawed, cubed
1/4 cup (50 mL) sherry, divided
1   can (19 ozs./ 540 mL) raspberry pie filling
    Additional whipped cream
    Fresh raspberries
    Mint leaves

In large mixer bowl combine Eagle Brand and water. Add pudding mix; beat well. Chill until thickened, about 20 min. Fold in whipped cream. Spoon 2 cups (500 mL) of the pudding mixture into 3-quart (3 L) round glass serving bowl. Top with half the cake cubes. Sprinkle 2 Tbsp. (30 mL) of the sherry over cake. Top with half the pie filling and half the remaining pudding mixture. Repeat layering, ending with pudding mixture. Chill at least 4 hours. Garnish with additional whipped cream, fresh raspberries and mint leaves. Cover leftovers; refrigerate. Makes 8 to 10 servings.

SPICED LEMON PEARS

11/2 cups (375 mL) water
1   cup (250 mL) packed brown sugar
1/4 cup (50 mL) REALEMON Lemon Juice
2   cinnamon sticks
6   whole cloves
4   fresh pears, halved, pared, cored

In large saucepan, combine water, sugar, Realemon, cinnamon sticks and cloves. Bring to boil; cook and stir until sugar dissolves. Add pears; cover and simmer 10 min. or until pears are tender. Serve warm or chilled as a dessert, meat accompaniment or salad. Makes 4 servings.

Microwave: In 2-quart (2 L) microwave-safe bowl, combine all ingredients except pears. Cover with vented plastic wrap; microwave at HIGH (100%) 6 min. or until mixture boils. Stir; add pears. Re-cover. Microwave at HIGH (100%) 6 min. or until pears are tender. Proceed as above.

APPLE BREAD PUDDING WITH MAPLE RUM SAUCE

 4 cups (1 L) day-old French bread cubes
 2 cups (500 mL) pared, cored, chopped apples
1/2 cup (125 mL) raisins
 3 eggs
 1 can EAGLE BRAND Sweetened Condensed Milk
13/4 cups (425 mL) hot water
1/4 cup (50 mL) butter, melted
 1 tsp. (5 mL) maple extract
    Maple Rum Sauce

Preheat oven to 350°F (180°C). In large bowl combine bread cubes, apples and raisins. Place in greased 9-inch (2.5 L) square baking pan. In large bowl beat eggs; stir in Eagle Brand, water, butter and maple extract. Pour over bread cube mixture, completely moistening bread. Bake 45 to 50 min. or until knife inserted in centre comes out clean. Cool slightly. Serve warm with Maple Rum Sauce. Makes 8 servings.

Maple Rum Sauce: In medium saucepan melt 1/4 cup (50 mL) butter; stir in 1 cup (250 mL) packed brown sugar and 1/2 cup (125 mL) whipping cream. Over medium heat, cook and stir until mixture comes to a boil. Boil 2 to 3 min. Remove from heat; stir in 2 Tbsp. (30 mL) rum and 1/2 tsp. (2 mL) maple extract. Cool slightly. Makes about 1 cup (250 mL).

FUDGEY MILK CHOCOLATE FONDUE

2 cups (500 mL) chocolate topping sauce for ice cream
1 can EAGLE BRAND Sweetened Condensed Milk
    Pinch salt
1 1/2 tsp. (7 mL) vanilla
    Dippers*

In heavy saucepan, combine chocolate sauce, Eagle Brand and salt. Over medium heat, cook and stir until mixture *just* comes to a boil. Remove from heat; stir in vanilla. Serve warm with Dippers*. Cover leftovers; refrigerate. Makes about 3 1/4 cups (800 mL).

Microwave: In 1-quart (1 L) glass measure combine chocolate sauce, Eagle Brand and salt. Microwave, uncovered, at HIGH (100%) 3 1/2 to 4 min. or until hot, stirring every min. Stir in vanilla. Proceed as above.

* **Dippers**: Pound cake cubes, melon balls, cherries with stems, pineapple chunks, orange slices, strawberries, banana slices, apple wedges, grapes, dried apricots, peach chunks, plum slices, pear slices, angel cake cubes, kiwi fruit slices and marshmallows.

Note: Can be served warm or cold over ice cream. Can be made several weeks ahead. Store, tightly covered in refrigerator.

RASPBERRY SWIRL DESSERT

2 2/3 cups (650 mL) flaked coconut, toasted *
1/3 cup (75 mL) butter, melted
1 pkg. (425 g) frozen red raspberries in syrup, thawed
1 Tbsp. (15 mL) corn starch
1 envelope unflavoured gelatin
1/4 cup (50 mL) water
1 can EAGLE BRAND Sweetened Condensed Milk
1 cup (250 mL) sour cream
3 Tbsp. (45 mL) orange-flavoured liqueur
1 cup (250 mL) whipping cream, whipped

Combine coconut and butter; press firmly on bottom and side of 8 or 9-inch (20 to 23 cm) springform pan. Chill. In blender container, blend raspberries until smooth. In small saucepan, combine raspberries and corn starch; cook and stir over medium heat until mixture boils and thickens. Cool. In small saucepan sprinkle gelatin over water; let stand 1 min. Over low heat, stir until gelatin dissolves; set aside. In large mixing bowl, combine Eagle Brand, sour cream, liqueur and gelatin; mix well. Fold in whipped cream. Chill 10 min. or until mixture mounds slightly. Spread half the gelatin mixture into prepared pan; top with half the raspberry mixture in small amounts. Repeat layering. With metal spatula swirl raspberry mixture through cream mixture**. Chill 6 hours or until set. Garnish as desired. Cover leftovers; refrigerate. Makes 10 to 12 servings.

*   See page 132 for instructions on toasting coconut.

** See page 134 for instructions on marbling.

TANGY LEMON TARTS

24	frozen medium tarts shells, baked
2	cups (500 mL) sugar
3/4	cup (175 mL) butter
2/3	cup REALEMON Lemon Juice
6	eggs

In medium saucepan, combine sugar, butter, and Realemon. Over low heat, cook and stir until sugar dissolves and butter melts. In small bowl, beat eggs well. Gradually stir about 1/4 cup (50 mL) hot mixture into eggs; stir into remaining Realemon mixture. Over medium heat cook and stir until mixture thickens, about 8 to 10 min. Chill. Spoon into prepared tart shells. Cover leftovers; refrigerate. Makes 24 tarts.

Microwave: In 2-quart (2 L) glass measure microwave butter, uncovered, at HIGH (100%) 1 min. or until melted. Stir in Realemon and sugar. Microwave, uncovered, at HIGH (100%) 21/2 min. or until sugar dissolves, stirring every min. In small bowl beat eggs well. Gradually stir about 1/4 cup (50 mL) hot mixture into eggs; stir into remaining Realemon mixture. Microwave, uncovered, at MEDIUM HIGH (70%) 5 to 6 min. or until thick, stirring every min. Proceed as above.

CREME CARAMEL

1/2	cup (125 mL) sugar
4	eggs
13/4	cups (425 mL) water
1	can EAGLE BRAND Sweetened Condensed Milk
1/2	tsp. (2 mL) vanilla
	Pinch salt

Preheat oven to 300°F (150°C). In heavy frypan over medium heat, cook sugar, stirring constantly until melted and caramel-coloured. Pour into 4-cup (1 L) round shallow baking dish, immediately tilting to coat bottom of dish completely. In medium bowl beat eggs; stir in water, Eagle Brand, vanilla and salt. Pour through a fine sieve into prepared dish. Set dish in larger pan (eg. broiler pan). Fill pan with hot water to a depth of 1 inch (2.5 cm). Bake 45 to 50 min. or until knife inserted near centre comes out clean. Remove dish from water bath. Cool. Chill. To serve loosen side of custard with knife; invert onto serving dish with rim; cut into wedges. Cover leftovers; refrigerate. Makes 6 to 8 servings.

ICE CREAM AND FROZEN DESSERTS

FROZEN PEPPERMINT CHEESECAKE

1¼ cups (300 mL) chocolate wafer cookie crumbs (about 24 wafers)
1/4 cup (50 mL) sugar
1/4 cup (50 mL) butter, melted
1 pkg. (250 g) cream cheese, softened
1 can EAGLE BRAND Sweetened Condensed Milk
1 cup (250 mL) crushed hard peppermint candy
Red food colour (optional)
2 cups (500 mL) whipping cream, whipped

Combine crumbs, sugar and butter; press onto bottom and half way up side of 9-inch (23 cm) springform pan. Chill. In large mixer bowl, beat cream cheese until fluffy. Gradually beat in Eagle Brand. Stir in crushed candy and food colour if desired. Fold in whipped cream. Pour into prepared pan; cover. Freeze 6 hours or until firm. Garnish as desired. Wrap leftovers; return to freezer. Makes 1 cheesecake.

FROZEN MOCHA CHEESECAKE

1 1/4 cups (300 mL) chocolate wafer cookie crumbs (about 24 wafers)
1/4 cup (50 mL) butter, melted
1/4 cup (50 mL) sugar
1 pkg. (250 g) cream cheese, softened
1 can EAGLE BRAND Sweetened Condensed Milk
2/3 cup (150 mL) chocolate syrup
1 to 2 Tbsp. (15 to 30 mL) instant coffee granules
1 tsp. (5 mL) hot water
1 cup (250 mL) whipping cream, whipped
Additional chocolate wafer crumbs (optional)

Combine crumbs, butter and sugar; press firmly on bottom and up side of 8 or
9-inch (20 or 23 cm) springform pan. Chill. In large mixer bowl, beat cream
cheese until fluffy. Gradually beat in Eagle Brand and syrup until smooth. In
small bowl, dissolve coffee in water; add to cheese mixture. Mix well. Fold in
whipped cream. Pour into prepared pan; cover. Freeze 6 hours or until firm.
Garnish with chocolate crumbs if desired. Wrap leftovers; return to freezer.
Makes 1 cheesecake.

EASY HOMEMADE CHOCOLATE ICE CREAM

1	can EAGLE BRAND Sweetened Condensed Milk
2/3	cup (150 mL) chocolate syrup
2	cups (500 mL) whipping cream, whipped

In large bowl, combine Eagle Brand and syrup. Fold in whipped cream. Pour into foil-lined 9 x 5-inch (1.5 L) loaf pan; cover. Freeze 6 hours or until firm. Scoop ice cream from pan or remove from pan, peel off foil and slice. Wrap leftovers; return to freezer. Makes about 6 cups (1.5 L).

French vanilla: In large bowl, combine Eagle Brand, 2 Tbsp. (30 mL) water, 3 beaten egg yolks* and 4 tsp. (20 mL) vanilla. Fold in whipped cream. Proceed as above.

Mint chocolate chip: In large bowl, combine Eagle Brand, 2 tsp. (10 mL) peppermint extract, 3 to 4 drops green food colour and 2 Tbsp. (30 mL) water. Fold in whipped cream and 1/2 cup (125 mL) mini semi-sweet chocolate chips. Proceed as above.

Butter pecan: In small saucepan melt 2 Tbsp. (30 mL) butter: sauté 1/2 cup (125 mL) chopped pecans until golden; cool. In large bowl, combine Eagle Brand, 2 beaten egg yolks*, 1 tsp. (5 mL) maple extract and pecans. Fold in whipped cream. Proceed as above.

* Use only clean, uncracked eggs.

FROZEN FLUFFY STRAWBERRY DESSERT

2 1/2 cups (625 mL) flaked coconut, toasted *
1/3   cup (75 mL) butter, melted
1   pkg. (125 g) cream cheese, softened
1   can EAGLE BRAND Sweetened Condensed Milk
2 1/2 cups (625 mL) fresh or frozen strawberries, thawed, mashed or puréed
3   Tbsp. (45 mL) REALEMON Lemon Juice
1   cup (250 mL) whipping cream, whipped
       Additional fresh whole strawberries

Combine coconut and butter; press onto bottom and 1 1/2 inches (4 cm) up side of 9-inch (23 cm) springform pan. Chill. In large mixer bowl beat cream cheese until fluffy; gradually beat in Eagle Brand. Stir in puréed strawberries and Realemon. Fold in whipped cream. Pour into prepared pan. Freeze 6 hours or until firm. To serve, garnish with whole strawberries. Wrap leftovers; return to freezer. Makes 8 to 10 servings.

*   See page 132 for instructions for toasting coconut.

FROZEN MINT CHOCOLATE MOUSSE

1	can *EAGLE BRAND Sweetened Condensed Milk*
2/3	cup *(150 mL) chocolate syrup*
3/4	tsp. *(4 mL) peppermint extract*
1	cup *(250 mL) whipping cream, whipped*

In large bowl, combine Eagle Brand, syrup and peppermint extract. Fold in whipped cream. Spoon equal portions into 6 or 8 individual serving dishes. Freeze 3 to 4 hours or until firm. Garnish as desired. Serve immediately. Wrap leftovers; return to freezer. Makes 6 to 8 servings.

FROZEN PEANUT BUTTER PIE

- **1   Chocolate Crunch Crust**
- **1   pkg. (250 g) cream cheese, softened**
- **1   can EAGLE BRAND Sweetened Condensed Milk**
- **3/4   cup (175 mL) peanut butter**
- **2   Tbsp. (30 mL) REALEMON Lemon Juice**
- **1   tsp. (5 mL) vanilla**
- **1   cup (250 mL) whipping cream, whipped ***
- **   Chocolate Fudge Ice Cream Topping**

In large mixer bowl, beat cheese until fluffy; gradually beat in Eagle Brand then peanut butter until smooth. Stir in Realemon and vanilla. Fold in whipped cream. Pour into prepared crust. Drizzle topping over pie. Freeze 4 hours or until firm. Wrap leftovers; return to freezer. Makes one pie.

Chocolate crunch crust: In heavy saucepan, over low heat, melt 1/3 cup (75 mL) butter and 1 pkg. (175 g) semi-sweet chocolate chips. Remove from heat; gently stir in 21/2 cups (625 mL) toasted rice cereal until completely coated. Press onto bottom and up side of buttered 9-inch (23 cm) pie plate. Chill 30 min.

* Or substitute 1 container (500 mL) frozen non-dairy whipped topping, thawed.

LEMON ICE CREAM

3	egg yolks
1	can EAGLE BRAND Sweetened Condensed Milk
1/2	cup (125 mL) REALEMON Lemon Juice
	Few drops yellow food colour (optional)
2	cups (500 mL) whipping cream, whipped

In large bowl, beat egg yolks; stir in Eagle Brand, Realemon and food colour if desired. Fold in whipped cream. Pour into foil-lined 9 x 5-inch (1.5 L) loaf pan; cover. Freeze 6 hours or until firm. Scoop ice cream from pan or remove from pan, peel off foil and slice. Serve with warm Blueberry 'n' Spice Sauce. Wrap leftovers; return to freezer. Makes about 6 cups (1.5 L).

BLUEBERRY 'N' SPICE SAUCE

1/2	cup (125 mL) sugar
1	Tbsp. (15 mL) corn starch
1/2	tsp. (2 mL) ground cinnamon
1/4	tsp. (1 mL) ground nutmeg
1/4	cup (50 mL) hot water
2	Tbsp. (30 mL) REALEMON Lemon Juice
2	cups (500 mL) fresh or frozen blueberries, thawed, drained

In small saucepan combine sugar, corn starch, cinnamon and nutmeg; gradually stir in water and Realemon. Over medium heat, cook and stir until mixture boils and thickens. Add blueberries; cook and stir until mixture comes to a boil. Serve warm over ice cream or cake. Makes about 1 2/3 cups (400 mL).

(Also pictured – Margarita Pie, recipe pg. 97.)

FROZEN STRAWBERRY MARGARITA PIE

1 1/4 cups (300 mL) finely-crushed pretzel crumbs
1/2   cup (125 mL) butter, melted
1/4   cup (50 mL) sugar
1   can EAGLE BRAND Sweetened Condensed Milk
1   cup (250 mL) chopped fresh strawberries or frozen unsweetened
       strawberries, thawed
1/4   cup (50 mL) REALIME Lime Juice
3 to 4 Tbsp. (45 to 50 mL) tequila
2   Tbsp. (30 mL) triple sec or other orange-flavoured liqueur
2 to 4 drops red food colour (optional)
1   cup (250 mL) whipping cream, whipped *

Combine crumbs, butter and sugar; press firmly on bottom and side of lightly-
buttered 9-inch (23 cm) pie plate. Chill. In large mixing bowl, combine Eagle
Brand, chopped strawberries, Realime, tequila, liqueur and food colour, if
desired; mix well. Fold in whipped cream. Pour into prepared crust. Freeze
4 hours or until firm. Let stand 10 min. before serving. Garnish as desired. Wrap
leftovers; return to freezer. Makes one pie.

*   Or substitute 1 container (500 mL) frozen non-dairy whipped topping, thawed.

FROZEN LEMON SOUFFLÉ

1 1/2 cups (375 mL) sugar
3   Tbsp. (45 mL) corn starch
1   envelope unflavoured gelatin
1   cup (250 mL) water
2/3 cup (150 mL) REALEMON Lemon Juice
     Few drops yellow food colour (optional)
3   egg whites*
1   cup (250 mL) whipping cream, whipped
     Additional whipped cream (optional)
     Candy lemon drops (optional)
     Gum drop slices (optional)
     Raspberry Sauce (optional)

In large saucepan, combine sugar, corn starch and gelatin; add water and
Realemon. Over medium heat, cook and stir until mixture boils and thickens; stir
in food colour if desired. Cool. Chill until partially set, about 1 hour, stirring
occasionally. In small mixer bowl, beat egg whites until stiff but not dry; fold
with whipped cream into Realemon mixture. Tape or tie a 3-inch (8 cm) wax
paper or foil collar securely around rim of 1-quart (1 L) soufflé dish. Pour
mixture into dish. Freeze 6 hours or until firm. Remove collar. Garnish with
additional whipped cream, lemon drops or gum drop slices if desired or serve
with Raspberry Sauce. Wrap leftovers; return to freezer. Makes 6-8 servings.

Raspberry sauce: In blender container, purée 1 pkg. (425 g) frozen red
raspberries in syrup, thawed. Press through sieve to remove seeds. In small
saucepan smoothly combine raspberry purée and 1 tsp. (5 mL) corn starch.
Over medium heat, cook and stir until mixture boils and thickens. Cool. Makes
about 1 1/4 cups (300 mL).

* Use only clean, uncracked eggs.

Pictured clock-wise
from top: Coconut Rum
Balls, Chocolate Pecan Critters
(recipes page 120), Fruit Bonbons
(recipe page 118), Milk Chocolate Brandy
Balls, Buckeyes (recipes page 119), Foolproof Dark
Chocolate Fudge (recipe page 117), Peanut Butter Logs
(recipe page 121), Layered Mint Chocolate Candy (recipe
page 118).

CANDIES AND CONFECTIONS

FOOLPROOF DARK CHOCOLATE FUDGE

3 **pkgs. (175 g** each**) semi-sweet chocolate chips**
1 **can EAGLE BRAND Sweetened Condensed Milk**
Pinch salt
1/2 **cup (125 mL) chopped nuts**
1 1/2 tsp. (7 mL) vanilla

In heavy saucepan, over low heat, melt chips with Eagle Brand and salt. Remove from heat; stir in nuts and vanilla. Spread evenly into wax paper-lined 8 or 9-inch (20 or 23 cm) square pan. Chill 2 hours or until firm. Turn fudge onto cutting board; peel off paper; cut into squares*. Store loosely covered at room temperature. Makes about 2 lbs. (1 kg).

Microwave: In 2-quart (2 L) glass measure, combine chips with Eagle Brand. Microwave, uncovered, at HIGH (100%) 2 min. Stir until chips melt and mixture is smooth. Stir in remaining ingredients. Proceed as above.

* Fudge may be well wrapped and frozen for up to 6 weeks. Thaw at room temperature before cutting.

LAYERED MINT CHOCOLATE CANDY

1   pkg. (350 g) semi-sweet chocolate chips
1   can EAGLE BRAND Sweetened Condensed Milk, divided
2   tsp. (10 mL) vanilla
6   ozs. (175 g) white chocolate
1   Tbsp. (15 mL) peppermint extract
    Few drops green food colour (optional)

In heavy saucepan, over low heat, melt chips with 1 cup (250 mL) Eagle Brand. Remove from heat; stir in vanilla. Spread half the mixture into wax paper-lined 8 or 9-inch (2 or 2.5 L) square pan; chill 10 min. or until firm. Hold remaining chocolate mixture at room temperature. In heavy saucepan, over low heat, melt white chocolate with remaining Eagle Brand. Remove from heat; stir in peppermint extract and food colour if desired. Spread on chilled chocolate layer; chill 10 min. longer or until firm. Spread reserved chocolate mixture on mint layer. Chill 2 hours or until firm. Turn onto cutting board; peel off paper and cut into squares. Store loosely covered at room temperature. Makes about 13/4 lbs. (750 g).

FRUIT BONBONS

1   can EAGLE BRAND Sweetened Condensed Milk
2   pkgs. (400 g each) flaked coconut
1   pkg. (85 g) any fruit-flavoured jelly powder, divided
1   cup (250 mL) ground blanched almonds
1   tsp. (5 mL) almond extract
    Food colour (optional)

In large mixing bowl, combine Eagle Brand, coconut, 1/3 cup (75 mL) of the jelly powder, almonds, almond extract and enough food colour if desired, to colour mixture desired shade. Chill 1 hour or until firm enough to handle. Using about 11/2 tsp. (7 mL) mixture for each, shape into 1-inch (2.5 cm) balls. Sprinkle remaining jelly powder onto wax paper; roll each ball in jelly powder to coat. Place on wax paper-lined baking sheets; chill. Store covered at room temperature or in refrigerator. Makes about 5 dozen candies.

BUCKEYES

1   *pkg. (250 g) cream cheese, softened*
1   *can EAGLE BRAND Sweetened Condensed Milk*
2   *pkgs. (350 g* each*) peanut butter-flavoured chips*
1   *cup (250 mL) finely-chopped peanuts*
1   *pkg. (175 g) semi-sweet chocolate chips*
2   *Tbsp. (30 mL) shortening*

In large mixer bowl, beat cream cheese until fluffy. Gradually beat in Eagle Brand until smooth. In heavy saucepan, over low heat, melt peanut butter chips; stir into cheese mixture. Add nuts. Chill 2 to 3 hours; shape into 1-inch (2.5 cm) balls. In small saucepan, over low heat, melt chocolate chips with shortening. With wooden pick, dip each peanut ball into chocolate mixture, not coating completely. Place on wax paper-lined baking sheets until firm. Store covered, at room temperature or in refrigerator. Makes about 7 dozen candies.

MILK CHOCOLATE BRANDY BALLS

3   *cups (750 mL) vanilla wafer cookie crumbs*
5   *Tbsp. (75 mL) brandy*
1   *pkg. (300 g) milk chocolate chips*
1   *can EAGLE BRAND Sweetened Condensed Milk*
    Finely-chopped nuts

In medium mixing bowl, combine crumbs and brandy. In heavy saucepan, over low heat, melt chips. Remove from heat; add Eagle Brand. Gradually add crumb mixture; mix well. Let stand at room temperature 30 min. or chill. Shape into 1-inch (2.5 cm) balls; roll in nuts. Store tightly covered at room temperature. Makes about 5½ dozen candies.

Note: Flavour of these candies improves after 24 hours. They can be made ahead, wrapped well and stored in freezer.

COCONUT RUM BALLS

3   cups (750 mL) vanilla wafer cookie crumbs
11/3 cups (325 mL) flaked coconut
1   cup (250 mL) finely-chopped nuts
1   can EAGLE BRAND Sweetened Condensed Milk
1/4 cup (50 mL) rum
    Additional flaked coconut or icing sugar.

In large mixing bowl, combine crumbs, coconut and nuts. Add Eagle Brand and rum; mix well. Chill 4 hours. Shape into 1-inch (2.5 cm) balls. Roll in additional coconut. Store tightly covered in refrigerator. Makes about 8 dozen candies.

Note: Flavour of these candies improves after 24 hours. They can be made ahead, covered and stored in refrigerator several weeks.

CHOCOLATE PECAN CRITTERS

1   pkg. (300 g) milk chocolate chips
1   pkg. (175 g) semi-sweet chocolate chips
1/4 cup (50 mL) butter
1   can EAGLE BRAND Sweetened Condensed Milk
    Pinch salt
2   cups (500 mL) coarsely-chopped pecans
2   tsp. (10 mL) vanilla
    Pecan halves

In heavy saucepan, over medium heat, melt chips and butter with Eagle Brand and salt. Remove from heat; stir in nuts and vanilla. Drop by small spoonfuls onto wax paper-lined baking sheets. Top with pecan halves. Chill. Store tightly covered in refrigerator. Makes about 5 dozen candies.

Microwave: In 2-quart (2 L) glass measure, combine chips, butter, Eagle Brand and salt. Microwave, uncovered, at HIGH (100%) 21/2 to 3 min., stirring after 11/2 min. Stir until chips melt and mixture is smooth. Stir in remaining ingredients. Proceed as above.

SUPER MAPLE FUDGE

1   pkg. (350 g) butterscotch-flavoured chips
1   can EAGLE BRAND Sweetened Condensed Milk
1 1/4 cups (300 mL) icing sugar
1   tsp. (5 mL) maple extract
1/2 cup (125 mL) chopped nuts

In heavy saucepan, over low heat, melt chips with Eagle Brand. Remove from heat; stir in icing sugar, maple extract and nuts. Spread evenly in wax paper-lined 8-inch (20 cm) square pan. Chill 2 to 3 hours or until firm. Turn fudge onto cutting board; peel off paper;* cut into squares. Store loosely covered at room temperature. Makes about 2 lbs. (1 kg).

* Fudge may be wrapped well and frozen for up to 6 weeks. Thaw at room temperature before cutting.

PEANUT BUTTER LOGS

1   pkg. (350 g) peanut butter-flavoured chips
1   can EAGLE BRAND Sweetened Condensed Milk
1   cup (250 mL) miniature marshmallows
1   cup (250 mL) chopped peanuts

In heavy saucepan, over low heat, melt chips with Eagle Brand. Add marshmallows; stir until melted. Remove from heat; cool 20 min. or until cool enough to handle. Divide in half; place each portion on a 20-inch (50 cm) piece of wax paper. Shape each into 12-inch (30 cm) log. Roll in nuts. Wrap tightly; chill 2 hours or until firm. Remove paper; cut into 1/4-inch (6 mm) slices. Makes two 12-inch (30 cm) logs.

Microwave: In 2-quart (2 L) glass measure, combine chips, Eagle Brand and marshmallows. Microwave, uncovered, at HIGH (100%) 3 1/2 to 4 min., stirring after 2 min. Stir until chips and marshmallows are melted and mixture is smooth. Proceed as above.

Peanut Butter Fudge: Stir peanuts into mixture. Spread onto wax paper-lined 8 or 9-inch (2 or 2.5 L) square pan. Chill 2 hours or until firm. Turn fudge onto cutting board; peel off paper; cut into squares.

SUPER CHOCOLATE FUDGE

1   pkg. (350 g) semi-sweet chocolate chips
1   can EAGLE BRAND Sweetened Condensed Milk
1 1/4 cups (300 mL) icing sugar
**   Pinch salt**
1   tsp. (5 mL) vanilla
1/2 cup (125 mL) chopped nuts

In heavy saucepan, over low heat, melt chips with Eagle Brand. Remove from heat; stir in icing sugar, salt, vanilla and nuts. Spread evenly in wax paper-lined 8-inch (20 cm) square pan. Chill 2 to 3 hours or until firm. Turn fudge onto cutting board; peel off paper;* cut into squares. Store loosely covered at room temperature. Makes about 2 lbs. (1 kg).

Microwave: In 2-quart (2 L) glass measure, combine chips with Eagle Brand. Microwave, uncovered, at High (100%) 2 min. Stir until chips melt and mixture is smooth. Stir in remaining ingredients. Proceed as above.

* Fudge may be wrapped well and frozen for up to 6 weeks. Thaw at room temperature before cutting.

CHOCOLATE TRUFFLES

3   pkgs. (175 g each**) semi-sweet chocolate chips**
1   can EAGLE BRAND Sweetened Condensed Milk
1   Tbsp. (15 mL) vanilla
Coatings*

In heavy saucepan, over low heat, melt chips with Eagle Brand. Remove from heat; stir in vanilla. Chill 2 hours or until firm. Shape into 1-inch (2.5 cm) balls; roll in any of the coatings. Chill 1 hour or until firm. Store covered at room temperature. Makes about 6 dozen candies.

*   **Coatings**: Finely chopped nuts, flaked coconut, chocolate sprinkles, coloured sprinkles, unsweetened cocoa powder, icing sugar.

CHOCOLATE FRUIT BALLS

2 1/2 cups (625 mL) vanilla wafer cookie crumbs
1   can EAGLE BRAND Sweetened Condensed Milk
2   cups (500 mL) chopped dates
1   cup (250 mL) finely-chopped nuts
1/2 cup (125 mL) chopped glacé cherries
2   Tbsp. (30 mL) unsweetened cocoa powder
     Icing sugar or unsweetened cocoa powder
     Additional glacé cherries (optional)

In large mixing bowl, combine crumbs, Eagle Brand, dates, nuts, cherries and cocoa; mix well. Chill 1 hour. Shape into 1-inch (2.5 cm) balls. Roll in icing sugar. Store tightly covered in refrigerator. Garnish with additional cherries if desired. Makes about 10 dozen candies.

Note: The flavour of these candies improves after 24 hours. They can be made ahead and stored, covered in the refrigerator for several weeks.

124

SCOTCHY TURTLES

1   pkg. (175 g) butterscotch-flavoured chips
1   can EAGLE BRAND Sweetened Condensed Milk, divided
2   tsp. (10 mL) white vinegar
4   cups (1 L) pecan halves
1   pkg. (300 g) milk chocolate chips
1   tsp. (5 mL) vanilla

In heavy saucepan, over low heat, melt butterscotch chips with 1/3 cup (75 mL) Eagle Brand. Remove from heat; stir in vinegar. Drop by small spoonfuls onto wax paper-lined baking sheets. Arrange 3 pecans on each butterscotch drop. In large heavy saucepan, over low heat, melt milk chocolate chips with remaining Eagle Brand and vanilla. Remove from heat; hold chocolate mixture over hot water. Drop chocolate by heaping spoonfuls over pecan clusters. Chill 2 hours or until firm. Store loosely covered in refrigerator. Makes about 5 dozen candies.

Microwave: In 1-quart (1 L) glass measure, combine butterscotch chips and 1/3 cup (75 mL) Eagle Brand. Microwave, uncovered, at HIGH (100%) 1 1/2 min. Stir until chips melt and mixture is smooth. Add vinegar. Proceed as above. In 1-quart (1 L) glass measure, combine milk chocolate chips with remaining Eagle Brand. Microwave at HIGH (100%) 2 min. Stir until chips melt and mixture is smooth. Add vanilla. Proceed as above.

CHOCOLATE PEANUT CLUSTERS

1   pkg. (350 g) semi-sweet chocolate chips
1   can EAGLE BRAND Sweetened Condensed Milk
2   cups (500 mL) oven-toasted rice cereal
1   cup (250 mL) peanuts

In heavy sauce pan, over low heat, melt chips with Eagle Brand. Remove from heat; stir in cereal and peanuts. Drop by small spoonfuls onto wax paper-lined baking sheets. Chill 2 hours or until firm. Store loosely covered at room temperature. Makes about 4 dozen candies.

EAGLE BRAND
DESSERT MAKING HINTS

Eagle Brand is an all-natural concentrated blend of whole milk and cane sugar condensed by a special vacuum cooking process. It is entirely different from evaporated milk. Eagle Brand may become thicker and more caramel-coloured as its age or storage temperature increases. The performance of the product is not affected by these natural changes. The unopened product is safe and wholesome as long as the can seal remains intact. If the sweetened condensed milk becomes unusually thick, stir briskly before using. If the product has become very caramelized, use in recipes where the caramel flavour is compatible with other ingredients. The best storage for sweetened condensed milk is a cool, dry place.

Because it is a natural product, Eagle Brand may vary in colour and consistency from can to can. These two photos illustrate the normal differences which may occur in Eagle Brand over time.

Hints for using Eagle Brand

Remove entire end of can with can opener; then use rubber scraper to remove all of the sweetened condensed milk from the can.

To avoid lumps in a cream cheese base recipe, gradually beat sweetened condensed milk into beaten cream cheese. Always heat sweetened condensed milk and chocolate over low or medium heat, stirring constantly.

To avoid lumpy gelatin mixtures sprinkle unflavoured gelatin over cold water; let stand 1 minute. Cook and stir over *low* heat until dissolved.

Always store unused sweetened condensed milk in refrigerator in covered container. Use within a week.

Eagle Brand is presweetened

Because Eagle Brand contains sugar which has already been thoroughly dissolved in the manufacturing process, most Eagle Brand recipes require no additional sugar.

Eagle Brand and chocolate

When heated with chocolate, Eagle Brand quickly thickens to a velvety smooth consistency for candies and sauces that are never grainy or long cooking. There is no need for constant stirring or a candy thermometer.

Magic thickening

Because it is a precooked blend of milk and sugar, Eagle Brand thickens almost magically with the addition of acidic fruit juices to form delicious pie fillings, puddings and desserts *without cooking*. Lemon juice or orange juice concentrate works best.

Ice cream making

The thick creamy consistency of Eagle Brand helps to minimize the formation of large ice crystals in ice creams and frozen desserts.

A note about eggs

Some recipes in this book specify, «Use only clean, uncracked eggs.» This is a precaution given when uncooked eggs are called for as in meringues, pie fillings, etc.

How to caramelize Eagle Brand sweetened condensed milk

Oven method:Preheat oven to 425°F (220°C). Pour Eagle Brand into 8 or 9-inch (20 or 23 cm) pie plate. Cover with foil; place in larger shallow pan. Fill outer pan with hot water. Bake 1 to 11/2 hours or until thick and light caramel-coloured. Remove foil. Cool. Chill thoroughly. Cover leftovers; refrigerate.

Stovetop method: Pour Eagle Brand into top of double boiler; cover. Place over boiling water. Over low heat, simmer 1 to 11/2 hours or until thick and light caramel-coloured. Beat until smooth. Cool. Chill thoroughly. Cover leftovers; refrigerate.

Microwave method: Pour Eagle Brand into 2-quart (2 L) glass measure. Microwave, uncovered, at MEDIUM (50 %) 4 min., stirring after 2 min. Reduce power to MEDIUM LOW (30%) and microwave, uncovered, 12 to 16 min. or until thick and light caramel-coloured; stir briskly every 2 min. until smooth. Cool. Chill thoroughly. Cover leftovers; refrigerate.

To reheat: Place desired amount of caramel in 1 or 2-cup (250 or 500 mL) glass measure. Microwave, uncovered, at HIGH (100%) 40 to 50 sec. or until warm, stirring after 20 sec.

* Caution: Never heat unopened can.

Crumb crust

1½ *cups (375 mL) graham* or *chocolate wafer crumbs*
1/4 *cup (50 mL) sugar*
6 *Tbsp. (90 mL) butter, melted*

Combine crumbs, sugar and butter; mix well. Press firmly on bottom and side of 8 or 9-inch (20 or 23 cm) pie plate. Chill thoroughly or bake in preheated 375°F (190°C) oven 6 to 8 min. Cool before filling. Makes 1 crust.

Pastry shell

1 *cup (250 mL) all purpose flour*
1/2 *tsp. (2 mL) salt*
1/3 *cup (75 mL) shortening*
3 to 4 *Tbsp. (45 to 60 mL) cold water*

In medium mixing bowl, combine flour and salt; cut in shortening until mixture resembles coarse crumbs. Sprinkle with water, 1 tbsp. (15 mL) at a time, mixing until dough is just moist enough to hold together. Form dough into ball. Place on well-floured surface. Press down into a flat circle with smooth edges. Roll dough to a circle 1/8-inch (3 mm) thick and about 1½ inches (7 cm) larger than inverted pie plate. Ease dough into pie plate. Trim 1/2 inch (12 mm) beyond pie plate edge. Fold under; flute edge as desired. Makes 1 shell.

To bake without filling

Preheat oven to 450°F (230°C). Prick bottom and side of pastry shell with fork. Line pastry with foil; fill with dry beans or pie weights. Bake 5 min.; remove beans and foil. Bake 5 to 7 min. longer or until golden.

To keep unfilled pastry shell from puffing or shrinking during baking, line with aluminium foil and fill with dry beans.

To bake with filling

Preheat oven as directed in recipe. Do not prick pastry shell. Fill and bake as directed.

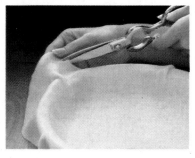

Use kitchen shears or sharp knife to trim dough 1/2 inch (12 mm) beyond pie plate edge. Fold under extra dough to form rim.

Flute edge as desired.

For successful meringue

Weather affects meringues. When the humidity is high, the sugar in the meringue absorbs moisture from the air, making the meringue gooey and limp. Meringues should be made on sunny dry days.

Carefully separate egg whites from yolks (they separate best when cold).

Mixing bowls and beaters should be completely grease-free. Egg whites should come to room temperature before beating. This increases the volume.

Sugar should be added *gradually*. Continue beating until sugar is completely dissolved.

Cool meringue slowly, away from drafts to prevent shrinking and weeping.

Meringue

3   egg whites
1/4   tsp. (1 mL) cream of tartar
6   Tbsp. (90 mL) sugar

Preheat oven to 350°F (180°C). In small mixer bowl, beat egg whites with cream of tartar until soft peaks form; gradually add sugar, beating until stiff but not dry. Spread meringue on top of pie, sealing carefully to edge of pastry shell. Bake 12 to 15 min. or until golden brown. Cool. Chill thoroughly. For 8 or 9-inch (20 or 23 cm) pie.

1. Beat egg whites and cream of tartar to soft peaks before adding sugar.

2. *Gradually* add sugar, beating until *stiff* but not dry. Mixture should be glossy.

3. Spread meringue, sealing carefully to edge of pastry shell.

4. Brown meringue as directed. Cool *slowly*.

Tinting coconut

Dilute a few drops food colour with 1/2 tsp. (2 mL) water or milk. Add coconut; toss with fork until evenly tinted.

Toasting coconut and nuts

Spread coconut or nuts evenly in shallow pan. Toast in preheated 350°F (180°C) oven 7 to 15 min. or until golden. Stir frequently.

Frosting grapes

Dip small clusters of grapes into slightly beaten egg white; sprinkle with granulated sugar. Dry on wire racks.

Chocolate leaves

Coat undersides of real leaves lightly with vegetable oil. Melt semi-sweet chocolate and coat undersides of leaves thickly with chocolate using small spoon. Chill or freeze until firm, then peel away leaf.

Chocolate curls

With a vegetable peeler or thin, sharp knife, slice across block of sweet milk chocolate or large-size milk chocolate candy bar with long, thin strokes. Chocolate should be at room temperature.

Pastry egg wash

For a more golden crust on a 2-crust pie, beat 1 egg yolk with 2 Tbsp. (30 mL) water; brush evenly over pastry before baking.

How to split cake layer

To split cake layer, measure halfway up side; mark with toothpicks. Using long piece of thread, rest on picks. Cross thread and pull through to split layers.

For level layers, use a long thin serrated knife to slice off rounded or uneven top of cake.

Make-ahead whipped cream

Freeze dollops of whipped cream on wax paper-lined baking sheets. When frozen, store in tightly closed plastic bags for use on desserts or Irish coffee.

For baked alaskas

Ice cream must be very firm before it is covered with meringue and baked. Dessert can be frozen several days before serving.

Unmolding frozen desserts

For easy unmolding of ice cream desserts, line container with aluminium foil, extending foil beyond rim of container. When frozen, lift dessert from pan with foil. Remove foil.

Slicing hints

Use a wet knife for cutting desserts with meringue. Wipe off knife after each cut.

Use a damp knife with a thin blade for slicing cake rolls.

Use a damp knife with a firm blade for cutting fudge or candy.

Use a serrated knife for slicing angel food cakes.

Whipping cream

Chill beaters and bowl thoroughly.

Beat chilled whipping cream on high speed (overbeating or beating on low speed can cause cream to separate into fat and liquid).

Beat only until stiff. Whipping cream doubles in volume. To sweeten whipped cream, gradually beat in 1 to 2 Tbsp. (15 to 30 mL) granulated or icing sugar and 1/2 to 1 tsp. (2 to 5 mL) vanilla for each 1 cup (250 mL) unwhipped cream.

Beat whipping cream only until *stiff* peaks form.

To marble, gently swirl a narrow spatula through light and dark mixtures.

REALEMON COOKING TIPS

Realemon starts with fresh lemons

Realemon starts with the juice of fresh lemons, concentrated to a uniform strength. Enough filtered water is used to return this concentrate to the natural strength of fresh lemons. Lemon oil from the peel is added to enhance the natural taste of fresh lemons.

Realemon is more economical and more convenient than home-squeezed lemons. And since fresh lemons can differ in size, juiciness and strength, the uniformity of Realemon can be an advantage in preparing recipes that call for lemon juice. For recipes specifying the «juice of one lemon» use 2 to 3 Tbsp. (30 to 45 mL) Realemon.

Refreshing salad dressing

Use Realemon for a light-tasting alternative to vinegar when preparing your favourite homemade salad dressing or packaged mix. Just substitute an equal amount of Realemon for vinegar.

Mushroom lovers

In medium saucepan, bring 1/3 cup (75 mL) water, 2 Tbsp. (30 mL) Realemon, 1 Tbsp. (15 mL) butter and a pinch salt to a boil. Add whole or sliced fresh mushrooms. Cover and simmer 5 min.; stir occasionally. Serve as a garnish or side dish.

Refreshing water

Add Realemon to hot or cold water for a refreshing low calorie beverage.

Buttermilk substitution

When a recipe calls for buttermilk or sour milk, combine 1 Tbsp. (15 mL) Realemon plus milk to make 1 cup (250 mL). Let stand 5 min. and mixture will be thick and ready to use.

Low sodium tip

Cutting down on sodium? Try sprinkling Realemon instead of salt on vegetables to enhance flavour.

Reduce onion odors

To reduce onion and garlic odors, rinse hands and cutting board with Realemon and cold water when peeling, slicing or grating onions or garlic.

Reduce fish odors

To eliminate fishy odor and taste, brush fish with Realemon before cooking or add Realemon to cold oil or butter before frying.

Tea and lemon

Add a few drops Realemon to iced tea or hot tea to enhance flavour. Or freeze Realemon in ice cube trays to use in iced tea.

Diet soda perk-up

Add lemony freshness to diet sodas, club soda or other carbonated beverages by adding a few drops Realemon or Realime.

Apples for pie

To give ordinary eating apples the tartness of «pie apples», sprinkle 1 Tbsp. (15mL) Realemon over sliced apples.

Barbecue tip

When barbecuing or broiling chicken or other poultry, brush with Realemon for added flavour and moistness.

Warm Punch

To help keep warm punch warm and to «condition» a glass bowl for a hot punch, slowly pour very warm water into punch bowl and let stand until bowl is warmed.

Savory lemon ice cubes

To make ice cubes for unsweetened drinks, like Bloody Marys, combine 1 part water and 1 part Realemon in ice cube trays; place olive, pearl onion or celery in each section if desired. Freeze.

Punch ice ring

To make a fruited ice ring for punches, pour 1/2 inch (12 mm) Realemon into ring mold.

Arrange fruits and mint leaves in mold. Freeze.

Add water to fill mold. Freeze until solid.

To unmold ice ring, quickly dip in hot water. Turn into punch bowl.

Keep fruits bright

To keep fruit garnishes such as apple slices or wedges, banana slices, etc. from darkening, dip in Realemon.

Iced tea cubes

In 1-quart (1L) pitcher, combine 3 cups (750 mL) strong brewed tea, cooled, and 1/4 cup (50 mL) Realemon. Pour into ice cube trays.

(Continued next page.)

Place 1 piece of fruit (maraschino cherries, mandarin orange segments, etc.) in each section if desired. Freeze. Use in iced tea. Makes about 3 dozen.

Lemon ice cubes

Dissolve 3/4 cup (175 mL) sugar in 1 cup (250 mL) Realemon; add 3 cups (750 mL) water. Pour into ice cube trays. Place 1 piece fruit in each section. Freeze.

Blueberry spice freezer jam

4 1/2 *cups (1.125 L) crushed fresh* or *dry-pack frozen blueberries*
5   *cups (1.25 L) sugar*
1   *tsp. (5 mL) ground cinnamon*
1/2   *tsp. (2 mL) ground nutmeg*
2   *pouches (85 mL* each*) liquid pectin (Certo)*
3   *Tbsp. (45 mL) REALEMON Lemon Juice*

In large bowl, combine blueberries, sugar, cinnamon and nutmeg; mix well. Let stand 10 min. In small bowl, combine pectin and Realemon; pour over berries. Stir thoroughly 3 min. (a few sugar crystals will remain). Spoon into glass or plastic containers; cover. Let stand at room temperature until set (may take up to 24 hours). Store in freezer. Thaw to serve; store leftovers in refrigerator. Makes about 7 cups (1.75 L).

Strawberry freezer jam

1 3/4 *cups (425 mL) crushed fresh strawberries*
4   *cups (1 L) sugar*
1   *pouch (85 mL) liquid pectin (Certo)*
1/4   *cup (50 mL) REALEMON Lemon Juice*

In large bowl, combine strawberries and sugar; mix well. Let stand 10 min. In small bowl, combine pectin and Realemon; pour over strawberries. Stir thoroughly 3 min. (a few sugar crystals will remain). Spoon into glass or plastic containers; cover. Let stand at room temperature until set. (May take up to 8 hours). Store in freezer. Makes about 4 cups (1 L). Thaw to use; store leftovers in refrigerator.

Lemon marshmallow sauce

1   *jar (200 g) marshmallow cream*
3   *Tbsp. (45 mL) REALEMON Lemon Juice*

In small bowl combine marshmallow cream and Realemon; mix well. Chill to blend flavours. Serve over fruit, ice cream or cake. Makes about 1 cup (250 mL).

Lemon whipped cream

1   *cup (250 mL) whipping cream*
1   *Tbsp. (15 mL) REALEMON Lemon Juice*
2   *Tbsp. (30 mL) sugar*

In small mixer bowl, combine cream and Realemon; beat until soft peaks form. Gradually add sugar, beating *only* until stiff. Serve with fruit, baked or steamed puddings, pies or cakes. Cover leftovers; refrigerate. Makes about 2 cups (500 mL).

Horseradish lemon cream

1   *cup (250 mL) whipping cream*
1   *Tbsp. (15 mL) REALEMON Lemon Juice*
2   *tsp. (10 mL) prepared horseradish, drained*

In small mixer bowl, combine cream and Realemon; beat *only* until stiff. Fold in horseradish. Serve with roast beef, corned beef, ham or ham loaf. Cover leftovers; refrigerate. Makes about 2 cups (500 mL).

Lemon rice

For a refreshing flavour change, combine 1 cup (250 mL) long grain rice with 3/4 cup (175 mL) water, 1/4 cup (50 mL) Realemon and 1 chicken bouillon cube. Bring to a boil; cover and simmer 15 to 20 min. or until liquid is absorbed. Stir in chopped water chestnuts, pimento and parsley if desired.

Lemon and melon

Squeeze a few drops of Realemon or Realime onto a cantaloupe, honeydew or other melon to complement the fruit flavour.

On a diet?

Use Realemon on your salads instead of high calorie salad dressing. And try Realemon on seafood in place of tartar sauce.

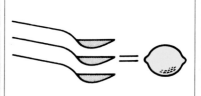

About 3 Tbsp. (45 mL) Realemon Lemon Juice equals the juice of one lemon.

143

144

ORDER FORM
BORDEN BEST RECIPES

● Makes a great gift for your favourite cook

● Comparable $12.95 retail value

For each book ordered, please send a cheque or money order for $5.95 plus applicable sales tax with your name and address to:

BORDEN RECIPE COLLECTION

P.O. Box 5053-B

Paris, Ontario

N3L 3W5

Please allow 4 - 6 weeks for delivery.

✂ —— ✂ —— ✂ —— ✂ —— ✂ —— ✂ —— ✂ ——

Yes, send me———— copies of 'Best Recipes'.

I have enclosed $5.95 plus applicable sales tax for each book ordered.

Language preferred   English   [ ]   French   [ ]

Number of copies ————   Amount enclosed $ ————

Name ————————————————————————

Street ———————————————— Apt. No. ————

City ———————————————— Province————

Postal Code————————

ORDER FORM

BORDEN BEST RECIPES

Yes, send me ——————— copies of 'Best Recipes'.

I have enclosed $5.95 plus applicable sales tax for each book ordered.

Language preferred   English   [ ]   French   [ ]

Number of copies ——————   Amount enclosed $ ——————

Name ————————————————————————————

Street ——————————————————   Apt. No. ——————

City ——————————————————   Province——————

Postal Code——————

✂ —— ✂ —— ✂ —— ✂ —— ✂ —— ✂ ——

● Makes a great gift for your favourite cook

● Comparable $12.95 retail value

For each book ordered, please send a cheque or money order for $5.95 plus applicable sales tax with your name and address to:

BORDEN RECIPE COLLECTION

P.O. Box 5053-B

Paris, Ontario

N3L 3W5

Please allow 4 - 6 weeks for delivery.

DINNER'S READY

DINNER'S READY

READY

Turn a Single Meal into a Week of Dinners

Andrew Schloss

with

Ken Bookman

William Morrow and Company, Inc. ✳ New York

To Karen, Dana, Ben, and Isaac,
who ate all the dinners that weren't ready for these pages.

To Ruth,
whose caring and support are all over this book.

It is the policy of William Morrow and Company, Inc., and its imprints and affiliates,
recognizing the importance of preserving what has been written, to print the books
we publish on acid-free paper, and we exert our best efforts to that end.

Library of Congress Cataloging-in-Publication Data
Schloss, Andrew, 1951-
Dinner's ready : turn a single meal into a week of dinners
/ by Andrew Schloss with Ken Bookman. — 1st ed.
p.   cm.
Includes index.
ISBN 0-688-12720-7
1. Dinners and dining.   2. Make-ahead cookery.   3. Menus.
I. Bookman, Ken.   II. Title.
TX737.S35   1995
641.5'55—dc20   94-26834
CIP

Printed in the United States of America

First Edition

1 2 3 4 5 6 7 8 9 10

BOOK DESIGN BY CLAIRE NAYLON VACCARO

Acknowledgments

Books of this complexity don't come easily—as this one did not. We are deeply grateful to the people who helped us shape it and who took on some of its difficulties.

We'd love to be able to say that our manuscript sailed effortlessly into print, but Susan Derecskey and Harriet Bell would know the truth. The truth is that Susan's editing was as meticulous and caring as an editing job can possibly be, and we can't thank her enough for her attention to every page—to the small details that she added and to the big mistakes that she kept out. Susan worked closely with William Morrow's editor, Harriet Bell, who nurtured a vision for this book from the moment it came to her attention. That kind of interest can't always be taken for granted and we thank her for giving it to us.

Judith Weber, our literary agent, has our gratitude, too, for taking our first, rough idea and elevating it into a plan that worked far better.

Finally, this book inflicted considerable disruption on the two homes in which it was put together, and it took great amounts of time from the people closest to us. Our thanks to them all—Dana, Ben, Isaac, and Karen Shain Schloss, and Ruth Adelman.

Introduction

This book is about time. Your time.

It is *not* a book about leftovers. If it were, it would be loaded with soups, stews, casseroles, and little else. We've got some of those, but that's not where we think you need help in the kitchen. This book will take you to the next level, and this paragraph is the first and last place in the book where you'll see the word *leftovers*.

Instead, we give you a different way to approach home cooking. We've assembled a year's worth of weekly cooking plans. Each chapter contains seven or eight interlocking recipes that, together, accomplish what every home cook wants but few ever achieve: the ability to leverage a single weekend dinner into a week's worth of meals that are delicious, that are varied, and that won't demand the one ingredient none of us has on a weeknight—time. If a single recipe catches your eye, and you want to prepare it, go ahead. You'll eat well. But you'll miss the ingenuity of this book.

The best part is how little you have to do—a single session of earnest cooking. Sunday is probably a day on which you do some earnest cooking anyway, perhaps as a family activity. So that's the way we begin every chapter, with a menu that we call "The Sunday Dinner," consisting of an entree and two or three side dishes, all of it very traditional Sunday Dinner fare. The trick is that you'll intentionally prepare those foods in large quantities. And why not? After all, once you're roasting a chicken, you might as well roast two. You'll be left with a Sunday meal for four people—plus a refrigerator full of the prepared meat, sauces, starches, and vegetables that will become the building blocks of what we call "The Weeknight Entrees."

That's the attraction of this book. You won't have to spend your all-too-short weeknights figuring out how to cook a good meal, because you'll have already cooked it. All you'll have to do is assemble the meal by mixing and matching those meats, sauces, vegetables, and starches with amazingly little new work—boiling water, perhaps, or reheating a couple of foods, or broiling a piece of fish or meat, or making a dressing. Those four diverse meals will be so delicious and so quick that you'll think you cheated. And the best part is that it's *not* recycled food, it's *new* food, meals so creative and original that no one would guess that they began life a few days before.

My co-author, Andrew Schloss, created these menus and recipes, using his food imagination, taste and flavor sense, and knowledge of how to make one recipe work with another, to create a recipe that keeps paying dividends days after you've prepared it. Those skills helped make him a highly acclaimed restaurant chef in Philadelphia during the late 1970s and early 1980s, and Schloss uses them to adapt the restaurant kitchen for the benefit of the home cook.

Next time you're dining in a small restaurant, the kind that has a constantly changing 10-appetizer-10-entree menu, look closely at the menu, and read between the lines a little. Notice some things that may not have been immediately apparent. The tomato sauce on the lasagna at the top of the menu could be the start of the stew at the bottom. The ranch dressing on the appetizer salad might be the marinade for a main-dish fish. The roast lamb on tonight's dinner menu could be the lamb pot-pie special for tomorrow's lunch.

Restaurant cooking is different from home cooking, but not so different that home cooks shouldn't look to restaurant kitchens for a few tricks that would make their lives easier. This book makes liberal use of those tricks.

Schloss is fascinated with how food works, with why it behaves as it does, and he's especially adept at fitting recipes to that food behavior. His interest in how food works was part of what took Schloss in 1982 from his restaurant kitchen to The Restaurant School in Philadelphia, where he spent ten years as culinary director before leaving to devote all his time to cookbook writing, food consulting, and occasional teaching.

Schloss and I have worked together since 1982, when he first tried his hand at food writing in the *Philadelphia Inquirer* at almost the same instant that I began eight years as that newspaper's food editor. I inherited his first article, but I enthusiastically commissioned the next four hundred or so. In 1990, we began collaborating on *Fifty Ways to Cook Most Everything: 2500 Creative Solutions to the Daily Dilemma of What to Cook,* a book that was inspired by one of his articles in the *Inquirer.*

The work on this, our second book, was an extension of our evolution as food journalists.

Give it a chance to respect both your time and your palate by following some of these chapters through their full five-dinner weeks. There's no fine print. It really works.

—Ken Bookman

Each chapter is divided into two sections, "The Sunday Dinner" and "The Weeknight Entrees." The two groups of recipes are meant to work with each other. **You'll see this special typeface with a ✪ used in almost every recipe. When this typeface appears in a Sunday recipe, it tells you to save that part of the recipe for a Weeknight entree. In the Weeknight recipes themselves, this same typeface designates ingredients that originated in one of the Sunday recipes.**

You can, of course, prepare a single recipe all by itself, without getting involved in a full week's cooking plan. It's easy enough to do. If it's a Sunday recipe, simply reduce the ingredient quantities to eliminate extra meat, fish, or poultry and to avoid making the extra sauces, broths, or dressings. If it's a Weeknight recipe, look for any ingredients that use **this special typeface**, then refer back to the Sunday recipe to see how those ingredients are prepared.

But remember: Once you're making a sauce or a broth or a dressing for one meal, you've already done so much of the work that you might as well let it take you further. That's the goal of this book.

The secret behind *Dinner's Ready* lies in the structure of the menus. Part of the structure is to use each Sunday meal to create the essential building blocks for assembling a week's worth of entrees. But it's also important to serve the weeknight dinners in the order in which they are listed. That way you'll know that all the prepared food will be wholesome and fresh on the night you serve it.

Although effort has been made to avoid consecutive meals with the same main ingredient, sometimes, such as with highly perishable ingredients like fish or cooked greens, back-to-back placement is unavoidable.

Almost all of the reserved ingredients in these menus should be stored tightly wrapped in the refrigerator. When refrigeration is unnecessary, it is noted in the reserved line at the end of the recipe.

If you need to skip or move a weeknight meal by a day or two, there is usually no harm in holding the reserved ingredients for that extra time. Be aware that proteins, like meat, fish, poultry, and meat juices, are quite perishable and should be used within three or four days of being cooked. Broths and juices are the most fragile and must be refrigerated as soon as possible and used within a few days. If there is a layer of fat on top of broth, do not remove it. In the refrigerator, this fat will solidify and form a seal that protects the broth against air and bacteria. Instead, scrape off the fat just before you use the broth. In all cases, trust your eyes and your nose over any set of written rules.

Soft foods, such as cooked greens, pasta, and grains, lose quality more quickly than the same ingredients raw and therefore should be used within two days of being cooked.

If a meal must be delayed more than two days beyond what is suggested, some of the reserved ingredients can be frozen. But be aware that some ingredients freeze better than others.

Cooked meats do not freeze well. They will become grainy and dry unless they have been cooked in liquid or are frozen with sufficient liquid surrounding them. In fact, any food cooked and held in liquid, such as soup or stew, can be frozen without compromising quality. Vegetables, grains, noodles, fruits, and herbs can be frozen after cooking.

If you are going to freeze a reserved ingredient, do so as soon as possible. Food stored in a refrigerator for several days and then frozen will not be as wholesome after defrosting as the same food that's frozen right away.

To protect from freezer burn, place ingredients in a close-fitting plastic container or wrap them tightly in paper and again in foil or plastic wrap. Label all frozen foods to indicate their contents and date of freezing and use them within a few weeks.

There's a chicken in every pot and skillet and oven in this country almost every night. We have become a nation of chicken-eaters, and we crave chicken recipes—quick, easy, delicious ways to turn the favored bird into a memorable meal.

Well, have I got a recipe for you. Perfumed with coriander leaf and seed, lemon, and garlic, this chicken emerges from the oven steaming with intoxicating smells. Best yet, the chicken and its side dishes—a Sicilian eggplant salad and pasta with a pungent rendition of pesto—form the groundwork for a week's worth of entrees.

Couscous and the stew that accompanies it are not opulent dishes, but, like most peasant fare, the traditional version can take the better part of a day to fix. Monday's Lemon Chicken Couscous speeds up the process without cutting corners. Because you've already developed the flavor of the sauce when you roasted the chicken, all that's left is to simmer the vegetables and steep the couscous. On Tuesday, the Caponata from Sunday's meal is transformed into an instant sauce niçoise to top a cod fillet, and on Thursday, it teams with some of Sunday's arugula pesto in a novel version of Soupe au Pistou. The same pesto provides the spark for Wednesday's unique cheeseburgers.

You'll notice in the recipe for Caponata that I have omitted the traditional step of salting the eggplant to extract its bitter juices before cooking it. In recent years, I have found this step not only undesirable but unnecessary. If the eggplants you are using are firm and not too big, bitterness is not a problem.

THE SUNDAY DINNER	THE WEEKNIGHT ENTREES
Roast Lemon and Coriander Chicken	Lemon Chicken Couscous
Caponata	Microwaved Cod Niçoise
Angel Hair Pasta with Arugula Pesto	Chèvre Cheeseburgers with Green Herb Salsa
	Soupe au Pistou

Roast Lemon and Coriander Chicken

6 cloves garlic, minced
Finely grated zest of 1 lemon
2 teaspoons ground cumin
1 tablespoon ground coriander
Salt and pepper to taste

6 tablespoons olive oil
2 chickens (about 4 pounds each)
3 lemons, halved
8 sprigs cilantro

Make a spice paste by combining the garlic, lemon zest, cumin, coriander, salt, pepper, and half the olive oil. Set aside.

Preheat the oven to 400°F.

Remove the giblets from the package inside the cavity of the chickens and scatter over the bottom of a large roasting pan. Remove visible fat from around the cavities. Wash inside and out and pat dry.

Rub plenty of salt and pepper into the walls of the cavities. Run your fingers under the skin of the breasts and legs of each chicken, gently separating it from the meat. Rub the spice paste under the skin, coating as much of the meat as you can reach. Rub the outside of the chickens with the remaining olive oil. Place the chickens, breast side down, in the roasting pan.

Roast for 30 minutes. Turn the chickens breast side up. Squeeze the lemons all over the chickens and stuff the empty lemon halves into the cavities of the chickens along with the cilantro sprigs. If any lemon halves won't fit inside, nestle them between the chickens.

Reduce the oven temperature to 350°F. and continue roasting the chickens for another 1½ hours, or until a thermometer inserted into the thickest part of the thigh registers 170°F. Let rest for 10 minutes before carving. Cut chickens into thigh, drumstick, wing, breast half, and back sections. Serve 2 breasts, 2 drumsticks, and 2 thighs.

Makes 4 servings, plus enough to:
✪ **Reserve 2 backs, 2 thighs, and 4 wings for Lemon Chicken Couscous.**
✪ **Reserve at least ½ cup drippings for Lemon Chicken Couscous.**

Caponata

2 medium-size firm eggplants, peeled and
  diced (about 1 pound each)
1⅓ cups diced celery (2 ribs celery)
1⅓ cups chopped onion (2 medium onions)
1 large green pepper, stemmed, seeded, and
  diced
¼ cup extra-virgin olive oil
2 cloves garlic, finely chopped
2 cups chopped, peeled, and seeded plum
  tomatoes (4 to 5 tomatoes)

2 teaspoons dried basil
½ teaspoon dried oregano
4 flat anchovies, minced
⅓ cup chopped pitted green olives (3 ounces)
1½ tablespoons capers, drained
3 tablespoons chopped flat-leaf parsley
3 tablespoons wine vinegar
Salt and pepper to taste

Cook the eggplants, celery, onion, and green pepper in the olive oil in a large skillet over
medium heat, stirring frequently, until the vegetables lose their raw look, about 5 minutes. Add the garlic, tomatoes, basil, and oregano. Cook until the vegetables are tender,
about 10 minutes. Remove from heat and stir in the anchovies, olives, capers, parsley,
vinegar, salt, and pepper. Serve warm or at room temperature.

Makes 4 servings, plus enough to:
✪ **Reserve 1 cup for Microwaved Cod Niçoise.**
✪ **Reserve 2 cups for Soupe au Pistou.**

Angel Hair Pasta with Arugula Pesto

2 cloves garlic, chopped
3 tablespoons pine nuts
Zest of ½ lemon, coarsely chopped
Pinch of crushed red pepper flakes
About 4 cups arugula leaves, washed and
  dried

About 1 cup flat-leaf parsley leaves, washed
  and dried
3 tablespoons olive oil
Salt to taste
¾ pound dried angel hair pasta or spaghettini
6 tablespoons freshly grated parmesan cheese

continued

3

Combine the garlic, pine nuts, lemon zest, and pepper flakes in the workbowl of a food processor and chop fine. Add the arugula and parsley leaves and process until coarsely chopped. Add the 3 tablespoons of oil and run the processor until the mixture is a thick paste. Season with salt. Set aside.

Bring a large pot of lightly salted water to a boil. Add the pasta. Boil until the pasta is tender, about 1 to 2 minutes for fresh, 5 for dried. Drain and toss the hot pasta with half the pesto (about ½ cup) and the parmesan. Serve immediately.

Makes 4 servings, plus enough to:
✪ **Reserve ¼ cup of Arugula Pesto for Chèvre Cheeseburgers.**
✪ **Reserve ¼ cup of Arugula Pesto for Soupe au Pistou.**

ADDING OIL TO PASTA WATER

Cooking pasta is about as simple as cooking gets, but even so, there are pitfalls—such as sticking and cooking time.

Pasta can stick when the noodle releases its starch, forming a film of paste that makes one strand of pasta adhere to another. Many cooks prevent this by adding a bit of oil to the water before the pasta is added. The oil floats on the water's surface and coats the pasta when it enters the pot or when the pasta is stirred. That seals the starch inside the pasta, where it cannot cause sticking.

Other cooks think the cure is more serious than the problem. These cooks *never, ever* add oil. They say it makes the pasta slick, preventing sauce from clinging to it. With tomato sauce, or other water-based sauces, this can be true, but when the sauce is oil- or cream-based, a film of oil on the pasta makes no difference.

I don't consider sticky pasta a big problem, and that's why I'm not adding oil to the cooking water. Your decision might be easier if you consider this: Sticking is a greater problem with some pasta brands than with others—and more with some shapes than with others. Small pastas, such as shells and elbows, have less of a tendency to stick than fettucine or lasagna noodles, because they have much less flat surface. For these shapes, you could omit the oil, if you wish.

Cooking time can also be a problem. Most pasta recipes in this book call for 10 minutes' cooking time. A better guideline, though, is a combination of the package directions and your testing. Consider fettuccine, for example. I checked different brands and found cooking times that varied from 7 to 14 minutes. Best bet: Bite into a strand or piece of pasta before the short end of the cooking range specified on the package, then test once or twice a minute until it's the way you like it.

Lemon Chicken Couscous

✪ **2 backs, 2 thighs, and 4 wings reserved from Roast Lemon and Coriander Chicken**
1 large onion, finely chopped
2 tablespoons olive oil
1 tablespoon ground coriander
2 teaspoons ground cumin
½ teaspoon crushed red pepper flakes
3 cloves garlic, minced
✪ **At least ½ cup pan drippings reserved from Roast Lemon and Coriander Chicken**

1 teaspoon ground turmeric
2 large carrots, cut into chunks
2 large ribs celery, quartered
1 large sweet potato, peeled and cut into chunks (12 ounces)
1 small winter squash, peeled, seeded, and cut into chunks (1-1½ pounds)
Salt and pepper to taste
2 cups couscous
2 tablespoons butter or margarine

Remove the larger pieces of meat from the reserved chicken backs, thighs, and wings. Save the bones for chicken broth, if desired, or discard. Set aside.

Sauté the onion in the oil in a large heavy saucepan over medium heat, until softened, about 2 minutes. Add the coriander, cumin, and pepper flakes. Cook another minute. Add the garlic and the chicken meat and toss gently. Add the reserved drippings mixed with enough water to make 2½ cups of liquid. Add the turmeric, carrots, celery, sweet potato, and squash. Season with salt and pepper. Simmer until the vegetables are completely tender, about 30 minutes.

Fifteen minutes before serving, bring 2½ cups of water to a boil. Add the couscous. Cover, remove from the heat, and allow to rest for 10 minutes. Toss with the butter or margarine. Serve the couscous with the stew spooned on top.

Makes 4 servings.

Microwaved Cod Niçoise

1 ½ pounds cod fillet
1 tablespoon olive oil
1 tablespoon finely grated orange zest
1 clove garlic, minced

Salt and pepper to taste
2 tablespoons lemon juice
✪ **I cup reserved Caponata**

Rub the cod and the interior of a 9 x 13-inch glass baking dish with the olive oil. Combine the orange zest, garlic, salt, and pepper. Rub all over the fish and place in the baking dish. Sprinkle the lemon juice over the fish and top with the reserved Caponata. Cover with plastic wrap and microwave at full power for 3 minutes 30 seconds. Poke the plastic wrap to release the steam, remove wrap, and serve immediately.

Or brown the cod fillet in the olive oil in a large skillet over medium-high heat on top of the stove. Add the orange zest, garlic, salt, pepper, lemon juice, and reserved Caponata. Cover and simmer for about 8 minutes, or until the fish flakes under gentle pressure.

Makes 4 servings.

Chèvre Cheeseburgers with Green Herb Salsa

1 ½ pounds ground beef, not extra-lean
¼ cup ice water
Salt and pepper to taste
✪ **¼ cup arugula pesto reserved from**
   Angel Hair Pasta with Arugula Pesto

¼ cup hot salsa, homemade
4 hamburger buns or soft round rolls, split
   and, if desired, toasted
2 ounces chèvre

Combine the ground beef, water, salt, and pepper in a mixing bowl and mix with your hands. Form the beef into four 6-ounce patties, 1 to 1½ inches thick. Do not pack too tightly. Grill or broil 4 inches from a hot fire until browned and cooked until done, about 3 to 5 minutes on each side for rare, 5 to 8 minutes for medium, 10 minutes for well done.

While the burgers are cooking, make the green herb salsa by combining the reserved pesto with the salsa. When the burgers are done, spoon 2 teaspoons of the salsa on the bottom half of each roll. Place a burger on each one. Top each burger with a portion of the chèvre and a portion of the remaining salsa. Cover with the top section of a roll and serve.

Makes 4 servings.

Soupe au Pistou

✪ **2 cups reserved Caponata**
3 cups chicken broth, canned or homemade
½ cup small pasta or broken-up spaghetti
1 cup cooked or canned white beans

✪ **¼ cup arugula pesto reserved from**
Angel Hair Pasta with Arugula Pesto
2 tablespoons freshly grated parmesan cheese

Combine the reserved Caponata and the chicken broth in a 3-quart heavy saucepan. Bring to a boil and stir in the pasta. Reduce the heat and simmer for 8 to 10 minutes, or until the pasta is tender. Add the beans and heat through. Meanwhile, mix the reserved pesto and the parmesan cheese. Ladle the soup into 4 bowls. Swirl the pesto into each bowl of soup and serve.

Makes 4 servings.

Sweet-and-sour, the enlightened pairing of sugar and vinegar, is the very antithesis of togetherness. The two refuse to combine. Instead they vibrate: *sweet-sour-sweet-sour-sweet-sour*. No sooner does the palate commit to one than the other takes over. Salty and sweet, hot and sour, sweet and sour—by combining flavors that strike opposing points on the palate, we increase the vibrancy of all the flavors manyfold.

This effect is evident throughout this week's menu. Sunday's Sweet-and-Sour Brisket is a standard, and the same flavor phenomenon is reinforced in the accompanying spinach salad, where the fruity tartness of red wine vinegar plays off lemony sweet red bell peppers and smoky saltiness in a smoked turkey breast.

In Monday's dinner, the same dressing is served chilled over hot grilled salmon for an equally intriguing attraction of opposites. Sunday's kasha fills a streamlined rendition of stuffed cabbage on Tuesday. The brisket's broth makes quick work of Wednesday's robust bean soup, which is brimming with vegetables and the rich meaty flavors that you created days before when you braised the brisket. The brisket itself forms the base for a one-dish meal of Beef Tostados on Thursday.

THE SUNDAY DINNER

Sweet-and-Sour Brisket

Mushroom Kasha

Spinach Salad with Red
Pepper Vinaigrette

THE WEEKNIGHT ENTREES

Grilled Salmon with Pickled Peppers

Microwaved Russian Stuffed Cabbage

Many Bean Soup

Beef Tostados

Sweet-and-Sour Brisket

3 pounds brisket of beef, trimmed of excess fat
1 tablespoon vegetable oil
2 medium onions, chopped
4 cloves garlic, minced
½ cup cider vinegar
6 tablespoons brown sugar

2 cups tomato puree
2 cups beef broth, canned or homemade
4 cups water
Salt and pepper to taste
1 pound carrots, thickly sliced
4 ribs celery, thickly sliced

Brown the brisket 4 inches from the flame of a broiler or over a very hot grill. Set aside.

Meanwhile, heat the oil over medium-high heat in a large iron skillet that has a lid or in a Dutch oven large enough to hold the brisket. When hot, add the onions and stir until they start to brown. Add the garlic and stir for 30 seconds.

Mix in the vinegar, brown sugar, tomato puree, beef broth, water, salt, and pepper. Bring to a boil. Place the brisket and any liquid that has collected around it in the skillet. Cover and simmer for 1½ hours, turning occasionally. Add the carrots and celery and simmer another 30 minutes, or until the vegetables and meat are tender.

Slice the brisket against the grain, skim the fat from the surface of the sauce, and return it to the sauce if you are holding it for any length of time. Transfer all but 6 to 8 slices of the brisket to a warm serving platter and cover with 2 cups of the sauce. Reserve enough vegetables and sauce for the rest of the week and serve the rest on the side.

Makes 4 servings, plus enough to:
- ✪ **Reserve 6 to 8 slices brisket for Beef Tostados.**
- ✪ **Reserve 3 cups sauce for Many Bean Soup.**
- ✪ **Reserve 2 cups sauce for Microwaved Russian Stuffed Cabbage.**
- ✪ **Reserve 1 cup vegetables for Microwaved Russian Stuffed Cabbage.**

Mushroom Kasha

3 tablespoons vegetable oil
1 medium onion, finely chopped
½ pound white mushrooms, stems trimmed,
    cleaned and sliced
3 cloves garlic, minced
2 tablespoons tomato paste
4 cups chicken broth, canned or homemade

1 box (13 ounces) whole-grain kasha
    (about 2 cups)
2 eggs, lightly beaten
Salt and pepper to taste
2 tablespoons chopped parsley
2 tablespoons chopped dill

Heat the oil in a heavy saucepan. Add the onion and mushrooms and sauté until soft-ened, about 3 minutes. Add the garlic and stir for 30 seconds. Add the tomato paste and broth, stir to blend, and bring to a boil.

Meanwhile, thoroughly mix the kasha with the beaten eggs in a mixing bowl. Turn into a dry large skillet and cook over medium heat until the kasha grains appear dry and separate. Add the liquid to the kasha. Season with salt and pepper. Stir once or twice and scatter the parsley and dill over the top. Cover the pan and simmer gently for 10 minutes. The kasha will puff and absorb all the liquid. Fluff with a fork, adjust season-ing, and serve all but 2 cups.

Makes 4 servings, plus enough to:
✪ **Reserve 2 cups for Microwaved Russian Stuffed Cabbage.**

Spinach Salad with Red Pepper Vinaigrette

1 package (10 ounces) fresh spinach leaves, washed, dried, and stemmed
6 scallions, white parts only, sliced
About 1 cup flat-leaf parsley leaves, washed and dried
¼ pound mushrooms, wiped clean and sliced
1 medium onion, finely chopped
¼ cup olive oil

2 large roasted red bell peppers, jarred or homemade, finely diced
2 cloves garlic, minced
¼ pound smoked turkey breast or ham, finely diced
2 tablespoons sugar
¼ cup red wine vinegar

Combine the spinach, scallions, parsley leaves, and mushrooms in a large salad bowl. Set aside.

Sauté the onion in the olive oil in a large skillet for 1 minute. Add the roasted peppers, garlic, smoked turkey or ham, sugar, and vinegar and heat through. Pour about half this dressing (1 cup plus 2 tablespoons) over the salad, toss, and serve.

Makes 4 servings, plus enough to:
✪ **Reserve 1 cup plus 2 tablespoons dressing for Grilled Salmon with Pickled Peppers.**

Grilled Salmon with
Pickled Peppers

4 salmon steaks (5 to 6 ounces each)
2 teaspoons olive oil
Salt and pepper to taste

✪ **1 cup plus 2 tablespoons dressing
reserved from Spinach Salad with Red
Pepper Vinaigrette**
1 lime, cut into 8 thin wedges

Rub the salmon with the oil and season both sides with salt and pepper. Broil or grill the fish 4 inches from a hot fire on an oiled rack or under a broiler for 3 to 4 minutes per side, depending on thickness, or until the surfaces are browned and the flesh flakes under gentle pressure. Spoon about a quarter of the reserved dressing over each salmon steak, garnish each with 2 lime wedges, and serve.

Makes 4 servings.

WHAT MAKES A FISH FLAKE?

However fish is cooked, one old cook's tale must be dispelled. A fish is *not* perfectly cooked when you can see it flake. It is overcooked. What the flaking rule means is that a properly cooked fish will show a flake when it is gently pressed, indicating that the connective membrane is soft but not yet fully dissolved.

Microwaved Russian Stuffed Cabbage

1 medium head of cabbage (see Note)
✪ **1 cup vegetables reserved from Sweet-and-Sour Brisket**

✪ **2 cups reserved Mushroom Kasha**
✪ **2 cups sauce reserved from Sweet-and-Sour Brisket**

Remove any torn and wilted leaves from the cabbage. Cut deeply to remove the core. Place the cabbage base down on a microwavesafe pie plate and microwave at full power for 8 minutes. Cool for a few minutes and remove 8 perfect large leaves. Set aside.

Finely chop half the reserved vegetables. Mix in the reserved kasha. Place about ⅓ cup of the mixture in the center of a cabbage leaf. Fold the sides of the leaf over the filling and roll up, starting at the stem end, into a neat bundle. Place the cabbage rolls, seam side down, in a 9 x 13-inch microwavesafe baking dish. Roll up the remaining cabbage leaves and pack snugly into the baking dish. Place remaining vegetables around the stuffed cabbage.

Pour the reserved sauce over the cabbage rolls and tightly cover the dish with plastic wrap. Microwave at full power for 15 minutes, or until the cabbage is tender. Pierce the plastic and allow the rolls to sit for 5 minutes before serving.

(If you do not have a microwave, I'd recommend skipping this recipe. It would take so long to prepare conventionally that it would not be feasible for a weeknight.)

Makes 4 servings.

Note: You will not need the entire head of cabbage for this dish, but you will need a cabbage of at least medium size in order to have leaves large enough for stuffing.

Many Bean Soup

4 strips bacon
1 medium onion, chopped
3 cloves garlic, minced
2 teaspoons ground cumin
¼ teaspoon crushed red pepper flakes
✪ **3 cups sauce reserved from Sweet-and-Sour Brisket**

2 cups beef broth, canned or homemade
Salt and pepper to taste
1 can (15 ounces) dark kidney beans, drained
1 can (15 ounces) light kidney or pinto beans
1 can (19 ounces) cannellini beans
2 tablespoons chopped parsley

Cook the bacon in a large heavy saucepan over medium heat until crisp, remove, and blot on paper towels. Crumble and set aside.

Add the onion to the bacon fat in the pan and cook over medium heat until softened, about 2 minutes. Add the garlic, cumin, and pepper flakes and stir for 30 seconds. Add the reserved sauce, beef broth, salt, and pepper and stir to combine. Bring the mixture to a boil, reduce the heat, and simmer for 5 minutes. Add all the beans and the parsley and stir to combine. Simmer another 5 minutes. Serve hot.

Makes 4 large servings.

Beef Tostados

1 cup instant refried beans (see Note)
1 cup boiling water
1 ripe avocado
1 teaspoon lemon juice
2 tablespoons salsa, homemade
1 small onion, finely chopped
2 teaspoons olive oil
2 cloves garlic, minced
✪ **6 to 8 slices brisket reserved from
Sweet-and-Sour Brisket, chopped**

2 teaspoons chili powder
2 tablespoons ketchup
8 (6-inch) corn tortillas
2 cups thinly shredded lettuce
2 tomatoes, diced
6 ounces monterey jack cheese, shredded
(1½ cups)

Combine the instant beans with the boiling water. Stir and let stand for at least 5 minutes. Cut the avocado lengthwise into quarters and discard the pit. Peel each quarter and dice. Mix the avocado with the lemon juice and salsa. Set aside.

Sauté the onion in the oil in a medium skillet over high heat until the onion is lightly browned, about 2 minutes. Add the garlic, brisket, and chili powder and cook for 2 minutes. Stir in the ketchup and remove from the heat.

Meanwhile, place the tortillas on a microwavesafe plate. Cover loosely with plastic wrap and microwave at full power for 1 minute. Or wrap the tortillas in foil and warm in a preheated 375°F. oven for 5 minutes.

Serve each tortilla topped with a layer of refried beans, a layer of the meat mixture, lettuce, tomatoes, cheese, and the avocado mixture.

Makes 4 servings.

Note: Instant refried beans are a dehydrated product sold in health-food stores and specialty groceries. Unlike canned refried beans, this product is fat-free.

Menu 3

The cacophony that is curry is the inspiration for this week's Sunday dinner. A stew of hearty winter vegetables is seasoned with a paste of warm curry spices, refreshing herbs, sautéed sweet onion, and a jolt of lemon juice. There are many kinds of curry seasoning mixtures; this one is fairly common. Its core is a premixed spice blend, called garam masala, which is sold in Indian groceries or the ethnic sections of some supermarkets. It comes in many styles, any of which is fine. Just be sure to buy one that is vacuum packed and to use it within four months of purchase, since it quickly goes stale. (For the longest shelf life, store it in a dry, dark, cool place.)

Accompanying Sunday's curry are Basmati Rice, a highly flavorful Asian grain, and a variety of side dishes that add color, texture, heat relief, and a different depth of flavor with each bite. Some, like the onion raita and minted cucumbers, are salads, which should be made the day of the dinner. Others, like the Eggplant Chutney and Toasted Cardamom Almonds, can be made days before and refrigerated for weeks after.

Sunday's salads recombine to form a fresh cucumber sauce for Monday's lamb chops. Bisteeya, an elaborate Moroccan pie usually reserved for the festival table, is made weeknight-easy with the help of Sunday's spiced almonds, Eggplant Chutney, and simmered vegetables for a vegetarian version of this extravaganza. On Wednesday, the vegetables become a stuffing for baked fish, and Sunday's lentil side dish cuts the usual hour of preparation time for lentil soup down to fifteen minutes on Thursday.

THE SUNDAY DINNER

Curry of Winter Vegetables

Basmati Rice

Red Onion Raita

Eggplant Chutney

Garlic Lentils

Cucumber Mint Salad

Toasted Cardamom Almonds

THE WEEKNIGHT ENTREES

Grilled Lamb with Creamy
Cucumber Sauce

Vegetable Bisteeya

Baked Fish Stuffed
with Vegetables

Lentil Soup with Italian Sausage

Curry of Winter Vegetables

2 large leeks
3 tablespoons vegetable oil
2 tablespoons mustard seed
4 large carrots, cut into chunks
2 sweet potatoes, peeled and cut into chunks
   (1 pound)
1 medium butternut squash, peeled and cut
   into chunks (2 pounds)
1 bulb fennel, trimmed, quartered, and thickly
   sliced
2 cups water
1 small cauliflower, broken into florets
1½ pounds broccoli, florets only

Salt and pepper to taste
1 large onion, finely chopped
4 cloves garlic, minced
2 tablespoons finely chopped gingerroot
3 tablespoons ground coriander seed
3 tablespoons ground cumin
⅛ teaspoon crushed red pepper flakes
3 tablespoons garam masala
1 tablespoon ground turmeric
Juice of 1 large lemon
1 cup yogurt
Basmati Rice (recipe follows)

Trim the leeks of the green and root sections. Cut the leeks lengthwise into quarters and run under a strong flow of cold water to wash out any dirt or grit. Shake off excess water and slice the leeks into small pieces.

Heat 2 tablespoons of the oil in a large heavy soup pot over medium-high heat. Add the mustard seed and cook, stirring frequently, until the seeds begin to pop. Add the carrots, sweet potatoes, squash, and fennel. Toss well, cover, and cook over medium heat for 5 minutes, stirring occasionally. Add the water, bring to a boil, reduce the heat, and simmer for 5 minutes. Add the cauliflower, broccoli, salt, and pepper. Simmer for 8 to 10 minutes more, or until everything is tender.

Meanwhile, sauté the onion in the remaining oil in a skillet over medium heat until softened, about 2 minutes. Add the garlic, gingerroot, coriander, cumin, pepper flakes, garam masala, and turmeric. Cook for 1 minute, stirring constantly. Add the lemon juice and remove from the heat.

Using a slotted spoon, set aside 4 cups of the cooked vegetables. Place the rest on a serving platter, leaving the cooking liquid in the pot. Add the spice mixture to the liquid in the pot. Boil for 2 minutes. Remove from the heat and stir in the yogurt. Pour the sauce over the vegetables on the platter. Set aside 1 cup of the sauced vegetables.

Serve each portion of curry on a bed of rice, surrounded by the side dishes.

Makes 4 servings, plus enough to:
✪ **Reserve 4 cups unsauced vegetables for Vegetable Bisteeya.**
✪ **Reserve 1 cup curried vegetables for Baked Fish Stuffed with Vegetables.**

YOUR OWN CURRY POWDER
Combine ¼ cup coriander seeds, 1 stemmed dried chili pepper, 1 teaspoon whole cloves, 1 tablespoon fenugreek seeds, 2 teaspoons cardamom seeds, and 1 tablespoon cumin seeds in a dry skillet. Cook over medium heat, stirring constantly, about 1 minute, or until the spices are very aromatic. Be careful not to let them burn. Grind to a fine powder in a spice grinder or in a mortar with a pestle.

Basmati Rice

5½ cups water
1 teaspoon salt

3 cups basmati rice

Combine the water and salt in a large saucepan, cover, and bring to a boil. Meanwhile, wash the rice in several changes of cold water. Drain the rice, stir into the boiling water, cover, and simmer over low heat for 15 minutes, or until all the water has been absorbed. Remove from the heat and let rest for 5 minutes. Fluff rice with a fork and serve all but 2 cups.

Makes 4 servings, plus enough to:
✪ **Reserve 2 cups for Baked Fish Stuffed with Vegetables.**

Red Onion Raita

½ large red onion, cut into paper-thin slices
Juice of ½ large lemon
1 teaspoon sugar

1 tablespoon chili powder
Salt to taste
2 tablespoons plain yogurt

Combine the onion, lemon juice, sugar, chili powder, salt, and yogurt. Refrigerate until ready to serve.

Makes 4 servings, plus enough to:
✪ **Reserve ⅓ cup for Grilled Lamb with Creamy Cucumber Sauce.**

Eggplant Chutney

¾ cup chopped onion (1 ½ medium onions)
1 tablespoon olive oil
1 medium eggplant, peeled and diced
    (1 pound)
1 clove garlic, minced
1 tablespoon garam masala or curry powder
½ teaspoon ground turmeric
1 teaspoon ground cumin

1 teaspoon chili powder
¾ cup chopped canned tomatoes
    (4 to 5 tomatoes)
1 ½ tablespoons sugar
¼ teaspoon ground saffron
3 tablespoons cider vinegar
⅓ cup roasted peanuts

Sauté the onion in the olive oil in a large heavy saucepan over medium-high heat until softened, about 2 minutes. Add the eggplant and cook for another 2 minutes, stirring constantly. Add the garlic, garam masala, turmeric, cumin, and chili powder and cook another minute. Add the tomatoes, sugar, saffron, and vinegar. Simmer for 15 minutes. Let cool and stir in the peanuts. Serve warm or at room temperature.

Makes 4 to 6 servings, plus enough to:
✪ **Reserve 3 tablespoons for Vegetable Bisteeya.**
✪ **Reserve ¾ cup for Baked Fish Stuffed with Vegetables.**

Garlic Lentils

1 tablespoon dried minced garlic   *3 cloves fresh garlic, minced*
2 teaspoons dried minced onion   *1 tablespoon minced gingerroot*
1 small dried chili   *¼ teaspoon turmeric*
1 cinnamon stick   *¼ cup olive oil*
1 pound lentils   *¼ cup orange juice*

Place the dried minced garlic, dried minced onion, dried chili, and cinnamon stick in a large pot of water and bring to a boil. Meanwhile, put the lentils in a large mixing bowl and wash in several changes of cold water. Drain and add to the boiling water. Simmer for 35 to 40 minutes, or until the lentils are tender. Drain and remove the chili and cinnamon stick. Add the fresh garlic, gingerroot, turmeric, olive oil, and orange juice and mix thoroughly.

Before serving, moisten with some of the cooking liquid from the curry and rewarm.

Makes 4 servings, plus enough to:
✪ **Reserve 2 cups for Lentil Soup with Italian Sausage.**

Cucumber Mint Salad

3 large cucumbers, peeled   *¼ cup chopped mint leaves*
¼ teaspoon salt   *Juice of ½ lime*
3 tablespoons olive oil   *1 to 2 teaspoons hot pepper sauce, to taste*
1 clove garlic, minced   *½ cup plain yogurt*

Cut the cucumbers lengthwise in half. Scoop out the seeds with a spoon and cut each cucumber half into thin slices. Toss with salt. Set aside for 10 minutes, then squeeze out excess water with your hands.

Combine the oil, garlic, mint, lime juice, hot pepper sauce, and yogurt. Mix in the cucumber slices. Refrigerate until ready to serve.

Makes 4 servings, plus enough to:
✪ **Reserve 1½ cups for Grilled Lamb with Creamy Cucumber Sauce.**

Toasted Cardamom Almonds

2 tablespoons vegetable oil
1 pound whole almonds with skins
1 tablespoon ground cardamom

2 teaspoons sugar
Salt and cayenne to taste

Heat the oil in a heavy skillet, add the almonds, and cook for 3 minutes, stirring frequently, until they start to crackle. Add the cardamom, sugar, salt, and cayenne. Cool to room temperature. Stir well and cook another minute, until almonds are uniformly toasted.

Makes 4 servings, plus enough to:
✪ **Reserve 2 cups for Vegetable Bisteeya.**

Grilled Lamb with Creamy Cucumber Sauce

8 loin lamb chops, each 1½ inches thick
2 tablespoons extra-virgin olive oil

✪ **1½ cups reserved Cucumber Mint Salad**
✪ **⅓ cup reserved Red Onion Raita**

Rub the lamb chops with half the olive oil and grill or broil 4 inches from a hot fire for 4 to 5 minutes per side.

Meanwhile, finely chop the reserved cucumber salad and raita and combine. Add the liquid from the 2 salads. Mix in the remaining olive oil. Divide the sauce among 4 plates, place 2 lamb chops on top of the sauce, and serve immediately.

Makes 4 servings.

Vegetable Bisteeya

✪ **4 cups vegetables reserved from Curry of Winter Vegetables**
¼ cup chopped cilantro
Juice of ½ lemon
✪ **3 tablespoons reserved Eggplant Chutney, finely chopped**
✪ **2 cups reserved Toasted Cardamom Almonds**

½ cup confectioners' sugar
4 teaspoons ground cinnamon
2 tablespoons butter
Olive oil spray
9 sheets frozen phyllo dough, defrosted (about ½ pound)

Combine the reserved vegetables, cilantro, lemon juice, and chutney. Set aside.

Coarsely chop the almonds in the workbowl of a food processor. Add ¼ cup of the confectioners' sugar, 2 teaspoons of the cinnamon, and the butter and process in pulses until the nuts start to adhere to each other but still maintain a crunchy consistency. Set aside.

Preheat the oven to 450°F.

To form the pie, spray the interior of a 10-inch deep-dish pie plate with the olive oil spray. Place a sheet of phyllo across the bottom of the pan with the edges hanging over the rim. Spray lightly with oil. Place another sheet perpendicular to the first and spray lightly with oil. Layer 4 more sheets in the same way. Scatter a layer of the almonds over the phyllo. Place the vegetable mixture on top of the almonds. Scatter the remaining almonds on top. Spray another sheet of phyllo with olive oil spray, fold in half, and place on top of the filling. Spray with oil. Repeat with the remaining 2 phyllo sheets. Fold the overhanging edges of phyllo inward so that they cover the edges of the top phyllo sheets all the way around. Spray with more oil. Bake for 20 minutes, or until the top is brown. Place a sheet pan on top and invert. Return to the oven and bake another 10 minutes. Allow to cool for 5 minutes.

Place the remaining confectioners' sugar in a strainer and sprinkle over the pie. Sprinkle with the remaining cinnamon. Slide onto a serving platter and cut into wedges.

Makes 4 large servings.

Baked Fish Stuffed with Vegetables

○ **1 cup vegetables reserved from Curry of Winter Vegetables**
○ **2 cups reserved Basmati Rice**
Salt and pepper to taste
2 whole fish, such as black bass, red snapper, porgy, bluefish, etc., scaled, gills removed, boned, and well washed (page 169) (1½ to 2 pounds each)

1 tablespoon olive oil
Juice of 1 lemon
○ **¾ cup reserved Eggplant Chutney**

If any of the reserved vegetables are in large pieces, cut them into bite-size pieces. Mix the vegetables and reserved rice and season with salt and pepper. Season the fish inside and out with salt and pepper and rub the skin with the olive oil.

Preheat the oven to 375°F.

Place the fish in a baking dish just large enough to hold them snugly. Lift the upper fillet of each fish and stuff the interior with half the rice mixture. Bake for 25 to 30 minutes, or until the fish flakes under gentle pressure. Using a large spatula, transfer the fish to a serving platter. Pour the lemon juice over all.

To serve, remove the head and tail and cut each fish into 2 pieces. Serve with the reserved chutney.

Makes 4 servings.

Lentil Soup with Italian Sausage

1 medium onion, chopped
¾ pound hot Italian sausage, chopped
✪ **2 cups reserved Garlic Lentils**

1 teaspoon ground cumin
2 cups canned vegetable juice
1½ cups chicken broth, canned or homemade

Cook the onion and sausage in a large saucepan over medium-high heat until the sausage loses its raw look and the onion has softened, about 4 minutes. Add the reserved lentils and the cumin and stir to combine. Mix in the vegetable juice and chicken broth. Simmer for 10 minutes. Serve hot.

Makes 4 servings.

Menu 4

When it comes to pork chops, forget everything you've ever learned about cooking. This isn't just "the other white meat"; it's a whole other animal. Pork is bred leaner and trimmed closer than it used to be. This is how most people profess to want their meat, but it has left us with pork chops that are hypersensitive to heat. The solution is not to give up on pork, for the traditional methods are all fine for lean pork, so long as you slow them down. Grill your pork chops, but keep the fire low and turn the meat frequently. Basting with sauce also helps restore some of the lost moisture without adding fat. Broiling is fine too, if the chops are marinated first and the rack of the broiler is lowered.

For the pork chops for this week's Sunday dinner, the flavors of an American classic are combined with a cooking method that has the chops gently simmering in a broth spiked with Worcestershire and herbs. The entree is accompanied by carrots in a cranberry glaze and sautéed cabbage fragrant with black pepper.

The cabbage becomes a bed for Tuesday's lemony seared scallops, and part of the filling for Mu Shu Linguine on Monday, in which a rendition of mu shu pork is served as a pasta sauce, rather than wrapped in a pancake. The full flavor of salmon stands up admirably to the sweet and pungent combination of cranberries and capers on Wednesday. On Thursday, Sunday's stuffing dresses up scallops of quickly sautéed turkey breast with a classic oyster dressing.

THE SUNDAY DINNER	THE WEEKNIGHT ENTREES
Stuffed Pork Chops	Mu Shu Linguine
Cranberry-glazed Carrots	Seared Scallops on Lemon-Dill Kraut
Black Pepper Cabbage	Salmon with Carrots, Bell Pepper, and Capers
	Turkey Rolls with Oyster Stuffing

Stuffed Pork Chops

1 rib celery, finely diced
1 medium onion, chopped
3 tablespoons vegetable oil
1 tablespoon butter
Salt and pepper to taste
1 sprig rosemary, leaves only
12 sage leaves
1 sprig thyme, leaves only

4 cups cubed crustless whole wheat or white
   bread (about 12 ounces)
2½ cups chicken broth, canned or homemade
6 pork chops, each 1½ inches thick, pockets
   cut in four of the chops
½ cup flour
Pinch of dried ground sage
Pinch of dried thyme
2 tablespoons Worcestershire sauce

Sauté the celery and half the onion in 1 tablespoon of the oil and the butter in a large skillet over medium heat until softened, about 2 minutes. Season with salt and pepper. Add the rosemary, sage, and thyme leaves and the bread cubes. Cook until the bread cubes are lightly browned, about 3 minutes. Stir in 1 cup of the chicken broth, tossing until all the bread has been moistened. Remove from heat and let cool. Reserve 1½ cups of the stuffing. Divide the remaining stuffing among the 4 pork chops that have the pockets. Press the pockets closed over the stuffing.

   Mix the flour with the dried sage, thyme, salt, and pepper. Dust all 6 chops with the seasoned flour, patting off any excess flour. Brown the chops in the remaining oil in the skillet over medium heat, about 5 minutes per side. Remove to a plate. Pour off all but about 2 teaspoons of the fat. Add the remaining onion to the pan and cook briefly until the onion has softened. Add the remaining chicken broth and the Worcestershire. Heat to a boil, add the browned chops, and simmer for 5 more minutes. Remove and reserve the unstuffed chops. Turn the stuffed chops and simmer 5 more minutes. Serve the stuffed chops with the sauce.

Makes 4 servings, plus enough to:
✪ **Reserve 1½ cups stuffing for Turkey Rolls with Oyster Stuffing.**
✪ **Reserve 2 unstuffed cooked pork chops for Mu Shu Linguine.**

Cranberry-glazed Carrots

1 ½ cups water
2 pounds carrots, spiral-cut
1 cup cranberries, fresh or frozen (see Note)

½ cup sugar
Salt to taste

Bring the water to a boil in a nonstick skillet. Add the carrots and cook until tender. There will be about ¼ cup water left in the pan. Remove ⅔ cup of the carrots and reserve.

Add the cranberries, sugar, and salt to the pan. Stir until the cranberries burst and the liquid in the pan thickens into a glaze on the surface of the carrots, 1 to 2 minutes.

Makes 4 servings, plus enough to:
✪ **Reserve ⅔ cup unglazed cooked carrots for Salmon with Carrots, Bell Pepper, and Capers.**

Note: Fresh cranberries can be frozen right in the bag; they will keep well in the freezer for up to 1 year.

CUTTING VEGETABLES

There are several ways of cutting vegetables to prepare them for cooking. Here are three:

Julienne. This is a ⅛ x ⅛ x 2-inch strip. Square off the vegetable and cut it into 2-inch lengths. Cut the lengths into ⅛-inch-thick slices. Stack up 3 slices and cut into ⅛-inch-thick strips.

Dice. These can vary in size. Cut them in much the same way as a julienne. Square off the vegetable and cut it into slices as thick as you want the diced vegetable to be. Large dice are about ¾ inch; medium dice, about ½ inch; small dice, about ¼ inch; fine dice, about ⅛ inch. Stack up a few slices and cut strips of the same width. Line up several strips and cut across into cubes.

Spiral-cut. This is an Asian technique usually associated with stir-fries. Cut the vegetable on a diagonal, then give it a quarter turn so that the cut surface faces up. Cut another diagonal slice across the cut face. Give the vegetable another quarter turn and slice again. Pieces will be multifaceted, like jewels.

Black Pepper Cabbage

3 tablespoons olive oil
1 medium onion, halved and thinly sliced
1 large head cabbage, quartered, cored, and
    very thinly sliced (2 to 3 pounds)

3 cloves garlic, minced
Salt to taste
1 tablespoon coarsely ground black pepper
1 tablespoon butter

Heat the oil in a large deep skillet. Add the onion and stir until softened, about 2 minutes. Add the cabbage, garlic, and salt. Cook, stirring, until the cabbage is barely tender, about 3 minutes. Add the pepper and cook another 2 minutes. Stir in the butter. Reserve 3 cups and serve the rest.

Makes 4 servings, plus enough to:
✪ **Reserve 2 cups for Seared Scallops on Lemon-Dill Kraut.**
✪ **Reserve 1 cup for Mu Shu Linguine.**

Mu Shu Linguine

½ cup boiling water
¼ ounce dried wild mushrooms (¼ cup)
3 tablespoons low-sodium soy sauce
3 tablespoons rice wine vinegar
1 tablespoon sugar
✪ **2 pork chops reserved from Stuffed Pork Chops**

1 tablespoon hoisin sauce
¾ pound dried linguine
1 teaspoon dark sesame oil
2 tablespoons vegetable oil
✪ **1 cup reserved Black Pepper Cabbage**
1 clove garlic, minced
6 scallions, white parts only, thinly sliced

Pour the boiling water over the mushrooms and set aside to soak for 10 minutes. Remove the mushrooms from the soaking water and cut into small pieces. Strain the soaking liquid through paper towels or cheesecloth set in a strainer. Set both aside.

Combine the soy sauce, vinegar, and sugar in a small bowl. Set aside.

Remove and discard the bones from the reserved chops. Cut the meat into thin strips 1 inch long. Toss the meat with half the soy sauce mixture and set aside. Add the hoisin sauce to the remaining soy sauce mixture. Set the hoisin-soy mixture aside.

Cook the linguine in a large pot of lightly salted boiling water until tender, about 10 minutes. Drain in a colander. Toss with seasame oil. Set aside.

Heat a large wok over high heat. Add the vegetable oil and heat until it is smoking. Add the reserved cabbage and the garlic and stir-fry for 30 seconds. Add the pork and its marinade and stir-fry for another minute. Add the mushrooms and their soaking liquid and bring to a boil. Add the linguine and stir-fry until heated through, about 1 minute. Add the hoisin-soy mixture and stir-fry until most of the liquid is absorbed, about 1 minute. Add the scallions and serve.

Makes 4 servings.

Seared Scallops on
Lemon-Dill Kraut

1½ pounds sea scallops
2 teaspoons olive oil
Salt and pepper to taste
6 tablespoons lemon juice

✪ **2 cups reserved Black Pepper Cabbage**
Zest of 1 lemon, finely chopped
1 tablespoon finely chopped dill
1 lemon, cut into 8 wedges

Trim any hard strips of muscle that may be attached to the sides of the scallops. Flatten the scallops gently but firmly between your palms so they are all about ½ inch thick. Rub the scallops with the oil and season them with salt and pepper. Drizzle 2 teaspoons of the lemon juice over the scallops and set aside for 10 minutes.

Heat a large heavy skillet over high heat for about 5 minutes. Sear the scallops for 1 to 2 minutes per side. Remove scallops to a platter. Turn off the heat. Add the reserved cabbage, lemon zest, and dill to the skillet and stir until the dill wilts and the cabbage is heated through, about 1 minute. Stir in remaining lemon juice and toss. Serve the scallops on a bed of cabbage garnished with lemon wedges.

Makes 4 servings.

Salmon with Carrots, Bell Pepper,
and Capers

4 salmon fillets, boned and skinned
    (about 5 ounces each)
Salt and pepper to taste
1 tablespoon olive oil
½ red bell pepper, stemmed, seeded, and
    diced
¼ cup chopped sweet onion, such as Vidalia
    or Bermuda

3 tablespoons capers, drained
✪ ⅔ **cup carrots reserved from
    Cranberry-glazed Carrots**
Juice of ½ lemon
1 tablespoon butter

Season the salmon with salt and pepper. Heat the olive oil in a nonstick skillet until smoking. Add the salmon and brown well on both sides, about 4 minutes per side. Add the pepper and onion and cook for another minute. Remove the salmon to a warm platter.

Add the capers and reserved carrots to the pan and stir until the capers brown lightly around the edges, about 2 minutes. Add the lemon juice and remove from heat. Stir in the butter and adjust seasoning with salt and pepper. Pour the vegetables over the salmon.

Makes 4 servings.

Turkey Rolls with Oyster Stuffing

8 turkey cutlets (3 to 4 ounces each)
1 pint shucked select oysters, drained

✪ **1½ cups stuffing reserved from Stuffed Pork Chops**
1 tablespoon vegetable oil

Place each turkey cutlet between sheets of plastic wrap. Pound with a smooth meat pounder, small heavy skillet, or saucepan to an even thickness of about ⅛ inch.

Cook the oysters in a small skillet until they plump, 1 to 2 minutes. Add the reserved stuffing to the pan and heat through.

Remove the top sheet of the plastic wrap or parchment from the cutlets. Divide the stuffing equally among the pieces of turkey and roll each cutlet around the stuffing. Heat the oil in a large nonstick skillet until very hot. Brown the turkey rolls in the oil, turning them 3 times and cooking the meat about 2 minutes per side. Serve 2 rolls per person.

Makes 4 servings.

Menu 5

Roasted garlic is so mild that it can be eaten by the spoonful, spread shamelessly on bread, or used to dress up a baked potato. Unlike sautéed garlic, whose pungency is prone to offend, the sweetness of roasted garlic enhances almost everything, and its nuance permeates this week's menu. It thickens the sauce for Sunday's braised sirloin tips, flavors the aïoli for Monday's bourride, and glazes the crackled skin of Thursday's Honey Garlic Chicken.

Bourride is the signature dish of the coastal towns in Languedoc in southern France. It is to that region what bouillabaisse is to neighboring Provence. It's a simple concoction of plainly cooked fish in broth, and its glory comes from aïoli (garlic mayonnaise) that is swirled into the broth near the end of cooking. The aïoli in this recipe breaks with tradition by using roasted, rather than fresh, garlic for its flavor.

Sunday's braised beef is accompanied by a garlicless version of traditional Middle Eastern bulgur salad and by fennel bulbs simmered in wine with the perfume of orange zest and the acrid briny intensity of black olives. These side dishes fuel Tuesday's skillet dinner of beef, fennel, and artichoke hearts and Wednesday's Middle Eastern pita sandwich filled with bulgur, chick peas, and sesame seeds.

THE SUNDAY DINNER

Braised Sirloin Tips Thickened with
Roasted Garlic

Herbed Bulgur with Tomatoes

Braised Fennel with Olives
and Orange

THE WEEKNIGHT ENTREES

Quick Bourride

Beef and Artichoke Provençale

Tabbouleh Tuna Salad in a Pita

Honey Garlic Chicken

Braised Sirloin Tips Thickened with Roasted Garlic

6 whole heads garlic
¼ cup olive oil
3 pounds sirloin tips or beef stew meat, trimmed
½ cup flour seasoned with salt and pepper to taste
1 medium onion, chopped
2 ribs celery, diced
1 medium carrot, diced

1 teaspoon dried thyme
1 teaspoon crumbled dried rosemary
1 teaspoon aniseed, ground
2 cloves garlic, minced
1 tablespoon tomato paste
2 cups red wine
4 cups water
Salt and pepper to taste
4 large pita breads

Preheat the oven to 400°F.

Rub the heads of garlic with 1 tablespoon of the olive oil and place in a small baking dish. Bake until soft, about 40 minutes.

Meanwhile, dredge the beef in the seasoned flour. Heat 2 tablespoons of the remaining oil in a large heavy saucepan until smoking. Add the meat in 2 or 3 batches and cook over medium-high heat until browned on both sides. Be sure not to crowd the pan. Remove the meat as it browns and set it aside. Add the remaining tablespoon of oil to the pan along with the onion and cook for 1 minute, or until softened. Add the celery and carrot and cook until the vegetables brown, stirring frequently, about 4 minutes. Add the thyme, rosemary, aniseed, minced garlic, and tomato paste. Stir to combine. Return the meat to the pan and add the red wine and water. Add salt and pepper to taste. Heat until simmering, cover, and simmer until the meat is completely tender, about 2 hours.

When the garlic is done, cut the heads in half crosswise. Squeeze the flesh from the skins and mash it with a fork. You should have about 1 cup of mashed roasted garlic.

Preheat the oven to 350°F.

Ten minutes before serving, heat the pitas in the oven. At the same time, mix ½ cup of the garlic puree into the stew. Serve 6 cups of the stew in a warm serving bowl, accompanied by the warm pitas.

Makes 4 servings, plus enough to:
- ✪ **Reserve 4 cups sirloin tips with sauce for Beef and Artichoke Provençale.**
- ✪ **Reserve ¼ cup mashed roasted garlic for Quick Bourride.**
- ✪ **Reserve ¼ cup mashed roasted garlic for Honey Garlic Chicken.**

THE FLAVORS OF OIL

You will notice that the recipes in this book call for a variety of oils. Most often, I use olive oil, both for its flavor and its reputed health benefits. When a pronounced olive flavor is essential for the recipe, such as in a dressing or in some Mediterranean preparations, I'll ask for extra-virgin olive oil. Virgin oils come from the first pressings of the fruit and are fuller-bodied and more aromatic. If those qualities don't mean much to you, use pure olive oil in place of extra-virgin.

When the flavor of the oil is not essential, I call for generic vegetable oil, by which I mean any nonassertive all-purpose oil. Use what you normally use: canola, peanut, corn, blended, or vegetable oil.

On special occasions, I recommend a rarer oil, like dark sesame oil, walnut oil, or hazelnut oil. There really is no substitute for these oils if you want the right flavor. Dark sesame oil is my all-purpose description of what is often sold as toasted sesame oil or Oriental sesame oil. It is not a designation that you'll find on a label. The important thing is to get an oil with a deep mahogany color rather than the pale yellow sesame oil sold in health-food stores that has very little sesame flavor.

Herbed Bulgur with Tomatoes

2 cups bulgur or fine-grain tabbouleh
2 cups water
¼ cup extra-virgin olive oil
Juice of 1½ lemons
Salt and pepper to taste

6 scallions, white parts only, finely sliced
¼ cup chopped parsley
¼ cup chopped mint
2 ripe tomatoes, cored and coarsely diced

Combine the bulgur, water, and oil in a mixing bowl and set aside for 30 minutes until all the water is absorbed. Add the lemon juice, salt, pepper, scallions, parsley, mint, and tomatoes. Stir. Refrigerate for at least 30 minutes. Serve 2 cups.

Makes 4 servings, plus enough to:
✪ **Reserve 2 cups for Tabbouleh Tuna Salad in a Pita.**

Braised Fennel with Olives and Orange

3 bulbs fennel, base and stalks trimmed
2 tablespoons olive oil
1 small onion, chopped
2 cloves garlic, minced
2 tablespoons julienned orange zest

1 cup white wine
Juice of 1 orange
Salt and pepper to taste
8 Greek olives, pitted and chopped

Cut each fennel bulb lengthwise into 5 thick slices. Heat the oil in a large skillet over medium-high heat and cook the fennel until browned on both sides. Remove fennel. Add onion to the skillet and cook for 1 minute, stirring constantly. Add the garlic, orange zest, wine, orange juice, salt, and pepper. Return fennel slices to the liquid in the pan. Cover and simmer over medium heat for 30 minutes, or until the fennel has softened. Scatter the olives over the top and simmer another 2 minutes. Serve each person 2 slices and a bit of sauce.

Makes 4 servings, plus enough to:
✪ **Reserve about 1½ cups for Beef and Artichoke Provençale.**
✪ **Reserve about 1 cup for Quick Bourride.**

Quick Bourride

✪ ¼ cup mashed roasted garlic reserved
   from Braised Sirloin Tips Thickened
   with Roasted Garlic
3 tablespoons mayonnaise
Juice of ½ lemon
1 tablespoon extra-virgin olive oil
1 teaspoon cornstarch
✪ About I cup reserved Braised Fennel
   with Olives and Orange

1 ½ pounds white fish fillet, such as flounder,
   orange roughy, red snapper, or black bass,
   skinned
½ cup flour seasoned with salt and pepper to
   taste
2 tablespoons olive oil
½ medium onion, chopped
¾ cup white wine
¾ cup bottled clam juice

Mix the reserved mashed roasted garlic with the mayonnaise, lemon juice, oil, and corn-starch and set aside. Chop the reserved fennel and set aside.

Cut the fish into 8 large pieces and dredge in the seasoned flour. Heat the olive oil in a skillet over medium-high heat. Add the fish, and cook until browned on both sides, about 2 minutes. Remove fish, and set aside. Add the onion to the pan and cook until softened, stirring frequently, about 1 minute. Add the wine and boil for 1 minute. Add the clam juice and the fennel and stir. Return the fish to the skillet and simmer for 4 minutes, or until the fish flakes to gentle pressure. Using a slotted spoon, transfer the fish to a warm serving bowl. Heat the liquid in the pan to a boil and boil vigorously for 1 minute. Over low heat, whisk in the garlic mixture and heat until lightly thickened, about 1 minute. Pour the sauce over the fish and serve.

Makes 4 servings.

Beef and Artichoke Provençale

✪ **4 cups reserved Braised Sirloin Tips Thickened with Roasted Garlic**
1 tablespoon olive oil
½ medium onion, chopped
1 teaspoon herbes de Provence
✪ **About 1½ cups reserved Braised Fennel with Olives and Orange**

2 tablespoons chopped parsley
1 jar (6 ounces) marinated artichoke hearts, coarsely chopped
12 ounces dried pasta, such as wagon wheels or medium shells

Pick out the meat from the reserved sirloin tips and cut into small pieces. Set aside.

Heat the olive oil in a large skillet. Add the onion and cook 2 minutes, or until softened. Add the herbes de Provence and reserved fennel and cook over medium heat for 30 seconds. Add the meat and the reserved sauce. Heat to a boil, stirring frequently. Stir in the parsley and artichokes and their marinade and heat through.

Meanwhile, cook the pasta in a large pot of salted boiling water until al dente, about 10 minutes. Drain and serve topped with the beef mixture.

Makes 4 servings.

Tabbouleh Tuna Salad in a Pita

1 can (about 6 ounces) water-packed white tuna, drained
1 clove garlic, minced
1 tablespoon olive oil
¼ teaspoon hot pepper sauce
✪ **2 cups reserved Herbed Bulgur with Tomatoes**

1 cup canned chick peas, drained and rinsed
2 tablespoons sesame seeds, toasted
Salt and pepper to taste
8 small or 4 large pita breads, opened as pockets

Crumble the tuna with a fork in a bowl. Mix in the garlic, oil, hot pepper sauce, reserved bulgur, chick peas, sesame seeds, salt, and pepper. Warm the pitas in a 350°F. oven or in a toaster oven for 8 to 10 minutes and serve filled with the tuna mixture.

Makes 4 servings.

Honey Garlic Chicken

2 Cornish hens, cut in half lengthwise with
    backbones removed (page 251), 2 chicken
    breasts, split, or 4 chicken legs
✪ **¼ cup mashed roasted garlic reserved
from Braised Sirloin Tips Thickened
with Roasted Garlic**

2 tablespoons olive oil
2 tablespoons honey
Salt and pepper to taste
1 tablespoon balsamic vinegar

Preheat the oven to 450°F.

    Place the Cornish hens in a roasting pan, bone side down. Roast for 30 minutes. Meanwhile, place the reserved mashed garlic in a bowl and whisk in the olive oil, honey, salt, pepper, and vinegar. Brush on the meat and roast another 15 minutes. Turn meat over and brush with remaining sauce. Roast another 15 minutes. Serve hot or at room temperature.

Makes 4 servings.

Menu 6

Braising is the technique least identified with fish cookery. Fish are more commonly poached. But if a fish can be poached, it can be braised. Braising calls for one preliminary step that makes an extraordinary difference: The fish is browned first, making it heartier and richer. After browning, liquid is added halfway up the fish, and it is simmered until done.

Sunday's braised cod steaks are served under an avalanche of wild mushrooms. They're accompanied by a visually striking bread spiraled with spinach and spices—and made in record time with help from a defrosted bread dough and two packages of chopped spinach. The side vegetable, strips of red pepper and carrot cooked together in a mixture of ginger, garlic, and orange juice, is equally stunning.

Monday's entree restructures the extra dough and filling from the spinach bread with the sautéed peppers and carrots for an unusual pizza that's prepared in just a couple of minutes. The spinach and cod make fast work of Seafood Stuffed Shells on Tuesday, and the julienned carrots and peppers transform easily into colorful nests for honey-glazed Cornish hens on Wednesday. The week finishes up with a simplified version of a classic French dish. Pounded veal scallops are wrapped around a mound of wild mushrooms into bundles meant to imitate small stuffed game birds.

THE SUNDAY DINNER

Cod Braised with Wild Mushrooms

Spinach Bread

Orange Braised Peppers and Carrots

THE WEEKNIGHT ENTREES

Red, Green, and White Pizza

Seafood Stuffed Shells

Broiled Cornish Hens in Vegetable Nests

Mushroom-stuffed Veal Birds

Cod Braised with Wild Mushrooms

3 slices bacon

3 pounds cod steaks

⅓ cup flour seasoned with salt and pepper
　to taste

1 medium onion, chopped

1 pound wild mushrooms, any variety, stems
　trimmed, cleaned, and sliced

1 pound white mushrooms, stems trimmed,
　cleaned and sliced

¼ pound ham, finely diced

3 cloves garlic, minced

1 tablespoon fresh rosemary leaves

1 tablespoon tomato paste

½ cup white wine

3 cups chicken broth, canned or homemade

Salt and pepper to taste

3 tablespoons chopped parsley

Juice of ½ lemon

Cook the bacon in a large heavy deep skillet over medium heat until crisp. Remove, drain on paper towels, crumble, and set aside. Pour off half the bacon fat. Set aside.

While the bacon is cooking, dredge the cod in the seasoned flour. Brown in the bacon fat remaining in the pan over medium-high heat for about 2 minutes per side. Remove with a slotted spatula and set aside. Add the onion to the fat remaining in the pan and cook over medium heat until softened, about 2 minutes. Add the mushrooms and ham. Cook, stirring constantly, until the mushrooms lose their raw look, about 4 minutes. Stir in the garlic, rosemary, and tomato paste and cook for 1 more minute. Add the wine and chicken broth. Bring to a simmer and season with salt and pepper. Return the cod steaks to the pan, cover, and simmer over medium-low heat until the cod flakes under gentle pressure, about 8 minutes. Remove the cod from the pan, place half of it on a deep-sided platter, and reserve one cup of mushrooms.

While the fish is cooking, stir 2 tablespoons of the flour remaining from the dredging into the bacon fat that was set aside and mix until smooth. Bring the liquid in the pan to a boil and spoon the bacon fat–flour mixture into the pan, 1 tablespoon at a time, whisking constantly. Simmer for 1 minute, or until the sauce thickens. Remove from the heat and stir in the parsley and lemon juice. Adjust seasoning. Pour 4 cups of sauce over the fish and serve.

After dinner, remove the skin and bones from reserved fish and break it into large pieces. You should have 2 cups.

Makes 4 servings, plus enough to:
- ✪ **Reserve 2 cups of flaked cod for Seafood Stuffed Shells.**
- ✪ **Reserve 1 cup mushrooms for Mushroom-stuffed Veal Birds.**
- ✪ **Reserve 2 cups sauce for Mushroom-stuffed Veal Birds.**
- ✪ **Reserve ¼ cup sauce for Seafood Stuffed Shells.**

Spinach Bread

1 medium onion, chopped
1 tablespoon olive oil
2 packages (10 ounces each) frozen chopped spinach, defrosted and squeezed dry
2 cloves garlic, finely chopped

Salt and pepper to taste
Pinch of ground allspice
2 pounds frozen bread dough, defrosted
Flour, for dusting
Cornmeal, for dusting the pan

Cook the onion in the olive oil in a skillet over medium heat until softened, about 2 minutes. Mix in the spinach, garlic, salt, pepper, and allspice. Pat and roll out half the bread dough on a lightly floured board with floured hands and rolling pin until it forms a rectangle about 8 x 10 inches. Spread ¾ cup of the spinach mixture over the surface of the bread, leaving a 1-inch border all around.

Preheat the oven to 400°F. Dust a baking sheet with cornmeal.

Starting on one of the 10-inch sides, roll up the bread, jellyroll style. Pinch the seam and ends closed, and place, seam side down, on the baking sheet. Cover loosely with plastic and set aside to rise for 30 to 45 minutes.

Make several slashes in the top of the loaf and brush with ice water. Bake for 35 minutes, brushing with more ice water after the first 5 minutes, until puffed and brown. Let cool for 10 minutes before serving. Cut a ¾-inch slice from each end of the bread and reserve. Cut the rest into thick slices and serve.

Makes 4 servings, plus enough to:
✪ **Reserve I cup spinach mixture for Red, Green, and White Pizza.**
✪ **Reserve ¼ cup spinach mixture for Seafood Stuffed Shells.**
✪ **Reserve I pound defrosted frozen bread dough for Red, Green, and White Pizza.**
✪ **Reserve 2 slices of Spinach Bread for Mushroom-stuffed Veal Birds.**

Orange Braised Peppers
and Carrots

4 red bell peppers, stemmed, seeded, and juli-
  enned
1 pound carrots, julienned
2 tablespoons olive oil
1 tablespoon finely chopped gingerroot

2 cloves garlic, finely chopped
½ cup orange juice
Salt and pepper to taste
6 scallions, white parts only, cut into strips

Cook the peppers and carrots in the olive oil in a skillet over medium heat for 3 minutes, stirring frequently. Add the gingerroot and garlic and cook for 1 minute more. Add the orange juice and simmer for 5 minutes or until most of the juice has evaporated. Season with salt and pepper and add the scallions. Stir until scallions wilt, about 1 minute. Serve ¾ cup to each person.

Makes 4 servings, plus enough to:
✪ **Reserve 2 cups for Broiled Cornish Hens in Vegetable Nests.**
✪ **Reserve 1 cup for Red, Green, and White Pizza.**

Red, Green, and White Pizza

Cornmeal, for dusting the pan
✪ **I pound defrosted frozen bread dough
reserved from Spinach Bread**
3 cups shredded mozzarella (8 ounces)

✪ **I cup spinach mixture reserved from
Spinach Bread**
✪ **I cup reserved Orange Braised Peppers
and Carrots**

If you have a pizza stone, place it in the oven and preheat to 425°F. for at least 30 minutes. If you don't have a stone, simply preheat the oven as you normally would. Dust a baking sheet or pizza pan with cornmeal.

Knead the reserved dough into a ball. Pat, pinch, roll, throw, or whirl the dough into something that looks like a pizza crust. Place on the baking sheet or pan. Scatter the mozzarella over the pizza, concentrating the cheese closer to the perimeter than to the center. Distribute the reserved spinach and the reserved peppers and carrots evenly over the top.

If you have a stone, slide the pizza from the sheet or pan directly onto the hot stone. If not, bake on the sheet or pan. Bake for 30 minutes, or until the filling is bubbling and the crust is puffed and brown. Serve at once.

Makes 4 servings.

Seafood Stuffed Shells

12 to 16 jumbo pasta shells
✪ **2 cups flaked cod reserved from Cod
Braised with Wild Mushrooms**
✪ **¼ cup spinach mixture reserved from
Spinach Bread**

✪ **¼ cup sauce reserved from Cod
Braised with Wild Mushrooms**
2 cups canned vegetable juice
Juice of ½ lemon

Cook the pasta shells in a large pot of boiling salted water until just tender, about 10 minutes. Do not overcook. Drain.

Preheat the oven to 350°F.

While the pasta is cooking, flake the reserved cod. You should have about 2 cups. Combine the cod, the reserved spinach mixture, and the reserved sauce. Stuff the shells and place them, stuffed side up, in a large baking pan. Combine the vegetable juice and lemon juice and pour over the shells. Bake for 25 minutes, or until heated through. The shells may also be microwaved at full power for 6 minutes.

Makes 4 servings.

Broiled Cornish Hens in Vegetable Nests

3 cloves garlic, minced
1 tablespoon finely chopped gingerroot
1 teaspoon honey
1 tablespoon dark sesame oil
2 teaspoons soy sauce

2 Cornish hens, split in half lengthwise with backbones removed (page 251)
✪ **2 cups reserved from Orange Braised Peppers and Carrots**

Combine the garlic, gingerroot, honey, sesame oil, and soy sauce in a small saucepan. Heat, stirring frequently, until the honey melts, about 1 minute. Pour over the Cornish hen halves. Turn to coat thoroughly. Refrigerate for at least 1 hour.

Remove the hens from the marinade and grill or broil them 4 inches over a hot fire for 10 minutes per side. After turning the hens, warm the reserved peppers and carrots in a skillet just until heated through. Keep warm.

To serve, mound ½ cup of the vegetables in the center of each of 4 plates. Spread out each mound slightly, forming an indentation in the center of each one. Place a hen half on each of the vegetable nests and serve.

Makes 4 servings.

Mushroom-stuffed Veal Birds

8 veal scallops
1 tablespoon vegetable oil
✪ **2 slices reserved from Spinach Bread, chopped**
✪ **1 cup mushrooms reserved from Cod Braised with Wild Mushrooms**

1 teaspoon olive oil
✪ **2 cups sauce reserved from Cod Braised with Wild Mushrooms**
½ cup beef broth, canned or homemade
Salt and pepper to taste

Rub the veal with the vegetable oil and place between sheets of wax paper or plastic wrap. Pound until paper thin. Set aside. Mix the chopped reserved bread with the reserved mushrooms and finely chop by hand or in a food processor.

To make a veal bird, place a small mound (about 2 tablespoons) of the mushroom mixture slightly off center on one of the veal scallops. Fold the side flaps over the filling as if you were wrapping a package and roll the meat up around the filling, securing the end with a toothpick.

Place a nonstick skillet over high heat for 1 minute. Add the olive oil and brown the veal bundles on both sides. Add the reserved sauce and the beef broth and simmer for 10 minutes, or until the veal is tender. Season with salt and pepper and serve.

Makes 4 servings.

Garlic is so essential to almost every flavor system that even perfectly crafted dishes lack luster when it's missing. Despite its popularity, though, it most often plays a supportive role. Not this week.

Sunday's chicken is overcome with garlic, which is spread under the skin, directly on the meat, to permeate every part of this roast. The chicken is served with smashed baked potatoes flavored with pureed celery root. Celery root (also called celeriac and knob celery) is probably one of the ugliest vegetables you are likely to see. Large, gnarled, and dirty, celery root must be peeled deeply to get it clean, but once that's done, it cooks quickly, lending a sweet celery flavor and creamy texture to whatever it touches. The green vegetable for Sunday is sautéed green beans, paired with walnuts instead of the usual almonds.

Sunday's garlic mixture infuses Monday's catfish with the flavors of Provence in less than 10 minutes. On Tuesday, pasta reaps the garlic advantage with some of the chicken's pan juices along with a mixture of canned beans and Sunday's green bean side dish. Wednesday's chicken soup, exploding with lemon and garlic, has an interesting twist: It calls for an envelope of unflavored gelatin, replacing the natural gelatin that was drawn out of the chicken during roasting. The week finishes up with gnocchi, which, by using Sunday's potatoes, are practically assembled before you begin.

THE SUNDAY DINNER

Garlic Roast Chicken

Smashed Potatoes with Celery
Root Puree

Green Beans and Walnuts

THE WEEKNIGHT ENTREES

Braised Catfish with Olives
and Tomatoes

Ziti Fagiolini

Lemon Garlic Chicken Soup

Gnocchi with Walnut Pesto

Garlic Roast Chicken

1 chicken (about 6 pounds)
1½ teaspoons salt
1½ teaspoons freshly ground black pepper
2 tablespoons minced garlic (about 9 cloves)

¼ cup extra-virgin olive oil
2 cups canned salt-free vegetable juice, more if
    needed
Juice of 1 lemon

Remove giblet packages from the chicken and scatter giblets over the bottom of a large roasting pan. Remove visible fat from around the cavity. Wash inside and out and pat dry. Mix 1 teaspoon of the salt with 1 teaspoon of the pepper and rub the mixture into the walls of the cavity.

Preheat the oven to 400°F.

Run your fingers under the skin of the breast and legs, gently separating the skin from the meat underneath. Mix the minced garlic with the remaining salt and pepper and 3 tablespoons of the olive oil. Rub 3 tablespoons of this garlic-oil mixture under the skin, coating as much meat as you can reach. Run the remaining 1 tablespoon olive oil over the skin of the chicken. Reserve the remaining 2 tablespoons of the garlic-oil mixture.

Place the chicken, breast side down, on top of the giblets, and roast for 30 minutes. Reduce oven temperature to 375°F. and turn the chicken breast side up. Roast for 1 hour more. Pour the vegetable juice over the chicken and continue roasting for 30 minutes more, basting with the juice every 10 minutes, until skin is golden brown and a meat thermometer inserted into the thickest part of the thigh registers 170° to 175°F. Allow to rest for 10 minutes before carving.

While the chicken is resting, skim and discard as much fat as possible from the surface of the pan juices. Pour the skimmed juices into a large measuring cup. Add the lemon juice. You should have at least 2½ cups. If not, add enough additional vegetable juice to make 2½ cups. Heat to a simmer. Serve 1½ cups of the sauce with the chicken.

Makes 4 servings, plus enough to:
✪ **Reserve bones and remaining meat for Lemon Garlic Chicken Soup.**
✪ **Reserve 2 tablespoons garlic-oil mixture for Braised Catfish with Olives and Tomatoes.**
✪ **Reserve ½ cup pan juices for Braised Catfish with Olives and Tomatoes.**
✪ **Reserve ½ cup pan juices for Ziti Fagiolini.**

Smashed Potatoes with Celery Root Puree

6 large russet potatoes (about 4 pounds)
1 pound celery root, peeled and diced
¼ cup milk

½ cup light cream, half-and-half, or yogurt
4 tablespoons unsalted butter
Salt and pepper to taste

Preheat the oven to 400°F.

Bake the potatoes for 1 hour, or until tender. Or microbake them.

While the potatoes are baking, cook the celery root in boiling water for 12 minutes to soften. Drain well. Puree the celery root with the milk in a food processor or blender until smooth.

When the potatoes are tender, reserve two of them. Coarsely chop the other four and transfer to a large bowl. Add the cream in a slow, steady stream, beating by hand or with an electric mixer until light and fluffy. Beat in the butter and season well with salt and pepper. Beat in the celery root puree, reheat, and serve.

Makes 4 servings, plus enough to:
✪ **Reserve 2 baked potatoes for Gnocchi with Walnut Pesto.**

MICROBAKING POTATOES

Baked potatoes take an hour, and although microwaved "baked" potatoes need only a fraction of that time, they emerge without a trace of the crackled skin and fluffy flesh of a true baked potato. You can, however, use a microwave in conjunction with a conventional oven to get a perfectly fluffy and crisp-skinned potato in less than half an hour.

Preheat the oven to 450°F. Meanwhile, wash, dry, and oil four 8- to 10-ounce russet potatoes, pierce the skins with a fork, and place the potatoes on a glass baking dish. Cook potatoes in the microwave at full power for 7 minutes, then transfer them to the preheated oven and bake for 20 minutes.

Green Beans and Walnuts

1½ pounds green beans, stems removed
2 tablespoons olive oil
½ cup walnut pieces, finely chopped

1 clove garlic, minced
Salt and pepper to taste

Bring a large pot of lightly salted water to a boil over high heat. Add the green beans and boil until the beans turn bright green and tender but not soft, about 2 to 3 minutes. Drain and run under cold water or submerge in a bath of ice water until chilled. Drain and shake off excess water.

Warm the oil in a large skillet. Add the walnuts and stir until lightly browned. Add the blanched green beans, garlic, salt, and pepper. Toss and cook until heated through. Serve two thirds of the beans.

Makes 4 servings, plus enough to:
✪ **Reserve a third of the beans for Ziti Fagiolini.**

Braised Catfish with Olives and Tomatoes

1¾ *pounds catfish fillets, trimmed (page 269)*
✪ **2 tablespoons garlic-oil mixture reserved from Garlic Roast Chicken**
Salt and pepper to taste
1 teaspoon olive oil
½ small onion, finely chopped
½ cup white wine

2 large plum tomatoes, chopped
½ cup black olives, pitted and chopped
✪ **½ cup pan juices reserved from Garlic Roast Chicken**
or ½ cup canned vegetable juice
2 teaspoons chopped parsley

Rub the catfish with the garlic-oil mixture and season with salt and pepper. Heat the olive oil in a 10-inch nonstick skillet until smoking. Add the fish fillets and brown, about 1 to 2 minutes on each side. Remove to a plate and set aside.

Reduce heat. Add the onion to the pan and cook until softened. Return the fish to the pan and add the wine, tomatoes, olives, and pan juices. Cook over medium heat until the liquid simmers. Cover and cook for about 5 to 6 minutes, or until the fish barely flakes. Add the parsley, adjust seasonings, and serve.

Makes 4 servings.

Ziti Fagiolini

½ pound ziti or other tubular pasta
✪ **Reserved Green Beans and Walnuts**
1 teaspoon extra-virgin olive oil
2 cloves garlic, minced
Salt and pepper to taste

½ cup cooked or canned black beans or cannellini
✪ **½ cup pan juices reserved from Garlic Roast Chicken**
or ½ cup canned vegetable juice
¼ cup freshly grated parmesan cheese

Bring a large pot of lightly salted water to a boil. Add the ziti and stir. Return to a boil and simmer until the pasta is tender but not soft, about 10 minutes.

Meanwhile, chop the reserved green beans into pieces about 2 inches long. You should have about 1½ cups. Set aside.

About 5 minutes before the pasta is done, heat the olive oil in a heavy saucepan. Add the green beans, garlic, salt, and pepper. Toss thoroughly and heat through. Add the beans and stir to combine.

When the pasta is done, drain it. Add the reserved pan juices to the beans and heat to a boil. Add the pasta and toss to combine. Turn into a serving bowl and top with parmesan cheese.

Makes 4 servings.

Lemon Garlic Chicken Soup

✪ **Bones reserved from Garlic Roast
  Chicken**
¾ *cup white wine*
4 cups water
1 small onion, chopped
3 ribs celery, sliced
2 medium carrots, sliced
1 tablespoon olive oil
6 cloves garlic, finely chopped
1 teaspoon dried thyme

Zest of 1 lemon
4 cups chicken broth, canned or homemade
1 envelope (¼ ounce) unflavored gelatin
1 tablespoon chopped parsley
Salt and pepper to taste
½ cup long-grain rice
✪ **Meat reserved from Garlic Roast
  Chicken, skin removed**
Juice of 1 lemon

Place the reserved bones and the wine in a small saucepan and boil until the sharp smell of alcohol dissipates, about 2 minutes. Add the water and simmer for 15 minutes.

Meanwhile, sauté the onion, celery, and carrots in the olive oil in a large saucepan over medium heat for 1 minute, stirring constantly. Add the garlic, thyme, lemon zest, and chicken broth. Sprinkle the gelatin powder over the top of the liquid and whisk vigorously until all the powder has been incorporated. Heat until liquid simmers.

When the bone mixture has simmered for 15 minutes, strain the liquid into the larger saucepan of soup. Add the parsley, salt, and pepper. Stir in the rice and simmer for 12 minutes. Add the reserved chicken meat and lemon juice and cook until chicken is heated through and rice is tender. Adjust seasoning. Serve immediately or refrigerate and reheat.

Makes 4 to 6 servings.

Gnocchi with Walnut Pesto

PESTO

1 cup basil leaves
2 cloves garlic, coarsely chopped
¼ cup walnuts, finely chopped
¼ cup olive oil
¼ cup walnut oil
¼ cup freshly grated parmesan cheese
Salt and pepper to taste

GNOCCHI

✪ **2 baked potatoes reserved from Smashed Potatoes with Celery Root Puree**
2 egg yolks
¼ cup yogurt
2 tablespoons freshly grated parmesan cheese
2 tablespoons flour plus additional for forming gnocchi
Salt and pepper to taste

Coarsely chop the basil in the workbowl of a food processor, using 2 or 3 quick pulses. Add the garlic and walnuts and pulse the processor a few more times until everything is finely chopped. With the processor on, pour in the oils, cheese, salt, and pepper. Scrape into a bowl and set aside.

To prepare the gnocchi, remove the flesh from the reserved baked potatoes and mix in a bowl with the egg yolks, yogurt, cheese, 2 tablespoons of flour, salt, and pepper until well combined. Form the gnocchi in batches. Roll 12 heaping teaspoon-size mounds of the potato mixture in the additional flour. Then gently roll each mound, one at a time, between your hands into a small cylinder about 2 inches long.

To shape the gnocchi, place a long-tined table fork face up on the work surface. Place a potato cylinder on the inside curve of the fork, parallel to the handle. Flatten by lightly pressing an index finger into the center of the dough and slide it off the fork. Each piece will be decorated with ridges from the fork tines on 1 side and an indentation from your finger on the other. Continue shaping the gnocchi in this way until all have been formed. There should be about 4 dozen gnocchi in all.

Bring a large saucepan of salted water to a boil and add half the gnocchi. In a short time, about 1 minute, they will float to the surface. Cook just 10 seconds more and remove with a large slotted spoon to a serving platter. Keep warm while you cook the remaining batch. Toss the hot gnocchi with the pesto and serve.

Makes 4 servings.

One of my personal preferences when it comes to pork is a flavoring of rosemary and apples. It led to this Sunday dinner of a pork loin stuffed with prunes and apples and perfumed with rosemary, garlic, and pepper. The pork is served with lemony candied sweet potatoes, buttered noodles, and brussels sprouts with ricotta cheese.

I love brussels sprouts. I cook them in milk, which eliminates bitterness, then serve them in a sauce of sweet ricotta cheese and garlic that complements the vegetable's natural bitterness. The results are wonderful—and the extra ricotta cream you make gives you a head start on the Fettuccine with Smoked Salmon, Cucumbers, and Capers for the following night.

The rest of the week proceeds just as interestingly. On Tuesday, the centerpiece of the meal is grilled swordfish steak, sweetened with some of the sweet potatoes' lemon glaze and spiked with a shot of vodka. On Wednesday, slices of pork are microwaved in an avalanche of sauerkraut to produce a version of an Alsatian *choucroute* with the traditional cooking time cut from two hours to twenty-five minutes. And on Thursday, more of the roasted pork is combined with the sweet potatoes in a quick savory pot pie crusted with convenient frozen puff pastry.

THE SUNDAY DINNER

Roasted Pork Loin Stuffed with
Prunes and Apples

Buttered Noodles with Parsley

Brussels Sprouts with Ricotta Cream

Lemon-glazed Candied Sweet Potatoes

THE WEEKNIGHT ENTREES

Fettuccine with Smoked Salmon,
Cucumber, and Capers

Sweetly Spiked Swordfish

Microwaved Choucroute Alsacienne

Sweet Potato and Pork Pie

Roasted Pork Loin Stuffed with Prunes and Apples

1 small onion, finely chopped
2 cloves garlic, minced
1½ teaspoons dried rosemary, crumbled
1½ teaspoons dried thyme
1 teaspoon butter
1 teaspoon vegetable oil
2 large tart apples, peeled, cored, and cubed
2 teaspoons brown sugar
Salt and pepper to taste

24 pitted prunes, quartered
1 boneless pork loin roast, rolled and tied
   (4½ to 5 pounds)
½ teaspoon garlic powder
½ teaspoon rubbed dried sage
2½ to 3 cups apple cider
1 sprig fresh rosemary, leaves only
2 tablespoons flour

Cook the onion, garlic, ½ teaspoon of the rosemary, and ½ teaspoon of the thyme in the butter and oil in a skillet until the onion has softened. Add the apple pieces, brown sugar, salt, and pepper and cook for a few minutes until the apples have lost their raw look but are not yet fully softened. Stir in the prunes and remove from heat.

Preheat the oven to 425°F.

With a long sharp knife, cut a small pocket down the center of the pork loin. Set aside ¾ cup of the apple-prune stuffing and stuff the rest into this pocket and under the flap of meat that wraps around the outside of the roast. Don't worry about everything looking perfect; just get as much stuffing into the roast as possible. Mix the remaining rosemary and thyme with the garlic powder, sage, and a liberal amount of salt and pepper. Rub this mixture all over the surface of the pork and set the meat, fat side up, on a rack in a roasting pan.

Roast for 40 minutes. Pour 1½ cups of the apple cider over the meat and reduce the oven temperature to 350°F. Roast, basting occasionally with the liquid in the pan, for another hour to hour and 15 minutes, until a meat thermometer inserted into the thickest part of the meat registers 160°F. Transfer to a platter.

Pour the liquid from the pan into a large measuring cup, skim the fat from the surface, and save the fat in a separate bowl. Add enough of the remaining apple cider to the defatted liquid to equal 3 cups. Pour the mixture into a saucepan and add the fresh rosemary. Bring to a boil. Meanwhile, mix the flour with 2 tablespoons of the reserved skimmed fat. When the liquid boils, whisk in the fat-flour mixture and simmer until the sauce thickens lightly. Stir in the reserved apple-prune stuffing. Adjust seasoning.

Slice half the pork loin, and serve 2 or 3 slices to each person. Top each portion with ¼ cup of the gravy. Serve 1 cup additional gravy on the side.

Makes 4 to 6 servings, plus enough to:
✪ **Reserve 1 pound roasted pork for Microwaved Choucroute Alsacienne.**
✪ **Reserve 1 pound roasted pork for Sweet Potato and Pork Pie.**
✪ **Reserve 1¼ to 1½ cups gravy for Sweet Potato and Pork Pie.**

Buttered Noodles with Parsley

1½ pounds dried fettuccine, broken in half
1 tablespoon butter
2 tablespoons plus 1 teaspoon olive oil

1 tablespoon chopped parsley
Salt and pepper to taste

Bring a large pot of salted water to a rolling boil. Add the fettuccine, stir, making sure that the noodles are all separate, and cook until the noodles are al dente, about 10 minutes. Drain. Place a third of the fettuccine (about 4 to 5 cups) in a serving bowl and toss with the butter, 2 tablespoons oil, parsley, salt, and pepper. Wash the remaining fettuccine under cold running water until completely cool, shake off excess water, toss with the remaining 1 teaspoon olive oil, and refrigerate in a tightly closed container. Serve the buttered noodles immediately.

Makes 4 servings, plus enough to:
✪ **Reserve 8 to 10 cups fettuccine for Fettuccine with Smoked Salmon, Cucumber, and Capers.**

Brussels Sprouts with Ricotta Cream

1 pound brussels sprouts
1 teaspoon olive oil
Salt and pepper to taste

2 cloves garlic, minced
2 cups milk
1½ cups ricotta cheese

continued

Trim the stems and the loose leaves from the brussels sprouts. Use the point of a paring knife to cut a deep X into the base of any large sprouts. Cook the brussels sprouts in the olive oil in a heavy saucepan over medium heat for 1 minute, stirring constantly. Add salt, pepper, and half the garlic and stir to combine. Add the milk, stir once, cover the pan, and cook for 6 to 8 minutes, stirring occasionally, until the brussels sprouts are tender.

Remove the brussels sprouts with a slotted spoon, place in a serving bowl, and keep warm. Reduce the milk in the pan to about H cup. Remove from the heat. Add the remaining garlic and the ricotta cheese and stir until the mixture is smooth. Pour ½ cup of the ricotta cream over the brussels sprouts, toss to coat, and serve.

Makes 4 servings, plus enough to:

✪ **Reserve 1½ cups ricotta cream for Fettuccine with Smoked Salmon, Cucumber, and Capers.**

Lemon-glazed Candied
Sweet Potatoes

3 large orange sweet potatoes, peeled and cut into large chunks (2½ pounds)	*Zest of 1 lemon, finely grated*
1 cup water	*Juice of 1½ lemons*
¼ cup sugar	*2 tablespoons butter*
½ cup molasses	*1 teaspoon vanilla extract*
	Salt and pepper to taste

Preheat the oven to 350°F.

Boil the sweet potatoes in a large pot of salted water for 7 minutes. Drain and place in a large baking dish. Combine the water, sugar, molasses, lemon zest, lemon juice, butter, vanilla, salt, and pepper in a saucepan, bring to a boil, and pour over the sweet potatoes.

Bake for 1 hour, or until sweet potatoes are very soft and the liquid has reduced to about ¾ cup. Reserve 2 cups of the sweet potatoes and serve the rest. Spoon 1 tablespoon of the glaze over the top of each portion.

Makes 4 servings, plus enough to:

✪ **Reserve ½ cup glaze for Sweetly Spiked Swordfish.**
✪ **Reserve 2 cups sweet potatoes for Sweet Potato and Pork Pie.**

Fettuccine with Smoked Salmon, Cucumber, and Capers

1 cucumber, peeled, seeded, and diced
½ teaspoon salt
¼ cup olive oil
6 scallions, white parts only, sliced
1 clove garlic, minced
2 tablespoons capers, rinsed and drained
1 cup white wine

1 tablespoon chopped dill
✪ **8 to 10 cups cooked fettuccine reserved from Buttered Noodles with Parsley**
Freshly ground pepper to taste
✪ **1½ cups ricotta cream reserved from Brussels Sprouts with Ricotta Cream**
¼ pound smoked salmon, chopped

Toss the cucumber with the salt and let stand for 10 minutes. Rinse, squeeze out excess moisture, and set aside.

Heat the olive oil in a deep skillet or large wok and sauté the scallions, garlic, and capers for 20 seconds, or until the scallions have softened. Add the wine and reduce to a third of its volume. Add the dill, cucumber, and reserved cooked fettuccine and toss until the pasta is warmed through, about 3 minutes. Reduce heat to low, season with pepper, and toss in the reserved ricotta cream and the smoked salmon. Serve at once.

Makes 4 servings.

Sweetly Spiked Swordfish

✪ **½ cup glaze reserved from Lemon-glazed Candied Sweet Potatoes**
2 tablespoons cider vinegar
2 tablespoons vodka

½ teaspoon hot pepper sauce
Salt and pepper to taste
2 swordfish steaks (about 10 ounces each)

Mix the reserved glaze with the vinegar, vodka, hot pepper sauce, salt, and pepper in a small bowl. Cut each fish steak in half, place the pieces in this marinade, and turn to coat. Cover and refrigerate for at least 20 minutes. Remove swordfish from the marinade and grill on an oiled rack or broil 3 inches from a hot fire for about 4 minutes per side, or until the fish springs back after a gentle prod. Serve immediately.

Makes 4 servings.

Microwaved Choucroute Alsacienne

4 strips bacon, quartered
1 medium onion, sliced
8 small red-skin potatoes, scrubbed and
    quartered
1 bay leaf
4 juniper berries, crushed
Pinch of ground clove
1 teaspoon ground ginger
1 teaspoon ground coriander
Freshly ground pepper to taste

3 cloves garlic, coarsely chopped
1 pound sauerkraut, drained and rinsed
    thoroughly
1 bottle (12 ounces) beer
✪ **1 pound meat reserved from Roasted
    Pork Loin Stuffed with Prunes and
    Apples**
2 knockwurst or frankfurters, sliced ¾ inch
    thick (optional)
⅓ cup spicy brown mustard

Scatter the bacon pieces in a 3-quart microwavesafe casserole. Cover with a sheet of wax paper and microwave at full power for 3 minutes. Remove the paper, add the onion and potatoes, and microwave at full power for 8 minutes more. Add the bay leaf, juniper berries, ground clove, ginger, coriander, pepper, garlic, sauerkraut, and half the bottle of beer (about ¾ cup). Mix, cover with wax paper, and microwave at full power for 6 minutes.

Slice the reserved pork into 8 slices. Remove the wax paper, and arrange the pork over the sauerkraut. Scatter the knockwurst, if desired, over all. Cover with plastic wrap or a lid, and microwave at full power for 4 minutes. Uncover and serve with the mustard on the side.

To make the choucroute on the stovetop, brown the bacon in a large deep skillet over medium heat. Add the onion and potatoes and cook for 5 minutes, stirring frequently. Add the spices and garlic, sauerkraut, and the full bottle of beer. Slice the pork. Heat the sauerkraut to a boil, arrange the pork and sausage, if using, over the top, cover, and simmer for 20 minutes. Uncover and serve, moistening each portion with some of the liquid in the pan.

Makes 4 servings.

Sweet Potato and Pork Pie

- ✪ 1 pound meat reserved from Roasted
  Pork Loin Stuffed with Prunes and
  Apples
- ✪ 2 cups reserved Lemon-glazed Candied
  Sweet Potatoes

- ✪ 1¼ to 1½ cups gravy reserved from
  Roasted Pork Loin Stuffed with Prunes
  and Apples
- *1 small or medium egg or 1 egg white or yolk*
- *1 tablespoon water*
- *1 sheet (8 ounces) frozen puff pastry, defrosted*

Preheat the oven to 425°F.

Cut the reserved pork meat into chunks. Combine the pork, reserved sweet potatoes, and reserved gravy in a 1½-quart microwavesafe casserole. Cover with plastic wrap and microwave at full power for 3 minutes. Remove plastic and stir. Or warm the pork, sweet potatoes, and gravy in a large heavy saucepan over medium heat, stirring occasionally, to remove the chill. Transfer to a casserole.

Mix the egg and water in a small bowl and brush the rim of the casserole dish with this mixture. Trim the pastry sheet so that it is slightly larger than the top of the dish. Place the pastry over the top of the casserole and press down on the edge to help it adhere to the rim. With a sharp knife, make tiny slits around the perimeter of the pastry. Make 3 small slits in the center of the pastry to act as steam vents. Brush the surface of the pastry with the rest of the egg wash. Bake for 25 minutes, or until the pastry is browned and the contents of the casserole are bubbling. Serve immediately.

Makes 4 servings.

Menu 9

Everyone knows what goes into lasagna: noodles, red meat sauce, and white cheese sauce all tangled together in a web of mozzarella. That's it, but is that all it can be? For an inventive cook, the techniques involved in producing a tried-and-true lasagna are just as useful when creating an inspired new version, which may share little more with the original than its structure and its name.

This week's Sunday entree, White Turkey Lasagna, is a case in point. Bands of pasta are layered with a broth-enriched white sauce, a paste of spinach and ricotta, sautéed turkey breast, mozzarella, and asiago cheese. The recipe is no more difficult than a traditional lasagna, but the finished product is anything but conventional.

More important is how the lasagna's building blocks become material for upcoming entrees. Its white sauce means that Monday's Smoked Salmon White Bean Chowder will be on the table six minutes after it's begun. The spinach mixture transforms seared scallops into Scallops Florentine on Tuesday. Some of the sautéed turkey breast becomes Southwest Turkey Salad with Chili Vinaigrette on Thursday, and the pesto tomatoes served with the lasagna on Sunday are the base for a fresh tomato sauce to top pork medallions Wednesday night.

THE SUNDAY DINNER

White Turkey Lasagna

Broiled Pesto Tomatoes

Lemon Asparagus Scattered
with Smoked Salmon

THE WEEKNIGHT ENTREES

Smoked Salmon White Bean Chowder

Scallops Florentine

Pork Medallions with Pesto
Tomato Sauce

Southwest Turkey Salad with
Chili Vinaigrette

White Turkey Lasagna

NOODLES
1 tablespoon olive oil
12 lasagna noodles (about ¾ pound)

SAUCE
2 tablespoons olive oil
1 medium onion, chopped
5 tablespoons flour
2 cloves garlic, minced
½ cup white wine
1 can (about 14 ounces) chicken or vegetable
    broth
3 cups milk
Salt and pepper to taste

SPINACH
2 packages (10 ounces each) frozen chopped
    spinach, defrosted
1 cup ricotta cheese
Salt and pepper to taste
Pinch of freshly grated nutmeg

TURKEY
3½ pounds boneless and skinless turkey
    breast, diced (about 5½ cups)
¼ cup cornstarch
About ¼ cup olive oil
1 medium onion, chopped
Pinch of crushed red pepper flakes
½ teaspoon dried oregano
2 cloves garlic, minced
Juice of ½ lemon

FOR ASSEMBLING
1 tablespoon olive oil
1 cup freshly grated asiago, parmesan, or
    romano cheese (about 2¾ ounces)
1½ cups shredded mozzarella cheese
    (about 6 ounces)

Bring a large pot of lightly salted water to a boil, add the 1 tablespoon of oil and noodles, and cook until the noodles are tender, about 10 minutes. Drain and run under cold water until the noodles have cooled. Set the noodles aside, placed side by side on dampened towels and covered, while you make the sauce and filling.

Heat the 2 tablespoons of oil in a large heavy saucepan for 30 seconds. Add the onion and cook over medium heat until softened, about 2 minutes. Add the flour and cook for another minute, stirring continuously. Add the garlic and wine and stir until smooth. Boil for 1 minute. Stir in the broth until the sauce is smooth and thickened. Stir in the milk until smooth and lightly thickened. Season with salt and pepper. Set aside.

Squeeze the excess moisture from the spinach through a clean towel or fine-mesh strainer. Mix with the ricotta cheese and 1 cup of the sauce in a medium bowl and season with salt, pepper, and nutmeg. Set aside.

Toss the turkey with the cornstarch. In a large skillet, brown the turkey in batches in the olive oil, using 1 to 2 tablespoons of oil per batch. Set aside. Pour off all but a thin film of oil from the skillet. Add the onion, pepper flakes, and oregano and cook over medium heat until the onion has lightly browned, about 3 minutes. Add the garlic and return the turkey to the pan. Toss to combine, add the lemon juice, and toss again. Remove from the heat and set aside.

Preheat the oven to 400°F.

To assemble, drizzle the olive oil over the bottom of a large rectangular baking pan. Spread ¼ cup of the sauce over the bottom of the baking dish. Cover with 4 overlapping noodles. Spread with another ¼ cup of the sauce, 1 cup of the spinach mixture, 1¼ cups of the turkey, ⅓ cup of the grated cheese, and another ¼ cup of sauce. Top with 4 more noodles, another ¼ cup sauce, 1 cup spinach, 1¼ cups turkey, ⅓ cup grated cheese, and another ¼ cup sauce. Top with the last 4 noodles, the mozzarella, and the remaining grated cheese. Bake for 30 minutes, or until the cheese is melted and the lasagna is bubbling. Let stand for 5 minutes before serving.

Makes 4 to 6 servings, plus enough to:
✪ **Reserve 1 cup sauce for Smoked Salmon White Bean Chowder.**
✪ **Reserve ½ cup sauce for Pork Medallions with Pesto Tomato Sauce.**
✪ **Reserve ½ cup sauce for Scallops Florentine.**
✪ **Reserve 1 cup spinach for Scallops Florentine.**
✪ **Reserve 3 cups turkey for Southwest Turkey Salad with Chili Vinaigrette.**

Broiled Pesto Tomatoes

3 cups basil leaves
3 cloves garlic, coarsely chopped
¼ cup extra-virgin olive oil
¼ cup freshly grated parmesan cheese

Salt and pepper to taste
3 very ripe large tomatoes, cored
2 tablespoons seasoned bread crumbs

Finely chop the basil and the garlic in a food processor. Add the olive oil, parmesan, salt, and pepper and process in pulses until well blended.

Cut each tomato into 4 thick slices and place the slices on a broiler tray. Spread 1½ teaspoons of the basil mixture on each slice. Top 4 slices with ½ tablespoon of bread crumbs each. Broil all the slices 6 inches from a high flame until lightly browned, about 3 minutes. Serve each person one of the tomato slices with the bread crumbs.

Makes 4 servings, plus enough to:
✪ **Reserve 8 pesto-grilled tomato slices for Pork Medallions with Pesto Tomato Sauce.**

Lemon Asparagus Scattered with Smoked Salmon

1 pound asparagus, trimmed of hard ends
Zest of 2 lemons, julienned
4 ounces smoked salmon, cut into thin strips

2 teaspoons olive oil
Freshly ground black pepper to taste

Poach the asparagus in a skillet filled with simmering water just until bright green, about 2 minutes for thin to medium asparagus. Meanwhile, toss together the lemon zest and smoked salmon. Remove asparagus with tongs and transfer to a platter. Drizzle with olive oil, season with pepper, and scatter 3 tablespoons of the salmon mixture over the top. Serve immediately.

Makes 4 servings, plus enough to:
✪ **Reserve ½ cup smoked salmon mixture for Smoked Salmon White Bean Chowder.**

Smoked Salmon White Bean Chowder

1 tablespoon olive oil
1 medium onion, finely chopped
1 clove garlic, minced
♻ **I cup sauce reserved from White Turkey Lasagna**
1 bottle (8 ounces) clam juice

1 can (about 16 ounces) white beans
1 teaspoon dried dillweed
♻ **½ cup salmon mixture reserved from Lemon Asparagus Scattered with Smoked Salmon**

Warm the oil in a large heavy saucepan over medium heat for 30 seconds. Add the onion and cook until softened, about 2 minutes, stirring constantly. Add the garlic and stir to combine. Add the reserved sauce and clam juice and stir to combine. Bring to a boil. Add the beans and dill and simmer for 3 minutes, stirring occasionally. Add the salmon mixture and heat through. Serve immediately.

Makes 4 servings.

Scallops Florentine

1 ½ pounds sea scallops, trimmed and cut in half horizontally
Salt and pepper to taste
Pinch of freshly grated nutmeg
1 tablespoon olive oil

♻ **I cup spinach reserved from White Turkey Lasagna**
♻ **½ cup sauce reserved from White Turkey Lasagna**
About ½ cup milk
1 lemon, cut into 8 thin wedges

Season the scallops with salt, pepper, and nutmeg. Heat the oil in a large nonstick skillet until smoking. Add the scallops and cook until lightly browned and barely firm, about 2 to 3 minutes. Remove scallops to a warm plate. Reduce heat to medium. Add the reserved spinach and reserved sauce. Stir and heat through. Adjust seasoning with salt and pepper and adjust the consistency with milk until sauce just coats a spoon. Divide the sauce among 4 plates. Place equal portions of the scallops on each plate and garnish each with 2 of the lemon wedges.

Makes 4 servings.

Pork Medallions with Pesto Tomato Sauce

8 boneless thin-cut pork chops
   (about 1 pound)
¼ cup flour seasoned with salt and pepper
   to taste
2 tablespoons olive oil

✪ **8 tomato slices reserved from Broiled Pesto Tomatoes**
✪ **½ cup sauce reserved from White Turkey Lasagna**
2 tablespoons tomato paste

Dust the pork chops with the seasoned flour. Heat the oil in a large nonstick skillet over high heat for 1 minute. Reduce heat to medium and brown the pork on both sides, about 3 minutes per side. Meanwhile, coarsely chop the reserved tomatoes. When the pork has browned, add the tomatoes, the reserved sauce, and tomato paste to the pan. Stir to combine and heat to a simmer. Serve the pork topped with the sauce.

Makes 4 servings.

Southwest Turkey Salad with Chili Vinaigrette

½ teaspoon onion powder
¼ teaspoon garlic powder
2 teaspoons ground cumin
1 tablespoon chili powder
¼ cup ketchup
2 tablespoons apple cider vinegar
¼ cup vegetable oil
1 teaspoon hot pepper sauce

○ 3 cups turkey reserved from White Turkey Lasagna
1 can (11 ounces) corn kernels, drained
2 jarred roasted red bell peppers, diced
6 scallions, trimmed of tops and roots, thinly sliced
½ head iceberg lettuce, cleaned and thinly sliced

Combine the onion powder, garlic powder, cumin, and chili powder in a small mixing bowl. Mix in the ketchup. Whisk in the vinegar, oil, and hot pepper sauce and keep whisking until the mixture is smooth. Toss the turkey, corn, roasted peppers, and scallions in a salad bowl. Add the dressing and mix thoroughly. Serve on a bed of lettuce.

Makes 4 servings.

GARLIC POWDER AND CULINARY CORRECTNESS

Although no processed product can replace a plump clove of freshly chopped garlic, there actually are times when dried garlic, a much maligned ingredient, makes more sense than fresh.

When seasoning a flour or a bread-crumb coating for sautéed or fried food, for example, fresh garlic will not distribute evenly, regardless of how finely it is chopped. I'd even argue that dried products are sometimes better for seasoning grilled meats since they dissolve into the meat juices and permeate the flesh better than fresh garlic. Nor do they burn from exposure to a flame.

Dried garlic commonly comes in three forms—minced, powdered, and blended with salt. Minced garlic is preferred by many who find a bitter or spoiled taste in garlic powders. True enough, the finer a dried herb or spice is ground, the more quickly it will spoil. If this is a concern, buy dried garlic in minced form and grind it in a spice grinder as you need it.

Menu 10

hat is a short rib? Where does it come from? And why does it taste so good? Depending on the amount of exercise a particular muscle group of an animal gets, its meat is usually flavorful or tender. A few cuts are both. Short ribs are such a cut. Short ribs are the part of the rib cage of a steer that corresponds to the spareribs on such smaller animals as calves, lambs, or pigs. The muscles of this section are somewhat tough to help support the ribs and the internal organs, but not as tough as the shoulder and hip muscles that are in constant motion.

The recipe for Sunday's braised short ribs yields more than just a single serving of melt-in-the-mouth richness. Its broth is a base for Wednesday's hearty onion soup and for Thursday's red wine sauce for sautéed chicken livers, and its meat is the core of Monday's chili. But the interconnections don't stop there.

The chili utilizes one of Sunday's side dishes as well. On Sunday, the short ribs are accompanied by cole slaw and an unusual succotash. Succotash, a Native American corn stew, is typically thought to contain lima beans and little spicing. In fact, it can contain any bean and has a wide range of flavorings. In this menu, the succotash uses kidney beans and Tex-Mex seasoning, making it perfect for fleshing out Monday's chili. The succotash and cole slaw join forces Tuesday for a vegetarian taco simple enough to go from cutting board to table in about five minutes.

THE SUNDAY DINNER	THE WEEKNIGHT ENTREES
Braised Short Ribs	Braised Beef Chili
Bok Choy Cole Slaw	Soft Veggie Tacos
Chili Succotash	Beefed-up Onion Soup
	Chicken Livers in Red Wine Sauce

Braised Short Ribs

1 ½ teaspoons chili powder
1 ½ teaspoons paprika
½ teaspoon salt
Pinch of dried oregano
8 beef short ribs (about 6 pounds)
1 tablespoon vegetable oil
1 medium onion, chopped
1 medium carrot, diced

1 rib celery, diced
1 tablespoon flour
1 teaspoon dried thyme
1 bay leaf
4 cups water
1 cup canned salt-free vegetable juice
Salt and pepper to taste
2 tablespoons red wine vinegar

Combine the chili powder, paprika, salt, and oregano and rub the mixture into all surfaces of the short ribs. Broil or grill the ribs 4 inches from a hot fire for 4 minutes per side, or until browned.

Heat the oil in a large saucepan or small soup pot over medium heat. Add the onion and cook until softened, about 2 minutes. Add the carrot and celery and cook for 4 more minutes, stirring frequently, until lightly browned. Add the flour and cook 3 more minutes, stirring constantly.

Add the thyme, bay leaf, water, vegetable juice, salt, pepper, and vinegar. Place the short ribs in the liquid and cover. Simmer until ribs are fork-tender, about 2 hours. Spoon off fat and reserve.

Serve 1 rib per person, moistened with a spoonful of broth.

Makes 4 servings, plus enough to:
✪ **Reserve 2 ribs for Braised Beef Chili.**
✪ **Reserve 2 ribs for Beefed-up Onion Soup.**
✪ **Reserve 2 tablespoons skimmed fat for Beefed-up Onion Soup.**
✪ **Reserve 2 cups broth for Beefed-up Onion Soup.**
✪ **Reserve 1 cup broth for Braised Beef Chili.**
✪ **Reserve 1 cup broth for Chicken Livers in Red Wine Sauce.**

Bok Choy Cole Slaw

2 tablespoons mayonnaise
2 tablespoons apple cider vinegar
2 tablespoons olive oil
1 teaspoon salt
1 teaspoon ground cumin
1 teaspoon hot pepper sauce

1 pound Chinese cabbage, cored and
    shredded
3 medium carrots, shredded
1 large red bell pepper stemmed, cored, and
    shredded

Whisk the mayonnaise, vinegar, olive oil, salt, cumin, and hot pepper sauce together in a large serving bowl until smooth. Add the cabbage, carrots, and bell pepper and toss to coat with the dressing. Refrigerate until ready to serve.

Makes 4 servings, plus enough to:
✪ **Reserve 2 cups for Soft Veggie Tacos.**

Chili Succotash

2 tablespoons vegetable oil
½ large onion, chopped
1 large red bell pepper, stemmed, cored, and
    diced
1 jalapeño, stemmed, seeded, and minced

1 tablespoon ground cumin
1 tablespoon chili powder
3 cans (11 ounces each) corn kernels, drained
2 cans (about 16 ounces) kidney beans
About 3 tablespoons chopped cilantro leaves

Heat the oil in a large saucepan or skillet. Add the onion and bell pepper and stir until the vegetables have softened slightly, about 2 minutes. Add the jalapeño, cumin, and chili powder and cook another 30 seconds. Add the corn and bring to a boil. Simmer for 2 minutes. Add the beans and cilantro and return to a boil. Remove from heat. Serve 2½ cups.

Makes 4 servings, plus enough to:
✪ **Reserve 2 cups for Soft Veggie Tacos.**
✪ **Reserve 2 cups for Braised Beef Chili.**

Braised Beef Chili

✪ **2 short ribs reserved from Braised Short Ribs**
1 tablespoon vegetable oil
½ medium onion, chopped
1 jalapeño, stemmed, seeded, and minced
2 teaspoons ground cumin
2 teaspoons chili powder

1 ripe tomato, cored and coarsely chopped
1 clove garlic, minced
✪ **I cup broth reserved from Braised Short Ribs**
✪ **2 cups reserved Chili Succotash**
Salt and pepper to taste

Remove and discard the fat from the reserved short ribs and cut the meat into cubes. Set aside.

Heat the oil in a heavy saucepan over medium-high heat. Add the onion and cook for 1 minute. Add the jalapeño, cumin, and chili powder and cook 30 seconds more. Add the meat and stir for 1 minute. Add the tomato, garlic, and reserved broth and bring to a boil. Simmer for 2 minutes. Add the reserved succotash and heat through. Season with salt and pepper and serve.

Makes 4 servings.

Soft Veggie Tacos

1 avocado
Juice of ½ lemon
12 (6-inch) flour tortillas
✪ **2 cups reserved Chili Succotash**

4 ounces jalapeño cheddar cheese, shredded (about 1 cup)
✪ **2 cups reserved Bok Choy Cole Slaw**
1 large tomato, cored and chopped

Cut the avocado lengthwise into quarters and discard the pit. Strip off the peel from each quarter. Dice the flesh into small pieces and toss with the lemon juice. Set aside.

Wrap the tortillas in a dampened towel and warm in a microwave oven at full power for 1 minute or in a 350°F. oven for 10 minutes.

Heat the reserved succotash in a heavy saucepan over medium heat, stirring frequently. Or heat in a microwave at full power for 3 minutes.

Serve the tortillas, succotash, shredded cheese, cole slaw, and chopped tomato for each person to assemble tacos.

Makes 4 servings.

Beefed-up Onion Soup

- ❂ **2 short ribs reserved from Braised Short Ribs**
- ❂ **2 tablespoons skimmed fat from Braised Short Ribs**
- 2 large onions, thinly sliced
- 2 tablespoons flour
- ½ teaspoon dried thyme

- ❂ **2 cups broth reserved from Braised Short Ribs**
- 1 can (about 14 ounces) low-salt beef broth
- ¾ cup water
- 1 tablespoon red wine vinegar
- Salt and pepper to taste

Remove and discard the fat from the reserved short ribs and dice the meat. Set aside.

Melt the skimmed fat in a heavy saucepan. Add the onions and cook over medium heat until lightly browned, about 10 minutes, stirring frequently. Add the meat and cook 2 more minutes. Add the flour and cook 3 more minutes, stirring constantly. Add the thyme, reserved broth, canned broth, water, and vinegar. Heat until simmering. Season with salt and pepper and simmer for 5 minutes. Serve hot.

Makes 4 servings.

Chicken Livers in Red Wine Sauce

1 tablespoon olive oil
1 medium onion, chopped
1 pound chicken livers, quartered, fat and
    tendon removed
½ teaspoon dried thyme
1 cup red wine

✪ **1 cup broth reserved from Braised
    Short Ribs**
1 teaspoon cornstarch
1 tablespoon water
2 cups medium pasta or rice, cooked

Heat the olive oil in a large skillet over medium-high heat. Add the onion and cook until softened, about 1 minute. Add the livers and cook until browned. Add the thyme and wine and bring to a boil. Boil vigorously for 1 minute. Add the reserved broth and simmer for 2 more minutes. Meanwhile, thoroughly dissolve the cornstarch in the water. Add the mixture to the simmering broth and stir until lightly thickened. Serve over hot pasta or rice.

Makes 4 servings.

Menu 11

I f you've never swooned over rice, you haven't eaten risotto. As basic to the cuisines of northern Italy as spaghetti is to the south, risotto's creamy consistency erases forever the notion that the sole measure of rice perfection is in the puffed autonomy of each grain.

Unlike most American rice dishes, which are made with long-grain rice, risotto calls for short-grain varieties. Arborio is the most commonly available Italian rice for making risotto. Though risotto is not difficult to prepare, the traditional method does require frequent stirring and constant attention. Risotto made in the microwave bypasses most of that labor.

Sunday's dinner surrounds risotto with roasted Cornish hens, lacquered with a unique glaze that pairs the often disparate flavors of sweet and hot. It is made easily by mixing a traditional spicy barbecue sauce with orange marmalade. The vegetable for Sunday is asparagus, flavored with lemon. The use of acid-free lemon zest instead of lemon juice ingeniously avoids discoloration, a problem that occurs when any green vegetable comes in contact with an acid.

It is commonly thought that risotto does not reheat well, and, in fact, is disastrous when kept overnight, but Thursday's dinner, baked peppers stuffed with risotto, shows that every rule has an exception. As it absorbs moisture from the steaming pepper, the risotto regenerates into a silken, cheese-laced custard. Risotto also flavors and thickens the sauce in Monday's Chicken Pot Pie with Fennel and Apples. The sauce from Sunday's Cornish hens becomes the base for Tuesday's barbecued ribs, and Wednesday's easy elegant fish gets its flavor from the same lemon oil that graced Sunday's asparagus.

THE SUNDAY DINNER

Spicy Fruit-glazed Cornish Hens

Microwaved Rosemary Risotto

Asparagus with Lemon Oil

THE WEEKNIGHT ENTREES

Chicken Pot Pie with Fennel
and Apples

Old Bay Barbecued Ribs

Lemon Garlic Fish en Papillote

Herb-stuffed Peppers

Spicy Fruit-glazed Cornish Hens

4 Cornish hens
1 tablespoon salt
1 teaspoon freshly ground black pepper
½ cup spicy barbecue sauce, prepared or
   homemade

½ cup orange marmalade
¼ cup fruit vinegar, such as raspberry, blueberry, or citrus vinegar

Preheat the oven to 450°F.

Wash the hens inside and out and pat dry. Combine the salt and pepper and rub the mixture over the walls of the cavity. Place the hens, breast side down, on an oiled rack in a large roasting pan and roast for 20 minutes. Meanwhile, combine the barbecue sauce, marmalade, and vinegar in a large mixing bowl. Set aside.

Remove hens from the oven and place them, one at a time, in the sauce. Coat thoroughly and return them to the rack on the roasting pan, breast side up.

Reduce the oven temperature to 350°F. Return the hens to the oven and roast for 30 minutes more, basting with any remaining sauce halfway through the roasting. Serve half a hen to each person.

Makes 4 servings, plus enough to:
✪ **Reserve 2 hens for Chicken Pot Pie with Fennel and Apples.**
✪ **Reserve fat from drippings, for Chicken Pot Pie with Fennel and Apples.**
✪ **Reserve ½ cup pan drippings for Old Bay Barbecued Ribs.**

MAKE YOUR OWN BARBECUE SAUCE

Barbecue sauce is sold in every grocery store in the country, but the mixture is so easy to whip up yourself and lends itself so well to endless effortless variations that it seems ridiculous to not have one or two barbecue concoctions up one's sleeve.

Here's a basic formula: Combine ¾ cup ketchup, ¼ cup grated onion, 2 tablespoons cider vinegar, and 1 tablespoon *each* mustard, molasses, Worcestershire, and hot pepper sauce, in a saucepan and bring to a simmer. This makes 1⅓ cups.

And here are two variations. For a mustard-molasses barbecue paste, combine ¼ cup brown mustard, 2 tablespoons peanut oil, 2 tablespoons lemon juice, and 1 tablespoon molasses. And for teriyaki barbecue sauce, heat ¼ cup each soy sauce, rice wine vinegar, honey, and water with 1 tablespoon grated gingerroot until the honey dissolves.

Microwaved Rosemary Risotto

3 tablespoons extra-virgin olive oil
1 medium onion, finely chopped
1 tablespoon fresh rosemary leaves
1 teaspoon dried thyme
1 bay leaf
2 cloves garlic, minced

2 cups Arborio rice
½ to 1 cup white wine
4½ to 6 cups hot chicken broth, canned or
    homemade
3 tablespoons freshly grated parmesan cheese
1 tablespoon butter

To make the risotto in the microwave, pour the olive oil into a 9-inch deep-sided glass pie plate and microwave at full power for 3 minutes. Add the onion, 2 teaspoons of the rosemary, the thyme, bay leaf, and garlic. Stir and microwave at full power for 2 minutes. Add the rice and stir. Microwave 1 minute more. Add ½ cup of wine and 2¼ cups of chicken broth and microwave at full power for 10 minutes. Stir in 2¼ more cups of the broth and the remaining rosemary leaves and microwave at full power for 8 more minutes. Let rest for 3 minutes. Stir in the parmesan cheese and butter. Serve immediately.

To make the risotto on the stovetop, heat the oil in a large heavy saucepan for 1 minute. Add the onion, 2 teaspoons of the rosemary, the thyme, bay leaf, and garlic. Stir and cook over medium heat until the onions have softened, 2 minutes. Stir in the rice and cook another minute, stirring frequently. Add 1 cup of wine and stir until it has been absorbed. Add 6 cups of chicken broth, 1 cup at a time, stirring frequently and waiting until it has been absorbed before adding the next cup. This will take about 30 minutes. When the last cup has been half absorbed, remove from the heat and stir in the parmesan cheese and butter. Serve immediately.

Makes 4 servings, plus enough to:
✪ **Reserve 1 cup for Chicken Pot Pie with Fennel and Apples.**
✪ **Reserve 2 cups for Herb-stuffed Peppers.**

Asparagus with Lemon Oil

Zest of 1 lemon, finely grated
½ cup olive oil
Juice of 1 lemon
Salt and pepper to taste

2 quarts salted water
1 pound medium asparagus, trimmed of
hard ends

Place the lemon zest in a small saucepan and cover with water. Bring to a boil and drain through a fine-mesh strainer. Mix the lemon zest with the olive oil and lemon juice. Season with salt and pepper and set aside.

Bring the 2 quarts of salted water to a boil in a deep skillet. Submerge the asparagus in the boiling water, reduce the heat, and simmer until the asparagus is bright green and barely tender, 3 to 4 minutes. If the asparagus is thin, simmer no more than 2 minutes. Using tongs, remove the asparagus from the water. Drain well and arrange on a platter. Whisk the lemon oil until well blended and spoon half of it over the asparagus.

Makes 4 servings, plus enough to:
✪ **Reserve 6 tablespoons lemon oil for Lemon Garlic Fish en Papillote.**

Chicken Pot Pie with Fennel and Apples

✪ **2 Cornish hens reserved from Spicy Fruit-glazed Cornish Hens**
1 medium onion, coarsely chopped
4 stalks fresh fennel, coarsely diced
✪ **2 tablespoons fat reserved from Spicy Fruit-glazed Cornish Hens**
1½ teaspoons herbes de Provence
2 cloves garlic, minced
✪ **I cup reserved Microwaved Rosemary Risotto**

2 Granny Smith apples, peeled, cored, and cubed
1 cup apple cider
1 cup chicken broth, canned or homemade
Salt and pepper to taste
2 tablespoons chopped parsley
½ pound (1 sheet) frozen puff pastry, defrosted
1 egg
1 tablespoon water

Cut up the reserved Cornish hens, remove and discard the skin, and remove the meat from the bones. Cut the meat into large chunks and set aside. You should have about 2 cups.

Cook the onion and fennel in the reserved fat in a skillet over medium heat until softened, about 2 minutes. Add the herbes de Provence, garlic, and reserved risotto and stir briskly for 1 minute. Add the apples and toss. Add the cider and chicken broth and stir to combine, scraping the bottom of the pan. Simmer until lightly thickened, about 2 minutes. Remove from the heat and season with salt and pepper. Fold in the meat and the parsley. Transfer mixture into a 2-quart casserole. Set aside.

Preheat the oven to 425°F.

Trim the sheet of puff pastry so that it just fits inside the rim of the casserole. Beat the egg and water together and brush over the top of pastry. Cut a few decorative slits in the top and bake for 25 minutes, or until puffed and brown.

Makes 4 servings.

Old Bay Barbecued Ribs

1½ tablespoons Old Bay seasoning
2 to 2½ pounds country ribs, split between the
bones, or 8 pork chops, each ¾ inch thick

✪ **½ cup drippings reserved from Spicy**
Fruit-glazed Cornish Hens
½ cup beer, preferably flat

Rub the Old Bay seasoning on all sides of the pork and let stand for 10 minutes.

Brown the meat on a grill or under a broiler, 4 inches from a hot fire, for about 3 minutes per side. Place in a baking dish or casserole just large enough to hold the meat in a single layer. Mix the drippings with the beer and pour over the meat.

Preheat the oven to 375°F. for 25 minutes until tender enough to pierce easily with a fork, turning the pork at least once. Transfer the meat to a platter and serve.

Makes 4 servings.

Lemon Garlic Fish en Papillote

✪ **6 tablespoons lemon oil reserved from**
Asparagus with Lemon Oil
2 cloves garlic, minced

4 fish fillets (5 to 6 ounces each)
Salt and pepper to taste
1 lemon, cut into 8 wedges

Preheat the oven to 375°F.

Combine the lemon oil and the garlic and set aside. Season the fish fillets on both sides with salt and pepper.

Cut four 12 x 16-inch sheets of parchment paper into heart shapes and spoon 1 teaspoon of the lemon oil onto 1 side of each sheet. Place a fish fillet on the oiled side and spoon a little more than 1 tablespoon of the lemon oil over each fillet. Fold the parchment over the fish and seal the package by folding the 2 edges together. To do this, start at the rounded end and make small, crisp folds, making sure that each fold overlaps the previous one. When you get to the pointed end, lock the chain of folds in place by twisting the point tightly. Repeat with the remaining packages.

Place the packages on a sheet pan and bake for 8 to 10 minutes, or until the parchment is puffed and browned and the liquid inside is bubbling. Snip open the parchment and slip the contents onto a plate. Squeeze the juice of a lemon wedge over each portion of fish and serve the remaining wedges on the side.

Makes 4 servings.

Herb-stuffed Peppers

✪ **2 cups reserved Microwaved Rosemary Risotto**
1 cup grated mozzarella (4 ounces)
2 tablespoons chopped fresh herbs (such as parsley, sage, savory, or basil)

4 large red and/or yellow bell peppers
¾ cup chicken broth, canned or homemade
1 tablespoon tomato paste

Mix the risotto with the mozzarella and herbs. Slice the tops off the peppers and reserve. Cut out the seeds and ribs from inside the peppers. Stuff the peppers with the rice mixture and secure the tops with a toothpick. Stand or place the peppers on their sides in a 9-inch microwavesafe baking dish. Combine the chicken broth and the tomato paste and pour over the peppers. Cover with plastic wrap and microwave at full power for 20 minutes, turning the peppers twice.

Or bake the peppers in a covered baking dish at 350°F. for 50 minutes, or until the peppers are tender. Serve 1 pepper per person with some of the sauce.

Makes 4 servings.

Menu 12

The problem with most turkeys is that they're just too big. One way around a turkey that refuses to quit is to start with a bird of modest proportions and to rely on its accompaniments, rather than on the turkey alone, for future inspiration. The first three weeknight entrees in this menu find their flavors in Sunday's sauce and side vegetables, rather than in the roast.

Sunday's roast turkey is filled with bread and cranberry stuffing and basted with apple cider to create a sauce brimming with meaty richness and a sweet tang of fruit. The stuffing is served as a side dish along with souffléed twice-baked potatoes and spinach sautéed in bacon fat with walnuts.

The potatoes and spinach meet again on Monday for an easy dish of gnocchi (Italian potato dumplings) tossed with olive oil and cheese. On Tuesday, scallops are braised in white wine and apple cider, a traditional combination in northwestern France. And on Wednesday, trout is stuffed with a mixture of crabmeat and Sunday's bread stuffing. The mole poblano on Thursday is a classic Mexican stew, in which turkey is simmered with chilies and spices, creating a sauce that is richly thickened with a bit of unsweetened chocolate as it finishes.

THE SUNDAY DINNER

Traditional Roast Turkey with
Apple Cider Gravy

Souffléed Sour Cream Baked Potatoes

Spinach Sautéed with Bacon and Walnuts

THE WEEKNIGHT ENTREES

Potato and Spinach Gnocchi with
Garlic, Parmesan, and Bacon

Bay Scallops Braised in Apple Cider

Baked Stuffed Trout

Mole Poblano with Corn

Traditional Roast Turkey with Apple Cider Gravy

¾ pound bread, cubed (about 4 cups)
1 turkey, with giblets (about 10 pounds)
   (see Note)
1½ cups chicken broth, canned or homemade
1 large onion, finely chopped
2 ribs celery, diced
1 tablespoon butter
2 tablespoons vegetable oil
1 cup fresh or frozen cranberries, coarsely
   chopped

1 tablespoon sugar
1 teaspoon rubbed dried sage
½ teaspoon dried thyme
Pinch of freshly grated nutmeg
2 teaspoons chopped parsley
Salt and pepper to taste
4 cups apple cider
1 tablespoon cornstarch
2 tablespoons water

Preheat the oven to 400°F.

Arrange the bread cubes in a single layer on a rimmed sheet pan, and bake for 10 minutes, or until lightly toasted. Meanwhile, wash the turkey inside and out with cold water. Pat dry. Coarsely chop the gizzard and heart. Place them in a small saucepan with the chicken broth and simmer for 15 minutes.

Sauté the onion and celery in the butter and half the oil in a skillet, until the vegetables are softened, about 1 minute. Add the cranberries, sugar, sage, thyme, nutmeg, and parsley and cook 1 more minute. Season with salt and pepper. Add the bread cubes and the cooked giblets with their cooking liquid. Stir to combine. Reserve 1 cup of this stuffing. Spoon the remaining stuffing into the cavity of the turkey and rub skin with remaining oil.

Turn the oven temperature up to 450°F. Place the turkey on an oiled rack, breast side down, in a roasting pan and roast for 30 minutes. Baste with ¼ cup of the apple cider and roast for another 30 minutes. Turn the turkey breast side up, and reduce the oven temperature to 350°F. Return the turkey to the oven and roast for another 2 hours, or until a meat thermometer inserted into the thickest part of a breast registers 170°F. or a thigh registers 180°F. After the first hour, pour 2¾ cups of the remaining apple cider over the turkey and baste with the liquid every 15 minutes until the turkey is done.

Transfer the turkey to a serving platter or carving board. Pour the liquid from the roasting pan into a 4-cup measuring cup and skim off the fat. Add enough of the remaining apple cider to make 4 cups. Transfer to a saucepan and bring to a boil. Stir the

cornstarch into the water until dissolved. Whisk the cornstarch mixture into the boiling juices and cook for 1 minute, or until the gravy thickens lightly. Carve turkey and serve 3 cups of the gravy on the side.

Makes 4 or 5 servings, plus enough to:
- ✪ **Reserve about a quarter of the turkey, preferably dark meat, for Mole Poblano with Corn.**
- ✪ **Reserve 1 cup gravy for Bay Scallops Braised in Apple Cider.**
- ✪ **Reserve 1 cup stuffing for Baked Stuffed Trout.**

Note: A turkey up to 12 pounds would work with this recipe, although you'll end up with more meat. A 12-pound turkey will need about 30 minutes more cooking time. Use the internal temperature of the meat as your guide.

Souffléed Sour Cream Baked Potatoes

*6 large russet potatoes, scrubbed and dried
  (about 4 pounds)
4 eggs, separated*

*¼ cup sour cream (see Note)
1 clove garlic, minced
Salt and pepper to taste*

Preheat the oven to 450°F.

Pierce the skins of the potatoes in several places with the tines of a fork. Bake for 45 to 50 minutes, or until tender. This can be done together with the turkey during the initial roasting period. Remove the potatoes from the oven and allow them to cool for 20 minutes until they are easy to handle. Using a serrated knife, cut a thin slice from one of the wider sides of each potato. Using a towel to protect your hand, hold each potato cut side up and scoop out the flesh. Place it in a mixing bowl and mash with a fork until nearly smooth. Add the egg yolks, sour cream, garlic, salt, and pepper and mix thoroughly. Reserve 2 cups of this mixture.

Beat the egg whites with a pinch of salt in a clean bowl until the whites are thick enough to hold a shape. Mix ½ cup of the egg whites into the potatoes remaining in the mixing bowl and fold the remaining whites into the 2 cups of reserved potatoes.

Preheat the oven to 400°F. Lightly oil a baking pan.

Spoon the potatoes from the mixing bowl into four potato skins, heaping the potato mixture. Place the potatoes, opening up, on the pan and bake for 30 minutes, or until puffed and browned. Serve immediately.

Makes 4 servings, plus enough to:
✪ **Reserve 2 cups potato mixture for Potato and Spinach Gnocchi with Garlic, Parmesan, and Bacon.**

Note: Yogurt may be substituted for the sour cream.

Spinach Sautéed with Bacon and Walnuts

4 slices bacon, finely chopped
¼ cup chopped walnuts

1½ pounds fresh spinach leaves, washed, shaken dry, and coarsely chopped
Salt and pepper to taste

Cook the bacon in a large skillet over medium heat until crisp. Add the walnuts and toss until lightly browned, about 30 seconds. Add the spinach and toss until the spinach has wilted, about 45 seconds. Remove from the heat and season with salt and pepper. Serve half the spinach, about 1½ cups.

Makes 4 servings, plus enough to:
✪ **Reserve 1½ cups for Potato and Spinach Gnocchi with Garlic, Parmesan, and Bacon.**

Potato and Spinach Gnocchi with Garlic, Parmesan, and Bacon

GNOCCHI

○ **2 cups potato mixture reserved from Souffléed Sour Cream Baked Potatoes**

○ **1½ cups reserved Spinach Sautéed with Bacon and Walnuts**

2 tablespoons freshly gated parmesan cheese

2 tablespoons flour

Salt and pepper to taste

Additional flour for forming gnocchi

SAUCE

2 tablespoons freshly grated parmesan cheese

2 teaspoons extra-virgin olive oil

½ clove garlic, minced

Salt and pepper to taste

Mix the reserved potato, reserved spinach, parmesan cheese, flour, salt, and pepper in a bowl until well combined. Form gnocchi in batches of 12. Take 1 teaspoon of the potato mixture and roll it in flour. Gently roll each mound between your hands into a cylinder about 2 inches long. Place a long-tined fork face up on a work surface. Place a potato cylinder on the inside curve of the fork, parallel to the handle. Gently flatten by pressing an index finger into the center of the dough and slide it off the fork. Each piece will be decorated on one side with ridges from the fork tines and with an indentation from your finger on the other. Continue shaping the gnocchi in this way until all have been formed. You should have about 48 gnocchi.

Bring a large saucepan of salted water to a boil. Add half the gnocchi to the boiling water. In a short time, they will float to the surface. Cook just 10 seconds more and remove with a large slotted spoon to a serving platter. Keep warm while you cook the remaining gnocchi.

For the sauce, combine the cheese, olive oil, garlic, salt, and pepper. Toss with the gnocchi and serve.

Makes 4 servings.

Bay Scallops Braised in Apple Cider

2 leeks, white parts only, thinly sliced
1 tablespoon butter
1½ pounds bay scallops
Salt and pepper to taste
1 cup white wine

✪ **1 cup gravy reserved from Traditional Roast Turkey with Apple Cider Gravy**
1 tablespoon apple cider vinegar
¼ cup sour cream or yogurt

Sauté the leeks in the butter in a large nonstick skillet over medium-high heat until softened. Add the scallops and cook until they begin to lose their raw look, about 1 to 2 minutes. Season with salt and pepper. Add the white wine and simmer until the scallops are just firm, about 30 seconds. Remove the scallops with a slotted spoon and set aside.

Add the reserved gravy and the vinegar and cook over high heat until lightly thickened, about 2 minutes. Return the scallops to the pan and heat through. Remove from the heat and stir in the sour cream or yogurt.

Makes 4 servings.

Baked Stuffed Trout

3 scallions, chopped
1 clove garlic, minced
8 ounces backfin crabmeat, cleaned
✪ **1 cup stuffing reserved from Traditional Roast Turkey with Apple Cider Gravy**

Pinch of cayenne
4 brook trout, preferably with head and tail on, boned
Salt and freshly ground pepper to taste
1 tablespoon olive oil

Preheat the oven to 350°F.

Combine the scallions, garlic, crabmeat, reserved stuffing, and cayenne in a small bowl. Season the interior of the fish with salt and pepper and divide the stuffing equally among the 4 fish, completely filling the cavity of each. Fold the top fillet of fish over the stuffing, gently pressing stray bits of stuffing in place to conform to the shape of the fish.

Lightly coat a baking dish large enough to hold the fish in a single layer with 1 teaspoon of the oil and arrange the fish in the dish. Coat the top of the fish with the remaining oil. Bake for 30 minutes, or until the fish flakes when gently pushed. Serve 1 fish per person.

Makes 4 servings.

Mole Poblano with Corn

2 medium onions, chopped
4 cloves garlic, minced
2 tablespoons corn oil
1 tablespoon chili powder, preferably ancho
    chili (see Note)
2 teaspoons ground cumin
1 teaspoon dried oregano
1 teaspoon dried thyme
½ teaspoon ground cinnamon

2 tablespoons canned crushed tomatoes
1 tablespoon tomato paste
2 tablespoons cornmeal
2½ cups chicken broth, canned or homemade
1 can (11 ounces) corn kernels, drained
✪ **Turkey reserved from Traditional Roast
    Turkey with Apple Cider Gravy**
½ ounce semisweet chocolate, finely chopped
2 tablespoons chopped cilantro or parsley

Cook the onions and garlic in the oil over medium heat, stirring constantly, until softened. Add the chili powder, cumin, oregano, thyme, cinnamon, crushed tomatoes, tomato paste, and cornmeal and cook for 1 more minute, stirring constantly. Stir in the chicken broth and continue stirring until the liquid begins to boil. Reduce the heat and simmer for 15 minutes. Add the corn and turkey and heat through. Stir in the chocolate and the cilantro or parsley. Serve hot.

Makes 4 servings.

Note: Ancho chilies are dried ripe poblanos.

Provençale cooking is rustic and unpretentious, and though the flavors are sometimes complex, they are never belabored. This week's menu invites you to bask in the sun-drenched foods of the south of France. For Sunday's dinner, fillets of orange roughy (or any firm white-meated fish) are baked in a quickly prepared fresh tomato sauce. The dish is served with potatoes roasted with garlic and grilled vegetables marinated in olive oil and wine vinegar.

Monday's meal is fish cakes. Fish cakes are usually laborious when made from scratch, but these have been streamlined with Sunday's fish and potatoes. They're given a Creole kick with a mixture of mayonnaise, hot pepper sauce, and ketchup—exceptionally easy and delicious. On Tuesday, marinated grilled vegetables turn a simple spinach salad into a one-dish meal that is a collection of opposites. All at once it's crisp and tender, spicy and sweet, chilled and warm. On Wednesday, lamb is braised with olives in the tomato sauce you made for the fish, and Thursday delivers an unconventional stir-fry of potatoes, sweet onion, and chunks of turkey breast.

THE SUNDAY DINNER

Baked Fish Provençale

Roasted Garlic Potatoes

Roasted Vegetables Vinaigrette

THE WEEKNIGHT ENTREES

Spicy Sweet Creole Fish Cakes

Smoky Spinach Salad

Mediterranean Braised Lamb

Turkey, Potatoes, and Sweet Onions

Baked Fish Provençale

2 tablespoons olive oil
1 medium onion, chopped
4 stalks fresh fennel, diced
1 teaspoon herbes de Provence
4 cloves garlic, finely chopped
15 plum tomatoes, diced (about 3 pounds)

1 cup orange juice
¼ cup chopped basil leaves
2 pounds orange roughy fillets
Salt and pepper to taste
8 anchovy fillets, finely chopped

Preheat the oven to 375°F.

Heat 1 tablespoon of the olive oil in a large skillet or saucepan and sauté the onion and fennel until softened, about 3 minutes. Add the herbes de Provence and garlic and cook 1 more minute, stirring constantly. Add the tomatoes and stir until the tomatoes soften and release their moisture, about 3 minutes. Add the orange juice and basil and bring to a boil. Remove from heat.

Meanwhile, rub the fish fillets with salt and pepper. Brush the remaining oil in a baking dish just large enough to hold the fish in a single layer. Arrange the fish in the dish and scatter the anchovies over the top.

Reserve 3 cups of the tomato sauce. Spoon the remaining sauce over the fish, and bake for 20 minutes, or until the fish flakes to gentle pressure. Reserve a third of the fish (about 2¾ cups), broken into flakes, and serve the rest in large pieces.

Makes 4 servings, plus enough to:
✪ **Reserve 2¾ cups flaked fish for Spicy Sweet Creole Fish Cakes.**
✪ **Reserve 3 cups tomato sauce for Mediterranean Braised Lamb.**

Roasted Garlic Potatoes

*8 large russet potatoes, scrubbed
    (about 5 pounds)*
Olive oil spray

2 cloves garlic, finely chopped
Salt and pepper to taste

Preheat the oven to 450°F.

Cut each potato lengthwise into 8 pieces. Spray 2 large rimmed sheet pans or baking pans with the olive oil spray. Arrange the potatoes on the pans and spray again. Scatter the chopped garlic over the top and season liberally with salt and pepper. Toss well. Roast for 45 to 50 minutes, turning every 15 minutes or so, or until the potatoes are tender and well browned.

Makes 4 servings, plus enough to:
✪ **Reserve 24 pieces for Turkey, Potatoes, and Sweet Onions.**
✪ **Reserve 8 pieces for Spicy Sweet Creole Fish Cakes.**

Roasted Vegetables Vinaigrette

2 small heads garlic
3 ears corn, unhusked
3 bell peppers, assorted colors
*3 leeks, white parts only, halved lengthwise
    and washed thoroughly*
1 eggplant, stemmed and thickly sliced

*8 large white mushrooms, stems trimmed and
    cleaned*
½ cup olive oil
¼ cup red wine vinegar
Salt and pepper to taste
¼ cup chopped basil leaves

Place the garlic, unhusked corn, and bell peppers on a lightly oiled grill 4 inches from a hot fire. Grill for 6 minutes, turning once.

Meanwhile, toss the leeks, eggplant slices, and mushrooms with 1½ tablespoons of the olive oil. Grill the leeks for 2 minutes, then add the eggplant and mushrooms. At the same time, give the garlic, corn, and peppers a quarter turn, and grill 4 more minutes. Turn everything on the grill, and cook another 4 minutes. The vegetables are done when they are well browned and tender. Test the corn by peeling back a portion of a husk and checking the kernels for tenderness.

Husk the corn and cut the kernels from the ears by holding the ear upright and cutting down several rows of kernels with a sharp knife. Transfer to a bowl. Halve, stem, and seed the peppers. Cube the peppers and the eggplant. Slice the mushrooms and leeks. Add vegetables to the bowl with the corn and set aside.

Cut the garlic in half and push out the soft cloves into a small mixing bowl. Whisk in the remaining olive oil, the vinegar, salt, pepper, and basil. Reserve ¼ cup of the dressing. Pour the remaining dressing over the vegetables. Allow to marinate at least 20 minutes. Reserve 2 cups of the marinated vegetables and serve the rest.

Makes 4 servings, plus enough to:
✪ **Reserve 2 cups marinated roasted vegetables for Smoky Spinach Salad.**
✪ **Reserve ¼ cup dressing for Mediterranean Braised Lamb.**

Spicy Sweet Creole Fish Cakes

½ cup mayonnaise
3 tablespoons hot pepper sauce
1 teaspoon ketchup
2 scallions, white parts only, finely chopped
✪ **8 pieces reserved Roasted Garlic Potatoes**

½ bell pepper, stemmed, seeded, and finely diced
✪ **2¾ cups flaked fish reserved from Baked Fish Provençale**
1¼ to 1½ cups Italian-style bread crumbs
2 to 4 tablespoons olive oil

Combine the mayonnaise and hot pepper sauce in a mixing bowl. Divide in half. Add the ketchup and scallions to 1 portion of the mayonnaise mixture and set aside.

Finely chop the reserved potatoes. Add potatoes, the bell pepper, and reserved fish to the second portion of the mayonnaise mixture and toss to combine.

Place the bread crumbs in a bowl. Form the fish cakes by scooping up a mound of the fish mixture with an ice cream scoop. Place the scoop of fish in the bread crumbs, sprinkle more crumbs over the fish, and carefully lift the crumb-coated cake in 1 hand. Pat into a burger shape using more crumbs to get an evenly crumbed surface. Repeat with the remaining fish mixture and crumbs. You should have 8 or 9 cakes.

Cook the fish cakes in 2 batches. Sauté the first batch in 2 tablespoons of the oil over medium heat until they are golden brown and heated through, about 4 minutes per side. If necessary, add the remaining oil to cook the second batch. Serve with the mayonnaise sauce.

Makes 4 servings.

Smoky Spinach Salad

2 packages (10 ounces each) fresh spinach, stemmed and cleaned

1 medium sweet onion, preferably Vidalia, halved and thinly sliced (Bermuda onion could be used, too)

2 ribs celery, finely diced

6 white mushrooms, stems trimmed, cleaned, and sliced

⅓ cup olive oil

6 ounces smoked ham, cubed (about 1¼ cups)

1 jalapeño, stemmed, seeded, and finely chopped

2 cloves garlic, minced

✪ **2 cups reserved marinated roasted vegetables from Roasted Vegetables Vinaigrette**

2 tablespoons sugar

Salt and pepper to taste

¼ cup wine vinegar

Toss the spinach, onion, celery, and mushrooms in a large salad bowl. Set aside.

Combine the oil, ham, and jalapeño in a skillet over medium heat and cook for 2 minutes, stirring constantly. Add the garlic and reserved vegetables and stir for another minute. Add the sugar, salt, pepper, and vinegar and bring to a boil. Pour the hot dressing over the spinach, toss to combine, and serve.

Makes 4 servings.

Mediterranean Braised Lamb

1 tablespoon olive oil

4 shoulder lamb chops (about 2 pounds)

¾ cup white wine

✪ **3 cups tomato sauce reserved from Baked Fish Provençale**

12 pitted black olives, coarsely chopped

✪ **¼ cup dressing reserved from Roasted Vegetables Vinaigrette**

Heat the oil in a large skillet over high heat until smoking. Add the lamb and brown on both sides, about 8 minutes. Add the wine and boil for 3 minutes. Add the tomato sauce and the olives. Cover and simmer for 25 to 30 minutes, or until the lamb is fork-tender. Spoon off fat and stir in dressing.

Makes 4 servings.

Turkey, Potatoes, and Sweet Onions

6 tablespoons apple cider vinegar

1 tablespoon sugar

1 tablespoon light soy sauce

1 teaspoon hot pepper sauce

3 tablespoons vegetable oil

1 medium sweet onion, preferably Vidalia, cut into thin wedges (Bermuda onion could be used, too)

✪ **24 pieces reserved Roasted Garlic Potatoes**

1 pound skinless and boneless turkey breast, cut into 1-inch chunks

2 cloves garlic, minced

½ teaspoon salt

Combine the vinegar, sugar, soy sauce, and hot pepper sauce in a small bowl. Set aside.

Heat the oil in a hot wok over medium-high heat until smoking. Add the onion and stir-fry until golden brown, about 3 minutes. Transfer the onion to a bowl with a slotted spoon. Add the reserved potato pieces to the wok and stir-fry until crisp, about 3 minutes. With a slotted spoon, transfer the potatoes to the bowl with the onion. Add the turkey chunks to the wok and stir-fry until lightly browned, about 3 minutes. Add the vinegar mixture, the onion, and the potatoes and stir-fry until the turkey is firm and the liquid has lightly thickened, about 2 minutes. Toss in the garlic and the salt. Mix well.

Makes 4 servings.

Menu 14

Much of this week's menu plays off the unusual triumvirate of spicy mustard, sweet honey, and sour lemon. The pungency of the mustard is mellowed by the honey, and the honey's cloying finish is cut by the sweet and sour spark of the lemon, which in turn lends the mustard its fruity perfume.

This gastronomic trio is used on Sunday as a glaze for baked squash, but it appears throughout the week, too, lending spice to Monday's sausage and peas, sweetness to Tuesday's barbecued pork, and pungency to the glaze for Wednesday's baked bluefish.

Braised pork leads off the Sunday meal. It's rubbed with chili, cinnamon, and thyme and its pungent crust is sweetened with a splash of apple cider. Blended together, these ingredients create a sauce that is at once spicy hot, aromatic, and sweet, a playful combination that is further intensified when combined with the extra lemon-honey-mustard mixture for Tuesday's pork barbecue sandwich. Sunday's pork is served with peppery greens and Glorious Garlic Mushrooms. The greens become a bed for peas and sausage on Monday, and the mushrooms join in a clam sauce for rice pilaf that wraps up the week.

THE SUNDAY DINNER

Pork Loin Braised in Cider

Lemon-Mustard Squash

Black Pepper Greens

Glorious Garlic Mushrooms

THE WEEKNIGHT ENTREES

Black-eyed Peas, Smoked Sausage,
and Greens

Barbecued Pork Grinders

Pungent Baked Bluefish

Garlic Basmati Rice with
White Clam Sauce

Pork Loin Braised in Cider

2 teaspoons salt
1 teaspoon ground black pepper
2 teaspoons dried thyme
½ teaspoon ground cinnamon
1 teaspoon chili powder
1 clove garlic, minced

1 boneless pork loin roast (4 pounds)
1 medium onion, chopped
2 ribs celery, chopped
2 apples, any variety except Red Delicious,
    chopped
2 cups apple cider

Preheat the oven to 375°F.

Combine the salt, pepper, thyme, cinnamon, chili powder, and garlic. Rub the pork with the mixture. Spread the onion, celery, and apple on the bottom of a roasting pan and place the pork on the vegetables, fat side up. Roast for 45 minutes.

Pour the cider over the pork and reduce the temperature to 325°F. Roast for 1 more hour, basting with pan juices every 10 minutes, until done, or when a thermometer inserted in the center of the roast registers between 155°F. and 160°F. for medium, between 165°F. and 170°F. for well done.

Allow pork to rest for 10 minutes and degrease the braising liquid. Cut into thin slices. Serve two thirds of the roast (10 to 12 slices) and spoon ¾ cup of the liquid over the sliced pork.

Makes 4 servings, plus enough to:
✪ **Reserve about I pound pork for Barbecued Pork Grinders.**
✪ **Reserve I cup braising liquid for Barbecued Pork Grinders.**

Lemon-Mustard Squash

2½ pounds winter squash, such as butternut,
    acorn, or buttercup, peeled, seeded, and
    cut into 2-inch chunks
½ cup water

2 tablespoons plus 1 teaspoon Dijon mustard
2 tablespoons plus 1 teaspoon honey
2 tablespoons plus 1 teaspoon lemon juice

continued

Preheat the oven to 375°F.

Place the squash chunks in a large baking dish and pour the water over the top. Bake until the squash just begins to soften, about 20 minutes. Remove from oven and pour off excess water.

While the squash is baking, combine the mustard, honey, and lemon juice. Drizzle 3 tablespoons of this mixture over the drained squash. Reduce oven temperature to 325°F. and bake for 30 minutes more, or until the squash is very tender. Remove from the oven and keep warm.

Just before serving, baste with some of the liquid in the pan and place under the broiler for 3 minutes to brown.

Makes 4 servings, plus enough to:
- ✪ **Reserve 3 tablespoons lemon-mustard sauce for Pungent Baked Bluefish.**
- ✪ **Reserve 2 teaspoons lemon-mustard sauce for Barbecued Pork Grinders.**
- ✪ **Reserve 1 teaspoon lemon-mustard sauce for Black-eyed Peas, Smoked Sausage, and Greens.**

Black Pepper Greens

3 pounds greens, such as small leaves of kale, chard, dandelion, mustard, or a combination
1 medium onion, finely chopped
¼ pound smoked meat, either pork, turkey, or beef, diced

2 tablespoons olive oil
Salt to taste
1 teaspoon ground black pepper
Pinch of cayenne

Discard any yellowed or wilted leaves from the greens, remove stems from the rest, and chop coarsely. Wash thoroughly in plenty of cold water. Shake off some of the water but leave the greens wet.

Cook the onion and smoked meat in the olive oil in a large soup pot over medium-high heat until softened. Put greens in the soup pot, pushing them down so they all fit into the pot. Cover and cook for 1 minute. Toss. Cover and cook for 1 more minute. Repeat until all the greens have softened, about 4 minutes. (Cook up to 5 minutes longer if leaves are large or tough.)

Season liberally with salt, stir in the black pepper and cayenne, and serve half.

Makes 4 servings, plus enough to:
- ✪ **Reserve 3 cups for Black-eyed Peas, Smoked Sausage, and Greens.**

Glorious Garlic Mushrooms

3 tablespoons olive oil
1 ½ pounds white mushrooms, stems trimmed,
   cleaned, and halved or quartered
4 cloves garlic, minced
Pinch of crushed red pepper flakes

3 scallions, white parts only, sliced
½ cup water
Salt and pepper to taste
1 tablespoon chopped parsley
2 tablespoons lemon juice

Heat the oil in a large saucepan or skillet. Add the mushrooms and cook until they lose their raw look, stirring frequently, about 3 minutes. Add the garlic, pepper flakes, and scallions. Toss well. Add the water, salt, and pepper and heat until simmering. Cover and simmer until mushrooms are tender, about 5 minutes. Stir in the parsley and lemon juice. Serve 2 cups of mushrooms.

Makes 4 servings, plus enough to:
- **Reserve I cup cooking liquid for Garlic Basmati Rice with White Clam Sauce.**
- **Reserve I cup mushrooms for Garlic Basmati Rice with White Clam Sauce.**

Black-eyed Peas, Smoked Sausage, and Greens

1 tablespoon vegetable oil
✪ **3 cups reserved Black Pepper Greens**
1 medium onion, chopped
*4 smoked sausages, each cut in 3 or 4 pieces
  (about 12 ounces)*

*1 can (14 ounces) black-eyed peas, drained
  and rinsed*
2 cloves garlic, minced
✪ **1 teaspoon lemon-mustard sauce
  reserved from Lemon-Mustard Squash**

Heat 1 teaspoon of the oil in a large nonstick skillet over medium-high heat. Add the reserved greens and stir until heated. Arrange in a ring on a serving platter. Keep warm.

Add the rest of the oil to the skillet and heat. Add the onion and stir until softened, about 2 minutes. Add the sausages and cook for 3 or 4 more minutes, stirring frequently until browned evenly. Reduce heat to medium and stir in the black-eyed peas and garlic. Heat through, about 1 minute. Stir in the lemon-mustard sauce and mound in the center of the ring of greens.

Makes 4 servings.

Barbecued Pork Grinders

✪ **Reserved Pork Loin Braised in Cider**
1 small onion, chopped
2 teaspoons vegetable oil
✪ **1 cup braising liquid reserved from Pork
  Loin Braised in Cider**

4 torpedo rolls (long Italian rolls), split
¼ cup ketchup
1 teaspoon apple cider vinegar
✪ **2 teaspoons lemon-mustard sauce
  reserved from Lemon-Mustard Squash**

Preheat the oven to 350°F.

Cut the reserved pork into small dice. You should have about 4 cups.

Cook the onion in the oil in a skillet until lightly browned, about 2 minutes. Add the pork and toss. Add the reserved braising liquid and simmer for about 8 minutes. Meanwhile, warm the rolls in the oven for 5 minutes.

Add the ketchup, vinegar, and reserved lemon-mustard sauce to the skillet. Stir to combine. Serve the barbecued pork heaped in the warm rolls.

Makes 4 servings.

Pungent Baked Bluefish

1½ pounds bluefish fillets
2 teaspoons olive oil
Salt and pepper to taste

✪ **3 tablespoons lemon-mustard sauce reserved from Lemon-Mustard Squash**

Preheat the oven to 400°F.

Rub the fish fillets with the olive oil. Place, skin side down, in a single layer in a large baking dish. Season with salt and pepper. Bake for 10 minutes. Brush with the reserved lemon-mustard sauce and bake another 5 to 8 minutes, or until the fish flakes to gentle pressure.

Makes 4 servings.

Garlic Basmati Rice with White Clam Sauce

2 cups water
½ teaspoon salt
¼ teaspoon pepper
✪ **1 cup cooking liquid reserved from Glorious Garlic Mushrooms**

1½ cups basmati rice, washed
✪ **1 cup reserved Glorious Garlic Mushrooms**
2 tablespoons chopped parsley
1 can (10½ ounces) white clam sauce

Combine the water, salt, pepper, and reserved mushroom cooking liquid in a medium-size heavy saucepan. Bring to a simmer, add the rice, stir to separate, cover pan, and simmer over low heat until all the liquid has been absorbed, about 15 minutes. Meanwhile, slice the reserved mushrooms. When the rice is done, stir in the mushrooms, parsley, and clam sauce and heat through, about 1 minute. Adjust seasoning with salt and pepper.

Makes 4 servings.

RICE: TO WASH OR NOT TO WASH

Mot brands of rice come prewashed, but some imported rices, basmati for one, do not and must be washed at home. Prewashed rice has a very smooth surface and looks somewhat translucent. Unwashed rice has a slightly powdery white surface.

To wash rice, place it in a very large bowl or pot and fill it with cold water. Swirl the rice around until the water becomes quite cloudy. Drain through a strainer. Repeat until the water is almost clear.

The rib roast is etched in my mind as the most regal of roasts, yet I don't think I've seen one in the meat case of my market or butcher for the better part of a decade. I ordered one for this week's menu and was amazed at how its lushness seems even greater now.

Because opulence knows no boundaries, I've gilded Sunday's roast with an equally lavish sauce, chunky with wild mushrooms and bits of fresh herbs. Its cost is tempered by using some white mushrooms to fill out the mixture. The roast is accompanied by traditional roasted potatoes that have been peppered with capers, by an eggless version of Caesar salad, and by a Mexican rendition of stewed tomatoes. These are seasoned with chipotle peppers, which are smoked jalapeños. Because the pepper oil can be very irritating to your skin, wash your hands well with lots of soap and water after you touch these peppers.

Unlike the other menus in this book, this one's weeknight entrees are more casual than their Sunday source. First, the Caesar dressing becomes a quick scampi sauce on Monday, then, along with the stewed tomatoes, it reappears as one of two piquant sauces for Wednesday's simple supper of chilled beef slices. Tuesday is pasta night, utilizing the chipotle stewed tomatoes for a quick fresh tomato sauce over spaghetti, and Thursday brings an opulent stew of chicken breast and wild mushrooms, miraculously ready in less than 10 minutes.

This Sunday dinner is more of a special-occasion feast than a family affair. Therefore, the recipes have been fashioned to yield eight to ten portions, plus enough for making the weeknight entrees.

THE SUNDAY DINNER

Rib Roast of Beef with Braised
Wild Mushrooms

Roasted Potatoes with Capers

Eggless Caesar Salad

Tomatoes Sautéed with Chipotle

THE WEEKNIGHT ENTREES

Broiled Scampi Romano

Mexican Spaghetti

Cold Roast Beef with Two Sauces

Chicken and Mushroom Stew

Rib Roast of Beef with Braised Wild Mushrooms

BEEF

2 teaspoons salt
1 teaspoon black pepper
3 cloves garlic, minced
1 rib roast of beef (about 9 pounds)

MUSHROOMS

1 ounce dried wild mushrooms,
   any kind
2 cups warm water
1 cup beef broth, homemade or canned

2 leeks, white parts only, thoroughly washed
   and finely chopped
2 tablespoons butter
¾ pound fresh wild mushrooms, any kind,
   stems trimmed, cleaned, and sliced
1 pound white mushrooms, stems trimmed,
   cleaned, and sliced
1 teaspoon dried rosemary leaves
2 tablespoons chopped parsley
4 plum tomatoes (¾ pound), finely chopped
Salt and pepper to taste

Preheat the oven to 475°F.

Combine the salt, pepper, and garlic and rub the mixture into the surface of the beef. Place the beef in a roasting pan, fat side up, and roast for 1 hour. Reduce the oven temperature to 400°F. and continue roasting for about 1½ hours, or until a meat thermometer inserted into the center of the meat registers 130°F. for medium-rare, 140°F. for medium.

About 30 minutes before the meat will be done, begin preparing the mushrooms. Soak the dried mushrooms in the warm water until they are soft and completely rehydrated, about 15 minutes. Squeeze out the mushrooms, rinse well, and set aside. Strain the soaking liquid through a coffee filter. Combine the strained soaking liquid and the beef broth in a saucepan, place over high heat, and reduce to 1 cup. Set aside.

Sauté the leeks in the butter in a large deep skillet until softened. Add the fresh wild mushrooms, white mushrooms, soaked wild mushrooms, rosemary, and parsley. Cook until the mushrooms begin to release their moisture. Add the tomatoes and the reduced soaking liquid. Season with salt and pepper and simmer for 5 minutes. Set aside.

When the beef is done, remove it from the oven and allow it to rest for 10 minutes before slicing. Cut the meat from the rack of bones and into ⅛-inch slices. Reheat the mushroom sauce to a simmer and serve with the meat.

Makes 8 to 10 servings, plus enough to:
✪ **Reserve 8 slices (about 1 pound) meat for Cold Roast Beef with Two Sauces.**
✪ **Reserve 2 to 2½ cups mushrooms for Chicken and Mushroom Stew.**

Roasted Potatoes with Capers

4½ pounds red-skin potatoes, scrubbed and
*   halved or quartered*
1 medium onion, finely chopped
2 cloves garlic, minced

Salt and pepper to taste
⅓ cup fat from pan drippings of Rib Roast of
*   Beef, or olive oil*
2 tablespoons capers, drained

Preheat the oven to 400°F.

Toss the potato pieces with the onion, garlic, salt, and pepper. Place in a wide shallow baking pan. Skim fat from the drippings of the roast beef in the roasting pan. Pour the fat over the potatoes, and toss to coat. Roast for 40 minutes, turning the potatoes 2 or 3 times. Scatter the capers over the top and roast another 10 to 15 minutes, or until the potatoes are crisp on the outside and tender inside. Reserve 1 cup and serve the rest.

Makes 8 to 10 servings, plus enough to:
✪ **Reserve 1 cup for Chicken and Mushroom Stew.**

Eggless Caesar Salad

3 cloves garlic, coarsely chopped
9 anchovy fillets
4 teaspoons spicy brown mustard
½ cup red wine vinegar
1 cup olive oil

Salt and pepper to taste
2 heads romaine lettuce, torn into bite-size
*   pieces*
¼ cup freshly grated parmesan cheese
2 cups garlic croutons

Mash the garlic and anchovies in a large wooden salad bowl with the back of a fork. Mix in the mustard and vinegar. Slowly beat in the olive oil. Season with salt and pepper. Reserve ¾ cup of this dressing and toss the lettuce with the rest. Sprinkle with the parmesan cheese and the croutons and toss again. Serve immediately.

Makes 8 to 10 servings, plus enough to:
✪ **Reserve 6 tablespoons dressing for Broiled Scampi Romano.**
✪ **Reserve 6 tablespoons dressing for Cold Roast Beef with Two Sauces.**

Tomatoes Sautéed with Chipotle

1 dried chipotle pepper, stemmed and seeded
¼ cup olive oil
30 plum tomatoes (about 5 ½ pounds)
1 medium onion, chopped

1 clove garlic, minced
Salt and pepper to taste
¼ teaspoon red wine vinegar
¼ cup chopped cilantro

Cover pepper with boiling water and soak for 10 minutes. Remove and finely chop. Mix in 2 tablespoons of the olive oil. Core the tomatoes and slice them ½ inch thick. Place the slices in the oil-chipotle mixture, turning to coat them. Sauté the onion in the remaining 2 tablespoons of olive oil in a large skillet until barely softened. Add the tomatoes and sauté until seared on both sides. Add the garlic, the remaining 2 teaspoons of chipotle sauce, salt, pepper, vinegar, and cilantro and cook for 1 more minute. Serve 5 or 6 slices per portion.

Makes 8 to 10 servings, plus enough to:
✪ **Reserve 1 cup for Mexican Spaghetti.**
✪ **Reserve 1 cup for Cold Roast Beef with Two Sauces.**

Broiled Scampi Romano

✪ **6 tablespoons dressing reserved from Eggless Caesar Salad**
2 tablespoons freshly grated parmesan cheese

1½ pounds large shrimp, peeled and deveined
Rice or pasta, for serving

Combine the reserved dressing and the cheese. Toss the shrimp with this marinade, cover, and refrigerate for at least 1 hour.

Remove shrimp from the marinade and grill or broil 4 inches from a hot fire for 1 to 2 minutes per side, basting with additional marinade when you turn the shrimp. Cook until the shrimp are firm and opaque. Serve with rice or pasta.

Makes 4 servings.

Mexican Spaghetti

1 pound spaghetti
1 medium onion, chopped
2 teaspoons olive oil
1 clove garlic, minced
✪ **1 cup tomatoes reserved from Tomatoes Sautéed with Chipotle**

2 cups canned crushed tomatoes (about 1-pound can)
Salt and pepper to taste
1 avocado, peeled, pitted, and finely diced

Cook the spaghetti in a large pot of boiling salted water for about 10 minutes, or until tender but not soft.

Meanwhile, cook the onion in the olive oil in a skillet until softened, about 2 minutes. Add the garlic and cook another 30 seconds. Add the reserved tomatoes, the canned tomatoes, salt, and pepper. Bring to a simmer and cook 8 to 10 minutes.

Drain the spaghetti in a colander or large strainer. Ladle a bit of sauce into a large bowl. Add half the pasta and toss to coat. Add the remaining pasta and top with the remaining sauce. Toss to combine. Scatter the diced avocado over top.

Makes 4 servings.

Cold Roast Beef with Two Sauces

1 tablespoon finely grated lemon zest, fresh or
   dried
1 clove garlic, minced
Salt and pepper to taste
✪ **8 slices meat reserved from Rib Roast
   of Beef with Braised Wild Mushrooms**
✪ **1 cup tomatoes reserved from
   Tomatoes Sautéed with Chipotle**

1 tablespoon olive oil
1 teaspoon red wine vinegar
1 teaspoon tomato paste
✪ **6 tablespoons dressing reserved from
   Eggless Caesar Salad**
1 tablespoon freshly grated parmesan cheese
2 tablespoons mayonnaise

Combine the lemon zest, garlic, salt, and pepper in a small bowl. Slice the reserved meat and arrange on a platter. Scatter the lemon-garlic mixture over the meat. Set aside while you make the sauces.

Finely chop the reserved tomatoes, and mix with the oil, vinegar, and tomato paste. Season with salt and pepper. Set aside. In a separate bowl, whisk the reserved Caesar salad dressing with the cheese and mayonnaise. Season with salt and pepper. Serve the roast beef with the sauces on the side.

Makes 4 servings.

Chicken and Mushroom Stew

*1 pound skinless and boneless chicken breast,
    cut into 1-inch chunks*
2 tablespoons vegetable oil
✪ **2 to 2½ cups mushrooms reserved
    from Rib Roast of Beef with Braised
    Wild Mushrooms**

*2 cups homemade chicken broth or 1 can
    (about 14 ounces) chicken broth*
✪ **1 cup reserved Roasted Potatoes with
    Capers**
½ cup canned crushed tomatoes
1 tablespoon flour

Cook the chicken in 1 tablespoon of the oil in a 3-quart saucepan until the meat loses its raw look. Add the reserved mushrooms, the chicken broth, reserved potatoes, and the tomatoes and stir to combine ingredients. Heat to a simmer and continue simmering until the chicken pieces are firm and opaque, about 5 minutes. Mix the flour with the remaining 1 tablespoon of oil and whisk into the stew. Simmer another minute until the liquid in the pan thickens lightly.

Makes 4 servings.

What nature fails to provide, meat marketers create, presenting us with new cuts of meat that allow us to cook quicker and eat leaner. One of the most versatile of their latest creations has to be Turkey London Broil. It's nothing more than a butterflied boneless turkey breast, yet it provides admirably what one would expect of a London broil.

For the meal for this Sunday, you'll work ahead by marinating a butterflied boneless turkey breast in a simple mixture of olive oil, lemon juice, and garlic for a Turkey London Broil. Turkey breast is tender enough to be grilled like London broil, and it can be sliced in any direction without concern about grain. The marinade does double duty as a marinade for Escabeche of Grilled Salmon the next night. And the grilled turkey meat makes it possible to bring Tuesday's Warm Turkey Salad on Escarole with Salsa Vinaigrette to the table in twenty minutes, even less if you use boxed croutons instead of the home-made. Wednesday's meal is a Chinese-style stir-fry of shrimp, green beans, and almonds in a ginger glaze. Thursday features an extravagant presentation of baked trout stuffed with cornbread, red bell pepper, and glazed onions—and the dish comes together almost instantly when you use Sunday's Confetti Cornbread with boned farm-raised trout.

THE SUNDAY DINNER

Lemon Turkey London Broil

Confetti Cornbread

Green Beans with Smokehouse Almonds

THE WEEKNIGHT ENTREES

Escabeche of Grilled Salmon

Warm Turkey Salad on Escarole
with Salsa Vinaigrette

Stir-fried Shrimp with Ginger
Green Beans

Trout with Cornbread-Almond Stuffing

Lemon Turkey London Broil

2 pounds skinless and boneless turkey breast,
butterflied
⅔ cup extra-virgin olive oil
2 cloves garlic, minced

Zest of 1 lemon, finely grated
Juice of 3 large lemons
Salt and pepper to taste

Place the turkey in a nonmetallic pan large enough to hold the turkey snugly but comfortably. Whisk together the olive oil, garlic, lemon zest, lemon juice, salt, and pepper in a large measuring cup. Pour half the marinade over the turkey, turning to coat it completely. Refrigerate at least 20 minutes. Reserve the remaining marinade.

Place the turkey breast on a lightly oiled rack set 4 inches from a hot fire. Grill or broil for 20 minutes, turning 3 times during the cooking. The turkey breast is done when it is just barely pink in the center of its thickest section. Cut about half the turkey into thin diagonal slices, and serve.

Makes 4 servings, plus enough to:
✪ **Reserve ⅔ cup of marinade for Escabeche of Grilled Salmon.**
✪ **Reserve about ⅔ pound turkey for Warm Turkey Salad on Escarole with Salsa Vinaigrette.**

Confetti Cornbread

1 medium onion, finely chopped
¼ cup corn oil
1 red bell pepper, stemmed, seeded, and diced
1 teaspoon ground cumin
1 tomato, cored, seeded, and diced
2 tablespoons chopped parsley
1 can (7 ounces) corn kernels, drained, or
kernels from 2 ears cooked corn

⅔ cup flour
1⅓ cups yellow cornmeal
2 tablespoons sugar
½ teaspoon salt
2 teaspoons baking powder
1 extra-large egg
1 cup milk
Vegetable oil spray

Preheat the oven to 425°F. and place a medium cast-iron skillet in it while you make the batter.

continued

Cook the onion in the corn oil in another skillet over medium heat until softened, about 2 minutes. Add the bell pepper, and cook for 1 more minute. Add the cumin and tomato and stir to heat through. Remove from the heat and stir in the parsley and corn. Sift together the flour, cornmeal, sugar, salt, and baking powder and mix into the vegetables. Add the egg and milk and mix just until thoroughly blended.

Using a heavy pot holder, remove the skillet from the oven and coat the interior with vegetable oil spray. Pour the batter into the hot pan. Bake for 30 minutes until puffed, brown, and firm in the center. Allow to cool in the pan for 5 minutes. Invert onto a plate and invert back onto a cutting board. With a serrated knife, cut and set aside a quarter of the cornbread. Cut the remainder into 8 wedges.

Makes 4 servings, plus enough to:
✪ **Reserve one-quarter of the cornbread for Trout with Cornbread-Almond Stuffing.**

Green Beans with Smokehouse Almonds

1¾ pounds green beans, ends trimmed
3 tablespoons butter

1 cup Smokehouse almonds, coarsely chopped
Pinch of cayenne

Bring a large pot of water to a boil and add the green beans. Cook the beans until barely tender and bright green, about 3 to 4 minutes. Drain beans and run under cold water to stop the cooking. Set aside.

Just before serving, heat the butter in a skillet over moderate heat. Add the almonds and cayenne and cook for 30 seconds, stirring frequently. Reserve ¼ cup. Add the green beans and heat through. Serve half.

Makes 4 servings, plus enough to:
✪ **Reserve 3 cups for Stir-fried Shrimp with Ginger Green Beans.**
✪ **Reserve ¼ cup almonds for Trout with Cornbread-Almond Stuffing.**

Escabeche of Grilled Salmon

1 pound salmon fillet
4 teaspoons olive oil
1 medium onion, halved and thinly sliced
Pinch of crushed red pepper flakes

2 cloves garlic, minced
✪ **2/3 cup marinade reserved from Lemon Turkey London Broil**
Juice of 1 orange

Cut the salmon fillet into 4 pieces. Rub the pieces with half the oil and grill or broil on a lightly oiled rack 4 inches from a hot fire until browned on both sides, about 2 minutes per side. Set aside.

Meanwhile, sauté the onion in the remaining oil in a skillet over medium heat until softened, about 2 minutes. Add the pepper flakes and garlic and cook another 30 seconds, stirring frequently. Add the reserved marinade and the orange juice. Heat to a boil, add the fish to the pan, and simmer for 2 minutes. Remove from heat and transfer the fish and cooking liquid to a deep dish. Allow to cool for at least 30 minutes or refrigerate overnight, if desired.

Makes 4 servings.

Warm Turkey Salad on Escarole
with Salsa Vinaigrette

Olive oil spray
3 cups cubed bread, any type (see Note)
1 teaspoon garlic salt
1 head escarole leaves, washed and dried
1 red bell pepper, stemmed, seeded, and diced
6 scallions, finely sliced

✪ **2/3 pound turkey reserved from Lemon Turkey London Broil**
1/3 cup olive oil
1/4 cup apple cider vinegar
2 cloves garlic, finely chopped
6 tablespoons salsa, storebought or homemade

Preheat the oven to 375°F. and spray a rimmed sheet pan with olive oil.

Scatter the bread cubes over the pan and spray again. Sprinkle the cubes evenly with the garlic salt. Bake for 15 minutes, turning every 5 minutes, or until the cubes are crisp and brown.

continued

Meanwhile, toss the escarole, bell pepper, and scallions in a large salad bowl and set aside. Thinly slice the reserved turkey on the diagonal and set aside.

Combine the olive oil and turkey breast in a saucepan. Cook for 1 minute over medium heat, stirring constantly. Add the vinegar and garlic. Bring to a boil. Remove from heat, stir in the salsa, and toss with the vegetables in the salad bowl. Scatter the croutons over the salad, and serve.

Makes 4 servings.

Note: Storebought garlic croutons may be substituted for homemade ones.

Stir-fried Shrimp with Ginger Green Beans

1 pound large shrimp, peeled and deveined
1 tablespoon cornstarch
3 tablespoons vegetable oil
○ **3 cups reserved Green Beans with Smokehouse Almonds**
1 tablespoon finely chopped gingerroot

2 cloves garlic, minced
6 scallions, white parts only
¼ cup dry sherry
2 teaspoons sugar
1 tablespoon soy sauce

Wash the shrimp well with cold water and shake off excess water. Toss the shrimp in a bowl with the cornstarch until it completely coats the shrimp. Heat a large wok over high heat for 1 minute. Add the oil and heat until smoking. Add the shrimp and stir briskly until the shrimp are firm and lightly browned. Remove with a slotted spoon and transfer to a colander to drain off excess oil.

Return wok to heat. Add the reserved green beans, the gingerroot, and garlic to the oil remaining in the wok. Stir briskly for 1 minute until heated through. Add the scallions, sherry, sugar, soy sauce, and shrimp. Toss all ingredients together quickly. Cook no more than 30 seconds. Transfer to a serving bowl and serve.

Makes 4 servings.

Trout with Cornbread-Almond Stuffing

1 small onion, finely chopped
⅛ teaspoon dried oregano
2 tablespoons corn oil
1 to 2 teaspoons hot pepper sauce
✪ **Reserved Confetti Cornbread**

✪ **Reserved almonds from Green Beans
with Smokehouse Almonds**
4 brook or rainbow trout (6 to 8 ounces each),
boned
1 lemon, cut into 8 wedges

Crumble the cornbread and set aside.

Cook the onion and oregano in 1 tablespoon of the oil in a small skillet over medium heat until onion has softened, about 2 minutes. Stir in the hot pepper sauce. Mix into the cornbread and almonds. Divide the mixture into 4 equal portions, and stuff a portion into each of the 4 trout.

Preheat the oven to 375°F. and spread half the remaining oil over a sheet pan.

Place the trout on the pan and drizzle the remaining oil over the fish. Bake for 25 minutes, or until the fish flakes to gentle pressure. Serve 1 fish per person, garnished with 2 lemon wedges.

Makes 4 servings.

Menu 17

The spirit of feasting is in the stuffing. Not only do stuffings bring instant cachet to simple preparations, they provide both entree and side dish—or, in this case, a week's worth of opulent entrees—from the labor of a single dinner.

The success of the stuffing here depends largely on the quality of the rice. Although brown rice is hardly new, mass commercialization began only in the late 1980s. If you still cannot find good-quality brown rice in your supermarket, try a health-food store; there you can usually find several kinds.

Sunday's stuffing fills the interiors of two large sea bass, which are baked and simply seasoned with a squeeze of lemon. The fish and its built-in side dish are supported by a succotash of corn, black beans, and sweet pepper and by spinach simmered with capers.

The rice and fruit stuffing from Sunday's fish becomes the bed for roasted Cornish hens glazed with a spicy orange syrup made from some of the dressing from the Chili Tomato Salad. The same tomato salad is teamed with Sunday's beans, corn, and peppers for a Seafood Chili whose subtle mix of flavors belies its five-minute preparation time. More of the tomato salad is pureed as a base for the sauce for Wednesday's Lamb Chops with Tomato Vinaigrette. Sunday's stir-fried spinach reappears in a pasta sauce for Ravioli Strung with Greens on Thursday.

THE SUNDAY DINNER

Whole Baked Sea Bass with
Fruit and Rice Stuffing

Black Beans with Corn and
Red Peppers

Stir-fried Spinach and Capers

Chili Tomato Salad

THE WEEKNIGHT ENTREES

Seafood Chili

Orange-glazed Stuffed Cornish Hens

Lamb Chops with Tomato Vinaigrette

Ravioli Strung with Greens

Whole Baked Sea Bass with Fruit and Rice Stuffing

STUFFING
6 ounces mixed dried fruit, chopped
1 cup boiling water
1 large onion, diced
1 tablespoon minced gingerroot
2 teaspoons ground coriander
1 teaspoon dried thyme leaves
2 cloves garlic, minced
3 tablespoons butter
2 cups brown rice

4¼ cups boiling chicken stock, canned or
  homemade
Salt and pepper to taste

FISH
1 tablespoon olive oil
2 whole sea bass, cleaned and scaled
  (3 to 4 pounds each)
Juice of 1 lemon

Soak the dried fruit in the boiling water until the fruit has absorbed the water and is fully rehydrated, about 30 minutes. Set aside.

Cook the onion, ginger, coriander, thyme, and garlic in the butter in a large saucepan until softened. Add the rice and toss well. Add the chicken stock, stir once, cover, and simmer gently for 40 to 45 minutes, or until all the broth has been absorbed. Season with salt and pepper. Mix in the soaked dried fruit.

Preheat the oven to 400°F.

Brush a rimmed sheet pan with half the oil and rub the remaining oil over the top of the fish. Fill the cavities of the fish with 3 cups of the stuffing. Pour the lemon juice over the fish and bake for 25 to 30 minutes, or until the thickest part of the fish flakes to gentle pressure. Fillet at the table, and serve three quarters of 1 fillet to each person.

Makes 4 servings, plus enough to:
✪ **Reserve I cup flaked fish for Seafood Chili.**
✪ **Reserve 2 cups stuffing for Orange-glazed Stuffed Cornish Hens.**

MINCING GARLIC: KNIFE VERSUS PRESS

To peel and chop garlic, break as many cloves from the head as you need. Place the cloves on a flat surface and press down on them with the heel of your hand or the flat side of a kitchen knife until you hear the skin crack. Peel it away and chop the flesh to the desired fineness. If you are planning to mince the clove, hasten the process by smashing it under the side of the knife. The clove will flatten and the peel can be pulled away easily before you start chopping.

To use a garlic press, place an unpeeled garlic clove in the chamber of the press, insert the tamper, and close the press until the garlic oozes from the holes. Scrape off any bits clinging to the press with a small knife. When you lift the tamper, the peel should come up with it. Remove it and clean the press right away by running it under a forceful stream of water. If you don't, bits of garlic will dry in the holes, and they will be difficult to remove. Garlic presses are available at all kitchenware stores.

Black Beans with Corn and Red Peppers

1 tablespoon olive oil
1 medium onion, chopped
1 large red bell pepper, stemmed, seeded, and
   diced
1 tablespoon ground cumin
Pinch of crushed red pepper flakes

Salt and pepper to taste
1 tablespoon tomato paste
2 cans (11 ounces each) corn kernels
1 can (19 ounces) black beans
2 tablespoons chopped parsley
1 teaspoon red or white wine vinegar

Heat the olive oil in a saucepan over medium heat. Add the onion and red pepper and cook until softened. Add the cumin, pepper flakes, salt, pepper, and tomato paste and cook 30 seconds, stirring constantly. Add the corn, beans, parsley, and vinegar. Heat through and adjust seasoning with salt and pepper. Serve 2 cups.

Makes 4 servings, plus enough to:
✪ **Reserve 2 cups for Seafood Chili.**

Stir-fried Spinach and Capers

1 tablespoon olive oil
2 pounds fresh spinach leaves, washed and
 shaken dry
2 cloves garlic, minced

Pinch of crushed red pepper flakes
 Salt and pepper to taste
2 tablespoons capers, drained

Heat a large wok or skillet over high heat for 1 minute. Add the oil and the spinach and stir until the spinach wilts, about 1 minute. Add the garlic, pepper flakes, salt, pepper, and capers. Stir and transfer to a serving plate. Serve about 2 cups.

Makes 4 servings, plus enough to:
✪ **Reserve 1½ cups for Ravioli Strung with Greens.**

Chili Tomato Salad

¼ cup olive oil
6 scallions, white parts only, finely sliced
1 tablespoon chili powder
1 tablespoon ground cumin
2 tablespoons ketchup

1 tablespoon red wine vinegar
Salt and pepper to taste
4 large tomatoes, cored and thickly sliced
2 tablespoons chopped parsley

Warm the oil, scallions, chili powder, and cumin in a small skillet or saucepan over low heat for 1 minute. Transfer to a serving bowl and stir in the ketchup, vinegar, salt, and pepper. Cut the tomato slices into narrow strips and toss in the dressing. Toss again with the parsley. Serve 3 cups.

Makes 4 servings, plus enough to:
✪ **Reserve 2 cups for Seafood Chili.**
✪ **Reserve 1 cup for Lamb Chops with Tomato Vinaigrette.**
✪ **Reserve 2 tablespoons chili dressing for Orange-glazed Stuffed Cornish Hens.**

Seafood Chili

- **2 cups reserved Black Beans with Corn and Red Peppers**
- **2 cups reserved Chili Tomato Salad**

1 bottle (8 ounces) clam juice

- **1 cup flaked fish reserved from Whole Baked Sea Bass with Fruit and Rice Stuffing**

Salt and pepper to taste

Combine the reserved bean mixture, reserved tomato salad, and clam juice in a saucepan over medium-high heat. Bring to a boil, add the reserved fish, and stir. Season with salt and pepper. Serve hot.

Makes 4 servings.

Orange-glazed Stuffed Cornish Hens

- **2 tablespoons chili dressing reserved from Chili Tomato Salad**

6 tablespoons orange juice
1 tablespoon honey
2 Cornish hens, split in half lengthwise with backbones removed (page 251)

Salt and pepper to taste

- **2 cups stuffing reserved from Whole Baked Sea Bass with Fruit and Rice Stuffing**

Preheat the oven to 400°F.

Combine the reserved chili dressing, orange juice, and honey and set aside. Rub the bone side of each Cornish hen half with salt and pepper. Cut a 12 by 12-inch sheet of foil into 4 squares. Place on a rimmed baking sheet, and mound ½ cup of stuffing on each piece of foil. Place half a hen over each mound and bake for 10 minutes. Baste with some of the chili-orange mixture and bake another 20 minutes, basting every 5 minutes. Serve half a hen per person.

Makes 4 servings.

Lamb Chops with Tomato Vinaigrette

Salt and pepper to taste
¼ teaspoon ground ginger
8 rib or loin lamb chops, each 1 inch thick
✪ **1 cup reserved Chili Tomato Salad**
1 tablespoon red wine vinegar

1 tablespoon extra-virgin olive oil
1 clove garlic, minced
1 tablespoon oil, preferably olive oil
2 tablespoons chopped parsley or basil
   (optional)

Combine the salt, pepper, and ginger and rub the lamb chops with the mixture. Set aside. Puree the reserved tomato salad, vinegar, olive oil, garlic, salt, and pepper in a food processor or blender. Transfer to a saucepan, heat to a simmer, and keep warm.

Heat the oil in a large skillet until it smokes. Space the lamb chops evenly around the skillet. Do not crowd. If the skillet isn't large enough, cook chops in 2 batches, using more oil if necessary. Cook the lamb chops until browned on both sides, about 3 to 4 minutes per side for medium-rare. Add the parsley to the sauce, if desired. Serve 2 chops per person, with some of the sauce.

Makes 4 servings.

Ravioli Strung with Greens

1 package (28 ounces) frozen ravioli
✪ **1½ cups reserved Stir-fried Spinach and Capers**
2 tablespoons chopped sundried tomatoes in oil

1 clove garlic, minced
Salt and pepper to taste
1 tablespoon extra-virgin olive oil
2 tablespoons freshly grated parmesan cheese

Bring a large pot of lightly salted water to a boil. Add the ravioli, and cook until tender, 10 to 12 minutes. Meanwhile, coarsely chop the reserved spinach and warm it in a small skillet or saucepan. Add the tomatoes, garlic, salt, and pepper and remove from the heat. Drain the ravioli and toss with the spinach mixture, the oil, and parmesan cheese.

Makes 4 servings.

A pot of hot water is probably the most versatile cooking tool in a kitchen. Boost it to a rolling boil, and it will cook an endless array of noodles, grains, and vegetables. Stop it at a simmer, and it becomes a vehicle for soups and stews. Coax it just beneath a bubble, and it will poach fragile fish or eggs.

Poaching is the method of choice for cooking delicate proteins, like seafood and white-meat poultry, which can easily overcook and dehydrate if heated too harshly. Because poaching temperatures are kept low and liquids never bubble vigorously, poached foods literally warm to doneness without having the exterior of the food overcook before the interior gets done.

This week's Sunday dinner takes advantage of the benefits of cooking in water. Poached salmon is served with a lowfat white wine sauce that uses yogurt as a thickener. The salmon and its sauce then play triple duty—as a simple salad sparkling with lime juice and rosemary on Monday, in a sophisticated pasta sauce teamed with capers and tomato on Wednesday, and as the base for a classic velouté served with turkey scaloppine on Thursday.

Sunday's side dishes are also major players during the week. The maltaise dressing for Sunday's asparagus derives from another French sauce, béarnaise. Maltaise is a béarnaise, but with orange instead of lemon. In this menu, the flavors of a maltaise are applied to a vinaigrette to become the seasoning for Tuesday's beef stir-fry. The stir-fry is served over a bed of rice and mushrooms made easily from Sunday's warm rice salad and is powerful with the rich flavor and meaty texture of portobello mushrooms.

THE SUNDAY DINNER

Poached Salmon with White Wine Sauce

Asparagus Maltaise

Warm Portobello Mushroom
and Rice Salad

THE WEEKNIGHT ENTREES

Salmon Salad with Lime-Rosemary Vinaigrette

Stir-fried Beef with Asparagus,
Orange, and Walnuts

Fettuccine with Salmon, Capers, and Tomato

Turkey Scaloppine with Cranberries Velouté

Poached Salmon with White Wine Sauce

4 cups white wine
2 cups water
1 medium carrot, diced
1 rib celery, diced
½ medium onion, diced
Salt and pepper to taste
2 tablespoons chopped parsley

½ lemon
2½ pounds salmon fillet
2 tablespoons butter
2 tablespoons flour
¼ cup whole-milk or lowfat yogurt, not
    nonfat yogurt

Combine the wine, water, carrot, celery, onion, salt, pepper, and parsley in a fish poacher or in a pan large enough to hold the salmon in a single layer. Squeeze the juice from the lemon half into the pan, then add the lemon half. Bring to a boil, reduce the heat, and simmer for 10 minutes. Remove the lemon half.

Add the fish to the liquid and adjust heat so that the liquid barely shivers. Poach for about 10 to 12 minutes (8 minutes per inch of thickness, measuring at the thickest part of the fillet). Remove the fish. Place half of it on a serving platter and keep in a warm low oven. Reserve the rest.

Boil the liquid in the pan over high heat until it reduces to 2½ cups. While the liquid is reducing, mash the butter with the flour. After the liquid has reduced, stir the butter-flour mixture into the boiling liquid bit by bit, stirring constantly. When all has been incorporated, simmer for 4 minutes. Strain liquid and whisk in the yogurt.

Reserve 1½ cups of the sauce. Pour the remaining sauce on top of the fish and serve a portion to each person. Break the reserved fish into large flakes.

Makes 4 servings, plus enough to:
✪ **Reserve 3 cups flaked fish for Salmon Salad with Lime-Rosemary Vinaigrette.**
✪ **Reserve 1 cup flaked fish for Fettuccine with Salmon, Capers, and Tomato.**
✪ **Reserve 1½ cups sauce for Turkey Scaloppine with Cranberries Velouté.**

Asparagus Maltaise

32 medium asparagus, trimmed of hard ends
   (about 2 pounds)
1 tablespoon walnut oil
1 tablespoon butter
Zest of 1 orange, finely chopped

½ cup coarsely chopped walnut pieces
1 clove garlic, minced
Juice of ½ orange
Salt and pepper to taste

Half fill a large skillet with lightly salted water. Bring to a boil, add the asparagus, and simmer until tender, about 4 minutes. Transfer the asparagus to a platter and keep warm. Discard water from pan and wipe it dry.

Heat the oil and butter in the skillet over medium heat until the butter melts. Add the zest, walnuts, and garlic and heat for 30 seconds. Add the orange juice. Stir to combine, season with salt and pepper, and pour over the asparagus. Serve 16 of the sauced asparagus.

Makes 4 servings, plus enough to:
✪ **Reserve 16 asparagus and half the sauce for Stir-fried Beef with Asparagus, Orange, and Walnuts.**

Warm Portobello Mushroom and Rice Salad

5 cups water
1 teaspoon salt
2½ cups long-grain white rice
2 large portobello mushrooms, wiped clean
1 small red bell pepper, stemmed, seeded, and
   diced

½ medium onion, diced
5 tablespoons olive oil
2 cloves garlic, minced
¼ cup red wine vinegar
Salt and pepper to taste
¼ cup chopped parsley

Bring the water and salt to a boil in a large heavy saucepan. Add the rice, stir, cover, and simmer 15 to 20 minutes, or until all the water is absorbed and the rice is tender. Remove from the heat and uncover. Fluff with a fork and cover pan with a towel. Replace the pot lid on top of the towel and let stand for 10 minutes.

Meanwhile, trim and discard the ends from the mushroom stems. Separate the stems from the caps and dice. Set aside.

Cook the bell pepper and onion in the olive oil in a skillet until softened, about 3 minutes. Add the mushrooms and cook 2 more minutes, stirring frequently. Add the garlic and vinegar, and season liberally with salt and pepper. Toss the contents of the skillet with 3 cups of the rice, and mix in the parsley. Serve warm.

Makes 4 servings, plus enough to:
✪ **Reserve 4½ cups cooked rice for Stir-fried Beef with Asparagus, Orange, and Walnuts.**

Salmon Salad with Lime-Rosemary Vinaigrette

3 scallions, trimmed and sliced
Zest of 1 lime, finely chopped
Juice of 1½ limes
2 teaspoons fresh rosemary leaves
¼ cup extra-virgin olive oil
Salt and pepper to taste
✪ **3 cups flaked salmon reserved from Poached Salmon with White Wine Sauce**

1 head Boston lettuce leaves, washed and dried
6 ounces watercress, stemmed, washed, and dried
½ cucumber, peeled and thinly sliced

Mix the scallions, lime zest, lime juice, rosemary, olive oil, salt, and pepper in a mixing bowl. Add the reserved salmon and toss lightly. Make a bed of Boston lettuce leaves on each of 4 plates. Scatter the watercress over the top. Place a mound of the salmon mixture on each of the plates, garnish with the cucumber slices, and serve.

Makes 4 servings.

Stir-fried Beef with Asparagus, Orange, and Walnuts

¾ *pound top round sandwich steak, fresh or
frozen, cut into thin strips*
1 *tablespoon cornstarch*
1 *teaspoon ground ginger*
1 *tablespoon soy sauce*
✪ **16 asparagus and sauce reserved from
Asparagus Maltaise**

1 *clove garlic, minced*
✪ **4½ cups rice reserved from Warm
Portobello Mushroom and Rice Salad**
1½ *tablespoons vegetable oil*
⅔ *cup orange juice*

If the steak is frozen, allow it to thaw for about 10 minutes. Toss the beef, cornstarch, ginger, and soy sauce in a large mixing bowl. Set aside. Cut the asparagus into 1-inch pieces. In a separate bowl, toss the asparagus with the orange and walnut sauce surrounding them and mix in the garlic. Set aside.

Warm the rice in a microwave oven at full power for about 4 minutes or with 3 tablespoons of water on the stove in a large heavy pot, stirring occasionally.

Place a wok over high heat until smoking. Add the oil and heat for 10 seconds. Add the beef mixture and toss vigorously, separating the pieces as much as possible. Stir-fry until the beef browns well, about 3 minutes. Add the asparagus mixture and toss until heated through, about 1 minute. Add the orange juice and bring to a boil. Serve over the rice.

Makes 4 servings.

Fettuccine with Salmon, Capers, and Tomato

12 ounces dried fettuccine
1 medium onion, finely chopped
2 tablespoons olive oil
1 clove garlic, minced
1 tablespoon coarsely chopped dill
12 plum tomatoes, cored and finely chopped
    (about 3 pounds)

1 tablespoon tomato paste
2 tablespoons capers, drained
Juice of ½ lemon
✪ 1 cup flaked poached salmon reserved
    from Poached Salmon with White Wine
    Sauce
Salt and pepper to taste

Boil the fettuccine in a large pot of lightly salted water until tender, about 10 minutes.

Meanwhile, cook the onion in the oil in a skillet over medium-high heat until softened, about 2 minutes. Add the garlic and dill and toss. Add the tomatoes and cook until they begin to release their liquid. Stir in the tomato paste, capers, and lemon juice. Boil 1 minute. Fold in the salmon.

Drain the pasta and season liberally with salt and pepper. Toss with the salmon and sauce and serve.

Makes 4 servings.

Turkey Scaloppine with Cranberries Velouté

½ cup dried cranberries
8 turkey cutlets (3 to 4 ounces each)
¼ cup flour seasoned with salt and pepper to
   taste
2 tablespoons olive oil

1 medium onion, finely chopped
1 clove garlic, minced
✪ **1½ cups sauce reserved from Poached
   Salmon with White Wine Sauce**
2 tablespoons finely chopped parsley leaves

Soak the cranberries in about 1 cup of hot water for at least 15 minutes. Drain and set aside. Dredge the turkey cutlets in the seasoned flour. Pat off excess flour. Set aside.

Heat the olive oil in a large skillet over high heat until smoking. In 2 batches, brown the turkey for about 1 minute per side. Transfer to a warm platter. Pour off all but 2 teaspoons of the oil. Add the onion to the pan and cook, stirring frequently, until softened, about 2 minutes. Add the garlic and the soaked cranberries and cook another 30 seconds. Add the reserved sauce and the parsley and bring to a boil. Adjust the seasoning and pour over the turkey.

Makes 4 servings.

London broils vary from recipe to recipe and even from steak to steak. Although originally a flank steak, London broil now almost always means a piece of top round. Where a flank fits perfectly into a single recipe, rounds are huge and, depending on where on the round a London broil is cut from, its texture and grain can differ. Marination helps to smooth out the difference and creates a uniform texture.

Sunday's London broil is marinated in brandy and pepper. The acid in the liquor helps to soften tough fibers, while its sweetness and aroma blend with cracked pepper to infuse the steak with flavor. The meat is surrounded by garlicky and lumpy "smashed" potatoes and a technicolor salad of red and yellow tomatoes.

These dishes are transposed during the week into a breathtaking stir-fry of beef and Szechuan pepper on Monday. Tuesday's fish fillets are fried in a garlicky crust made from Sunday's potatoes. The sauce and vegetables for Wednesday's gorgonzola-and-tomato grinders and Thursday's chicken stew are all ready. They've been developing flavor in their marinade since you made the tomato salad on Sunday.

THE SUNDAY DINNER

London Broil in a Crust of Brandied Pepper

Garlic Smashed Potatoes

Red and Yellow Tomato Salad

THE WEEKNIGHT ENTREES

Szechuan Scallion Beef

Spud-crusted Fish Puffs

Warm Gorgonzola and Tomato Grinders

Mediterranean Braised Chicken Legs

London Broil in a Crust of Brandied Pepper

1 tablespoon cracked black pepper
2 teaspoons brandy
2 pounds top round, prepared for London broil
(see below)

Salt to taste
2 teaspoons extra-virgin olive oil

Mix the cracked pepper and brandy. Rub both sides of the meat with salt and press the brandied pepper into 1 side of the meat. Set aside for at least 20 minutes or, preferably, overnight.

Grill the meat 4 inches from a hot fire for 8 minutes per side, starting with the side that has no pepper. Transfer meat to a cutting board, drizzle with oil, and allow to rest for 5 minutes. Thinly slice the meat against the grain. Set aside a third of the meat, about 12 slices. Serve the rest.

Makes 4 servings, plus enough to:
✪ **Reserve 12 slices for Szechuan Scallion Beef.**

THE LONDON BROIL MONSTER

London broil is a marketing term originally devised to help sell flank steak. The term referred to the fact that flank was the only tough cut of meat that could be cooked rare under a broiler and then cut against its grain into slices thin enough to tenderize it. This was possible because the meat fibers in a flank all run perfectly parallel to one another.

London broil's popularity soon outran the number of available flanks, so butchers were forced to find new sources for the Frankenstein they had created. London broil soon became the name for any cut of beef that was boneless, about 1½ inches thick, and relatively rectangular. Round steak was the most obvious alternative, and now London broil is almost always cut from the top round of beef. The meat fibers of the round, however, are not as evenly spaced as those of the flank, which makes slicing more of a problem.

Garlic Smashed Potatoes

1 head garlic
2 tablespoons plus 1 teaspoon olive oil
2½ pounds russet or Yukon Gold potatoes,
*   quartered*

Salt and pepper to taste
1 cup yogurt

Preheat the oven to 375°F.

Rub the garlic with 1 teaspoon of olive oil. Place on a small baking dish or pie pan and bake for 45 minutes. Or grill or broil 4 inches from a hot fire for 15 minutes, turning every 4 to 5 minutes. Set aside. Meanwhile, cook the potatoes in a large pot of boiling water for 30 minutes, or until fork-tender. Drain and set aside.

Cut the garlic head in half at its widest point. Squeeze each half, forcing the cloves from the skin into a large mixing bowl. Mash the garlic with a fork. Add the potatoes to the garlic and mash coarsely with a fork. Mix in the salt, pepper, remaining 2 table-spoons of olive oil, and yogurt. Reserve 1½ cups. Rewarm the remaining potatoes if necessary and serve.

Makes 4 servings, plus enough to:
✪ **Reserve 1½ cups for Spud-crusted Fish Puffs.**

Red and Yellow Tomato Salad

2 tablespoons olive oil
1 tablespoon red wine vinegar
2 cloves garlic, minced
Salt and pepper to taste
4 large ripe red tomatoes, cored and cut into
    large dice (about 2 pounds)

2 large ripe yellow tomatoes, cored and cut
    into large dice (about 1 pound)
1½ cups basil leaves, coarsely chopped

Combine the olive oil, vinegar, garlic, salt, and pepper in a large bowl. Add the tomatoes and basil and toss. Reserve 4 cups and serve the rest.

Makes 4 servings, plus enough to:
✪ **Reserve 2½ cups salad for Mediterranean Braised Chicken Legs.**
✪ **Reserve 1½ cups salad for Warm Gorgonzola and Tomato Grinders.**

Szechuan Scallion Beef

2 tablespoons oyster sauce
1 teaspoon soy sauce
½ teaspoon garlic chili paste
1 teaspoon sugar
✪ **12 slices meat reserved from London Broil in a Crust of Brandied Pepper**

1 tablespoon vegetable oil
¼ teaspoon Szechuan peppercorns
1 cup thinly sliced white mushrooms
2 cloves garlic, minced
6 scallions, cut into 2-inch strips
2 teaspoons sherry

Mix the oyster sauce, soy sauce, chili paste, and sugar in a small bowl. Set aside. Cut the reserved meat into strips. Set aside.

Heat a wok until smoking. Add the peanut oil and the Szechuan peppercorns. Stir for a few seconds, add the mushrooms, and stir-fry vigorously until they begin to soften, about 1 minute. Add the garlic and the meat strips and stir-fry for 1 minute. Add the oyster-sauce mixture and scallions and toss for 1 more minute. Remove from the heat and add the sherry. Turn onto a platter and serve.

Makes 4 servings.

Spud-crusted Fish Puffs

Oil, for frying
✪ **1½ cups reserved Garlic Smashed Potatoes**
2 eggs
3 tablespoons flour for dredging
½ teaspoon salt

Pinch of cayenne
¼ teaspoon ground black pepper
½ cup flour seasoned with salt and pepper to taste
4 catfish fillets (about 2 pounds)
1 lemon, cut into 8 wedges

Heat the oil in a deep-fat fryer to 375°F. or heat about 2 inches of oil in a large heavy saucepan to 375°F., or until a bread cube dropped into the hot oil sizzles immediately. While the oil is heating, place the reserved potatoes, the eggs, 3 tablespoons of flour, the salt, cayenne, and freshly ground black pepper in the bowl of a food processor and puree. When smooth, transfer to a bowl. Set aside.

continued

Cut the catfish fillets down their center lines and cut each half into 2 pieces. Dredge the fish pieces in the seasoned flour. Pat off excess flour. Set aside.

When the oil is at the right temperature, coat the floured fish pieces with the potato batter. Fry in 3 or 4 batches, or until the fish is puffed and golden brown, about 4 minutes per batch. Drain the fish on paper towels and keep warm until all the fish has been cooked. Serve with lemon wedges.

Makes 4 servings.

Warm Gorgonzola and Tomato Grinders

✪ **1½ cups reserved Red and Yellow Tomato Salad**
8 ounces gorgonzola cheese, crumbled

12 fresh basil leaves, coarsely chopped
4 long Italian rolls
3 tablespoons olive oil

Preheat the oven to 400°F.

Combine the tomato salad, gorgonzola, and basil leaves in a bowl. Set aside. Slit the rolls open lengthwise. Brush the interior of the rolls with the olive oil. Divide the tomato-cheese mixture among the rolls. Close the rolls and wrap each sandwich in a sheet of aluminum foil. Bake for 15 minutes.

Makes 4 servings.

Mediterranean Braised Chicken Legs

12 chicken drumsticks, skinned
Flour seasoned with salt and pepper, for
    dredging
3 tablespoons extra-virgin olive oil
1 medium onion, chopped
2 cloves garlic, minced

✪ 2½ cups reserved Red and Yellow
    Tomato Salad
¼ cup chopped pitted black olives, preferably
    oil-cured
¼ cup chopped basil leaves

Dredge the chicken in the seasoned flour. Pat off excess flour. Heat half the oil in a deep skillet until smoking. Brown half the chicken in the oil and set aside. Brown the remaining chicken in the remaining oil and set aside. Spoon off all but 1 tablespoon of the oil.

Add the onion to the oil in the pan and cook over medium heat until softened, about 2 minutes. Add the garlic, reserved tomato salad, olives, and browned chicken legs. Simmer over medium heat for 30 minutes, or until the chicken is cooked through. Add the basil, stir, and simmer for 5 more minutes.

Makes 4 servings.

Menu 20

hen you can't stand the heat, one of the best roads out of the kitchen leads to the barbecue. But a few hints are in order before you light the coals. Chicken is notorious for burning on the surface before it is done through. A barbecue cover can help contain the heat and cook the chicken more evenly. All grills have hot and cool spots, so move the chicken pieces around the grill as you turn them. Sweet barbecue sauces, such as the one in this menu, will scorch easily; a spray bottle of water will help douse flareups. (Get the chicken pieces out of the way before you spray.)

The grill is the inspiration for Sunday's chicken entree, as well as for the accompanying side dishes. The corn is grilled right in its husk, where it will steam while absorbing a smoky redolence. The squash is really a warm salad, a harmony of roasted aromas, wine vinegar, and fragrant olive oil.

Starting off with a gala cookout creates the foundation for a week's worth of menus—and no one will guess that Monday's Ziti with Grilled Vegetables sprang practically full-grown from the vegetables grilled the previous night. No one will ever know that the Corn and Black Bean Gumbo simmered for only thirty minutes because its ingredients had been prepared days ahead. The Sweet Peppered Tuna Steaks will seem a novelty, even though the inspiration was the barbecue sauce that graced dinner several nights before.

THE SUNDAY DINNER

Barbecued Chicken

Roasted Corn with Spicy Tomato Butter

Grilled Summer Squash Vinaigrette

THE WEEKNIGHT ENTREES

Ziti with Grilled Vegetables

Charred Chicken Salad

Corn and Black Bean Gumbo

Sweet Peppered Tuna Steaks

Barbecued Chicken

1½ cups cider vinegar
2¼ cups ketchup
¾ cup honey
4 teaspoons chili powder
1 bay leaf, crumbled

¼ teaspoon dried oregano
Salt and pepper to taste
2 chickens, each cut into 8 pieces
    (about 4 pounds each)

Combine the vinegar, ketchup, honey, chili powder, bay leaf, oregano, salt, and pepper in a heavy saucepan. Bring to a simmer, remove from heat, and let cool. Use about 3 cups of the sauce to marinate the chicken pieces for at least 1 hour in the refrigerator.

Remove the chicken from the sauce and grill over medium heat until firm, about 25 to 30 minutes for legs and wings, 15 to 20 minutes for breasts. Turn chicken frequently to keep it from burning, basting it with sauce after each turn. Serve half the chicken.

Makes 4 servings, plus enough to:
- **Reserve 1 cup sauce for Sweet Peppered Tuna Steaks.**
- **Reserve 4 or 5 chicken pieces, especially any pieces that may have burned, for Charred Chicken Salad.**
- **Reserve 3 or 4 chicken pieces for Corn and Black Bean Gumbo.**

Note: If you wish to serve the sauce in which the chicken was marinated, boil it first for at least 3 minutes.

Roasted Corn with Spicy Tomato Butter

5 tablespoons softened butter
2 tablespoons vegetable oil
2½ tablespoons tomato paste

1 teaspoon chili paste
½ teaspoon garlic salt
12 ears unhusked corn

Combine the butter, oil, tomato paste, chili paste, and garlic salt in a small bowl. Place ¼ cup of this mixture in a small dish to serve with the corn. Place the corn over a high fire on a grill or under a broiler and cook for 10 to 12 minutes, turning every 3 or 4 minutes. Allow to cool for 2 minutes. Remove the husks and silks. Serve 8 ears of the corn with the tomato butter.

Makes 4 servings, plus enough to:
✪ **Reserve ¼ cup Spicy Tomato Butter for Ziti with Grilled Vegetables.**
✪ **Reserve 3 tablespoons Spicy Tomato Butter for Sweet Peppered Tuna Steaks.**
✪ **Reserve 4 ears roasted corn for Corn and Black Bean Gumbo.**

Grilled Summer Squash Vinaigrette

½ cup olive oil
¼ cup red wine vinegar
3 tablespoons lemon juice
1 clove garlic, minced
Pinch of cayenne

Salt and pepper to taste
4 zucchini, stemmed and sliced lengthwise,
  into ½-inch-thick slices
4 yellow summer squash, stemmed and sliced
  lengthwise, into ½-inch-thick slices

Whisk together the oil, vinegar, lemon juice, garlic, cayenne, salt, and pepper. Marinate the zucchini and yellow squash in this dressing for 10 minutes. Grill for 2 to 4 minutes per side over a hot fire and toss with enough dressing to moisten. Serve half.

Makes 4 servings, plus enough to:
✪ **Reserve half the squash for Ziti with Grilled Vegetables.**

Ziti with Grilled Vegetables

1 pound ziti
✪ **Squash reserved from Grilled Summer Squash Vinaigrette**
1 roasted red bell pepper, jarred or homemade
1 clove garlic, minced
2 tablespoons minced onion
1 tablespoon olive oil

Salt and pepper to taste
✪ **¼ cup Spicy Tomato Butter reserved from Roasted Corn with Spicy Tomato Butter**
⅓ cup freshly grated parmesan cheese
2 tablespoons chopped basil
2 tablespoons chopped parsley

Boil the ziti in a large pot of lightly salted boiling water until tender, about 12 minutes.

While the pasta is cooking, dice the reserved squash and the roasted pepper. Sauté the garlic and onion in the olive oil until softened, about 10 seconds. Do not allow them to brown. Add the squash and bell pepper and heat through. Season liberally with salt and pepper.

When the pasta is ready, drain well and toss with the vegetables, tomato butter, cheese, basil, and parsley. Season with more salt and pepper if needed and serve.

Makes 4 servings.

Charred Chicken Salad

✪ **4 or 5 chicken pieces reserved from Barbecued Chicken**
4 strips bacon
2 red peppers, stemmed, seeded, and diced
¼ pound mushrooms, cleaned and sliced
1 small head romaine lettuce leaves, washed and dried
2 scallions, sliced

2 cloves garlic, minced
½ medium onion, minced
¼ cup cider vinegar
1 tablespoon Worcestershire sauce
½ teaspoon hot pepper sauce
2 tablespoons sugar
Salt and pepper to taste

Let the chicken come to room temperature before preparing the salad.

Cook the bacon in a large skillet over medium heat until all the fat has been rendered. Drain the bacon on paper towels, leaving the fat in the skillet. While the bacon is cooking, prepare the chicken for the salad. Leave the burnt skin on unless it's bitter tasting. Remove the bones. Cut the chicken into thin slices and place in a mixing bowl. Add the peppers and mushrooms, crumble in the bacon, and toss. Tear the romaine into bite-size pieces. Toss with the scallions in the bottom of a large salad bowl.

Add the garlic and onion to the hot bacon fat in the skillet and cook over medium heat until softened, about 10 seconds. Add the vinegar, Worcestershire, hot pepper sauce, and sugar. Bring to a boil, season with salt and pepper, and whisk to blend.

Pour three quarters of the hot dressing over the chicken mixture and toss to coat. Pour the remainder over the greens and toss. Make a well in the center of the greens, and put the chicken salad in the well. Serve immediately.

Makes 4 servings.

Corn and Black Bean Gumbo

3¾ cups water
2 cups long-grain white rice
✪ **4 ears roasted corn reserved from**
   Roasted Corn with Spicy Tomato Butter
4 slices bacon
1 medium onion, chopped
2 ribs celery, chopped
½ red bell pepper, stemmed, seeded, and
   chopped
¼ cup flour
2 cloves garlic, minced
Pinch of crushed red pepper flakes

4 cups chicken broth
Salt and pepper to taste
½ pound smoked sausage, sliced
1 package (10 ounces) frozen sliced okra
✪ **3 or 4 chicken pieces reserved from**
   Barbecued Chicken, skinned, meat
   removed from bone, and cut into bite-
   size pieces
2 cups cooked or canned black beans
6 scallions, trimmed and sliced
¼ cup chopped parsley

Bring the water to a boil, add the rice, stir, cover, lower the heat, and simmer for 15 to 20 minutes, or until all the water has been absorbed. Fluff with a fork. Remove from heat and keep warm.

While the rice is cooking, remove kernels from reserved ears of corn. Then cook the bacon in a large saucepan over medium heat for 2 minutes. Add the onion, celery, and red bell pepper and continue to cook until the vegetables have softened, about 3 minutes. Discard bacon. Add the flour and cook over medium heat, stirring constantly, until the flour turns a deep golden brown, about 5 minutes. Add the garlic and pepper flakes and cook another 30 seconds. Add half the chicken broth and stir, scraping any browned flour stuck to the bottom and sides of the pot into the liquid. Add the remaining broth and bring to a simmer. Season with salt and pepper. Add the sausage, corn, and okra, and simmer for 10 minutes, stirring occasionally. Add the chicken and beans to the gumbo and heat through.

Serve the gumbo in large bowls over the rice, garnishing the top with scallions and parsley.

Makes 4 servings.

Sweet Peppered Tuna Steaks

✪ **I cup sauce reserved from Barbecued Chicken**
Juice of 1 lemon
4 tuna steaks, each 1 inch thick
 (6 to 8 ounces each)

✪ **3 tablespoons Spicy Tomato Butter reserved from Roasted Corn with Spicy Tomato Butter**

Combine reserved barbecue sauce and lemon juice. Marinate tuna in this mixture for 20 minutes.

Grill on an oiled rack or broil 4 inches from a hot fire until browned and firm, about 4 to 5 minutes per side, basting the tuna with sauce 2 or 3 times on each side. Remove the tuna to a platter and top each piece with 2 teaspoons of the reserved tomato butter. Serve immediately.

Makes 4 servings.

Menu 21

Sauces don't always show. Even when they carry the flavor and richness of a recipe, they often do so hidden deep within the heart of a dish.

This week's Sunday meal is brimming with sauce, but most of it is invisible. It starts with a soufflé made from a white sauce that's flavored with spinach and cheddar cheese. That sauce branches in four directions, each of them becoming a weeknight meal. On Monday, it turns a boneless breast of chicken into a classic chicken stew. On Tuesday, it is mounded with hazelnuts and garlic to become a novel sauce for Coquilles Saint-Jacques. Wednesday finds the same sauce disguised as a stuffing for baked trout. And on Thursday, it gives moisture to a meat loaf laced with cheddar cheese.

Sunday's side dishes—a red pepper relish, a garlic and hazelnut baguette, and a salad with hot bacon dressing—play supporting roles during the week, too, by seasoning the sauce for Tuesday's scallops and the meat mixture for Thursday's meat loaf.

THE SUNDAY DINNER

Spinach Cheddar Soufflé
with Red Pepper Relish

Garlic and Hazelnut Baguette

Romaine and Escarole Salad
with Hot Bacon Dressing

THE WEEKNIGHT ENTREES

Blanquette of Chicken

Coquilles Saint-Jacques aux Noix

Trout Florentine

Cheesy Meat Loaf

Spinach Cheddar Soufflé with Red Pepper Relish

SOUFFLÉ
½ medium onion, finely chopped
6 tablespoons olive oil
1 cup flour
5 cups hot milk
1¾ teaspoons salt
½ teaspoon freshly ground black pepper
¼ teaspoon dry mustard
Pinch of cayenne
2 packages (10 ounces each) frozen spinach, defrosted and drained

8 eggs, separated
2 cups shredded cheddar cheese (8 ounces)
6 tablespoons finely grated parmesan cheese

RELISH
2 large roasted peppers, homemade or jarred, finely chopped
¾ cup basil leaves, finely chopped
1 large clove garlic, minced
3 tablespoons extra-virgin olive oil
Salt and pepper to taste

Cook the onion in the olive oil in a large heavy saucepan over medium heat until softened, about 2 minutes. Add the flour and stir until well blended. Cook for 1 minute, stirring constantly. Whisk in the hot milk just until smoothly blended. Stir with a wooden spoon until very thick, about 3 to 5 minutes. Season with 1 teaspoon of the salt, half the black pepper, the mustard, and cayenne. Reserve 2 cups of this white sauce.

Combine the remaining 2 cups of the sauce with the spinach, egg yolks, ½ teaspoon of the salt, and the remaining pepper. Transfer 1 cup of this spinach mixture to a bowl and reserve. Add the cheddar cheese and 4 tablespoons of the parmesan to the rest of the spinach mixture. Let cool.

Preheat oven to 400°F. Grease a 3-quart soufflé dish and dust it with the remaining 2 tablespoons of parmesan.

Beat the egg whites with the remaining ¼ teaspoon salt until they hold a shape. Stir a quarter of the beaten egg whites into the spinach-cheese mixture. Fold in the remaining whites until well mixed but still fluffy. Turn this soufflé batter into the prepared dish and bake for 15 minutes. Reduce the oven temperature to 350°F. and bake for 20 minutes.

While the soufflé is baking, make the relish by mixing the roasted peppers, basil, garlic, and olive oil. Season to taste with additional salt and pepper.

When the soufflé is finished, serve immediately, scooping out portions and serving them with 2 to 3 tablespoons of relish per person.

continued

Makes 4 servings, plus enough to:
- ✪ Reserve 1 cup white sauce for Blanquette of Chicken.
- ✪ Reserve ½ cup white sauce for Coquilles Saint-Jacques aux Noix.
- ✪ Reserve ½ cup white sauce for Cheesy Meat Loaf.
- ✪ Reserve 1 cup spinach mixture for Trout Florentine.
- ✪ Reserve ¼ cup relish for Cheesy Meat Loaf.

SOUFFLÉS: A CULINARY CON

The soufflé is one of the great culinary con jobs. It is reputedly temperamental, but in truth it is a simple, humble casserole—not an egg dish, as many think, but a sauce.

A thick, white sauce (*béchamel* in classic French terms) is the base for almost all soufflés. It needs to be very thick, like day-old gruel. If the sauce is not starchy enough, it will slip from the aerated whites as they inflate and you will end up with a crown of meringue floating on a limpid sea of sauce.

Season liberally. When a sauce inflates, the flavorings must grow as well.

Next, add egg yolks while the sauce is still hot, so the heat from the sauce starts to set up the protein in the egg yolks. Otherwise, the liquid of the yolk will thin the sauce, making the soufflé mixture too slack. Many recipes alert you to the opposite pitfall, warning that the yolks could curdle if added when the sauce is too hot. But unless the sauce is near bubbling, this won't happen.

Finally, don't overbeat the egg whites. Their sole function is to transfer air into the sauce mixture, where it can expand in the oven and push the soufflé aloft. Too much beating will make them brittle, causing them to break and release their air when you try to mix them into the sauce. Stop beating while the aerated whites are still soft and they will flow into the sauce readily. They'll combine more easily, the air will be dispersed evenly throughout the sauce, and you'll get an even rise.

Garlic and Hazelnut Baguette

½ cup hazelnuts, toasted and finely chopped
1 clove garlic, finely chopped
3 tablespoons olive oil

3 tablespoons hazelnut oil
Salt and pepper to taste
1 baguette, about 24 inches long

Preheat the oven to 350°F.

Combine the hazelnuts, garlic, olive oil, hazelnut oil, salt, and pepper. Slice the baguette ½ inch thick without cutting all the way through. Spread ¼ cup of the nut mixture over the inside surfaces. Close up the loaf and wrap it in foil. Bake for 15 minutes. Cut into 4 portions and serve.

Makes 4 servings, plus enough to:
✪ **Reserve ½ cup hazelnut mixture for Coquilles Saint-Jacques aux Noix.**

Romaine and Escarole Salad with Hot Bacon Dressing

1 small head romaine lettuce leaves, washed, dried, and broken into bite-size pieces
1 small head escarole leaves, washed, dried, and broken into bite-size pieces
⅓ cup flat-leaf parsley leaves, coarsely chopped
6 white mushrooms, stems trimmed, cleaned, and thinly sliced

6 slices bacon, chopped
1 small onion, finely chopped
2 cloves garlic, minced
½ cup cider vinegar
2 tablespoons sugar
2 tablespoons tomato paste
Salt and pepper to taste

Toss together the romaine, escarole, parsley, and mushrooms in a salad bowl. Refrigerate.

Cook the bacon in a large heavy saucepan over medium heat until crisp. Add the onion and stir until softened, about 2 minutes. Add the garlic, vinegar, sugar, and tomato paste. Stir to blend and season liberally with salt and pepper. Toss the salad with half of the hot dressing and serve.

Makes 4 servings, plus enough to:
✪ **Reserve ½ cup bacon dressing for Coquilles Saint-Jacques aux Noix.**

Blanquette of Chicken

½ cup white wine

1 cup chicken broth, canned or homemade

2 large red-skin potatoes, cut into medium dice

¾ pound skinless and boneless chicken breast, cut into chunks

¼ pound large white mushrooms, stems trimmed, cleaned, and quartered

✪ **I cup white sauce reserved from Spinach Cheddar Soufflé with Red Pepper Relish**

1 package (10 ounces) frozen peas and pearl onions

Rice or crusty black bread for serving

Heat the wine and chicken broth to a simmer in a large saucepan. Add the potatoes and cook over high heat for 5 minutes. Reduce heat to medium-low, add the chicken, and simmer until the chicken is firm and potatoes almost tender, about 10 minutes. Add the mushrooms and simmer another 4 minutes. Stir in the reserved white sauce and the peas and onions and cook, stirring constantly, until the sauce thickens slightly. Serve with rice or crusty black bread, if desired.

Makes 4 servings.

Coquilles Saint-Jacques aux Noix

1 teaspoon extra-virgin olive oil

1½ pounds sea scallops, trimmed and cut in half horizontally

✪ **½ cup hazelnut mixture reserved from Garlic and Hazelnut Baguette**

✪ **½ cup bacon dressing reserved from Romaine and Escarole Salad with Hot Bacon Dressing**

✪ **½ cup white sauce reserved from Spinach Cheddar Soufflé with Red Pepper Relish**

Pasta or rice, for serving

Heat the oil in a large nonstick skillet over medium-high heat until smoking. Add the scallops and cook until lightly browned and barely firm, about 1 minute. Add the reserved hazelnut mixture and stir for 30 more seconds. Add the reserved bacon dressing and reserved white sauce, and bring to a simmer. Serve with pasta or rice.

Makes 4 servings.

Trout Florentine

1 tablespoon olive oil
4 boned rainbow trout (6 to 8 ounces each)
Juice of ½ lemon
Salt and pepper to taste

✪ **1 cup spinach mixture reserved from Spinach Cheddar Soufflé with Red Pepper Relish**

Preheat the oven to 375°F. Brush half the olive oil over the bottom of a large rectangular baking dish.

Open the trout and season the insides with the lemon juice, salt, and pepper. Place ¼ cup of the reserved spinach mixture in each fish, and close the fish around the stuffing. Place the fish in a single layer in the prepared baking dish. Drizzle the remaining oil over the trout. Bake for 15 minutes. Or use a glass dish and microwave at full power for 4 minutes.

Makes 4 servings.

Cheesy Meat Loaf

1½ pounds ground-meat combination for
meat loaf or ¾ pound each ground turkey
and ground beef

✪ **½ cup white sauce reserved from**
Spinach Cheddar Soufflé with Red
Pepper Relish

✪ **¼ cup relish reserved from Spinach**
Cheddar Soufflé with Red Pepper Relish

1 extra-large egg, lightly beaten

½ cup fresh bread crumbs

1 cup shredded cheddar cheese (4 ounces)

Preheat the oven to 400°F.

Combine all the ingredients. On a rimmed sheet pan, form the mixture into a long loaf. Bake for 45 minutes. Transfer to a platter and serve.

Makes 4 servings.

Some fish stews are thin as soup and others are so chock-full of shellfish that there is hardly enough room in the pot for broth. One thing almost all fish stews have in common is speed. The method is usually to make a broth first and then poach the stew ingredients in it just until they are cooked through. This means that once the broth is made, the preparation of a fish stew can take less than five minutes.

This week's Sunday dinner is a classic fish stew cloaked in the mystique of French Mediterranean cuisine. Let the arguments rage over what goes into a true bouillabaisse. The best thing you can do is get the freshest, brightest fish that's available and cook it in a broth infused with the flavors of the region—fresh garlic, good olive oil, basil, fennel, citrus, and tomato.

Sunday's bouillabaisse is accompanied by warm sourdough bread slathered with dried figs and ground fennel and a simple green salad glazed in an equally simple dressing of olives, red wine vinegar, and a good-quality virgin olive oil. These elements recombine throughout the week. On Monday, the broth and pesto from the bouillabaisse are spiked with the dressing to become a multilayered broth for braising sweet Italian sausage. On Tuesday, the olive vinaigrette transforms into a Caesar dressing for a salad of romaine, poached shellfish, and croutons made from Sunday's sourdough. The bouillabaisse broth and pesto make an elaborate spur-of-the-moment pasta sauce Wednesday, and the dressing returns Thursday as olive aïoli to grace a grilled turkey cutlet.

THE SUNDAY DINNER

Bouillabaisse

Sourdough Bread Baked with
Figs and Fennel

Mixed Lettuce Salad with
Olive Vinaigrette

THE WEEKNIGHT ENTREES

Braised Mediterranean Sausage

Seafood Caesar Salad with
Fragrant Croutons

Pasta with Pesto Red Sauce

Grilled Turkey Breast with Olive Aïoli

Bouillabaisse

1 large onion, coarsely chopped
1 bulb fennel, trimmed and diced
3 tablespoons olive oil
2 teaspoons fennel seed, ground
4 cloves garlic, minced
1 bay leaf
1 cup white wine
1 teaspoon turmeric
Zest, finely grated, and juice of 1 large orange
1 can (28 ounces) tomatoes, drained and chopped
4 cups fish broth, or 1 bottle (8 ounces) clam juice and 3 cups water

Salt and pepper to taste
2 cups basil leaves
¼ cup parsley leaves
1 pound oily fish fillet, such as tuna, salmon, bluefish, mackerel, blowfish, or shark, skinned and cut into bite-size chunks
12 mussels, scrubbed
1½ pounds large shrimp, peeled and deveined
1 pound sea scallops, trimmed and cut in half horizontally

Sauté the onion and diced fennel in 2 teaspoons of the olive oil in a large soup pot until barely softened, about 2 minutes. Add the fennel seed, half the garlic, and the bay leaf and cook 30 seconds more. Add the wine and turmeric, and boil vigorously for 1 minute. Stir in the orange zest and juice, the tomatoes, fish broth, salt, and pepper. Heat until boiling, reduce the heat, and simmer for 10 minutes.

Meanwhile, combine the basil, parsley, remaining garlic, and remaining olive oil in a food processor and chop fine. Set aside.

A few minutes before serving, add the fish to the soup and simmer for 2 minutes. Add the mussels and cook 1 more minute. Add shrimp and scallops. Cover and simmer for 1 to 2 more minutes or until the mussels open and the shrimp and scallops are firm.

Serve 3 mussels, 6 shrimp, ¼ cup scallops, and ⅓ cup fish in each of 4 large soup bowls. Ladle 1½ cups of broth into each bowl and top each with 1 tablespoon of the basil paste.

Makes 4 servings, plus enough to:
- ✪ **Reserve 2 cups seafood for Seafood Caesar Salad with Fragrant Croutons.**
- ✪ **Reserve 1½ cups broth for Braised Mediterranean Sausage.**
- ✪ **Reserve 1½ cups broth for Pasta with Pesto Red Sauce.**
- ✪ **Reserve 1 tablespoon basil mixture for Braised Mediterranean Sausage.**
- ✪ **Reserve 1 tablespoon basil mixture for Pasta with Pesto Red Sauce.**

Sourdough Bread Baked with Figs and Fennel

4 dried Calimyrna figs, stems removed and
    chopped
1½ tablespoons orange juice
2 teaspoons fennel seed, ground

2 cloves garlic, minced
Pinch of crushed red pepper flakes
¼ teaspoon salt
1 large sourdough bread (about 2 pounds)

Preheat the oven to 375°F.

Process the figs, orange juice, fennel seed, garlic, pepper flakes, and salt in a blender or food processor until almost smooth. Slice the bread ½ inch thick without cutting all the way through. Spread 1 side of each slice with the fig mixture. Close up the bread and wrap in foil. Bake for 20 minutes. Serve half the bread.

Makes 4 servings, plus enough to:
✪ **Reserve ½ loaf for Seafood Caesar Salad with Fragrant Croutons.**

Mixed Lettuce Salad with Olive Vinaigrette

18 black olives, pitted and finely chopped
3 large cloves garlic, finely chopped
Large pinch of crushed red pepper flakes
½ cup extra-virgin olive oil
6 tablespoons red wine vinegar
Salt and pepper to taste
1 head green-leaf lettuce leaves, washed and dried

1 head red-leaf lettuce leaves, washed and dried
6 ounces arugula leaves, stems removed, washed and dried
½ cup parsley leaves

Combine the olives, garlic, pepper flakes, oil, vinegar, salt, and pepper. Set aside. Tear the lettuce and arugula into bite-size pieces. Toss together with the parsley in a large salad bowl. Whisk the dressing vigorously and toss the salad with ¼ cup of it. Serve immediately.

Makes 4 servings, plus enough to:
✪ **Reserve 2 tablespoons dressing for Braised Mediterranean Sausage.**
✪ **Reserve ¼ cup dressing for Seafood Caesar Salad with Fragrant Croutons.**
✪ **Reserve 6 tablespoons dressing for Grilled Turkey Breast with Olive Aïoli.**

Braised Mediterranean Sausage

1 tablespoon olive oil

1½ pounds sweet Italian sausage, in 1 piece, coiled

✪ 1½ cups broth reserved from Bouillabaisse

✪ 2 tablespoons dressing reserved from Mixed Lettuce Salad with Olive Vinaigrette

✪ 1 tablespoon basil mixture reserved from Bouillabaisse

Heat the olive oil in a large skillet over medium-high heat and brown the sausage on both sides. Add the reserved broth, reserved dressing, and reserved basil mixture and stir to combine. Cover and simmer until the sausage is cooked through, about 15 minutes, turning the sausage once halfway through the cooking. Cut the sausage into 8 pieces and serve with the sauce.

Makes 4 servings.

Seafood Caesar Salad with Fragrant Croutons

✪ ½ loaf reserved Sourdough Bread Baked with Figs and Fennel

6 tablespoons olive oil

1 egg yolk (see Note)

1 large clove garlic, finely chopped

3 anchovy fillets, finely chopped

1 teaspoon spicy brown mustard

✪ ¼ cup dressing reserved from Mixed Lettuce Salad with Olive Vinaigrette

1 large head romaine lettuce leaves, washed and dried

✪ 2 cups seafood reserved from Bouillabaisse

Preheat the oven to 375°F.

Cut the reserved bread into cubes, toss with 1 tablespoon of the olive oil in a large baking pan, and toast for 15 minutes, turning halfway through. Set aside.

Meanwhile, whisk the egg yolk, garlic, anchovies, and mustard in a large salad bowl. In a slow steady stream, whisk in the reserved dressing and 4 tablespoons of the olive oil. Break the lettuce leaves into bite-size pieces and refrigerate.

continued

Just before serving, heat the remaining tablespoon of oil in a large nonstick skillet. Add the reserved seafood and cook until steaming, no more than 1 to 2 minutes. Toss the salad and croutons with the dressing in the bowl. Pour the seafood over the top.

Makes 4 servings.

Note: If you do not want to use a raw egg yolk, you can omit it, but the dressing will not be thick.

Pasta with Pesto Red Sauce

1 pound dried pasta shells
✪ **1½ cups broth reserved from Bouillabaisse**
1½ cups tomato pasta sauce, any type

✪ **1 tablespoon basil mixture reserved from Bouillabaisse**
2 tablespoons grated parmesan cheese

Cook the pasta in a large pot of rapidly boiling salted water until done. Meanwhile, combine the reserved broth and the pasta sauce and heat until simmering. Combine the reserved basil mixture and the parmesan. When the pasta is ready, drain well and toss with the sauce and the basil mixture. Serve immediately.

Makes 4 servings.

Grilled Turkey Breast
with Olive Aïoli

○ **6 tablespoons dressing reserved from
Mixed Lettuce Salad with Olive
Vinaigrette**
*1 egg yolk or 3 tablespoons mayonnaise
(see Note)*
3 tablespoons olive oil

Salt and pepper to taste
Flour, for dredging
1 teaspoon garlic powder
¼ teaspoon rubbed dried sage
8 turkey cutlets (3 to 4 ounces each)

Beat the dressing into the egg yolk or mayonnaise in a slow, steady stream until the mixture is smooth. Beat in half the olive oil and season with salt and pepper. Set aside.

Season the flour with salt, pepper, garlic powder, and sage. Dredge the turkey cutlets in the seasoned flour and pat off excess.

Heat the remaining oil in a large skillet over high heat until smoking. In 2 batches, brown the turkey, about 2 minutes per side. Serve with a dollop of sauce.

Makes 4 servings.

Note: Use mayonnaise if you don't wish to use a raw egg yolk.

Menu 23

etting a duck that's crisp of skin, tender of flesh, and void of fat is difficult. Unlike chicken and turkey, birds that can go from raw to glorious in an oven alone, a duck needs both moist and dry heat to find perfection. I suggest steaming it in a microwave or in a steamer to rid it of fat, then roasting it traditionally to get a golden lacquered skin.

The Sunday entree is accompanied by kasha, or buckwheat, the heartiest of grains. Kasha comes in different grinds. Although this recipe calls for coarsely ground kasha, you can use any size, so long as you know that the finer the grind, the softer the cooked grain will be. The menu has two vegetable side dishes. You've probably seen the white-veined burgundy leaves of radicchio in salads, but you may not have cooked with it. This member of the endive family develops a rich aroma and subtle bitter bite when braised. If available, the bullet-shaped Treviso radicchio has a better shape for braising than the round-headed Rosa variety. For the peas and peppers, I recommend frozen peas. They offer more consistent quality than fresh peas and they're much easier to cook.

Sunday's menu explodes into a week of diverse dinners. The spice mixture from the duck doubles as a dry rub for Monday's steak. Save some of the juices and fat from the duck; they're essential in giving Tuesday's Stir-fried Szechuan Duck over Soba much of its flavor and creamy consistency. Kasha is the main attraction for Wednesday's dressed-up latkes (Yiddish for pancakes), which are studded with specks of smoked salmon and served with sautéed medallions of fresh salmon. And Sunday's vegetables make fast work of an aromatic minestrone with a vibrant cheese and endive crostini on Thursday.

THE SUNDAY DINNER

Fragrant Pepper Duck

Kasha with Browned Onions

Braised Balsamic Radicchio

Peas and Sweet Peppers

THE WEEKNIGHT ENTREES

Great Grilled Steak

Stir-fried Szechuan Duck over Soba

Salmon with Smoked Salmon
and Buckwheat Latkes

Minestrone with Grilled Endive Crostini

Fragrant Pepper Duck

3 *dried ancho chilies, stems removed*
2 *tablespoons cumin seed*
2 *teaspoons ground coriander*
½ *teaspoon ground cinnamon*
1½ *teaspoons salt*

2 *teaspoons ground black pepper*
1 *tablespoon sugar*
2 *ducks (about 4 pounds each)*
Juice of 2 limes, halves reserved

Grind the chilies and cumin to a fine powder in a spice grinder or blender or in a mortar with a pestle. Mix with the coriander, cinnamon, salt, black pepper, and sugar. Set aside.

Remove and discard the giblets and visible fat from the cavity of the ducks. Cut off any extra skin and wash the ducks well, inside and out, under cold running water. Dry thoroughly.

Reserve 2 tablespoons of the spice and mix the rest all over the outside of the ducks. Rub half the lime juice over the walls of the cavity of each duck. Place the lime halves in the cavities. Arrange the ducks, breast side down, in a large oblong glass baking dish. Microwave at full power for 10 minutes. Turn the ducks over, breast side up, pour the remaining lime juice over the top, and microwave another 5 minutes. Pour off and reserve the fat and juices. Or steam the ducks on a rimmed platter in a large steaming basket over simmering water for 30 minutes, turning the ducks after the first 15 minutes.

Preheat the oven to 375°F.

Transfer the ducks to the oven and roast for 1 hour and 15 minutes, or until the duck skin is crisp and the drumstick moves slightly when twisted. Carve 1½ of the ducks into drumstick, thigh, wing, and breast sections.

Makes 4 servings, plus enough to:
✪ **Reserve 2 tablespoons spice mixture for Great Grilled Steak.**
✪ **Reserve ½ duck for Stir-fried Szechuan Duck over Soba.**
✪ **Reserve 2 tablespoons duck fat for Stir-fried Szechuan Duck over Soba.**
✪ **Reserve ½ cup roasting juices for Stir-fried Szechuan Duck over Soba.**

Kasha with Browned Onions

3 tablespoons vegetable oil
1 large onion, quartered and thinly sliced
3 cloves garlic, minced
4 cups chicken broth, canned or homemade
1 box (13 ounces) coarse-grind kasha
   (about 2 cups)

2 eggs, lightly beaten
Salt and pepper to taste
2 tablespoons chopped parsley
2 tablespoons chopped dill

Heat the oil in a heavy saucepan over low heat. Add the onion and cook until browned, about 10 minutes. Add the garlic and stir for 30 seconds. Add the broth, stir to blend, and bring to a boil.

Meanwhile, mix the kasha thoroughly with the beaten eggs in a mixing bowl. Turn into a large dry skillet, and cook over moderate heat until the grains of kasha appear dry and separate. Add the broth and onions to the kasha. Season with salt and pepper. Stir once or twice, scatter the parsley and dill over the top, cover the pan, and simmer gently for 10 minutes. The kasha will puff and absorb all of the liquid. Fluff with a fork, adjust seasoning, and serve 5 cups.

Makes 4 servings, plus enough to:
✪ **Reserve 3 cups kasha for Salmon with Smoked Salmon and Buckwheat Latkes.**

Braised Balsamic Radicchio

4 small heads radicchio, cored and quartered
2 tablespoons olive oil
½ medium onion, finely chopped
2 cloves garlic, minced

1 cup red wine
2 tablespoons balsamic vinegar
Salt and pepper to taste
3 sprigs fresh rosemary

Preheat the oven to 375°F.

Brown the radicchio on all sides in 1 tablespoon of the oil in a skillet. Transfer to a baking dish just big enough to hold the radicchio in a single layer. Add the onion, garlic, and remaining oil to the skillet and cook for 1 to 2 minutes until the onion has softened but not browned. Add the wine and vinegar and bring to a boil. Pour over the radicchio, season with salt and pepper, and place the rosemary over the top. Bake for 40 minutes, or until the radicchio is tender. Remove rosemary and serve.

Makes 4 servings, plus enough to:
✪ **Reserve 3 pieces radicchio for Minestrone with Grilled Endive Crostini.**
✪ **Reserve ¼ cup cooking liquid for Minestone with Grilled Endive Crostini.**

Peas and Sweet Peppers

½ medium onion, chopped
1½ tablespoons extra-virgin olive oil
1 red bell pepper, stemmed, seeded, and diced
1 yellow bell pepper, stemmed, seeded, and diced

2 cloves garlic, minced
½ teaspoon dried thyme leaves
2 packages (10 ounces each) frozen peas, defrosted

Cook the onion in the oil in a skillet over medium heat until softened, about 2 minutes. Add the red and yellow peppers and cook for 2 more minutes. Add the garlic, thyme, and peas, and heat through.

Makes 4 servings, plus enough to:
✪ **Reserve 2 cups for Minestrone with Grilled Endive Crostini.**

Great Grilled Steak

✪ **2 tablespoons spice mixture reserved from Fragrant Pepper Duck**
2 large cloves garlic, minced

2 tablespoons extra-virgin olive oil
4 sirloin steaks (6 ounces each)

Combine the spice mixture, garlic, and oil. Rub into the steaks and set aside for 10 minutes. Grill the steaks 4 inches from a hot fire for 4 to 5 minutes per side for medium.

Makes 4 servings.

Stir-fried Szechuan Duck over Soba

8 ounces Japanese soba udon (buckwheat noodles)
2 tablespoons garlic chili paste
2 tablespoons low-sodium soy sauce
2 tablespoons dry sherry
1 teaspoon sugar
1 tablespoon Chinese black or balsamic vinegar
✪ **½ duck reserved from Fragrant Pepper Duck**
✪ **2 tablespoons duck fat reserved from Fragrant Pepper Duck**

1 medium onion, finely chopped
2 tablespoons minced gingerroot
1 teaspoon Szechuan peppercorns, crushed
½ red bell pepper, stemmed, seeded, and diced
1 large rib celery, peeled and diced
✪ **½ cup roasting juices reserved from Fragrant Pepper Duck**
2 cloves garlic, minced

Cook the noodles in a large pot of boiling water until tender, about 4 minutes. Drain and cool under cold running water. Set aside.

Mix the chili paste, soy sauce, sherry, sugar, and vinegar in a small bowl. Set aside. Remove the reserved duck meat from the bones and cut it into bite-size pieces. Set aside.

Melt 1 tablespoon of the reserved duck fat in a large wok or skillet over high heat. Add the onion, gingerroot, and Szechuan peppercorns and stir until the onion browns lightly, about 30 seconds in a wok, longer in a skillet. Add the bell pepper and celery and stir 20 to 30 seconds. Add the remaining duck fat and the noodles and stir-fry for 1 minute. Add the reserved roasting juices and the chili-paste mixture and toss until the liquid comes to a boil. Add the duck meat, and heat through. Stir in the garlic and serve.

Makes 4 servings.

Salmon with Smoked Salmon and Buckwheat Latkes

❂ **3 cups reserved Kasha with Browned Onions**
2 eggs
2 tablespoons flour
¼ pound smoked salmon, diced
Salt and pepper to taste

1 pound salmon fillet, skinned
2 teaspoons lemon juice
⅓ cup sour cream or crème fraîche
1 small clove garlic, minced
3 tablespoons olive oil

Combine the reserved kasha, eggs, and flour in a mixing bowl. Blend well. Stir in the smoked salmon and season with salt and pepper. Set aside.

If the salmon fillet is 1 inch thick or thicker, slice it in half horizontally. Cut salmon into 12 pieces. Season with salt and pepper. Set aside.

Mix the lemon juice, sour cream, and garlic. Set aside.

Heat 2 tablespoons of the olive oil in a large nonstick skillet until smoking. Drop twelve ¼-cup mounds of the kasha mixture into the hot fat, and flatten lightly with a spatula. Cook over moderate heat for 2 to 3 minutes per side, until well browned. Drain on paper towels and keep warm while cooking the remaining latkes.

Discard any pieces of latke remaining in the pan. Add the remaining 1 tablespoon of oil to the pan and heat until smoking. Sauté the salmon pieces until browned on both sides and barely flaking to the touch, 3 to 4 minutes.

To serve, place a piece of fish on each latke and top with a small spoonful of the sour cream mixture.

Makes 4 servings.

Minestrone
with
Grilled Endive Crostini

SOUP

1 medium onion, chopped

2 tablespoons olive oil

1 medium carrot, sliced

2 ribs celery, sliced

¼ teaspoon crumbled dried rosemary

¼ teaspoon dried oregano

1 teaspoon dried basil

¼ teaspoon rubbed dried sage

3 cloves garlic, minced

*2 plum tomatoes, fresh or canned, peeled,
    seeded, and chopped*

*3 cups chicken or vegetable broth, canned or
    homemade*

1 teaspoon red or white wine vinegar

2 teaspoons tomato paste

Salt and pepper to taste

✪ **2 cups reserved Peas and Sweet
    Peppers**

CROSTINI

✪ **3 pieces reserved Braised Balsamic
    Radicchio**

✪ **¼ cup cooking liquid reserved from
    Braised Balsamic Radicchio**

1 clove garlic, minced

Salt to taste

Pinch of cayenne

2 tablespoons extra-virgin olive oil

4 thick slices Italian bread

4 teaspoons freshly grated parmesan cheese

¼ cup freshly grated parmesan cheese

For the soup, cook the onion in the olive oil in a large soup pot over medium heat until softened, about 2 minutes. Add the carrot and celery and cook for 2 minutes. Add the rosemary, oregano, basil, sage, and garlic and cook 1 more minute, stirring constantly. Add the tomatoes, broth, vinegar, tomato paste, salt, and pepper. Bring to a boil, reduce the heat, and simmer for 5 minutes. Add the reserved peas and peppers and simmer 2 more minutes.

For the crostini, finely chop the reserved radicchio in a food processor or blender. Mix with the reserved cooking liquid, garlic, salt, cayenne, and 1 tablespoon of the olive oil. Set aside.

Spread one side of each slice of the bread with the remaining olive oil, and broil, grill, or toast in the oven until lightly browned. Spread the radicchio mixture on each piece of bread and top with 1 teaspoon parmesan cheese. Broil for 1½ minutes, or until cheese melts.

Sprinkle the soup with parmesan cheese. Serve the soup with the crostini.

Makes 4 servings.

Menu 24

The convenience of prepared Chinese ingredients is the inspiration for this week's meals. Unlike Western cooking, which often depends on hours of simmering or roasting to enhance the flavors of meats and vegetables, Chinese recipes call for ingredients to be quickly cooked, ensuring crisp textures and bright colors. Then the dish is flavored with a syrup of hoisin, oyster, or soy sauce infused with ginger, garlic, hot peppers, and sugar.

Sunday's meal starts with a traditional American dish—roast chicken—transformed by a glaze of hoisin and honey. It is served in the style of Peking duck, deboned and rolled in pancakes. The Peking Chicken is surrounded by broccoli stir-fried with toasted pine nuts and fresh ginger and a pilaf made from an ancient South American grain called quinoa. Quinoa (pronounced KEE-nwah) is available in health-food stores and many groceries. It is very high in protein and cooks similarly to rice. As it simmers, it swells and produces a tiny curly tail. Even after cooking, quinoa has a pleasant nutlike flavor and al dente snap. On Tuesday, Sunday's pancakes are turned into wrappers for vegetable blintzes, little fried packets filled with farmer cheese, stir-fried broccoli, and some of the vegetables from Sunday's Quinoa Pilaf. For Wednesday's entree the quinoa is mixed with canned clam sauce and lemon as a stuffing for baked fish. The broccoli is paired with some of the roasted chicken for an instant Chinese chicken salad on Monday. The hoisin glaze reappears on Thursday to be slathered on a ham steak and caramelized over a charcoal fire.

THE SUNDAY DINNER

Peking Chicken

Ginger Pancakes

Stir-fried Broccoli with
Garlic and Pine Nuts

Quinoa Pilaf

THE WEEKNIGHT ENTREES

Chinese Chicken Salad

Vegetable Blintzes

Whole Baked Fish with Clam
and Quinoa Stuffing

Caramel Grilled Ham Steak

Peking Chicken

CHICKEN
2 chickens (about 4 pounds each)
2 tablespoons dark sesame oil
1 cup honey
6 tablespoons hoisin sauce
1 cup boiling water

FOR SERVING
12 Ginger Pancakes (recipe follows)
⅓ cup hoisin sauce
Juice of ½ lemon

Preheat the oven to 450°F.

Remove giblet packages from the chickens and reserve for another use, such as making chicken broth. Remove visible deposits of fat from around the cavities of the chickens. Wash the chickens inside and out and pat dry. Run your fingers under the skin of the breast and legs, gently separating it from the meat underneath. Rub the sesame oil over the breast and leg meat of both chickens. Rub any remaining oil all over the outside of the chicken. Place the chicken, breast side down, on a rack set above a rimmed sheet pan or baking pan and roast for 20 minutes.

Meanwhile, combine the honey, the 6 tablespoons of hoisin sauce, and the boiling water. Reserve 1 cup. Brush a thin film of the remaining sauce over the bottoms of both chickens, and roast for another 10 minutes. Turn the chickens breast side up. Brush with more of the honey sauce. Reduce oven temperature to 375°F., and roast for another 45 minutes, basting with the honey sauce every 10 minutes until all the sauce has been used up.

While the chickens are roasting, cook the pancakes and keep them warm. Mix the ⅓ cup of hoisin sauce with the lemon juice in a small bowl and set aside.

When the chickens are done roasting, remove the skin and let the chickens rest. Place the skin on the roasting rack and return to the oven for 10 minutes to crisp. Remove the meat from one of the chickens and cut into chunks. Slice the crisped chicken skin into thin strips. Wrap the second chicken and reserve in the refrigerator.

Serve the chunks of chicken, all the skin strips, the hoisin-lemon sauce, and the 12 pancakes. To assemble, spread a teaspoon of the hoisin sauce on a pancake, put a few pieces of chicken and skin strips on top, and roll the meat up in the pancake. Eat with your hands.

Makes 4 servings, plus enough to:
✪ **Reserve 1 chicken for Chinese Chicken Salad.**
✪ **Reserve 1 cup honey sauce for Caramel Grilled Ham Steak.**

Ginger Pancakes

2 cups flour
6 extra-large eggs
2 cups milk
¼ cup vegetable oil

1½ tablespoons sugar
2 teaspoons ground ginger
12 scallions, white parts only, thinly sliced
Vegetable oil spray

Using a whisk, mix the flour and eggs until the mixture is smooth. Heat the milk until it steams and whisk it into the flour mixture. Whisk in oil, sugar, ginger, and scallions. Cover and refrigerate for at least 1 hour.

Coat an 8-inch nonstick skillet with oil spray. Place over high heat until smoking. Pour 3 to 4 tablespoons of batter into the pan, tilting the pan so that the batter runs over the bottom. Pour any excess batter back into the bowl. Cook over high heat until the batter sets, about 40 seconds. Flip and cook another 20 seconds. Transfer to a plate. Make the remaining pancakes in the same way. You will need to regrease the pan every 3 or 4 pancakes.

Makes 24 to 26 pancakes, enough to use 12 pancakes for Peking Chicken, plus enough to:
✪ **Reserve 12 pancakes for Vegetable Blintzes.**

Stir-fried Broccoli with Garlic and Pine Nuts

1½ pounds broccoli
6 cloves garlic
1 tablespoon vegetable oil
¼ cup pine nuts

½ cup water
Salt and pepper to taste
2 teaspoons finely chopped gingerroot

Trim the ends from the broccoli stalks. Peel the stems with a vegetable peeler. Thinly slice the stems all the way up to the florets. Thinly slice 5 garlic cloves and mince the sixth.

Heat the peanut oil in a wok over high heat until smoking. Add the pine nuts and stir until lightly browned, about 20 seconds. Remove with a slotted spoon and set aside. Add the broccoli and sliced garlic to the wok and stir-fry for 1 to 2 minutes, or until the color of the broccoli heightens. Add the water, toss briefly, cover the wok, and steam the broccoli for 2 to 3 minutes, or until tender. Uncover and cook over high heat until any water in the wok evaporates. Season liberally with salt and pepper and toss in the minced garlic and gingerroot. Transfer to a serving platter and scatter the pine nuts over the top. Serve half.

Makes 4 servings, plus enough to:
✪ **Reserve ½ cup for Vegetable Blintzes.**
✪ **Reserve 2 cups for Chinese Chicken Salad.**

Quinoa Pilaf

2 cups quinoa
1 medium onion, chopped
1 cup diced celery
3 medium carrots, chopped
2 tablespoons vegetable oil

6 cups finely sliced green or white cabbage
4 cups hot vegetable broth or chicken broth,
    canned or homemade
Salt and pepper to taste

Wash the quinoa in several changes of cold water. Drain well and set aside.

Sauté the onion, celery, and carrots in the oil in a heavy 4-quart saucepan over medium heat until softened. Add the cabbage and stir until slightly softened. Remove and reserve 1 cup of the vegetables. Add the quinoa to the remaining vegetables and stir to distribute evenly. Add the hot broth, salt, and pepper. Stir briefly, reduce the heat, cover, and simmer for 15 minutes, or until the quinoa has absorbed all the liquid. Fluff with a fork and serve.

Makes 4 servings, plus enough to:
✪ **Reserve 2 cups pilaf for Whole Baked Fish with Clam and Quinoa Stuffing.**
✪ **Reserve 1 cup cooked vegetables for Vegetable Blintzes.**

Chinese Chicken Salad

- ✪ 1 chicken reserved from Peking Chicken
- 5 scallions, white parts only, thinly sliced
- ½ red bell pepper, sliced
- ✪ 2 cups reserved Stir-fried Broccoli with Garlic and Pine Nuts
- 1 tablespoon honey

- 3 tablespoons rice vinegar
- 1½ tablespoons dark sesame oil
- 1½ tablespoons low-sodium soy sauce
- ¾ teaspoon hot pepper sauce
- 1½ tablespoons vegetable oil

Cut the reserved chicken meat into 1-inch chunks. You should have about 5 cups. Place in a microwavesafe dish, cover with plastic, and warm in a microwave oven at full power for 2 minutes. Or remove the chicken from the refrigerator 30 minutes before preparing the salad to let it come to room temperature.

Meanwhile, toss the scallions, bell pepper, and reserved broccoli in a large salad bowl. Mix the honey, vinegar, sesame oil, soy sauce, hot pepper sauce, and peanut oil in a small bowl. Toss the chicken and vegetables with the dressing and serve.

Makes 4 servings.

Vegetable Blintzes

- 4 ounces farmer cheese
- 1 egg
- 1 clove garlic, finely chopped
- ✪ 1 cup cooked vegetables reserved from Quinoa Pilaf

- ✪ ½ cup reserved Stir-fried Broccoli with Garlic and Pine Nuts
- ✪ 12 reserved Ginger Pancakes
- 2 tablespoons vegetable oil
- ½ cup sour cream

Combine the cheese, egg, garlic, reserved vegetables, and reserved broccoli in a medium mixing bowl. Set aside.

Place the reserved pancakes on a microwavesafe plate, cover with plastic wrap, and microwave at full power for 1 minute. Or wrap pancakes in foil and warm in a 375°F. oven for 10 minutes.

Place a pancake on a clean work surface. Place 3 tablespoons of the cheese mixture on the pancake, a little bit off-center. Tuck in 2 opposite sides, and roll up loosely so that the filling is completely covered by the pancake. Place, seam side down, on a cookie sheet or tray while you form the remaining blintzes.

Heat about 2 teaspoons of the peanut oil in a large nonstick skillet over medium heat. Place 4 blintzes, seam side down, in the pan and brown on top and bottom. Do not handle too much; the blintzes break easily. When heated through, carefully remove from pan with a spatula and keep warm while you brown the remaining blintzes. Serve with sour cream.

Makes 4 servings.

Whole Baked Fish with Clam and Quinoa Stuffing

1 can (10½ ounces) white clam sauce
✪ **2 cups reserved Quinoa Pilaf**
1 egg, lightly beaten
2 whole fish, such as black bass, red snapper, porgy, or bluefish, scaled, gills removed, boned, and well washed (1½ to 2 pounds each)

Salt and pepper to taste
1 tablespoon olive oil
Juice of 1 lemon

Preheat the oven to 375°F.

Bring the clam sauce to a boil. Combine half the clam sauce, the reserved pilaf, and the egg.

Season the fish inside and out with salt and pepper and rub the skin with the olive oil. Place the fish in a baking dish just large enough to hold them snugly. Lift the upper fillet of each fish and stuff with half the quinoa mixture. Bake for 15 minutes. Pour the remaining clam sauce over the top and bake for another 10 to 15 minutes, or until the fish flakes to gentle pressure. Transfer the fish to a serving platter. Pour the lemon juice over all. Strain the cooking juices through a fine-mesh strainer and serve on the side. To serve, remove the head and tail if still on and cut each fish into 2 pieces.

Makes 4 servings.

BONING A WHOLE FISH

Here's how to ready a whole fish for stuffing and slicing. Lay the fish on its side. Using a sharp thin knife, slit down the back of the fish from head to tail on the top side of the dorsal fin. Keeping the knife parallel to the fin with one side of the blade against the fish's center bone structure, cut the top fillet from the bones, leaving it attached at the head and the tail. Flip the fish over and repeat to separate the second fillet. Remove the center skeleton by cutting through the backbone just behind the head and just in front of the tail with a pair of shears. Lift out the bones.

Caramel Grilled Ham Steak

○ **1 cup honey sauce reserved from
   Peking Chicken**
½ teaspoon hot pepper sauce
1 teaspoon cider vinegar

1 clove garlic, minced
*4 ham steaks, each ½ inch thick
   (about 6 ounces each)*

Combine the reserved sauce, the hot pepper sauce, vinegar, and garlic. Brush the ham steaks with this marinade and grill 4 inches from a medium-hot fire, turning 2 to 3 times and basting frequently with more marinade until the ham browns lightly on both sides, about 4 minutes per side.

Makes 4 servings.

Menu 25

There are three methods of frying—sautéing, pan-frying, and deep-frying. Of the three, pan-frying is best suited to thick or slow-cooking ingredients, like chicken parts. The critical element in all frying is temperature. If it's too low, the food will absorb grease; if it's too high, the surface will scorch before the interior cooks through. When the temperature is just right, the surface of the food sears on contact, the interior gently steams, and the skin becomes brown and crisp.

For pan-frying chicken, oil is heated to 375°F. and breaded or batter-dipped chicken pieces are placed in it and browned on all sides. Then the heat is lowered to keep a constant temperature of about 350°F.—high enough to keep the chicken pieces sizzling but not so hot that they brown before the meat is cooked through.

Since there is little difference in taste or texture between chicken fried with its skin or without it and since most of the fat in chicken is attached to its skin, fried skinless chicken is featured as this week's Sunday entree. It has less than half the fat content of a chicken roasted with its skin attached.

The fried chicken is accompanied by mashed potatoes seasoned with anchovies and olive oil rather than with butter and cream. This combination might sound bizarre but reserve judgment until you taste it. It's not only lower in fat and calories than the original but the salty pungency of the anchovies works perfectly with the blandness of the potatoes. Broccoli tossed with asiago cheese, which is similar to romano, completes the menu.

During the week, the chicken gravy is transformed into the base for Monday's double mushroom soup, which combines the dark, rich flavor of dried wild mushrooms with a slew of sliced white mushrooms. Tuesday's dinner uses pieces of the fried chicken for a quick rendition of chicken Caesar salad, and Sunday's broccoli helps Wednesday's stir-fry be ready in minutes. The anchovy flavor of Sunday's potatoes is perfect for Thursday's quiche, redolent with bits of sautéed leek and fresh goat cheese.

THE SUNDAY DINNER

Fried Chicken and Gravy

Anchovy Mashed Potatoes

Broccoli with Asiago

THE WEEKNIGHT ENTREES

Mushroom Mushroom Soup

Warm Chicken Caesar Salad

Stir-fried Scallops with Broccoli
and Caramelized Hazelnuts

Potato, Leek, and Goat Cheese Quiche

Fried Chicken and Gravy

2 cups buttermilk
3 cloves garlic, minced
1 teaspoon crushed red pepper flakes
2 teaspoons dried rosemary, crumbled
2½ teaspoons rubbed dried sage
Salt and pepper to taste
16 pieces chicken parts, skin removed
    (5 to 6 pounds)

3 cups flour
¼ cup vegetable oil
2 tablespoons ground coriander
4 cups chicken broth, canned or homemade
Juice of 1 lemon
3 tablespoons chopped cilantro
Oil, for frying

Combine the buttermilk, garlic, pepper flakes, 1 teaspoon of the rosemary, 1 teaspoon of the sage, salt, and pepper in a medium mixing bowl. Toss the chicken pieces in the mixture to coat. Refrigerate for at least 1 hour.

Mix the flour with salt and pepper to taste, the remaining rosemary, and 1 teaspoon of sage. Lift the chicken from its marinade, shaking off any excess, and dredge in the seasoned flour until well coated. You might have to dredge the chicken twice to ensure a thorough coating. Set the chicken pieces on a rack placed over a sheet pan to air-dry for at least 15 minutes.

While the chicken is resting, make the gravy. In a heavy saucepan, mix the ¼ cup of oil with 5 tablespoons of the flour remaining from dredging the chicken. Cook over moderate heat for 1 minute, stirring constantly. Add the remaining ½ teaspoon sage, the coriander, and the chicken broth and simmer for 15 minutes. Add the lemon juice, 1 tablespoon of the cilantro, and salt and pepper to taste. Keep warm.

Heat ¾ inch of oil in a large skillet to 375°F., or until a bread cube dropped into the hot oil sizzles immediately. Preheat the oven to 300°F. Line a baking sheet with several layers of paper towels.

Add the drumsticks and thighs to the oil and adjust the heat so that the chicken sizzles constantly. Cook for about 15 minutes, turning every few minutes, or until the chicken is golden brown and cooked through. Transfer to the baking sheet and place in the oven. Add the breast and wing pieces to the hot oil and fry, turning every few minutes, until done, about 10 minutes. Remove to paper towels to drain.

Place 12 pieces of the chicken on a serving platter. Sprinkle the remaining cilantro over the chicken. Serve 1¾ cups of the gravy on the side.

Makes 4 servings, plus enough to:
✪ **Reserve 4 pieces fried chicken for Warm Chicken Caesar Salad.**
✪ **Reserve 1¾ cups gravy for Mushroom Mushroom Soup.**

Anchovy Mashed Potatoes

6 large russet potatoes
1 tin (2 ounces) flat anchovy fillets in olive oil
2 tablespoons extra-virgin olive oil

2 cloves garlic, minced
3 tablespoons freshly grated parmesan cheese
Salt and pepper to taste

Preheat the oven to 400°F.

Bake the potatoes for 1 hour, or until tender. While the potatoes are baking, finely chop the anchovy fillets. Set aside the anchovies and the oil from the can.

Cut the potatoes in half lengthwise and scoop out the flesh into a large bowl. Beat in the chopped anchovies, anchovy oil, olive oil, garlic, and parmesan cheese. Season with salt and pepper, keeping in mind that anchovies are quite salty. A pinch of salt will probably do. Reheat all but 2 cups in a heavy saucepan and serve.

Makes 4 servings, plus enough to:
✪ **Reserve 2 cups for Potato, Leek, and Goat Cheese Quiche.**

Broccoli with Asiago

2 pounds broccoli
½ cup grated asiago or parmesan cheese

1 small clove garlic, minced
1 teaspoon olive oil

Bring a large pot of lightly salted water to a boil. Meanwhile, trim off about 3 inches of stem from each stalk of broccoli. Peel the skin from the stems, using a small paring knife. Place the peeled stalks in the water, stem end down with the heads floating above the water's surface. Simmer for 4 minutes. Do not let the water boil. Remove with tongs or a slotted spoon.

While the broccoli is cooking, mix the cheese with the garlic. Place half the broccoli on a serving plate. Drizzle the olive oil over the top and sprinkle with the cheese mixture. Serve half.

Makes 4 servings, plus enough to:

✪ **Reserve 4 cups broccoli for Stir-fried Scallops with Broccoli and Caramelized Hazelnuts.**

THE BROCCOLI DILEMMA

Unlike most vegetables, of which we eat either root, leaf, flower, or stem, broccoli has a split personality. A stalk of broccoli is part stem and part flower bud. Leaf vegetables, such as spinach, or stem vegetables, such as celery, cook through evenly because they have the same water content, fiber density, and toughness throughout.

Because the stems of broccoli are more fibrous than the buds, they need longer, more intense cooking. So a cook who wants to keep the broccoli stalk intact faces the no-win prospect of undercooking the stem or overcooking the flower. The trick is to peel the tough skin from the stem and cook the broccoli in a pan deep enough to hold the stalks upright. That way the peeled stems are simmered under water while the flowers steam gently on the surface.

Mushroom Mushroom Soup

¼ ounce dried wild mushrooms, any type
2 cups hot water
1 pound white mushrooms, stems trimmed
and cleaned
2 teaspoons butter
1 medium onion, chopped

✪ 1¾ cups gravy reserved from Fried
Chicken and Gravy
Salt and pepper to taste
1 tablespoon chopped parsley leaves
(optional)

Soak the dried mushrooms in the hot water in a bowl until softened, about 20 minutes. Remove the mushrooms from the water and finely chop them. Strain soaking liquid through a paper towel set in a strainer or a coffee filter. Set aside both the mushrooms and the soaking liquid. Meanwhile, slice half the white mushrooms and finely chop the rest. Set both aside.

Melt the butter in a large soup pot or saucepan over medium heat and cook the onion in it until softened, stirring frequently, about 2 minutes. Add the sliced mushrooms and cook until lightly browned. Add the remaining fresh mushrooms and the chopped wild mushrooms and cook until the mushrooms release their liquid, about 4 minutes. Add the reserved gravy and soaking liquid and heat through. Season with salt and pepper and stir in the parsley, if desired.

Makes 4 servings.

Warm Chicken Caesar Salad

1 large head romaine lettuce leaves, washed
and dried
✪ 4 pieces chicken reserved from Fried
Chicken and Gravy
1 cup olive oil
3 cups bread cubes, any type
2 egg yolks (see Note)

5 flat anchovy fillets, finely chopped
2 cloves garlic, minced
Juice of 1 lemon
1 tablespoon red wine vinegar
1 teaspoon spicy brown mustard
Salt and pepper to taste

Remove the tough ribs from the lettuce leaves, and tear the leaves into bite-size pieces. Place in a large salad bowl. Set aside. Remove the chicken meat from the bones and cut into bite-size chunks. Set aside.

Heat 2 tablespoons of the oil in a large skillet over medium-high heat until hot. Add the bread cubes and toss until lightly browned, about 2 minutes. Place on top of the lettuce. Add 2 more tablespoons oil to the skillet. Add the chicken and toss gently until heated through and slightly browned, about 3 minutes. Place on the lettuce. Remove skillet from heat.

Whisk the egg yolks with the chopped anchovies, garlic, lemon juice, vinegar, and mustard in a mixing bowl.

Add the remaining oil to the skillet. Slowly pour the contents of the pan into the egg-yolk mixture, whisking constantly. The sauce will thicken. Season with salt and pepper and pour over the salad. Toss to combine. Serve immediately.

Makes 4 servings.

Note: The oil will be hot enough to cook the egg yolk.

Stir-fried Scallops with Broccoli and Caramelized Hazelnuts

4 teaspoons peanut oil
1 cup blanched hazelnuts
2 tablespoons sugar
1 pound bay scallops
2 tablespoons cornstarch
✪ **4 cups broccoli reserved from Broccoli with Asiago**

2 cloves garlic, minced
4 scallions, thinly sliced
1-inch piece of gingerroot, peeled and grated
   or finely chopped
Pinch of crushed red pepper flakes
2 tablespoons hoisin sauce
2 teaspoons dark sesame oil

Heat 2 teaspoons of the oil in a large wok until smoking. Add the hazelnuts and toss quickly until nuts are lightly browned, about 45 seconds. Add the sugar and continue stirring until the sugar melts and browns to a deep caramel color. Using heavy oven mitts or pot holders, pick up the wok and pour the nuts and the caramelized sugar onto a clean sheet pan. Be very careful; the caramel can burn you mercilessly should it come in contact with your skin. Spread out the nuts in an even layer using a spoon. Wash the excess caramel from the wok with hot water and dry the wok. Allow the nuts to cool until the caramel sets, about 10 minutes. Break into individual pieces and set aside.

While the nuts are cooling, toss the scallops and cornstarch in a mixing bowl. Set aside. Cut the broccoli into bite-size pieces. Set aside. Mix the garlic with the scallions. Set aside.

Place the wok over high heat until smoking hot, about 1 minute. Add the remaining peanut oil and the gingerroot. Toss. Add the scallops and stir-fry until they lose their raw look, about 1 to 2 minutes. Add the pepper flakes, reserved broccoli, and hoisin sauce. Heat through. Stir in the garlic and scallions. Remove from heat and stir in the sesame oil. Transfer to a platter, scatter the caramelized hazelnuts over the top, and serve.

Makes 4 servings.

Potato, Leek, and Goat Cheese Quiche

3 leeks
1 tablespoon olive oil
1 clove garlic, minced
✪ **2 cups reserved Anchovy Mashed Potatoes**

2 eggs
⅔ cup milk
5 ounces chèvre cheese
1 ready-to-bake 9-inch pie shell
2 tablespoons freshly grated parmesan cheese

Preheat the oven to 450°F.

Trim off the dark green leaves and root ends from the leeks, split the leeks lengthwise, and wash thoroughly in plenty of cold water. Chop the leeks. Heat the oil in a large skillet over medium heat and sauté the leeks until softened, about 3 minutes. Add the garlic and cook another 30 seconds. Set aside. Beat the leeks into the reserved potatoes. Beat in the eggs and milk until thoroughly incorporated. Break the goat cheese into small pieces and fold into the potatoes. Pour the mixture into the pie shell. Sprinkle the top with the parmesan.

Reduce the oven temperature to 375°F. and bake the quiche for 35 to 40 minutes, or until set and browned.

Makes 4 servings.

Menu 26

ooks are incessant matchmakers, coupling ingredients with the zeal of professional marriage-brokers. Sometimes accident does all the work, as when there's nothing in the cupboard but a bottle of hot sauce and some blue cheese dressing. Legend has it that that's exactly what happened to Teressa Bellissimo, owner of the Anchor Bar in Buffalo, New York, who, in 1964 decided to serve an excess of chicken wings in a glaze of hot sauce. Her Buffalo chicken wings, served with blue cheese dressing and a celery-stick garnish, were an instant success.

This week's menu owes its inspiration to the folks at the Anchor Bar. It starts with a rendition of the original wing recipe with bacon added to the blue cheese and a little honey to the hot-sauce mix. The celery sticks are stir-fried with carrots, and a tomato-mint salad adds a refreshing note. During the week, the wing sauce ignites a grilled burger and the blue cheese is paired with Sunday's baked potatoes in a hearty, creamy casserole. The stir-fried celery and carrots make easy work of Monday's flounder, and the sauce undergoes an ethnic transformation on Thursday to become the flavoring for stir-fried shrimp.

THE SUNDAY DINNER

Sweet Heat Chicken Wings with
Bacon–Blue Cheese Dressing

Stir-fried Celery and Carrot Sticks

Minted Tomato Salad

Baked Potatoes with Basil Butter

THE WEEKNIGHT ENTREES

Herbed Flounder en Papillote
with Julienned Vegetables

Grilled Buffalo Burgers

Crocked Blue Cheese Potatoes and Ham

Stir-fried Red Hot Shrimp

Sweet Heat Chicken Wings with Bacon–Blue Cheese Dressing

DRESSING

4 slices bacon
2 tablespoons finely chopped onion
1 large clove garlic, minced
Salt and pepper to taste
6 ounces blue cheese, crumbled
⅔ cup yogurt or sour cream
½ cup milk

WINGS

Oil, for frying
24 chicken wings, cut into sections with wing
    tips discarded (about 4 pounds)
4 tablespoons butter, melted
½ cup vegetable oil
½ cup Durkee Red Hot Sauce (see Note)
¼ cup honey

For the dressing, cook the bacon in a skillet over medium heat until barely crisp. Remove bacon, drain, crumble, and reserve.

Add the onion to the bacon fat and cook just until onion has softened, about 30 seconds. Remove from heat and transfer the onion and bacon fat to a mixing bowl. Stir in the garlic, salt, pepper, blue cheese, yogurt or sour cream, and milk. Mix until well blended and stir in the crumbled bacon. Set aside.

Heat 2 to 3 inches of oil in a fryer or deep heavy saucepan to 375°F. or until a cube of bread tossed into the oil begins to sizzle almost on contact.

Fry the wings in 2 or 3 batches without overcrowding until golden brown and cooked through, about 8 minutes per batch. Drain the wings on paper towels and keep warm while you fry the remaining wings.

While the wings are frying, combine the butter, oil, hot sauce, and honey. Stir to mix thoroughly. Just before serving, mix the sauce again, toss the cooked wings in ¾ cup of the sauce, and serve with 1 to 1¼ cups (about half) of the blue cheese dressing on the side for dipping.

Makes 4 servings, plus enough to:
✪ Reserve 1 cup bacon–blue cheese dressing for **Crocked Blue Cheese Potatoes and Ham.**
✪ Reserve ½ cup sweet hot sauce for **Stir-fried Red Hot Shrimp.**
✪ Reserve ¼ cup sweet hot sauce for **Grilled Buffalo Burgers.**

Note: For most foods, the brand of hot sauce makes no difference, but when cooking Buffalo style, only Durkee Red Hot Sauce will do.

WING DIVISION

There is an ongoing debate over whether Buffalo wings should be separated into sections, and, if so, just how many sections. Where wings are divided into 3 segments, only the 2 meatier parts are served, with the bony wing tip discarded or saved for the stockpot. This way the pieces fry quickly and evenly and are less messy to serve and eat.

To section wings (or legs, for that matter), spread the joint open as far as possible. Make a slit through the skin and meat at the inside of the joint. Pull the bones backward, away from the cut, until the joint pops. Cut through the joint and separate the pieces.

Stir-fried Celery and Carrot Sticks

1 tablespoon olive oil
1 small onion, finely chopped
1 teaspoon fennel seed
½ teaspoon celery seed
6 medium carrots, julienned

5 ribs celery, julienned
⅓ cup chicken broth, canned or homemade
2 cloves garlic, minced
Salt and pepper to taste

Heat the oil in a large skillet over medium-high heat. Add the onion and stir until softened, about 1 minute. Add the fennel seed, celery seed, carrots, and celery. Toss the vegetables to coat with oil and cook for 3 minutes, stirring occasionally. Add the broth, cover, and cook for 3 more minutes. Uncover, stir in the garlic, salt, and pepper, and boil until most of the liquid in the pan has evaporated. Serve ½ cup to each person.

Makes 4 servings, plus enough to:
✪ **Reserve 1½ cups for Herbed Flounder en Papillote with Julienned Vegetables.**

Minted Tomato Salad

⅓ cup fresh mint leaves
¼ cup olive oil
¼ cup orange juice
1 tablespoon balsamic vinegar

1 clove garlic, minced
Salt and pepper to taste
2 pounds perfectly ripe tomatoes (4 to 6)

Wash, dry, and finely chop the mint leaves. Combine the mint, olive oil, orange juice, vinegar, garlic, salt, and pepper in a glass or ceramic serving bowl. Slice the tomatoes and place in the dressing, turning the slices to coat evenly. Refrigerate for at least 1 hour.

Makes 4 servings, plus enough to:
✪ **Reserve 4 slices tomato for Grilled Buffalo Burgers.**

Baked Potatoes with Basil Butter

8 large russet or Yukon Gold potatoes
  (about 5 pounds)
1 tablespoon vegetable oil
¼ cup chopped basil leaves

1 clove garlic, minced
3 tablespoons olive oil
4 tablespoons butter, softened
Salt and pepper to taste

Preheat the oven to 400°F.

Scrub the potatoes, pat dry, and rub with a light film of vegetable oil. Bake the potatoes for 1 hour, or until tender. Cook the basil leaves and garlic in the olive oil until wilted, about 30 seconds. Mix into the butter and season liberally with salt and pepper. Serve 4 potatoes with 8 tablespoons basil butter.

Makes 4 servings, plus enough to:
✪ **Reserve 4 potatoes for Crocked Blue Cheese Potatoes and Ham.**
✪ **Reserve 3 tablespoons basil butter for Herbed Flounder en Papillote with Julienned Vegetables.**

Herbed Flounder en Papillote with Julienned Vegetables

✪ **3 tablespoons basil butter reserved from Baked Potatoes with Basil Butter**

2 large flounder fillets (about 12 ounces each), halved lengthwise

Salt and pepper to taste

✪ **1½ cups reserved Stir-fried Celery and Carrot Sticks**

Preheat the oven to 400°F.

Cut 4 large pieces (about 15 inches square) of parchment paper, fold each in half, and cut a heart shape from each piece, using the fold line as the center axis. Open the hearts and spread about 2 teaspoons of the reserved basil butter on half of each heart, leaving a border of at least 1½ inches unbuttered. Place a fish fillet half on the buttered side and season with salt and pepper. Place a quarter of the reserved carrot and celery over each piece of fish. Fold the other side of the parchment over the top and secure each package. Starting with the rounded end, fold the parchment in small, crisp creases along its open edge, making sure each fold overlaps the one before it, locking it in place. When you get to the pointed end of the heart, lock the chain of folds in place by twisting the point tightly.

Place the packages on a baking sheet and bake for 10 to 12 minutes. Slit open the parchment and serve.

Makes 4 servings.

Grilled Buffalo Burgers

1 ½ pounds ground beef
½ teaspoon garlic powder
½ teaspoon onion powder
Salt and pepper to taste
4 kaiser rolls, split

✪ **¼ cup sweet hot sauce reserved from Sweet Heat Chicken Wings with Bacon–Blue Cheese Dressing**
✪ **4 slices tomato reserved from Minted Tomato Salad**

Combine the ground beef, garlic powder, onion powder, salt, and pepper. Form into 4 burgers. Grill or broil the burgers close to a hot flame, turning once, until done as desired, 10 to 15 minutes total. Lightly toast the rolls by placing them, opened up, near the fire for a minute.

When the burgers are done, mix the reserved sauce again and dip the burgers into it. Place each burger on a roll and drizzle any remaining sauce over top. Top each burger with 1 slice of the reserved tomato.

Makes 4 servings.

Crocked Blue Cheese Potatoes and Ham

1 medium onion, chopped
2 tablespoons butter
2 tablespoons flour
1 ¾ cups milk
✪ **I cup bacon–blue cheese dressing reserved from Sweet Heat Chicken Wings with Bacon–Blue Cheese Dressing**

1 egg
Salt and pepper to taste
✪ **4 potatoes reserved from Baked Potatoes with Basil Butter**
½ pound thinly sliced ham

Preheat the oven to 400°F.

Cook the onion in the butter in a small saucepan over medium heat until softened, about 2 minutes. Add the flour and stir for 2 minutes. Add the milk and stir until smooth. Simmer for 3 to 4 minutes, remove from the heat, and stir in the reserved dressing, the egg, salt, and pepper.

Place a few spoonfuls of the sauce in the bottom of a 2-quart casserole. Slice the potatoes and spread a layer of potato slices and a layer of ham on top of the sauce. Top with more sauce and continue layering potatoes, ham, and sauce until all have been used, finishing with a layer of sauce. Bake for 25 to 30 minutes, until bubbly, and serve at once.

Makes 4 servings.

Stir-fried Red Hot Shrimp

1½ pounds large shrimp, peeled and
   deveined
2 tablespoons cornstarch
1 tablespoon soy sauce
1 teaspoon ground ginger

1 tablespoon vegetable oil
✪ ½ cup sweet hot sauce reserved from
   Sweet Heat Chicken Wings with
   Bacon–Blue Cheese Dressing

Toss the shrimp with the cornstarch, soy sauce, and ginger. Heat a large wok or skillet over high heat until smoking. Add the oil and swirl to coat the bottom of the pan. Add the shrimp in 1 or 2 batches and stir-fry until the shrimp lose their raw look and begin to firm. Add the reserved sauce and toss while the sauce heats to a simmer. Serve immediately.

Makes 4 servings.

Smoked turkey, a frequent alternative to ham, has the same problems as its pork counterpart. The most readily available products are often the least desirable. These meats, usually sold in delis, are rubbery, overly salty, and lacking in smoky aroma. They may be adequate for sandwiches, but they're always disappointing as roasts. For this week's menu, I encourage you to seek out a good-quality smoked turkey breast at a local farmer's market or through your butcher. It will probably cost you no more per pound than what you get at the deli and you'll reap the benefits all week.

On Sunday, I glaze a boneless smoked turkey breast with mustard and maple syrup. Because the meat is already cooked, it needs only to be heated through, making preparation quick and easy. This is one of the rare dinners where the side dishes take longer than the entree. Honey-spiced sweet potatoes are roasted with parsnips and carrots in the same oven as the turkey breast. Chard is simmered with rosemary and mushrooms. And small Seckel pears are poached in white wine with sugar and cranberries.

Sunday's all-American sweet potatoes turn into a tropical stew on Monday with a spicing of chili, cumin, and ginger, a chopped tomato, and a pile of shrimp. They meld into a distinctive sauce for pasta, teaming sweet potatoes, garlic, pine nuts, and parmesan cheese on Thursday. Smoked turkey seasons beans and Sunday's chard to become a bed for fried fish on Tuesday. And the pear compote makes an instant sauce for Wednesday's pork chops.

THE SUNDAY DINNER

Roasted Smoked Turkey with
Maple Mustard Glaze

Roasted Sweet Potatoes and Parsnips

Rosemary Chard and Mushrooms

Pear and Cranberry Compote

THE WEEKNIGHT ENTREES

Calypso Seafood Stew

Spicy Roughy with Smoky Greens and Beans

Fruited Pork Chops

Autumn Fettuccine

Roasted Smoked Turkey with Maple Mustard Glaze

2 pounds boneless smoked turkey breast
1 tablespoon spicy brown mustard

2 tablespoons maple syrup
1 clove garlic, minced

Preheat the oven to 350°F.

Place the turkey, skin side up, in a small roasting pan and roast for 30 minutes. Combine the mustard, maple syrup, and garlic, and brush on the surface of the turkey twice during roasting. Serve 2 slices to each person.

Makes 4 servings, plus enough to:
✪ **Reserve a quarter of the turkey for Spicy Roughy with Smoky Greens and Beans.**

Roasted Sweet Potatoes and Parsnips

2 tablespoons butter
1 medium onion, chopped
1 tablespoon ground coriander
1 teaspoon ground cardamom
Pinch of crushed red pepper flakes
1 clove garlic, minced
1 tablespoon honey

1 cup vegetable broth, canned or homemade
Salt and pepper to taste
2½ pounds orange sweet potatoes, peeled and cut into chunks
½ pound parsnips, cut into chunks
½ pound carrots, cut into chunks

Preheat the oven to 350°F.

Melt the butter in a small skillet over medium-high heat. Add the onion, and cook until softened, about 2 minutes. Add the coriander, cardamom, and pepper flakes and cook another 30 seconds. Stir in the garlic, honey, broth, salt, and pepper. Bring to a boil and pour into a large baking dish. Add the sweet potatoes, parsnips, and carrots and mix with the sauce. Bake for 1 hour and 15 minutes, or until tender, turning twice during baking. Serve ½ cup to each person.

Makes 4 servings, plus enough to:
✪ **Reserve 1½ cups for Calypso Seafood Stew.**
✪ **Reserve 1 cup for Autumn Fettuccine.**

Rosemary Chard and Mushrooms

2 pounds Swiss chard
3 tablespoons olive oil
1 small onion, finely chopped
½ pound white mushrooms, stems trimmed,
   cleaned and sliced

1 large sprig rosemary, leaves only
1 clove garlic, minced
Pinch of freshly grated nutmeg
Salt and pepper to taste

Thoroughly wash the chard. Shake off excess water but do not dry. Trim away the hard stem ends and coarsely chop the leaves and tender parts of the stems. Set aside.

Heat the oil in a large saucepan over medium heat, add the onion, and cook until soft, about 2 minutes . Add the mushrooms and cook another 2 minutes. Add the rosemary and cook another 30 seconds. Add the chard and toss well. Cover and cook until the chard wilts, about 3 minutes. Add the garlic, nutmeg, and plenty of salt and pepper. Cook another 2 minutes, uncovered.

Makes 4 servings, plus enough to:
✪ **Reserve 2 cups for Spicy Roughy with Smoky Greens and Beans.**

Pear and Cranberry Compote

12 Seckel pears, peeled, halved, and cored
Juice of 1 lemon
1 cup sugar
⅓ cup white wine

1 package (12 ounces) fresh or frozen
cranberries, rinsed and picked over
Salt to taste

Toss pear halves with lemon juice in a bowl. Set aside.

Combine ½ cup of the sugar and the wine in a large saucepan and bring to a boil. Remove from the heat and add the pears and lemon juice. Cover and return to a boil. Simmer for 2 minutes. Add the cranberries and the remaining sugar and stir. Boil for 3 minutes. Remove from the heat. Season with salt and allow to cool before serving.

Makes 4 servings, plus enough to:
✪ **Reserve 1 cup for Fruited Pork Chops.**

Calypso Seafood Stew

1 tablespoon vegetable oil
1 medium onion, chopped
1 clove garlic, minced
1 teaspoon ground ginger
Pinch of crushed red pepper flakes
1 teaspoon ground cumin
1 teaspoon chili powder

Salt and pepper to taste
1 pound large shrimp, peeled and deveined
1 large ripe tomato, cored and cubed
✪ 1½ cups reserved **Roasted Sweet Potatoes and Parsnips**
1 cup vegetable broth, canned or homemade

Heat the oil in a large saucepan over medium-high heat, add the onion, and cook until softened, about 2 minutes. Add the garlic, ginger, pepper flakes, cumin, chili powder, salt, and pepper and stir for 10 seconds. Stir in the shrimp and cook until they lose their raw look, about 1 minute. Add the tomato, reserved sweet potatoes, and the broth and heat until simmering. Simmer for 2 minutes. Adjust the seasoning and serve.

Makes 4 servings.

Spicy Roughy with Smoky Greens and Beans

¼ cup buttermilk
1 clove garlic, crushed
Salt and pepper to taste
1 teaspoon hot pepper sauce
1 teaspoon ground cumin
4 orange roughy fillets, trimmed
    (about 6 ounces each)
1 cup yellow cornmeal
Salt

Pinch of cayenne
✪ **Turkey reserved from Roasted Smoked Turkey with Maple Mustard Glaze**
¼ cup corn oil
✪ **2 cups reserved Rosemary Chard and Mushrooms**
1 cup canned black beans or black-eyed peas,
    drained and rinsed
1 orange, cut into 8 wedges (optional)

Combine the buttermilk, garlic, salt, pepper, hot pepper sauce, and cumin in a non-metallic pan large enough to hold the fish in a single layer. Place the fish in this mixture and turn to moisten. Set aside.

Toss the cornmeal with the salt and cayenne in a large pie pan. Dredge the moistened fish in the cornmeal, turning the fillets until they are well coated. Place on a rack over a sheet pan to dry for about 10 minutes.

Finely dice the reserved turkey; you should have about 1½ cups. Heat 1 tablespoon of the oil in a large skillet, add the turkey, and stir for 30 seconds. Add the reserved chard and mushrooms and the beans and cook until heated through. Transfer to a warm platter, cover, and keep warm.

Wipe out the skillet and add the remaining oil. Heat oil over medium-high heat and add the fish. Cook until browned and cooked through, about 3 to 4 minutes per side. Drain the fish on paper towels and serve on the greens. Garnish with wedges of orange, if desired.

Makes 4 servings.

Fruited Pork Chops

4 pork chops (about 6 ounces each)
Salt and pepper to taste
¼ cup flour
1½ tablespoons vegetable oil

½ cup chicken broth, canned or homemade
½ cup cranberry juice
✪ **1 cup reserved Pear and Cranberry Compote**

Season the pork chops with salt and pepper and dust lightly on both sides with the flour. Heat the oil in a large skillet over medium-high heat. Add the chops and brown on both sides, about 2 minutes per side. Add the chicken broth and cranberry juice. Heat until simmering, cover, and simmer for 5 to 6 minutes. Cut the pear halves in half. Add the pears and cranberries to the pan. Heat through. Serve chops with the sauce.

Makes 4 servings.

Autumn Fettuccine

1 pound dried fettuccine
✪ **1 cup reserved Roasted Sweet Potatoes and Parsnips**
2 tablespoons olive oil
2 cloves garlic, minced

¼ cup coarsely chopped flat-leaf parsley
Pinch of crushed red pepper flakes
Salt and pepper to taste
½ cup grated parmesan cheese
¼ cup pine nuts, toasted

Bring a large pot of salted water to a boil. Add the fettuccine and stir to separate the strands. Boil vigorously until al dente, about 10 minutes.

Meanwhile, mash the reserved sweet potatoes and parsnips with a fork. Heat the oil in a heavy saucepan. Add the sweet potatoes and parsnips, the garlic, parsley, pepper flakes, and 1½ cups of the pasta water. Stir and heat until boiling. Remove from the heat and season liberally with salt and pepper. Keep warm.

Drain the pasta and toss with the sauce and parmesan cheese. Serve on 4 dinner plates. Top each with 1 tablespoon pine nuts.

Makes 4 servings.

Whenever we think of reducing fat in a recipe, we must also think of how to preserve and boost the flavors that remain. That's when a good rub can help. Rubs are powders ground from flavorful ingredients, such as individual spices and herbs or seasoning blends. Rubs can be used as a dry marinade on steak or chicken, they can be sprinkled into a sauce or soup, or sautéed with vegetables.

Season a stew with a rub or steep one in simmering water to make a pungent broth for steaming fish or opening clams. Often the seasonings are toasted before they're ground to enrich their flavors. Toasting is usually done in a dry skillet over high heat for a minute or less, and the spices must be stirred constantly to prevent scorching, which would rob them of aroma and turn them bitter.

This Sunday's entree, swordfish steak, is marinated in an incendiary mix of chili peppers, cumin, and coriander, and served with contrasting salsas, one made from sweet red peppers, the other from avocados. The swordfish steak is tempered by a cooling balm of cole slaw unusually sweetened with orange marmalade and apples, and a sauté of corn seasoned with cumin.

Sunday's spice rub permeates the week, too, as a seasoning for grilled Cornish hens on Monday, a coating for Blackened Turkey Burgers on Wednesday, and, on Thursday, a spice blend for Crab and Corn Chowder made from Sunday's corn sautéed in its own cumin butter. The prepared swordfish and red salsa make fast work of Tuesday's fish cakes, which are sauced with the sweet and spicy dressing reserved from the cole slaw.

THE SUNDAY DINNER

Grilled Chilied Swordfish with Red Pepper and Green Avocado Salsas

Hot Sweet Cole Slaw

Cumin Corn

THE WEEKNIGHT ENTREES

Grilled Cornish Hens with Avocado Vinaigrette

Unbelievable Fish Cakes

Blackened Turkey Burgers

Crab and Corn Chowder

Grilled Chilied Swordfish with Red Pepper and Green Avocado Salsas

RUB AND SWORDFISH

*3 dried ancho chilies, stemmed and seeded
(see Note)*
*2 dried cayenne chilies, stemmed and seeded
(see Note)*
¼ cup whole cumin seed
¼ cup whole coriander seed
1 teaspoon onion powder
1 teaspoon garlic powder
1¼ teaspoons salt
1 teaspoon ground black pepper
Pinch of dried oregano
6 swordfish steaks (about 8 ounces each)
2 tablespoons olive oil

RED PEPPER SALSA

*2 medium red bell peppers, stemmed, seeded,
and chopped*
2 tomatoes, cored and chopped
½ medium onion, chopped
1 to 2 tablespoons chopped jalapeño
Salt and pepper to taste

GREEN AVOCADO SALSA

1 tomato, cored and chopped
½ small onion, chopped
1 tablespoon chopped jalapeño
Juice of 1 lime
2 cloves garlic, minced
Salt and pepper to taste
2 ripe California avocados

With your fingers, break the ancho chilies and the cayenne chilies into small bits. Combine with the cumin and coriander and toast in a dry heavy skillet over high heat until very aromatic and just beginning to color, about 30 to 60 seconds. Finely grind the mixture with a spice grinder, or in a mortar with a pestle. Strain to remove the coriander hulls. Mix the ground spices with the onion powder, garlic powder, salt, pepper, and oregano.

Rub 4 tablespoons of the spice powder into the swordfish steaks. Coat a nonmetallic pan large enough to hold the fish in a single layer with half the oil. Place the fish in the pan and drizzle with the remaining oil. Cover and refrigerate for at least 1 hour.

To make the red pepper salsa, combine the bell peppers, tomatoes, onion, jalapeño, salt, and pepper in a container. Cover and refrigerate.

To make the green avocado salsa, combine the tomato, onion, jalapeño, lime juice, garlic, salt, and pepper. Quarter the avocados and discard the pits. Peel and dice the quarters, toss gently with the other green-salsa ingredients, cover tightly, and refrigerate.

Grill on an oiled rack or broil the swordfish steaks 4 inches from a hot fire for 4 to 5 minutes per side, until firm to the touch. Serve 1 swordfish steak per person and top each steak with ¼ cup of each salsa.

Makes 4 servings, plus enough to:
- ✪ **Reserve 5 tablespoons spice mixture for Blackened Turkey Burgers.**
- ✪ **Reserve I teaspoon spice mixture for Grilled Cornish Hens with Avocado Vinaigrette.**
- ✪ **Reserve I teaspoon spice mixture for Crab and Corn Chowder.**
- ✪ **Reserve 2 swordfish steaks for Unbelievable Fish Cakes.**
- ✪ **Reserve drippings, if any, for Crab and Corn Chowder.**
- ✪ **Reserve I cup red pepper salsa for Unbelievable Fish Cakes.**
- ✪ **Reserve I cup green avocado salsa for Grilled Cornish Hens with Avocado Vinaigrette.**

Note: You can substitute ¼ cup chili powder spiked with a pinch of cayenne for the ground chilies.

Hot Sweet Cole Slaw

¼ cup sweet orange marmalade
2 tablespoons honey
½ cup mayonnaise
6 tablespoons sour cream
¼ cup ketchup
¼ cup hot pepper sauce
1 teaspoon salt
½ teaspoon ground black pepper

3 tablespoons red wine vinegar
2 large tart apples, such as Granny Smith, cored and coarsely shredded
1 medium cabbage, cored and shredded (about 2 pounds)
6 scallions, thinly sliced
2 large carrots, coarsely shredded

Combine the marmalade, honey, mayonnaise, sour cream, ketchup, hot pepper sauce, salt, and pepper. You should have about 1¾ cups of dressing. Combine ¾ cup of the dressing with the vinegar and toss with the apple, cabbage, scallions, and carrots. Refrigerate until ready to serve.

Makes 4 to 6 servings, plus enough to:
- ✪ **Reserve I cup dressing for Unbelievable Fish Cakes.**

Cumin Corn

1 tablespoon corn oil
4 teaspoons ground cumin
Pinch of cayenne

5 tablespoons lightly salted butter, softened
Salt and pepper to taste
6 large ears of corn, shucked

Warm the corn oil with the cumin and cayenne in a small skillet over medium heat for 30 seconds, stirring constantly. Let cool. Mix the spiced oil into the butter and season with salt and pepper.

Cook the corn in a large pot of boiling water for 3 to 4 minutes, or until tender. Remove and drain the corn. Serve four of the ears with 3 tablespoons of the cumin butter.

Makes 4 servings, plus enough to:
✪ **Reserve 1 tablespoon cumin butter for Unbelievable Fish Cakes.**
✪ **Reserve 1 tablespoon cumin butter for Crab and Corn Chowder.**
✪ **Reserve 4 teaspoons cumin butter for Blackened Turkey Burgers.**
✪ **Reserve 2 ears cooked corn for Crab and Corn Chowder.**

Grilled Cornish Hens with Avocado Vinaigrette

- ✪ 1 teaspoon spice mixture reserved from Grilled Chilied Swordfish with Red Pepper and Green Avocado Salsas
- 2 Cornish hens, split in half lengthwise with backbones removed (page 251)

- 2 tablespoons olive oil
- ✪ 1 cup green avocado salsa reserved from Grilled Chilied Swordfish with Red Pepper and Green Avocado Salsas
- 1 tablespoon red wine vinegar

Rub ¼ teaspoon of the spice mixture into each hen half and lightly coat each with ½ teaspoon of the olive oil. Broil or grill 4 inches from a hot fire for 10 minutes per side, checking every 5 minutes to see that they don't scorch.

While the hens are cooking, mix the remaining oil with the reserved avocado salsa and the vinegar. Serve the hens with a portion of avocado vinaigrette on the side.

Makes 4 servings.

Unbelievable Fish Cakes

- ✪ 1 cup dressing reserved from Hot Sweet Cole Slaw
- ✪ 1 cup red pepper salsa reserved from Grilled Chilied Swordfish with Red Pepper and Green Avocado Salsas
- 1 egg
- 1 tablespoon Worcestershire sauce
- ✪ 2 swordfish steaks reserved from Grilled Chilied Swordfish with Red Pepper and Green Avocado Salsas

- 2 to 3 slices bread, depending on size
- Salt and pepper to taste
- 1½ cups dried bread crumbs
- 3 tablespoons vegetable oil
- ✪ 1 tablespoon cumin butter reserved from Cumin Corn
- 1 tablespoon prepared horseradish

Combine half the reserved dressing with the reserved salsa, the egg, and Worcestershire sauce in a mixing bowl. Remove the skin from the reserved swordfish steaks and crumble the fish into the bowl. Tear the bread into small pieces and add them. Combine well and season with salt and pepper.

continued

Spread the bread crumbs on a plate. Scoop eight ½-cup portions of the fish mixture onto the plate, dredge the fish with bread crumbs, and form into patties.

Heat the oil with the reserved cumin butter in a large skillet. In 2 batches, brown the fish cakes for about 3 minutes per side. Drain on paper towels. Mix the horseradish with the remaining reserved dressing and serve as a sauce with the fish cakes.

Makes 4 servings.

Blackened Turkey Burgers

1 pound ground turkey
2 tablespoons ketchup
¼ cup bread crumbs
¼ cup water
2 teaspoons Worcestershire sauce
✪ **5 tablespoons spice mixture reserved
from Grilled Chilied Swordfish with Red
Pepper and Green Avocado Salsas**

2 teaspoons vegetable oil
✪ **4 teaspoons cumin butter reserved
from Cumin Corn**
Rolls (optional)

Using your hands, blend the ground turkey, ketchup, bread crumbs, water, and Worcestershire sauce until thoroughly mixed. Form 4 patties and dredge on both sides in the reserved spice mixture. Pat so the spices adhere to the sides of the patties, flattening them slightly.

Turn the hood fan to its highest setting. Heat a large iron skillet over high heat for 5 minutes. Add the oil (see Note). Cook the burgers over medium-high heat for 5 minutes. Flip and cook another 4 minutes. (As the burgers cook, the volatile oils in the spices will produce a strong smoke. The hood fan should draw most of it away, but small amounts of smoke can make you cough, so avoid standing too close to the stove.)

Serve each burger with a teaspoon of the reserved cumin butter. The burgers can be served on rolls, if desired.

Makes 4 servings.

Note: The pan must be very hot for the meat to blacken correctly, and it is possible that the oil may flame when it hits such a hot pan. Have a tight-fitting lid ready. If the oil should flame, cover the pan with the lid, and the flame will die immediately.

Crab and Corn Chowder

- ✪ 2 ears of corn reserved from Cumin Corn
- ✪ I tablespoon cumin butter reserved from Cumin Corn
- 1 small onion, chopped
- ✪ I teaspoon spice mixture reserved from Grilled Chilied Swordfish with Red Pepper and Green Avocado Salsas (see Note)

3 cups water
1 bay leaf
½ pound lump crabmeat, cleaned
2 tablespoons chopped parsley
Juice of 1 lemon
1 clove garlic, minced

Hold an ear of the reserved corn upright on a cutting board and slice down the ear, separating the corn from the cob. Repeat with the second ear. Break the corn apart into kernels and set aside. You should have about 2 cups of kernels.

Heat the reserved cumin butter in a large saucepan until it melts. Add the onion and cook until softened, about 2 minutes. Add the reserved corn and spice mixture, the water, and the bay leaf. Bring to a boil, reduce the heat, and simmer for 10 minutes. Add the crabmeat and parsley and heat through, about 1 minute. Add the lemon juice and garlic. Remove the bay leaf. Stir and serve.

Makes 4 servings.

Note: Two tablespoons drippings, if any, from the swordfish may be substituted for the spice mixture.

Though eggplant has been cultivated since antiquity, it has never gained much popularity in America beyond the notable exception of eggplant parmesan, which is the inspiration for a week's worth of diverse dishes, starting with a rendition that crosses elements of the original with lasagna. The casserole is formed from three distinct elements—a quick tomato sauce, a cheese-laden white sauce, and browned eggplant slices—that provide flavors that would otherwise take hours to concoct.

Sunday's eggplant casserole is accompanied by polenta, perfumed with parmesan and fresh poblano pepper, and a tossed salad of lettuces and toasted pine nuts in a simple vinaigrette dressing. The polenta becomes a spectacular filling for braised chicken breast that oozes cheese and creamy corn porridge with every bite.

The rest of the week owes its streamlining to Sunday's two sauces. The white sauce coats Monday's tortellini with parmesan, garlic, and cream. The same sauce is enriched with farmer cheese and diced browned eggplant and peppers to make the filling for Thursday's Vegetable Enchiladas. These are coated with some of the eggplant's tomato sauce, spiked for the occasion with ground chilies. A couple of nights before, the same tomato sauce was combined with oregano, black olives, and lamb to become a Greek-style lamb stew.

THE SUNDAY DINNER

Eggplant with Three Cheeses

Poblano Polenta

Green Salad with Garlic and
Pine Nut Dressing

THE WEEKNIGHT ENTREES

Tortellini with Parmesan and Garlic

Greek Lamb Stew

Chicken Breast Stuffed with Corn Porridge
and Cheddar

Vegetable Enchiladas

Eggplant with Three Cheeses

3 medium eggplants
Olive oil spray
3 red or yellow bell peppers, stemmed, seeded, and halved
⅓ cup olive oil
2 medium onions, chopped
4 cloves garlic, finely chopped
2 tablespoons flour
2 cups milk

Cayenne to taste
Salt and pepper to taste
1 can (28 ounces) crushed tomatoes
½ cup basil leaves, chopped
1 cup part skim-milk ricotta cheese
¼ cup freshly grated parmesan cheese
1 egg yolk
1 cup shredded mozzarella

Preheat the oven to 425°F.

Cut off both ends of each eggplant, and cut each eggplant across into 8 slices, each about 1 inch thick. Lightly spray 2 sheet pans with the oil. Place the eggplant slices and pepper halves on the oiled sheet pans and spray the vegetables with more oil. Bake for 25 minutes, turning halfway through the baking. Dice the peppers. You should have about 2½ cups. Set aside.

Meanwhile, heat 2 tablespoons of the olive oil in a medium saucepan over medium heat, add half the onion, and cook until softened, about 2 minutes. Add half the garlic and the flour, and cook for another minute, stirring constantly. Add the milk in 3 additions, stirring the sauce until smooth after each addition. Add some cayenne, salt and pepper and cook for another 10 minutes, stirring occasionally. You should have a little more than ⅓ cup white sauce. Set aside to cool.

Cook the remaining onion in 2 tablespoons of the remaining olive oil in another saucepan over medium heat until softened. Add 1½ cups of the diced peppers and cook for another minute, stirring frequently. Add the remaining garlic and the crushed tomatoes and simmer for 10 minutes. Stir in the basil and simmer another 2 minutes. You should have about 3½ cups tomato sauce. Set aside.

Mix the ricotta cheese with 3 tablespoons of white sauce, the parmesan cheese, egg yolk, and a bit more cayenne, salt, and pepper.

Grease a 3-quart baking dish with half the remaining olive oil. Spread ½ cup of tomato sauce over the bottom of the baking dish. Place eight of the larger eggplant slices in a single layer over the tomato sauce. Season lightly with salt and pepper to taste. Place about 3 tablespoons of the ricotta mixture on each eggplant slice. Top with eight more of the larger eggplant slices. Season with more salt and pepper, and drizzle with remaining olive oil. Spoon 2 more tablespoons of the tomato sauce over each eggplant slice, and top each with 2 tablespoons of the mozzarella. Reduce the oven temperature to 375°F. and bake for 30 minutes. Let stand for 5 minutes before serving.

Makes 4 servings, plus enough to:
- ✪ **Reserve 1 cup white sauce for Tortellini with Parmesan and Garlic.**
- ✪ **Reserve 3 tablespoons white sauce for Vegetable Enchiladas.**
- ✪ **Reserve 1 cup tomato sauce for Greek Lamb Stew.**
- ✪ **Reserve 1 cup tomato sauce for Vegetable Enchiladas.**
- ✪ **Reserve 8 slices eggplant for Vegetable Enchiladas.**
- ✪ **Reserve 1 cup diced bell pepper for Vegetable Enchiladas.**

Poblano Polenta

4 cups water
1 cup cornmeal
Salt and pepper to taste

¼ cup olive oil
1 poblano chili, stemmed, seeded, and diced
¼ cup grated parmesan cheese

Whisk together the water and cornmeal in a large heavy saucepan until the cornmeal is moistened. Stir in salt and pepper. Cook over medium heat, stirring frequently with a wooden spoon, until the mixture is very smooth and silky, about 15 minutes. To make polenta in a microwave, mix the water and cornmeal in a 2-quart soufflé dish. Microwave at full power for 7 minutes. Remove and whisk thoroughly. Mix in salt and pepper. Place a paper towel over the dish and microwave another 6 minutes.

Heat 1 tablespoon of the oil in a small skillet. Add the poblano and cook over medium heat until softened, about 2 minutes.

When the polenta is finished, mix in the poblano, remaining oil, parmesan cheese, and more salt and pepper to taste, and serve.

Makes 4 servings, plus enough to:
- ✪ **Reserve 1 cup for Chicken Breast Stuffed with Corn Porridge and Cheddar.**

Green Salad with Garlic and Pine Nut Dressing

⅓ cup pine nuts
1 large garlic clove, minced
Pinch of crushed red pepper flakes
Salt and pepper to taste
2 tablespoons red wine vinegar

3 tablespoons extra-virgin olive oil
8 cups washed mesclun or other mixed leaf
   lettuce (about 12 ounces)
¼ cup parsley leaves

Place a small skillet over high heat for 2 minutes, reduce the heat to low, add the pine nuts, and stir until they color, about 2 minutes. Or place the pine nuts in a microwavesafe pie plate or flat dish and microwave at full power for 3 minutes, stirring every minute.

Mix the garlic, pepper flakes, salt, pepper, vinegar, and olive oil in a salad bowl. Add the mesclun, parsley, and toasted pine nuts, toss, and serve.

Makes 4 servings.

Tortellini with Parmesan and Garlic

1 pound cheese tortellini
✪ **1 cup white sauce reserved from Eggplant with Three Cheeses**
1 cup half-and-half

Salt and freshly ground pepper to taste
½ cup freshly grated parmesan cheese
1 tablespoon chopped parsley

Cook the tortellini in a large pot of boiling water until tender, 8 to 10 minutes. Drain well.

Heat the white sauce and the half-and-half over medium heat until simmering. Season with salt and pepper. When the tortellini are done, toss in a serving bowl with the sauce, parmesan cheese, and parsley. Serve immediately.

Makes 4 servings.

Greek Lamb Stew

¼ cup flour
¼ teaspoon salt
¼ teaspoon ground black pepper
½ teaspoon dried oregano
½ teaspoon garlic powder
4 shoulder lamb chops, cut in half (about 3 pounds)
3 tablespoons olive oil
½ medium onion, coarsely chopped

6 large white mushrooms, stems trimmed, cleaned, and quartered
2 cloves garlic, minced
✪ **1 cup tomato sauce reserved from Eggplant with Three Cheeses**
1½ cups beef broth, canned or homemade
8 large brine-cured black olives, pitted and halved
¼ cup chopped parsley

Mix the flour, salt, black pepper, half the oregano, and the garlic powder on a plate. Dredge the lamb in the mixture and pat off any excess.

Heat the olive oil in a large skillet, brown the chops, then remove them to a plate. Add the onion, remaining oregano, and mushrooms and cook until lightly browned, about 2 minutes, stirring frequently. Add the garlic and stir. Add the reserved tomato sauce and the broth and bring to a boil. Reduce to a simmer and return the lamb to the pan along with any juices on the plate. Simmer for 20 minutes, or until the lamb is tender. Stir in the olives and parsley and serve.

Makes 4 servings.

Chicken Breast Stuffed with Corn Porridge and Cheddar

2 boneless and skinless chicken breasts, split
Salt and pepper to taste
✪ I cup reserved **Poblano Polenta**
2 ounces cheddar cheese, cut into 8 sticks
¼ cup flour

2 tablespoons cornmeal
1 tablespoon olive oil
½ cup white wine
1 cup chicken broth, canned or homemade

Remove the tenders from the chicken breasts. Remove the tendon running down the center of each tender by holding one end of the tendon and scraping up its length with a small sharp knife. Place the chicken breasts and tenders between sheets of plastic wrap and pound until uniformly ¼ inch thick. Season with salt and pepper. Spoon ¼ cup polenta down the length of each breast. Imbed 2 sticks of the cheese in the polenta on each breast half. Roll the breast around the filling, using a tender to cover any bare spots.

Mix the flour and cornmeal and season with additional salt and pepper to taste. Dredge the chicken rolls in the flour mixture, patting off any excess.

Heat the oil in a nonstick skillet. Brown the chicken rolls on all sides. Add the wine and chicken broth and simmer the chicken rolls for about 6 minutes, or until cooked through. Remove the chicken rolls to a serving plate.

Reduce the liquid in the pan over high heat until lightly thickened, about 4 minutes. Pour over the chicken and serve.

Makes 4 servings.

Vegetable Enchiladas

1 tablespoon chili powder

2 small jalapeños, stemmed, seeded, and minced

1 teaspoon ground cumin

2 cloves garlic, minced

2 teaspoons olive oil

✪ **1 cup tomato sauce reserved from Eggplant with Three Cheeses**

1 cup water

Salt to taste

4 ounces farmer cheese (½ cup)

✪ **3 tablespoons white sauce reserved from Eggplant with Three Cheeses**

✪ **8 slices eggplant reserved from Eggplant with Three Cheeses**

✪ **1 cup diced bell pepper reserved from Eggplant with Three Cheeses**

2 tablespoons minced onion

Pepper to taste

8 (6-inch) corn or flour tortillas

1 cup shredded cheddar cheese (4 ounces)

Mix the chili powder, jalapeños, cumin, garlic, and olive oil in a small skillet and cook over medium heat for 30 seconds, stirring constantly. Add the reserved tomato sauce, water, and salt. Heat to a simmer and simmer for 3 minutes. Turn into a pie plate and set aside.

Combine the farmer cheese and the reserved white sauce. Dice the reserved eggplant slices and add to the cheese mixture with the reserved bell pepper and the onion. Season to taste with salt and pepper, and stir to mix.

Preheat the oven to 375°F.

Place the tortillas on a microwavesafe plate, cover loosely with plastic wrap, and microwave at full power for 1 minute. Or wrap the tortillas in foil and warm in the preheated oven for 5 minutes.

Dip the tortillas in the chili-tomato sauce to coat both sides with a thin film of sauce. Place 2 to 3 tablespoons of the cheese mixture in the middle of each tortilla, roll, and place tortillas, seam side down, in an oblong baking dish large enough to hold them. Spread the remaining tomato sauce over the top and sprinkle with cheddar cheese. Bake for 30 minutes.

Makes 4 servings.

ommercially prepared salsa is convenient—and it has its place when it's sparking another sauce or layering up a spur-of-the-moment taco—but fresh salsa is easy to make and far better than its processed counterpart. As proof, I offer a meal infused with salsa.

Sunday starts with shrimp that is poached in herb tea and given flavor impact and color with three contrasting salsas—one made of tomato and ginger, another of corn and bell peppers, and a third that's a mixture of fresh fennel, orange, and avocado.

The shrimp is poached in hibiscus tea along with aromatic vegetables. Hibiscus, a component of many herbal teas, adds a subtle floral fragrance and seems to elevate other flavors around it. The shrimp is served with a casserole of scalloped potatoes pungent with specks of anchovy and layers of fresh chèvre cheese, and an assertive salad of arugula leaves tossed with onion, pecans, and a balsamic vinaigrette.

The arugula, sauced with some of its own dressing, becomes a bed for grilled turkey on Monday. And on Tuesday, the poaching liquid from Sunday's shrimp doubles as a broth for Shrimp and Potato Bisque, utilizing the cheesy potatoes to lend a creamy richness and full flavor. On Wednesday, the potatoes become crisp aromatic pancakes, served beneath braised garlic lamb chops, and on Thursday, two of Sunday's salsas are transformed into a full-bodied chili that takes barely 10 minutes to travel from refrigerator to table.

THE SUNDAY DINNER

Tea-poached Prawns with Three Salsas

Scalloped Potatoes with Chèvre and Anchovy

Arugula Salad with Red Onion and Pecans

THE WEEKNIGHT ENTREES

Turkey Scaloppine with Bitter Greens in Balsamic Glaze

Shrimp and Potato Bisque

Garlic Lamb Chops on Pommes Galettes

Garden Black Bean Chili

Tea-poached Prawns with Three Salsas

FENNEL-ORANGE SALSA

1 bulb fennel, trimmed of base and stalks
1 tablespoon chopped shallot
1 navel orange, peeled and cut into ½-inch
   pieces
Pinch of crushed red pepper flakes
1 tablespoon chopped basil leaves
Pinch of sugar
Salt and pepper to taste
2 teaspoons lemon juice
1 ripe California avocado, skinned, pitted,
   and diced

TOMATO-GINGER SALSA

2 large tomatoes, cored and finely chopped
2 tablespoons finely chopped gingerroot
½ small onion, finely chopped
1 clove garlic, minced
1 tablespoon finely chopped jalapeño

CORN SALSA

2 cooked ears of corn, kernels removed, or
   3 cups canned corn kernels
½ red bell pepper, stemmed, seeded, and
   diced
1 tablespoon chopped cilantro leaves
1 teaspoon finely chopped jalapeño
Salt and pepper to taste
1 teaspoon ground cumin

SHRIMP

40 to 44 medium shrimp (1½ pounds)
4 cups water
2 hibiscus or hibiscus blend tea bags
   (see Note)
¼ medium onion, chopped
1 rib celery, chopped
Juice of 1 lemon

For the fennel-orange salsa, finely dice the fennel and combine with the remaining ingredients for that salsa. Cover and refrigerate.

For the tomato-ginger salsa, combine all ingredients for that salsa. Cover and refrigerate.

For the corn salsa, combine all ingredients for that salsa. Cover and refrigerate.

Peel and devein the shrimp, reserving the shells. Wash the shells, place in a plastic bag, and refrigerate.

Meanwhile, bring the water to a boil in a medium saucepan. Add the tea bags, onion, and celery. Simmer for 5 minutes. Remove the tea bags and add the lemon juice. Bring the liquid in the pan to a boil. Add the shrimp, stir, and cover. Remove from heat and set aside for 2 minutes.

Using a slotted spoon, remove the shrimp from the poaching liquid. Mound 8 shrimp on each dinner plate and surround them with ¼ cup of each of the salsas.

Makes 4 servings, plus enough to:
- ✪ **Reserve 1 cup tomato-ginger salsa for Garden Black Bean Chili.**
- ✪ **Reserve 2 cups corn salsa for Garden Black Bean Chili.**
- ✪ **Reserve shrimp shells for Shrimp and Potato Bisque.**
- ✪ **Reserve 2 cups shrimp poaching liquid for Shrimp and Potato Bisque.**
- ✪ **Reserve 8 to 12 shrimp for Shrimp and Potato Bisque.**

Note: Hibiscus and hibiscus-blend tea bags are available wherever you would find a good selection of herbal teas.

Scalloped Potatoes with Chèvre and Anchovy

1 can (2 ounces) flat anchovies in olive oil
3 cloves garlic, minced
4 pounds potatoes, peeled, halved, and very thinly sliced
1 medium onion, halved and thinly sliced

8 ounces fresh chèvre or feta cheese
¼ cup flat-leaf parsley leaves
1½ cups light cream
Salt and pepper to taste

Preheat the oven to 375°F.

Finely chop the anchovies. Glaze the bottom of a 3-quart baking dish with 1 tablespoon of the anchovy oil and set aside the rest, about 1 tablespoon. Combine the garlic and the chopped anchovies and set aside.

Layer a quarter of the potato slices in the bottom of the baking dish. Scatter a third of the onion and a third of the anchovy mixture on top. Crumble a third of the cheese and a third of the parsley over all. Pour ⅓ cup of the light cream over everything. Continue layering the potatoes, onions, anchovy mixture, cheese, and cream in that order, ending with a layer of potatoes. Pour the remaining cream (about ½ cup) over the top. Drizzle with the remaining anchovy oil.

Bake, uncovered, for 50 minutes, or until potatoes are tender. Serve each person about 1 cup.

Makes 4 servings, plus enough to:
- ✪ **Reserve 3 cups for Shrimp and Potato Bisque.**
- ✪ **Reserve 3 cups for Garlic Lamb Chops on Pommes Galettes.**

Arugula Salad with Red Onion and Pecans

½ cup pecans
6 tablespoons extra-virgin olive oil
¼ cup balsamic vinegar
2 tablespoons red wine vinegar
1 tablespoon minced garlic

Salt and pepper to taste
1 pound arugula, stems removed, washed and
  dried
1 small red onion, thinly sliced

Toast the pecans in a small skillet over medium heat, stirring constantly until lightly browned and very aromatic, about 3 minutes. Or toast them in a flat microwavesafe dish in a microwave oven on full power for 2 minutes. Set aside.

Combine the olive oil, balsamic vinegar, red wine vinegar, garlic, salt, and pepper. Set aside.

Just before serving, whisk the dressing vigorously and pour ¼ cup of it over the arugula. Toss gently. Mound ¾ cup of the dressed greens on each of 4 plates. Top each with a quarter of the red onion and 2 tablespoons of the pecans and serve.

Makes 4 servings, plus enough to:
✪ **Reserve 1 cup dressed arugula for Turkey Scaloppine with Bitter Greens in Balsamic Glaze.**
✪ **Reserve ½ cup dressing for Turkey Scaloppine with Bitter Greens in Balsamic Glaze.**

Turkey Scaloppine with Bitter Greens in Balsamic Glaze

8 small turkey cutlets (about 3 ounces each), pounded thin
¼ cup flour seasoned with salt and pepper to taste
2 tablespoons olive oil

✪ ½ cup dressing reserved from Arugula Salad with Red Onion and Pecans
✪ 1 cup dressed arugula reserved from Arugula Salad with Red Onion and Pecans

Dredge the turkey in the seasoned flour and shake off any excess. Heat the oil in a non-stick skillet until smoking. Brown the turkey in the hot oil and transfer it to a platter, keeping it warm. Add the reserved dressing to the hot skillet and bring to a boil. Stir in the reserved arugula, pour the mixture over the turkey, and serve.

Makes 4 servings.

Shrimp and Potato Bisque

✪ **Shrimp shells reserved from Tea-poached Prawns with Three Salsas**
1 medium onion
1 tablespoon butter
✪ **2 cups poaching liquid reserved from Tea-poached Prawns with Three Salsas**
1 bottle (8 ounces) clam juice

✪ **3 cups reserved Scalloped Potatoes with Chèvre and Anchovy**
Salt and pepper to taste
2 cups milk
✪ **8 to 12 shrimp reserved from Tea-poached Prawns with Three Salsas**

Finely chop the shrimp shells and the onion in a food processor. Transfer to a large heavy saucepan, add the butter, and cook for 2 minutes, stirring frequently. Add the reserved poaching liquid and the clam juice. Bring to a simmer, and cook for 15 minutes. Strain and return broth to pan. Add the potatoes, salt, and pepper, reduce the heat, and simmer for 5 minutes.

Return the soup to the food processor or a blender and process until finely pureed. Return to the saucepan. Mix in the milk and the reserved shrimp and heat through. Serve immediately.

Makes 4 servings.

Garlic Lamb Chops on Pommes Galettes

4 lamb shoulder chops (about 8 ounces each)
Salt and pepper to taste
6 tablespoons olive oil
5 cloves garlic, thinly sliced
1 cup beef broth, canned or homemade

✪ **3 cups reserved Scalloped Potatoes with Chèvre and Anchovy**
1½ tablespoons flour
2 eggs, lightly beaten

Rub the lamb on both sides with salt and pepper. Set aside. Heat 2 tablespoons of the olive oil in a deep skillet until the oil is smoking. Add the lamb and brown on both sides. Add the garlic and broth, cover, and simmer for 15 minutes. Remove cover and simmer 5 more minutes. Transfer lamb to a warm platter. Reduce pan juices over high heat to ¾ cup.

Meanwhile, finely chop the reserved potatoes and mix with the flour and eggs. Season with salt and pepper. Heat 2 tablespoons of the remaining oil in a large nonstick skillet. Place small mounds of the potato mixture (about 2 to 3 tablespoons each) in the hot oil, and brown on both sides. Cook the pancakes in batches, using the remaining oil, if necessary. Blot the cooked potato cakes with paper towels and keep in a warm oven while the lamb finishes cooking.

Serve the lamb on the potato galettes, and top each serving with 3 tablespoons of the garlic pan sauce.

Makes 4 servings.

Garden Black Bean Chili

1 tablespoon corn oil
1 medium onion, chopped
2 tablespoons chili powder
1 tablespoon ground cumin
1 clove garlic, minced
3 tablespoons cornmeal, preferably blue
✪ **1 cup tomato-ginger salsa reserved from Tea-poached Prawns with Three Salsas**

✪ **2 cups corn salsa reserved from Tea-poached Prawns with Three Salsas**
2 cups canned vegetable juice
1 can (15 ounces) black beans
Salt and pepper to taste

Heat the corn oil in a large heavy saucepan and cook the onion until softened, about 2 minutes. Add the chili powder, cumin, garlic, and cornmeal and cook for 1 more minute, stirring constantly. Add the reserved salsas and the vegetable juice and simmer for 5 minutes. Add the canned beans, salt, and pepper and heat through. Serve immediately.

Makes 4 servings.

Polenta is magical mush. It's made of cornmeal, salt, and water, but it's alchemized into homespun silk, and one would think that the transformation could be realized only by sleight-of-hand. All it takes is a little elbow grease. In the traditional method of making polenta, cornmeal is slowly added to boiling water to prevent the meal from lumping. A much easier method is to combine the cornmeal and cold water. That way, the meal is moistened evenly and the mixture can be cooked without danger of lumping. It needs almost constant stirring as it cooks and has a tendency to sputter as it simmers. A much simpler method for making polenta in the microwave was developed by Barbara Kafka in her book *Microwave Gourmet*. A rendition of that technique is given as an alternate method in the recipe for Polenta with Roasted Shallots.

This Sunday, polenta plays a supporting role to an entree of bluefish baked with horseradish and mustard. Not many fish could stand up to such dominant condiments, but the sweet, meaty flesh of bluefish begs for a sauce that's equally assertive. The menu is completed with a gratin of broccoli seasoned with capers and with a garnish of apples sautéed with rosemary.

Spoon bread, Monday's entree, is typically a side dish. But here, this cross between a soufflé and a cornbread is turned into a balanced meal with the addition of cheddar cheese and Sunday's baked broccoli. Tuesday's Seafood Quesadillas use Sunday's bluefish to transform this typical Mexican appetizer into a filling main course. Wednesday's and Thursday's meals utilize some garnishes from Sunday to make stuffed pork chops and to make a sauce for grilled chicken.

THE SUNDAY DINNER

Baked Bluefish with Horseradish Mustard

Polenta with Roasted Shallots

Baked Broccoli with Caper Crumbs

Rosemary Apples

THE WEEKNIGHT ENTREES

Broccoli Cheddar Spoon Bread

Seafood Quesadillas

Pork Chops Stuffed with Apples
and Prunes

Grilled Chicken with Shallot Chutney

Baked Bluefish with Horseradish Mustard

2 pounds bluefish fillets
1 tablespoon olive oil
Salt and pepper to taste
Juice of 1 lemon

2 tablespoons spicy brown mustard
1 tablespoon prepared horseradish
1 large clove garlic, finely chopped
¼ cup buttermilk

Preheat the oven to 400°F.

Rub the fish fillets with the olive oil. Place, skin side down, in a single layer in a large baking dish. Season with salt, pepper, and lemon juice. Bake for 15 minutes, or until the fish flakes under gentle pressure. While the fish is cooking, combine the mustard, horseradish, garlic, and buttermilk in a small mixing bowl.

When the fish is done, reserve about a quarter of it. Place the rest on a warm serving platter. Mix any juices from the baking dish into the mustard mixture and serve with the fish.

Makes 4 servings, plus enough to:
✪ **Reserve 1 cup bluefish for Seafood Quesadillas.**
✪ **Reserve ¼ cup sauce for Broccoli Cheddar Spoon Bread.**

Polenta with Roasted Shallots

¾ pound shallots
3 tablespoons extra-virgin olive oil
2 teaspoons kosher salt
1 cup yellow cornmeal

4 cups cold water
Salt and pepper to taste
¼ teaspoon minced garlic
3 ounces cheddar cheese, grated (¾ cup)

Preheat the oven to 400°F.

Toss the shallots with 1 tablespoon of the oil and the kosher salt. Place in a large roasting pan and roast for 40 minutes. Cut the ends from the shallots and push the flesh from the peels. Set aside.

Mix the cornmeal with the water in a large heavy saucepan until the cornmeal is moistened. Stir in salt and pepper and cook over medium heat, stirring frequently with a wooden spoon until the mixture is very smooth and silky, about 15 minutes. Or mix the water and cornmeal in a 2-quart soufflé dish and microwave at full power for 7 minutes. Whisk thoroughly, mix in salt and pepper, place a paper towel over the soufflé dish, and microwave another 6 minutes.

Chop ¼ cup of the roasted shallots and mix into the cooked cornmeal. Add the remaining 2 tablespoons of olive oil, the garlic, and the cheddar cheese. Serve 3 cups of the polenta.

Makes 4 servings, plus enough to:
❂ **Reserve 2 cups polenta for Broccoli Cheddar Spoon Bread.**
❂ **Reserve ½ cup roasted shallots for Grilled Chicken with Shallot Chutney.**

Baked Broccoli with Caper Crumbs

3 pounds broccoli, peeled and cut into
   bite-size pieces
1 tablespoon olive oil
1 clove garlic, finely chopped

2 tablespoons capers, drained
½ cup seasoned bread crumbs
1 cup canned condensed broccoli soup

Cook the broccoli in a large pot of boiling water until bright green and barely tender, about 2 minutes. Drain and set aside. Heat the oil in a small skillet, add the garlic and capers, and cook for 10 seconds. Add the bread crumbs, remove from the heat, and mix thoroughly.

Preheat the oven to 350°F.

Mix the broccoli and the soup and turn into a large rectangular or oval baking dish. Top with the bread crumb mixture and bake for 20 minutes. Serve two thirds of the broccoli.

Makes 4 servings, plus enough to:
❂ **Reserve 1½ cups for Broccoli Cheddar Spoon Bread.**

Rosemary Apples

6 medium or large apples, any type except
   Red Delicious (about 3 pounds)
Juice of ½ lemon
1 small onion, finely chopped
1 teaspoon butter

2 sprigs rosemary, leaves only
1 clove garlic, minced
1 tablespoon sugar
Salt and pepper to taste

Peel, core, and thinly slice the apples, immediately tossing the peeled slices with the lemon juice.

Cook the onion in the butter in a large skillet until onion has softened, about 2 minutes. Add the rosemary and garlic and toss. Add the apple slices and sugar and cook over high heat until the apples are softened and lightly browned. Season with salt and pepper. Serve ½ cup per person.

Makes 4 servings, plus enough to:
✪ **Reserve 1 cup for Broccoli Cheddar Spoon Bread.**
✪ **Reserve ½ cup for Pork Chops Stuffed with Apples and Prunes.**

Broccoli Cheddar Spoon Bread

- 1½ cups reserved **Baked Broccoli with Caper Crumbs**
- 2 cups polenta reserved from **Polenta with Roasted Shallots**

4 eggs, separated
1 cup shredded aged cheddar cheese (4 ounces)
Salt and pepper to taste

Dash of cayenne
1 teaspoon vegetable oil
2 to 3 tablespoons yellow cornmeal
- 1 cup reserved **Rosemary Apples**
- ¼ cup sauce reserved from **Baked Bluefish with Horseradish Mustard**

¼ cup sour cream or yogurt

Finely chop the reserved broccoli. Combine the broccoli, reserved polenta, the egg yolks, cheese, salt, pepper, and cayenne in a mixing bowl. Set aside.

Preheat the oven to 400°F. Grease a 6-cup soufflé dish or casserole with the oil and dust it with the cornmeal. Set aside.

Beat the egg whites until they hold a soft shape. Mix a third of the whites into the polenta mixture. Fold in the remainder. Pour into the prepared baking dish and bake for 30 minutes.

Just before baking is finished, heat the reserved apples in a small skillet or saucepan. Remove from the heat and mix in the reserved bluefish sauce and the sour cream or yogurt.

Serve the spoon bread immediately with a large spoon or cut it into wedges in the dish. Serve with some of the sauce.

Makes 4 servings.

Seafood Quesadillas

6 scallions, white parts only, finely sliced

1 teaspoon olive oil

1 teaspoon ground cumin

2 teaspoons minced pickled jalapeño

1 clove garlic, minced

✪ **1 cup fish reserved from Baked Bluefish with Horseradish Mustard**

Juice of 1 lemon

8 (6-inch) flour tortillas

1 cup shredded monterey jack cheese
  (4 ounces)

1 to 2 teaspoons vegetable oil

1 to 1½ cups salsa, any type

Cook the scallions in the olive oil in a skillet over medium heat until softened, about 1 minute. Add the cumin, jalapeño, and garlic and cook another minute, stirring frequently. Remove from heat. Gently toss in the reserved bluefish and the lemon juice.

Place four of the tortillas on a work surface. Spread about 2½ tablespoons of the fish mixture over each tortilla. Top each with 2½ tablespoons of cheese and the remaining tortillas.

Heat half the vegetable oil in a large nonstick skillet over medium-high heat. Brown the quesadillas on both sides, about 45 seconds per side. You will be able to do only 1 or 2 quesadillas at a time. Keep each warm while you brown the next, using the remaining oil as needed. Serve 1 quesadilla to each person with salsa.

Makes 4 servings.

Pork Chops Stuffed with Apples and Prunes

4 boneless pork chops, each 1¼ to 1½ inches
   thick (about 6 ounces each)
✪ **½ cup reserved Rosemary Apples**
4 pitted prunes, chopped

¼ cup seasoned bread crumbs
1 tablespoon vegetable oil
2 cups apple cider or juice

Cut a deep wide pocket in each of the pork chops, keeping the slit about 1½ inches long. Mix half the reserved apples with the prunes. Stuff the pockets with the apple-prune mixture. Dust the surface of each pork chop with bread crumbs.

    Heat the oil in a large nonstick skillet over medium-high heat and brown the chops on both sides, about 3 minutes per side. Add the apple cider, cover, reduce the heat, and simmer for 15 minutes. Remove the chops to a warm platter.

    Over high heat, boil the juices in the pan for 3 to 4 minutes until they reduce to about ¾ cup. Add the remaining apples and boil another minute. Pour over the chops.

Makes 4 servings.

Grilled Chicken with Shallot Chutney

2 chicken breasts, split
2 teaspoons olive oil
Salt and pepper to taste
✪ **½ cup roasted shallots reserved from
   Polenta with Roasted Shallots**

1 tablespoon honey
2 teaspoons apple cider vinegar
1 teaspoon hot pepper sauce

Rub the chicken with the olive oil, salt, and pepper. Grill or broil the chicken breasts 4 inches from a hot fire, 10 to 12 minutes per side. Meanwhile, make the chutney by combining the roasted shallots, honey, vinegar, and hot pepper sauce. Serve the chicken accompanied by the chutney.

Makes 4 servings.

Menu 32

This week's menu is infused with the briny flavor of olives, but that doesn't mean that every dinner tastes the same. We start with a roast turkey rubbed with garlic and olive oil and served with a rendition of tapenade, a mixture of black olives, olive oil, and garlic that is the soul food of the Mediterranean. In this menu, green olives take the place of black for an effect that's a little milder.

Sunday's turkey is supported by a Provençale version of scalloped potatoes in which diced potatoes are simmered with onion, tomato, garlic, basil, and herbes de Provence, a blend of herbs that includes thyme, savory, rosemary, fennel seed, and lavender. All this intensity is tamed by a rich subtle dish of spinach simmered with wild mushrooms in cream.

The potatoes and tapenade reappear on Monday in the braising liquid for spice-coated fish. On Tuesday, the spinach and tapenade are baked with feta in puff pastry, for a haute cuisine version of Greek street food, a spanakopita turnover. Wednesday's meal combines Sunday's tapenade with jarred roasted peppers for a full-bodied condiment loaded with Mediterranean flavor that tops grilled shrimp. On Thursday, Sunday's turkey is reborn in a salad tossed with beans, tapenade, orange, and crisp endive.

THE SUNDAY DINNER

Garlic Roast Turkey Breast with
Green Olive Tapenade

Potato Ratatouille

Spinach Creamed with Wild Mushrooms

THE WEEKNIGHT ENTREES

Braised Catfish Castilian

Spanakopita Turnovers

Grilled Shrimp with Roasted
Pepper Relish

Turkey and White Bean Salad
over Endive

Garlic Roast Turkey Breast with Green Olive Tapenade

TURKEY

1 turkey breast (about 5 pounds)
3 large cloves garlic, each cut into about 8
   slices
Salt and pepper to taste
2 tablespoons extra-virgin olive oil

TAPENADE

2 cups pitted green olives (12 ounces)
5 cloves garlic, minced
½ cup extra-virgin olive oil
Salt and pepper to taste

Preheat the oven to 425°F.

Carefully peel back the skin of the turkey, leaving it attached at one end. Using a knife, make 12 evenly spaced deep punctures in the turkey breast. Season the sliced garlic liberally with salt and pepper and insert 2 slices into each slit in the turkey breast. Rub the surface of the turkey breast with the olive oil, and replace the skin. Place the turkey, bone side down, on a rack in a shallow roasting pan and roast for 30 minutes. Reduce the oven temperature to 325°F. and roast for 1 more hour, or until a thermometer inserted into the thickest part of the breast registers 170°F.

While the turkey is roasting, make the tapenade. Finely chop the olives and mix them with the minced garlic, olive oil, salt, and pepper.

When the turkey is done, remove it from the oven and allow it to rest for 10 minutes. Slice half the turkey and serve it with about half the tapenade.

Makes 4 servings, plus enough to:
✪ **Reserve 1 pound roasted turkey breast for Turkey and White Bean Salad over Endive.**
✪ **Reserve 3 tablespoons tapenade for Braised Catfish Castilian.**
✪ **Reserve 3 tablespoons tapenade for Grilled Shrimp with Roasted Pepper Relish.**
✪ **Reserve 3 tablespoons tapenade for Turkey and White Bean Salad over Endive.**
✪ **Reserve 1 tablespoon tapenade for Spanakopita Turnovers.**

Potato Ratatouille

1 large onion, chopped

1 green bell pepper, stemmed, seeded, and cut
  into strips

1 red bell pepper, stemmed, seeded, and cut
  into strips

¼ cup olive oil

3 pounds russet or Yukon Gold potatoes,
  scrubbed and sliced

Salt and pepper to taste

1 teaspoon herbes de Provence

1 cup water

3 large tomatoes, peeled, cored, and coarsely
  chopped

2 cloves garlic, minced

½ cup basil leaves, coarsely chopped

1 tablespoon red wine vinegar

Cook the onion and peppers in the olive oil in a large skillet over medium heat until softened, about 3 minutes. Add the potatoes and toss them to coat with oil. Season with salt, pepper, and herbes de Provence and cook until onion browns lightly, about 5 minutes, stirring often. Add the water and stir. Cover the pan and cook for 15 to 20 minutes, or until the potatoes are just tender, stirring occasionally. Add the tomatoes and garlic and cook another 5 minutes. Add the basil and vinegar and heat through. Serve hot or warm.

Makes 4 servings, plus enough to:
✪ **Reserve 3 cups for Braised Catfish Castilian.**

Spinach Creamed with Wild Mushrooms

¼ ounce dried wild mushrooms
1 cup warm water
3 packages (10 ounces each) frozen chopped
*   spinach, defrosted*
1 small onion, chopped
2 tablespoons butter

Pinch of dried marjoram or oregano
Pinch of freshly grated nutmeg
Salt and pepper to taste
½ cup light cream
¼ cup freshly grated parmesan cheese

Soak the mushrooms in the warm water for 20 minutes. Drain and coarsely chop the mushrooms. Set aside. Place the spinach in a strainer to drain off excess moisture. Set aside.

Cook the onion in the butter in a large skillet or wide saucepan over medium heat until softened, about 2 minutes. Add the marjoram and nutmeg and cook another 30 seconds. Add the spinach and mushrooms and stir until heated through. Season with salt and pepper and add the cream. Simmer until cream is absorbed. Remove from heat, stir in the parmesan cheese, and serve.

Makes 4 servings, plus enough to:
✪ **Reserve ¾ cup for Spanakopita Turnovers.**

Braised Catfish Castilian

1 tablespoon mild or hot paprika
2 teaspoons ground cumin
Salt and pepper to taste
2 pounds catfish fillets, trimmed
1 to 2 tablespoons extra-virgin olive oil

✪ **3 cups reserved Potato Ratatouille**
⅓ cup chicken or fish broth
✪ **3 tablespoons tapenade reserved from Garlic Roast Turkey Breast with Green Olive Tapenade**

Combine the paprika, cumin, salt, and pepper. Cut each piece of catfish in four and coat the pieces with the spice mixture. Heat the olive oil in a deep skillet. Brown the fish, in batches if necessary, and transfer to a plate. Add the reserved potatoes, broth, and reserved tapenade to the skillet and heat until simmering, stirring occasionally. Place the fish on top of the potatoes, cover, and simmer for 5 minutes, or until the fish is cooked through. Serve the fish on a bed of potatoes.

Makes 4 servings.

Spanakopita Turnovers

✪ **¾ cup reserved Spinach Creamed with Wild Mushrooms**
✪ **1 tablespoon tapenade reserved from Garlic Roast Turkey Breast with Green Olive Tapenade**

4 ounces feta cheese, crumbled
1 sheet (8 ounces) frozen puff pastry, defrosted
1 small egg, lightly beaten

Preheat the oven to 400°F.

Combine the reserved spinach, reserved tapenade, and feta cheese. Cut the sheet of puff pastry into 4 square pieces. Brush the pieces with some beaten egg. Place 3 tablespoons of the spinach mixture in the center of each square. Fold over a corner of each square to meet its opposite corner, forming a triangle that completely encloses the spinach filling. Using the tips of the tines of a fork, press the edges together. Place the turnovers on a sheet pan, and brush the tops with a thin coating of beaten egg. Bake for 20 minutes, or until puffed and golden brown. Allow to cool for 5 minutes before serving.

Makes 4 servings.

Grilled Shrimp with Roasted Pepper Relish

✪ **3 tablespoons tapenade reserved from Garlic Roast Turkey Breast with Green Olive Tapenade**

1 small jar (7 ounces) roasted red peppers, drained and finely chopped

Pinch of crushed red pepper flakes

Salt and pepper to taste

24 large shrimp, peeled and deveined (about 1 ¼ pounds)

¼ cup olive oil

Make the relish by combining the reserved tapenade, roasted peppers, pepper flakes, salt, and pepper. Set aside. Season the shrimp with salt and pepper, and toss with the oil. Grill the shrimp on an oiled mesh rack 4 inches from a hot fire for 1 to 2 minutes per side, or until they are opaque and firm. Serve 6 shrimp per person, topped with some of the relish.

Makes 4 servings.

Turkey and White Bean Salad over Endive

3 heads belgian endive, 1 head curly endive, or 2 heads raddichio, leaves washed, dried, and torn into bite-size pieces

✪ **1 pound roasted turkey breast reserved from Garlic Roast Turkey Breast with Green Olive Tapenade**

1 tablespoon olive oil

½ cup walnut pieces

Pinch of crushed red pepper flakes

Salt to taste

✪ **3 tablespoons tapenade reserved from Garlic Roast Turkey Breast with Green Olive Tapenade**

1 can (19 ounces) cannellini beans, drained and rinsed

½ cup orange juice

2 tablespoons red wine vinegar

3 large scallions, white parts only, sliced

1 clove garlic, minced

Place the endive in a large serving bowl, and chill. Cut the turkey into bite-size pieces.

Heat the oil in a skillet, add the walnuts, and stir for 1 minute, or until the walnuts start to toast. Add the turkey, pepper flakes, and salt. Cook another minute, or until the turkey is heated through. Add the tapenade, beans, orange juice, and vinegar and bring to a boil. Stir in the scallions and garlic. Pour over the endive, toss, and serve.

Makes 4 servings.

Menu 33

The flavors of the Mediterranean are a source of endless inspiration. Coriander and cumin in North Africa; lemon and mint in the Middle East; oregano, basil, fennel, and lavender along the northern coast; garlic and olives everywhere. Those intoxicating flavors are plumbed once again for this week's menu. Scallops, the Sunday entree, are poached in a delicate tomato sauce scented with orange and enriched with cream. A portion of the sauce, along with some of Sunday's braised fennel side dish, give Tuesday's veal chops instant Provençale cachet.

The scallops are accompanied by quinoa, an ancient grain that was cultivated widely by the Incas nearly five thousand years ago. It is still a common crop in the Andes and, since the mid-1980s, it has been grown in the Rocky Mountain states.

Quinoa is a small round seed resembling a sesame seed. The cooked grain has a beautifully textured appearance and a chewy resiliency. Quinoa is easy and fast to cook. Just simmer it in twice as much water as grain for about fifteen minutes.

Quinoa takes the place of bulgur in Monday's seafood salad redolent with Sunday's orange- and fennel-scented scallops. On Wednesday, the scallop sauce doubles as a sauce for conchiglie (shell-shaped pasta) tossed with small white beans, and on Thursday the olive paste that permeated Sunday's quinoa gives the essence of the Mediterranean to a grilled chicken breast.

THE SUNDAY DINNER

Poached Scallops with Orange-Tomato Sauce

Caramelized Fennel

Quinoa Niçoise

THE WEEKNIGHT ENTREES

Quinoa Seafood Salad

Provençale Veal Chops

Conchiglie with White Beans and Asiago

Grilled Chicken Breast with Olive Paste

Poached Scallops with Orange-Tomato Sauce

1 tablespoon olive oil
1 medium onion, chopped
Zest, finely grated, and juice of 1 large orange
1 teaspoon fennel seed, ground
Pinch of crushed red pepper flakes
5 large tomatoes or 15 plum tomatoes, peeled and chopped (3 pounds)

2 tablespoons tomato paste
Salt and pepper to taste
2 tablespoons chopped basil leaves
2 cloves garlic, minced
2 pounds sea scallops, trimmed
2 teaspoons cornstarch
⅓ cup heavy cream

Heat the olive oil in a large heavy skillet. Add the onion and cook over medium heat until softened, about 2 minutes. Add the orange zest, fennel seed, and pepper flakes and cook another 30 seconds, stirring constantly. Add the tomatoes and cook until the sauce simmers. Add the tomato paste, orange juice, salt, pepper, basil, and garlic and simmer another 2 minutes. While the sauce is simmering, cut the scallops in half or quarters, depending on their size. Remove 4 cups of the sauce from the skillet and reserve it.

Return the sauce to the heat, bring back to a simmer, and add the scallops. Cook until the scallops are barely firm, about 2 to 3 minutes. With a slotted spoon, transfer the cooked scallops to a serving bowl. Remove and reserve 1 cup of scallops.

Bring the sauce in the pan to a boil and boil vigorously for 2 minutes. Whisk together the cornstarch and cream until smooth. Whisk into the boiling sauce and return to a simmer. Pour the sauce over the scallops and serve.

Makes 4 servings, plus enough to:
✪ **Reserve 2 cups tomato sauce for Conchiglie with White Beans and Asiago.**
✪ **Reserve 2 cups tomato sauce for Provençale Veal Chops.**
✪ **Reserve 1 cup scallops for Quinoa Seafood Salad.**

THERE'S MORE THAN ONE WAY TO SKIN A TOMATO

With a peeler. For this you need a firm tomato and a good peeler; if you have a very ripe tomato use one of the other methods. Remove the core with a twist of the pointed end of a vegetable peeler. Remove the skin in parallel strips starting at the stem end and going down toward the blossom end.

With boiling water. Bring a large pot of water to a boil. While the water heats, cut a small **X** into each tomato skin across the rounded end. Place the tomatoes, a few at a time, in the boiling water, and cook for 30 to 40 seconds. Remove with a slotted spoon, and plunge into cold water for a minute. Peel off the skin with your fingers, starting from the **X**.

With a flame. Place tomatoes directly near the flame of a grill, broiler, or gas burner. Cook until the skin blisters and pops, about 10 seconds per side. Turn to heat evenly. Peel off the skin with your fingers. Don't worry if you miss a bit of skin here and there.

Caramelized Fennel

3 bulbs fennel
2 tablespoons extra-virgin olive oil
½ cup white wine
1 cup low-salt beef broth, canned or homemade
1 teaspoon balsamic vinegar

½ cup water
1 teaspoon tomato paste
½ medium onion, sliced
3 cloves garlic, minced
2 tablespoons fresh rosemary leaves
Salt and pepper to taste

Trim the base and dark stalks from each fennel bulb and cut it vertically into 4 slices. Heat the oil in a large heavy skillet over medium-high heat and brown the fennel slices for 2 to 3 minutes per side. While the fennel is browning, combine the white wine, beef broth, vinegar, water, and tomato paste. Set aside.

When the fennel is almost brown, add the onion and cook until the onion softens and begins to brown lightly, about 3 minutes. Add the garlic and rosemary and mix to blend. Add the reserved liquid ingredients and season with salt and pepper. Cover and simmer until the fennel is tender and most of the liquid has been absorbed, about 40 minutes, turning the fennel occasionally. Serve the larger pieces of fennel, reserving 1 cup of loose or broken pieces.

Makes 4 servings, plus enough to:
✪ **Reserve 1 cup fennel for Provençale Veal Chops.**

Quinoa Niçoise

2 cups quinoa
1 teaspoon olive oil
1 small onion, chopped
4 cups water
12 large brine-cured black Greek olives,
   pitted

2 cloves garlic, minced
2 tablespoons olive brine
1 tablespoon chopped basil leaves
Salt and pepper to taste

Place the quinoa in a strainer, and wash under a constant stream of cold water for about 2 minutes.

Heat the olive oil in a large heavy saucepan over medium heat, add the onion, and cook until it softens, about 2 minutes. Add the water and bring to a boil. Add the quinoa and stir several times. Simmer for 15 minutes, or until all the water has been absorbed and the quinoa is fluffy and tender.

While the quinoa is cooking, finely chop the olives, and mix with the garlic, olive brine, basil, salt, and pepper. Mix a third of this mixture into the cooked quinoa, and serve about 1 cup of the finished quinoa to each person.

Makes 4 servings, plus enough to:
✪ **Reserve 4 cups quinoa for Quinoa Seafood Salad.**
✪ **Reserve 2 tablespoons olive mixture for Provençale Veal Chops.**
✪ **Reserve ⅓ cup olive mixture for the Grilled Chicken Breast with Olive Paste.**

Quinoa Seafood Salad

- ✪ 1 cup scallops reserved from Poached Scallops with Orange-Tomato Sauce
- ✪ 4 cups reserved Quinoa Niçoise

1 large tomato, cored and diced

1 large cucumber, peeled, seeded, and diced
Juice of 1 large lemon
1 clove garlic, minced
Salt and pepper to taste

Cut each scallop into 2 or 3 pieces. Toss with the quinoa, tomato, and cucumber. Combine the lemon juice, garlic, salt, and pepper, and toss with the salad. Serve cold or at room temperature.

Makes 4 servings.

Provençale Veal Chops

- ✪ 1 cup reserved Caramelized Fennel

4 veal chops (6 to 8 ounces each)

- ✪ 2 tablespoons olive mixture reserved from Quinoa Niçoise

Salt and pepper to taste

1 tablespoon olive oil

- ✪ 2 cups tomato sauce reserved from Poached Scallops with Orange-Tomato Sauce

Coarsely chop the fennel. Set aside.

Rub the surfaces of the chops with half the olive mixture. Season with salt and pepper. Heat the olive oil in a large heavy skillet over high heat and brown the chops on both sides, about 2 to 3 minutes per side. Add the tomato sauce and the fennel and stir to combine. Simmer, partially covered, for 5 to 7 minutes. Remove chops to a platter. Boil the sauce for 2 minutes, remove from the heat, and stir in the remaining olive mixture. Pour the sauce over the chops and serve.

Makes 4 servings.

Conchiglie with White Beans and Asiago

12 ounces conchiglie (medium pasta shells)
1 tablespoon olive oil
½ medium onion, chopped
3 cloves garlic, finely chopped
✪ **2 cups tomato sauce reserved from Poached Scallops with Orange-Tomato Sauce**

1 tablespoon tomato paste
1 can (14 ounces) small white beans, drained and rinsed
¼ cup chopped parsley
Salt and pepper to taste
2 to 3 tablespoons freshly grated asiago or parmesan cheese

Bring a large pot of salted water to a boil and cook the pasta until tender, about 10 minutes. When the pasta is almost done, heat the oil in a saucepan. Add the onion and cook until softened, about 2 minutes. Add the garlic and stir. Add the tomato sauce, tomato paste, beans, and parsley and heat through. Season with salt and pepper. Drain the pasta, toss with the sauce and cheese, and serve.

Makes 4 servings.

Grilled Chicken Breast with Olive Paste

2 chicken breasts, split
Salt and pepper to taste

✪ **⅓ cup olive mixture reserved from Quinoa Niçoise**
3 tablespoons finely chopped parsley

Rub the chicken with salt, pepper, and a thin film of the oil from the olive mixture. Grill or broil the chicken breasts 4 inches from a hot fire for 10 to 12 minutes per side. Combine the olive mixture and the parsley and serve the chicken topped with this mixture.

Makes 4 servings.

Menu 34

The proof of the meatball is in the filler. Grinding meat extracts any juiciness or textural subtlety the meat once had; those qualities are restored by adding liquids and bread. Then you have meat that will retain its moisture and consistency during cooking better than a steak, chop, or roast.

Sunday's meatballs are simmered with sausages in a red hot tomato sauce that's tamed from three directions by its side dishes. The mashed potatoes act as a balm to sop up the sauce as well as some of its fire. Kale, a strong bitter green in the cabbage family, steps in with another assertive flavor that goes equally well with the meatball sauce and the potatoes. And the caramelized onions lend a roasted sweetness that's needed to balance the other strong-willed participants.

The meatballs and sausages on Sunday provide an instant sauce and hearty garnish for Monday's Spicy Spaghetti and Meatballs. They are also the reason that Tuesday's gumbo can go from cutting board to table in less than five minutes. And their exotic spice harmonizes with Sunday's kale and sweet onions to make Wednesday's scallop stew a powerhouse of flavors and color. Thursday's potato pancakes utilize all three of Sunday's side dishes to create a hearty meatless entree that needs only to be quickly combined and sautéed.

THE SUNDAY DINNER

Meatballs and Sausages with
Red Hot Red Pepper Sauce

Sage Mashed Potatoes

Braised Kale with Mushrooms

Caramelized Onions

THE WEEKNIGHT ENTREES

Spicy Spaghetti and Meatballs

Easy Gumbo

Spiced Scallop Stew

Cheddar Potato Pancakes Jardinière

Meatballs and Sausages with Red Hot Red Pepper Sauce

SAUCE

2 large red bell peppers, stemmed, seeded, and finely chopped

3 hot red chilies, such as cayenne or red jalapeño, stemmed, seeded, and minced

1 medium onion, finely chopped

3 cloves garlic, minced

Salt and black pepper to taste

2 teaspoons ground cumin

1 teaspoon ground coriander

1 tablespoon olive oil

1½ cups water

1½ tablespoons ketchup

1½ cups canned crushed tomatoes

MEATBALLS AND SAUSAGES

4 slices bread, crumbled

1 cup milk

1 pound ground beef

1 pound ground turkey, pork, or veal

2 cloves garlic, minced

1 small onion, grated

1 teaspoon dried basil

2 eggs or 3 egg whites

2 tablespoons tomato paste

1 tablespoon olive oil

1½ pounds sweet Italian sausage, thickly sliced into a total of 48 pieces

1 small onion, sliced

1 to 1½ cups water

For the sauce, combine the bell peppers, chilies, onion, garlic, salt, black pepper, cumin, coriander, and oil in a small heavy saucepan. Cook over medium heat until the vegetables begin to soften, about 2 minutes. Add the water and simmer until the vegetables are very soft and the liquid has reduced to about ¼ cup, about 15 minutes. Stir in the ketchup and tomatoes. Set aside.

For the meatballs, combine the bread and milk in a small bowl and let stand for 5 minutes.

Combine the ground meats, garlic, grated onion, basil, eggs, tomato paste, and soaked bread and milk in a large bowl. Using your hands, mix until thoroughly combined and form into 48 1-inch meatballs.

Heat the olive oil in a large skillet over medium-high heat and brown the sausage slices on both sides. Remove with tongs or a slotted spoon, and set aside. Brown the meatballs on all sides in the same oil. Remove with a slotted spoon and set aside.

Pour off all but a thin film of oil from the pan. Reduce heat to medium. Add the sliced onion and cook until lightly browned, about 3 minutes. Add the sausage, meatballs, and ¾ cup of water and simmer until all the water is gone, tossing frequently, about 10 minutes. When the pan is dry, the meatballs and sausage should be cooked through. Cut one open to check. If underdone, add another ½ cup water and cook some more. Transfer half the meatballs and sausages (about 4 cups) to a serving bowl, and toss with 1 cup of the sauce.

Makes 4 servings, plus enough to:
- ✪ **Reserve 24 pieces cooked sausage for Easy Gumbo.**
- ✪ **Reserve 24 meatballs for Spicy Spaghetti and Meatballs.**
- ✪ **Reserve ½ cup red pepper sauce for Spicy Spaghetti and Meatballs.**
- ✪ **Reserve ½ cup red pepper sauce for Easy Gumbo.**
- ✪ **Reserve ½ cup red pepper sauce for Spiced Scallop Stew.**
- ✪ **Reserve ½ cup red pepper sauce for Cheddar Potato Pancakes Jardinière.**

Sage Mashed Potatoes

3 pounds russet or Yukon Gold potatoes,
scrubbed
1 teaspoon rubbed dried sage
¼ teaspoon minced garlic

1 cup milk
1 tablespoon olive oil
1 teaspoon salt
¼ teaspoon ground black pepper

Cut each potato into eighths and cook in a large pot of boiling water for 15 to 20 minutes, or until tender. Drain potatoes, return them to the pot, and mash them coarsely with a potato masher. Add the sage, garlic, milk, oil, salt, and pepper. Continue to mash until well blended. The potatoes will be a bit lumpy. Serve half.

Makes 4 servings, plus enough to:
- ✪ **Reserve 3 cups for Cheddar Potato Pancakes Jardinière.**

Braised Kale with Mushrooms

2 pounds fresh kale
2 tablespoons olive oil
1 small onion, chopped
3 ounces ham, diced

1 pound white mushrooms, stems trimmed,
 cleaned and sliced
Salt and pepper to taste

Cut away the kale stems and discard. Toss the leaves in lots of cold water to remove any dirt. Remove the leaves, shaking off excess water. Set aside.

Heat the oil in a large heavy soup pot over medium heat. Add the onion, ham, and mushrooms, cooking until the vegetables lose their raw look, about 3 minutes. Remove and reserve 1 cup. Add the kale to the remaining mushroom mixture, cover, and simmer for 1 minute. Toss. Cover and cook another 2 minutes. Toss. Cover and cook another 8 to 10 minutes, or until the kale is tender, tossing every few minutes. Season liberally with salt and pepper. Serve 4 cups.

Makes 4 servings, plus enough to:
✪ **Reserve 1 cup mushroom mixture for Spiced Scallop Stew.**
✪ **Reserve 1 cup kale and mushrooms for Cheddar Potato Pancakes Jardinière.**

Caramelized Onions

2 packages (10 ounces each) fresh pearl
 onions, trimmed and peeled
2 tablespoons olive oil

Salt and pepper to taste
½ teaspoon dried thyme leaves
1 cup water

Cook the onions in the oil in a large skillet over medium-high heat until browned, about 3 minutes, stirring constantly. Season with salt, pepper, and thyme and add the water. Reduce heat to medium, cover, and simmer until the onions are tender and all the water has evaporated, about 12 minutes. Add more water as necessary. Adjust seasoning with salt and pepper. Serve 1⅓ cups.

Makes 4 servings, plus enough to:
✪ **Reserve ⅓ cup for Cheddar Potato Pancakes Jardinière.**
✪ **Reserve ⅓ cup for Spiced Scallop Stew.**

Spicy Spaghetti and Meatballs

*1 pound fresh or frozen spaghetti or 12 ounces
dried spaghetti*

1½ cups tomato sauce

✪ **½ cup red pepper sauce reserved from
Meatballs and Sausages with Red Hot
Red Pepper Sauce**

✪ **24 meatballs reserved from Meatballs
and Sausages with Red Hot Red Pepper
Sauce**

Boil the spaghetti in a large pot of lightly salted water until al dente, 3 to 4 minutes for
fresh, 5 to 6 minutes for frozen, 10 minutes for dried. Meanwhile, heat the tomato
sauce, reserved red pepper sauce, and reserved meatballs in a saucepan. Simmer until
the meatballs are warmed through, about 5 minutes. Thin with about ½ cup of pasta
water. Drain the pasta, toss with the sauce and meatballs, and serve immediately.

Makes 4 servings.

Easy Gumbo

1 tablespoon vegetable oil

1 medium onion, chopped

½ pound large shrimp, peeled and deveined

✪ **24 pieces cooked sausage reserved from
Meatballs and Sausages with Red Hot
Red Pepper Sauce**

1 cup sliced frozen okra, defrosted

½ cup canned crushed tomatoes

✪ **½ cup red pepper sauce reserved from
Meatballs and Sausages with Red Hot
Red Pepper Sauce**

Salt and pepper to taste

3 cups hot cooked rice

Heat the oil in a large nonstick skillet over medium-high heat, add the onion, and cook
until lightly browned, stirring constantly, about 3 minutes. Add the shrimp, and toss for
30 seconds. Add the sausage, okra, tomatoes, and pepper sauce. Bring to a boil, reduce
the heat, season with salt and pepper, and simmer for 1 minute. Serve over hot rice.

Makes 4 servings.

Spiced Scallop Stew

1 tablespoon extra-virgin olive oil
1 pound bay scallops
¼ cup white wine or water
✪ 1 cup mushroom mixture reserved
from Braised Kale with Mushrooms
✪ ⅓ cup reserved Caramelized Onions

✪ ½ cup red pepper sauce reserved from
Meatballs and Sausages with Red Hot
Red Pepper Sauce
1 tablespoon chopped parsley
Juice of ½ lemon
Salt and pepper to taste

Heat the oil in a large saucepan until smoking. Add the scallops and cook for 30 seconds. Add the wine or water and heat until simmering, about 30 seconds. Add the reserved mushrooms, reserved onions, and reserved red pepper sauce. Heat until simmering. Add the parsley and lemon juice and season to taste with salt and pepper.

Makes 4 servings.

Cheddar Potato Pancakes Jardinière

✪ ½ cup red pepper sauce reserved from
Meatballs and Sausages with Red Hot
Red Pepper Sauce
✪ ⅓ cup reserved Caramelized Onions
✪ 1 cup reserved Braised Kale with
Mushrooms
✪ 3 cups reserved Sage Mashed Potatoes

1 cup shredded sharp cheddar cheese
(4 ounces)
2 eggs
¼ cup flour
Salt and pepper to taste
2 to 4 tablespoons olive oil

Bring the reserved red pepper sauce to room temperature. Chop the reserved onions and reserved kale. Combine the onions, kale, reserved mashed potatoes, ½ cup of the cheddar, the eggs, flour, salt, and pepper in a mixing bowl. Blend well.

Preheat the oven to 300°F. Form the mixture into twelve 4-inch pancakes. Heat a thin film of oil in a large nonstick skillet over medium-high heat. Brown the pancakes on both sides, about 2 minutes per side. Do this in batches, transferring the finished pancakes to an ovensafe serving platter and keeping them warm in the oven. Sprinkle the remaining cheese over the top and leave in the oven until the cheese melts, about 5 minutes. Serve with dollops of the reserved red pepper sauce.

Makes 4 servings.

Menu 35

ood Barbecued Ribs aren't easy, and great ones require a commitment akin to fanaticism, for few dishes take more time and vigilance. The method used for this Sunday's dinner guarantees ribs that are permeated with spices, with meat sodden with sauce and practically falling from the bone. The slab of ribs is rubbed with dry spices and parcooked in simmering water for full flavor and complete tenderness. Because the sauce is applied and grilling takes place after the ribs have been cooked through, there is no scorching.

The spice rub from Sunday's ribs does double duty on Wednesday when it's used to season Wok-steamed Pepper Clams. Black-eyed Peas and Leeks and the broccoli from Sunday's side dishes are combined on Monday in a quick and distinctively flavored soup that's enriched with bits of feta cheese. Tuesday's Caribbean Pork Stew practically prepares itself by teaming some of the barbecue sauce with cooked rib meat. This stew is so fast that the only thing stretching preparation time is the fifteen minutes or so needed to cook the rice on which the stew is served. The week ends as it started, on the grill, with Cornish hens lacquered with a tangy-sweet cider glaze from the sauce made on Sunday for the broccoli side dish.

THE SUNDAY DINNER

Barbecued Ribs

Black-eyed Peas and Leeks

Broccoli with Spiced Apple Cider Sauce

THE WEEKNIGHT ENTREES

Creamy Broccoli Bean Soup

Caribbean Pork Stew

Wok-steamed Pepper Clams

Apple-glazed Cornish Hens

Barbecued Ribs

RIBS

1 tablespoon chili powder
½ teaspoon salt
¾ teaspoon cracked black pepper
2 teaspoons dried minced onion
¾ teaspoon dried minced garlic
2 racks pork spareribs (7 pounds)

SAUCE

2 cups apple butter
½ cup ketchup
½ cup cider vinegar
2 teaspoons salt
2 teaspoons cracked black pepper
4 teaspoons chili powder
2 cups water

Make a dry rub by combining the chili powder, salt, pepper, dried minced onion, and dried minced garlic. Reserve 1 tablespoon. Rub the remainder into both sides of both slabs of ribs. Set aside for at least 10 minutes.

Bring a large pot of water to a boil. Cut each slab of ribs in half between two of the middle ribs. Add the ribs to the water, reduce heat, and simmer until tender, about 20 minutes. Meanwhile, make the sauce. Whisk together the apple butter, ketchup, cider vinegar, salt, pepper, and chili powder in a saucepan. Mix in the water and bring to a boil. Set aside.

Preheat a grill until very hot.

Cut the ribs into 1- or 2-rib sections. Reserve 1 cup of the sauce in a separate container. Dip the ribs into the remaining sauce and brown on the grill, about 4 minutes per side, basting every 2 minutes with the sauce you dipped the ribs in. Serve as soon as possible.

Makes 4 servings, plus enough to:
○ **Reserve 8 ribs for Caribbean Pork Stew.**
○ **Reserve 1 cup sauce for Caribbean Pork Stew.**
○ **Reserve 1 tablespoon spice mixture for Wok-steamed Pepper Clams.**

Black-eyed Peas and Leeks

3 large leeks
6 tablespoons extra-virgin olive oil
Pinch of crushed red pepper flakes
3 cloves garlic, minced

4 cups cooked or canned black-eyed peas
   (page 346)
Salt and pepper to taste
Juice of 1 lemon

Trim the leeks of their green and root sections and cut them in quarters lengthwise. Run under a strong flow of cold water to wash thoroughly. Shake off excess water and slice the leeks into small pieces. Heat 2 tablespoons of the olive oil in a large saucepan or skillet over medium heat, add the leeks and pepper flakes, and cook until completely soft, about 2 minutes. Add the garlic and the black-eyed peas and heat through, stirring occasionally. Season liberally with salt and pepper. Stir in the lemon juice and the remaining oil and serve.

Makes 4 servings, plus enough to:
✪ **Reserve 1½ cups for Creamy Broccoli Bean Soup.**

Broccoli with Spiced Apple Cider Sauce

4 cups apple cider
4 cloves garlic, finely chopped
2 teaspoons finely chopped gingerroot

1 teaspoon dried rosemary, crumbled
¼ teaspoon cracked black pepper
3 pounds broccoli

Combine the cider, garlic, gingerroot, rosemary, and pepper in a medium saucepan. Boil over high heat for about 20 minutes, or until the liquid is reduced to 1½ cups. Strain.

Meanwhile, trim the ends from the broccoli stems. Peel the skin from the stems with a vegetable peeler or small sharp knife. Cut the stems into 2-inch-long sticks, and cut the florets into bite-size pieces. Bring a large pot of water to a boil and add the broccoli. Boil for 4 minutes, or until the broccoli is bright green and tender. Drain well, and shake off any excess water.

Arrange half the broccoli (about 3½ cups) on a platter, pour ½ cup of the sauce over it, and serve.

Makes 4 servings, plus enough to:
✪ **Reserve 1 cup sauce for Apple-glazed Cornish Hens.**
✪ **Reserve 3½ cups broccoli for Creamy Broccoli Bean Soup.**

Creamy Broccoli Bean Soup

- ✪ 1½ cups reserved Black-eyed Peas and Leeks
- ✪ 3½ cups broccoli reserved from Broccoli with Spiced Apple Cider Sauce

½ teaspoon dried thyme
4 cups chicken broth, canned or homemade
Salt and pepper to taste
4 ounces feta cheese, crumbled

Finely chop the reserved black-eyed peas and reserved broccoli in a food processor. Turn the mixture into a large heavy saucepan and add the thyme, chicken broth, salt, and pepper. Bring to a boil, reduce the heat, and simmer for 5 minutes. Reduce heat to low and stir in the cheese, mixing until it melts. Serve immediately.

Makes 4 servings.

Caribbean Pork Stew

- ✪ 8 ribs reserved from Barbecued Ribs

2 teaspoons soy sauce
3 cups water
1½ cups long-grain rice
1 medium onion, chopped
1 bell pepper, stemmed, seeded, and diced
1 tablespoon vegetable oil
Pinch of crushed red pepper flakes
1 teaspoon ground allspice
1 teaspoon ground cumin

¼ teaspoon dried thyme
½ teaspoon ground ginger
- ✪ 1 cup sauce reserved from Barbecued Ribs

1 cup beef or chicken broth, canned or homemade
8 plum tomatoes, canned or fresh, coarsely chopped
Salt and pepper to taste

Slice the reserved barbecued rib meat from the bones, trimming off most of the fat. Cut into bite-size pieces and set aside.

Combine the soy sauce and water in a heavy saucepan. Bring to a boil and add the rice. Stir once. Reduce heat and cover so the water simmers for 15 to 20 minutes.

Meanwhile, cook the onion and pepper in the vegetable oil in a saucepan or deep skillet over medium heat until softened. Add the pepper flakes, allspice, cumin, thyme, and ginger. Cook for 30 seconds, stirring constantly. Stir in the reserved sauce, broth, tomatoes, and meat. Bring to a simmer and cook for 5 minutes. Season with salt and pepper. Arrange the rice in a ring on a large platter and ladle the stew into the center.

Makes 4 servings.

Wok-steamed Pepper Clams

4 dozen littleneck clams
¼ cup cornmeal
✪ **I tablespoon spice mixture reserved
from Barbecued Ribs**
¼ teaspoon ground ginger
1 tablespoon vegetable oil

Pinch of crushed red pepper flakes
½ bell pepper, stemmed, seeded, and diced
½ cup water
3 scallions, thinly sliced
1 loaf crusty whole-grain bread, warmed

Place the clams in a large bowl and scatter the cornmeal over them. Fill the bowl with cold water and set aside for at least 15 minutes. Drain and rinse the clams well. Combine the spice mixture and ginger, and set aside.

Heat the oil in a large wok until smoking. Add the pepper flakes and bell pepper and stir-fry for 10 seconds. Add the clams, the spice mixture, and the water. Bring to a boil, cover, and cook for about 5 minutes, or until the clams open. Stir in the scallions and serve immediately with the warm bread.

Makes 4 servings.

Apple-glazed Cornish Hens

1 teaspoon dried rosemary
½ teaspoon dried thyme
½ teaspoon dried sage
1 teaspoon salt
½ teaspoon cracked black pepper

2 large Cornish hens, split in half lengthwise
with backbones removed (page 251)
✪ **I cup sauce reserved from Broccoli
with Spiced Apple Cider Sauce**

Combine the rosemary, thyme, sage, salt, and pepper, and grind until fine in a spice grinder, spice mill, or in a mortar with a pestle. Set aside. Rub the spice mixture into the interior of each hen half.

Grill 5 inches from a medium-hot fire for 10 minutes on each side, turning 3 times. Brush the hens with the reserved sauce and grill them for 15 minutes more, turning 3 more times and brushing with glaze each time the hens are turned. Serve immediately.

Makes 4 servings.

Menu 36

This week starts with a meal punctuated by pepper, garlic, and a creamy balm of blue cheese. The garlic and pepper–crusted steak, which is the center of the Sunday meal, is the groundwork for the Spiced Sirloin Strips with Peanut Sauce late in the week. Its pungent crust of peppercorns and garlic is set off by the hot, sweet bite of a Thai peanut sauce.

Roasted Buffalo Potatoes are my takeoff on Buffalo chicken wings. They are guaranteed to become a classic in your kitchen. They make instant work of the Spinach and Potato Gratin on Monday, and the extra hot-pepper sauce is all you need to flavor the Grilled Hot Pepper Catfish on Wednesday.

Sunday's Spinach Salad with Blue Cheese Vinaigrette uses the dip that traditionally accompanies Buffalo chicken wings to grace an elegant salad of fresh spinach, sweet onion, and a handful of toasted walnuts. The dressing is warmed on Tuesday into a creamy blue cheese sauce for grilled chicken paillard. To make paillards, boneless chicken breasts are pounded paper-thin so each one almost covers a dinner plate. When they're that thin, they need just a few seconds in a hot skillet.

THE SUNDAY DINNER

Grilled Sirloin Steak with a
Pepper and Garlic Crust

Roasted Buffalo Potatoes

Spinach Salad with Blue
Cheese Vinaigrette

THE WEEKNIGHT ENTREES

Spinach and Potato Gratin

Paillard of Chicken with Creamy
Blue Cheese Sauce

Grilled Hot Pepper Catfish

Spiced Sirloin Strips with Peanut Sauce

Grilled Sirloin Steak with a Pepper and Garlic Crust

1 tablespoon cracked black pepper
2 large cloves garlic, minced
1 teaspoon salt

¼ cup olive oil
2½ pounds boneless sirloin steak

Combine the pepper, garlic, salt, and oil and rub the mixture into the surface of the steak. Let stand for 30 minutes.

Grill or broil the steak until done, about 5 to 7 minutes per side for medium, depending on how thick it is. Allow to rest for 5 minutes before cutting. Serve half the steak.

Makes 4 servings, plus enough to:
✪ **Reserve remaining steak for Spiced Sirloin Strips with Peanut Sauce.**

Roasted Buffalo Potatoes

3 to 4 pounds russet potatoes, scrubbed and
*   dried*
1 tablespoon vegetable oil

Salt to taste
2 tablespoons butter, melted and hot
5 tablespoons Durkee Red Hot Sauce

Preheat the oven to 425°F.

Cut each potato into 8 to 10 wedges. Toss with the vegetable oil and place in a large roasting pan. Sprinkle with salt. Roast for 1 hour, turning with a spatula every 20 minutes. Remove and reserve half the potatoes.

Whisk together the butter and hot sauce. Pour 3 tablespoons of the sauce over the remaining potatoes, toss to coat evenly, and serve.

Makes 4 servings, plus enough to:
✪ **Reserve half the potatoes for Spinach and Potato Gratin.**
✪ **Reserve ¼ cup sauce for Grilled Hot Pepper Catfish.**

Spinach Salad with Blue Cheese Vinaigrette

3 cloves garlic, minced
6 tablespoons olive oil
4½ tablespoons red wine vinegar
¾ cup yogurt or sour cream
3 tablespoons milk
6 ounces blue cheese, crumbled

Salt and pepper to taste
1½ pounds fresh spinach leaves, washed and
   dried
½ small red onion, thinly sliced
¾ cup walnuts, toasted

Whisk together the garlic, olive oil, vinegar, yogurt, milk, cheese, salt, and pepper. Set aside. Toss two thirds of the spinach with the onion and refrigerate until ready to serve. Just before serving, toss the spinach and onion with ½ cup of the dressing and the walnuts.

Makes 4 servings, plus enough to:
✪ **Reserve ½ pound spinach for Spinach and Potato Gratin.**
✪ **Reserve 1 cup dressing for Paillard of Chicken with Creamy Blue Cheese Sauce.**

Spinach and Potato Gratin

½ small onion, finely chopped
Pinch of crushed red pepper flakes
2 tablespoons olive oil
1 clove garlic, minced
✪ **½ pound spinach leaves reserved from Spinach Salad with Blue Cheese Vinaigrette**
Salt and pepper to taste

½ cup seasoned bread crumbs
✪ **Reserved Roasted Buffalo Potatoes**
4 ounces aged cheddar cheese, shredded
2 eggs, lightly beaten
1 cup milk
1 teaspoon spicy brown mustard
1 tablespoon grated parmesan cheese

Sauté the onion and pepper flakes in 2 teaspoons of the olive oil in a skillet until softened. Add the garlic and reserved spinach and cook until the spinach wilts. Season liberally with salt and pepper. Set aside.

Preheat the oven to 350°F. Grease a 6-cup casserole and dust with half the bread crumbs.

Cut the reserved potatoes into large chunks and make a layer of potatoes in the bottom of the prepared casserole. Season with salt and pepper. Top with a third of the cheddar cheese and a third of the spinach mixture. Combine the eggs, milk, and mustard and pour a third over the top. Continue to layer the potatoes, salt and pepper, cheddar cheese, spinach, and milk mixture until all has been used up. Even the top. Mix the remaining bread crumbs with the parmesan cheese and sprinkle evenly over the top. Drizzle the remaining olive oil over all.

Bake for 25 minutes. Increase the oven temperature to 450°F. and bake another 10 minutes, or until mixture is bubbling and browned. Cut into wedges and serve.

Makes 4 to 6 servings.

Paillard of Chicken with Creamy Blue Cheese Sauce

2 skinless and boneless chicken breasts, split
1 tablespoon olive oil
Salt and pepper to taste

✪ **1 cup dressing reserved from Spinach Salad with Blue Cheese Vinaigrette**
8 sprigs watercress

Trim away all visible fat and tendons from the chicken breasts. Brush the chicken with the olive oil and season with salt and pepper. Pound each piece of chicken between sheets of plastic wrap to a thickness of ⅛ inch. Refrigerate until just before serving.

Just before cooking the chicken, warm the reserved blue cheese dressing in the top of a double boiler or in a microwave at 50 percent power, just long enough to melt the cheese. Do not overheat. Keep warm.

Heat an iron skillet, preferably one with ridges, until smoking. Brush with a thin film of oil. Remove plastic from one of the breasts and cook for 45 seconds per side, or until chicken is firm. Transfer to a plate and keep warm. Cook the rest of the chicken in the same way.

Serve each paillard on a dinner plate; it will nearly take up the whole center section of the plate. Pour a stream of the sauce across the center and garnish with 2 sprigs of watercress.

Makes 4 servings.

Grilled Hot Pepper Catfish

4 catfish fillets (about 6 ounces each)
1 tablespoon olive oil
1 tablespoon hot paprika
½ teaspoon garlic salt
¼ teaspoon onion powder
¼ teaspoon ground cumin

½ teaspoon ground black pepper
✪ ¼ cup sauce reserved from Roasted Buffalo Potatoes
1 clove garlic, minced
2 tablespoons coarsely chopped cilantro (optional)

Coat the fish fillets with the oil. Mix the paprika, garlic salt, onion powder, cumin, and pepper. Rub into the fish. Refrigerate for 20 minutes.

Heat the reserved sauce with the garlic until sauce is warm.

Grill on an oiled rack or broil the fish 4 inches from a hot fire, 3 to 4 minutes per side. Remove from heat and spoon sauce over top. Top with cilantro, if desired.

Makes 4 servings.

Spiced Sirloin Strips with Peanut Sauce

1 small onion, finely chopped
1 clove garlic, minced
2 teaspoons peanut oil
2 teaspoons grated fresh gingerroot
½ teaspoon ground cumin
½ teaspoon ground coriander
2 scallions, thinly sliced

1 teaspoon chili paste
2 teaspoons light soy sauce
¼ cup crunchy peanut butter
1 cup yogurt
✪ Reserved Grilled Sirloin Steak with a Pepper and Garlic Crust

Sauté the onion and the garlic in the oil until soft. Add the gingerroot, cumin, and coriander and cook another minute. Add the scallions, chili paste, soy sauce, and peanut butter and stir with a whisk until blended. Remove from heat and mix in the yogurt. Slice the steak into ¼-inch-thick strips, and toss with half the sauce. Set aside for 20 minutes.

Thread each strip on a 10-inch skewer, and grill over a hot fire until browned, about 2 minutes per side. Serve with remaining sauce as a dip.

Makes 4 servings.

Menu 37

Paella, a specialty of coastal Spain, is a hearty one-pot meal traditionally made over an open fire in a large flat pan that is also called a paella. If you don't have a paella (and most of us don't), a Dutch oven, a heavy roasting pan, or a deep skillet will also work. Just be sure the pan is wide enough to hold the meat and seafood in a single layer. Although the dish can be made with any combination of poultry, meat, and seafood, it depends on short- or medium-grain rice for its success. Paella is traditionally served alone, but I have added a refreshing cucumber salad and a side dish of Curried Sweet Potatoes. These Sunday dishes lead to the weeknight entrees, three out of four of which are themselves one-dish dinners. The seafood gets teamed with the sweet potato dish for an unusual pie with a spicy sweet potato crust. The poultry is perfumed with orange for Orange Saffron Chicken and Rice and the sausage is used in Tortellini with Hot Sausage and Broccoli. Thursday's grilled lamb steaks are sauced with Sunday's parsleyed cucumbers.

THE SUNDAY DINNER	THE WEEKNIGHT ENTREES
Paella	Spicy Seafood Pie
Curried Sweet Potatoes	Orange Saffron Chicken and Rice
Parsleyed Cucumber Salad	Tortellini with Hot Sausage and Broccoli
	Grilled Lamb Steaks with Cucumber Sauce

Paella

4 Cornish hens, quartered
Salt and pepper to taste
¼ cup olive oil
1 pound hot sausage (Italian or chorizo), cut in 12 pieces
¼ pound ham, diced
1 large onion, chopped
4 cloves garlic, minced
1 large red bell pepper, stemmed, seeded, and diced
1 large green bell pepper, stemmed, seeded, and diced
3½ cups short-grain white rice (about 1½ pounds)

1 teaspoon dried thyme
1 cup frozen peas
6 cups hot chicken broth, canned or homemade
½ teaspoon ground saffron
4 plum tomatoes, peeled, seeded, and coarsely chopped
1 bay leaf
¼ cup chopped parsley
60 medium shrimp, peeled and deveined (about 1¾ pounds)
1¾ pounds bay scallops

Season the Cornish hens all over with salt and pepper. Heat 3 tablespoons of the olive oil in a large Dutch oven or very large and deep skillet over medium-high heat until very hot. Brown the hen pieces in batches. Remove and set aside.

Add the remaining tablespoon of oil and cook the sausage, ham, and onion until the onion softens and the sausage loses its raw look, about 2 minutes. Add the garlic and bell peppers and cook another 3 to 5 minutes, or until all the vegetables have softened. Add the rice and thyme and toss with the vegetables for 1 minute. Add the peas, chicken broth, and saffron. Heat until simmering, stirring occasionally. Return the hen pieces to the pot, and submerge in the liquid. Add the tomatoes, bay leaf, and parsley. Cover and simmer for 15 to 20 minutes, or until the hen pieces are cooked through. Scatter the shrimp and scallops over the top, cover, and simmer another 5 minutes, or until all the liquid has been absorbed, the rice is tender, and the seafood is firm.

To serve, make a bed of rice on a large platter, using about two thirds of the rice. Top with 8 hen pieces, about two thirds of the shrimp (about 40), three fourths of the scallops, and 8 pieces of sausage.

Makes 4 servings, plus enough to:
✪ **Reserve 3 cups rice mixture for Orange Saffron Chicken and Rice.**
✪ **Reserve 8 pieces Cornish hen for Orange Saffron Chicken and Rice.**
✪ **Reserve 20 shrimp for Spicy Seafood Pie.**
✪ **Reserve 1 cup scallops for Spicy Seafood Pie.**
✪ **Reserve 4 pieces sausage for Tortellini with Hot Sausage and Broccoli.**

HEN DIVISION

To split a hen in half lengthwise, cut along both sides of the backbone with kitchen shears and remove the backbone (save it for making stock). Turn the hen over and cut through the center of the breastbone with a large knife. To quarter a hen, cut it in half, removing the backbone, then separate the leg from the breast-wing section by positioning the knife under the leg and cutting diagonally through the ends of the rib-cage bones, following the outside edge of the breast section.

Curried Sweet Potatoes

1 tablespoon vegetable oil	*8 sweet potatoes, peeled and cut into chunks*
1 large onion, chopped	*1 tablespoon sugar*
½ teaspoon ground ginger	*Salt and pepper to taste*
1 tablespoon curry powder	*1½ cups water*
1 small dried chili	*¾ cup milk*

Heat the oil in a large heavy saucepan over medium heat. Add the onion and cook, stirring frequently, for 1 minute. Add the ginger, curry, and chili and cook another 30 seconds. Add the sweet potatoes and toss. Add the sugar, salt, pepper, and the water. Cover and simmer until the potatoes are tender, about 15 to 20 minutes. Drain and mix in the milk. Serve about ¾ cup per person.

Makes 4 servings, plus enough to:
✪ **Reserve 3 cups for Spicy Seafood Pie.**

Parsleyed Cucumber Salad

2 large or 3 medium cucumbers	*1 clove garlic, minced*
2 tablespoons olive oil	*Salt and pepper to taste*
1 tablespoon lemon juice	*¼ cup chopped parsley*
1 tablespoon red or white wine vinegar	

Peel the cucumbers, split them in half lengthwise, scrape out the seeds, and slice thin. Toss with salt and set aside for 10 minutes. Squeeze cucumber slices gently and toss the slices with the olive oil, lemon juice, vinegar, garlic, salt, and pepper. Refrigerate for at least 15 minutes. Toss in the parsley. Serve ½ cup per person.

Makes 4 servings, plus enough to:
✪ **Reserve ½ cup for Grilled Lamb Steaks with Cucumber Sauce.**

Spicy Seafood Pie

✪ **3 cups reserved Curried Sweet Potatoes**
✪ **20 shrimp reserved from Paella**
1 medium onion, finely chopped
1 tablespoon vegetable oil
1 green bell pepper, stemmed, seeded, and diced

1 teaspoon finely chopped gingerroot
1 cup chopped canned tomatoes
Salt and pepper to taste
✪ **I cup scallops reserved from Paella**
½ cup yogurt

Preheat the oven to 375°F.

Press the potatoes in an even layer across the bottom and up the sides of a 9-inch pie plate. Set aside. Coarsely chop the reserved shrimp. Set aside.

Cook the onion in the vegetable oil in a skillet over medium heat until softened, about 1 minute. Add the bell pepper and the gingerroot and cook for another 2 minutes. Add the tomatoes and cook until thickened. Season with salt and pepper.

Stir in the shrimp, the reserved scallops, and yogurt. Fill the sweet-potato shell with the mixture. Bake for 20 minutes and serve.

Makes 4 servings.

Orange Saffron Chicken and Rice

1 cup orange juice
✪ **3 cups rice reserved from Paella**
Pinch of crushed red pepper flakes

✪ **8 pieces of Cornish hen reserved from Paella**

Heat the orange juice in a skillet until simmering. Add the reserved rice, stirring to separate clumps. Stir in the pepper flakes. Place the reserved pieces of Cornish hen on top and simmer until the orange juice has been absorbed and the chicken is heated through. Serve the hen pieces on a bed of the rice.

Makes 4 servings.

Tortellini with Hot Sausage and Broccoli

¾ pound broccoli
✪ **4 pieces sausage reserved from Paella**
1 pound frozen or refrigerated meat or cheese
  tortellini

1 clove garlic, finely chopped
2 tablespoons olive oil
3 tablespoons freshly grated parmesan cheese
Salt and pepper to taste

Peel the broccoli stalks and cut them in half lengthwise. Thinly slice the stems, and cut the tops into small florets. Set aside. Coarsely chop the sausage.

Cook the tortellini in a large pot of salted boiling water for 3 minutes if refrigerated, 5 minutes if frozen. Add the broccoli and cook 5 more minutes, until the tortellini and broccoli are tender. Add the reserved sausage and the garlic and heat through. Drain and toss in a bowl with the olive oil, parmesan cheese, salt, and pepper. Serve right away.

Makes 4 servings.

Grilled Lamb Steaks with Cucumber Sauce

2 lamb steaks, each 1 inch thick
Salt and pepper to taste
1 teaspoon garlic powder
✪ **½ cup reserved Parsleyed Cucumber Salad**

1 clove garlic, finely chopped
1 cup yogurt
½ teaspoon hot pepper sauce

Rub the lamb steaks with salt, pepper, and garlic powder. Refrigerate for at least 15 minutes or as long as several hours.

Coarsely chop the reserved cucumbers and mix with the garlic, yogurt, and hot pepper sauce. Season to taste with salt and pepper. Set aside.

Grill or broil the lamb very close to a hot fire, 3 minutes per side for rare, 2 to 3 inches from the fire for 5 minutes per side for medium, and 4 inches from the fire for 7 minutes per side for well done. Cut each steak in half and serve with the sauce.

Makes 4 servings.

merican cookbooks are full of boiled dinners completed in a single vessel, from corned beef and cabbage to cioppino. In France, you can have your pick—choucroute in the north, bouillabaisse in the south, and *pot au feu* everywhere. The Italian rendition of this feast in a pot is called bollito misto and it is the hub of this week's menu.

Like most boiled meals, bollito misto is simple, taking time but little attention. Meats and vegetables—in this case, brisket, potatoes, veal shanks, Cornish hens, carrots, turnips, and sausages—are set to simmer after lunch and uncovered for dinner ready to eat. The broth, rich with meat juices and fragrant with herbs, is served as a first course, followed by the boiled meats dressed with two pungent sauces (one red, made from chilies and sweet peppers; the other green, a combination of fresh herbs, garlic, and anchovy); and the vegetables tossed in garlic-infused olive oil.

Sunday's opulent dinner becomes the source of a variety of dishes. On Monday, a pack of fresh tortillas is all you need for the red sauce, boiled brisket, and vegetables to become a distinctive dinner of enchiladas. The hen and sausage combine with the garlic oil and canned white beans for an easy version of cassoulet on Tuesday, and Wednesday's bolognese sauce is assembled in minutes from Sunday's veal shanks, garlic oil, meaty broth, and red sauce. Thursday's is the easiest meal of all—a tuna potato salad that emerges by tossing Sunday's green sauce, garlic oil, and potatoes with a can of tuna. All you have to do is open the can.

THE SUNDAY DINNER	THE WEEKNIGHT ENTREES
Bollito Misto	Enchilada Grande
Tomato Rice Soup	Chicken Cassoulet
Mixed Vegetables with Garlic Oil	Twelve-Minute Pasta Bolognese
	Pungent Tuna Potato Salad

Bollito Misto

10 cups water
2 cups red or white wine
1 piece of brisket (about 2 pounds)
Salt and pepper to taste
1 pound carrots, cut into 2 or 3 pieces each
6 ribs celery, cut into 2 or 3 pieces each
2 whole cloves
2 medium onions, halved
1 teaspoon dried thyme
1 teaspoon dried rosemary

1 small dried chili
6 2–inch pieces veal shanks (about 4 pounds)
1 cup canned tomatoes, coarsely chopped
8 russet potatoes, halved (3 pounds)
4 turnips, quartered
2 Cornish hens, quartered (page 251)
1 pound sweet Italian sausage, cut into
   8 pieces
½ cup Red Sauce (recipe follows)
⅔ cup Green Sauce (recipe follows)

Combine the water and wine in a very large soup pot and bring to a boil. Season the brisket with salt and pepper and add to liquid. Return to a simmer and cook for 1 hour, skimming foam from the surface as needed. Add the carrots and celery. Stick the cloves into 2 pieces of the onion and add all the onion to the pot. Add the thyme, rosemary, chili, veal shanks, and tomatoes. Simmer for 1 more hour. Add the potatoes, turnips, Cornish hens, and sausage. Simmer for 1 more hour. Skim fat.

Set aside 6 cups of the broth to make the Tomato Rice Soup and serve as a first course. Set aside 4 cups of the vegetables for Mixed Vegetables with Garlic Oil to serve as a side dish with the meat. Serve each person 1 piece of veal shank, 2 slices of brisket, a quarter of a Cornish hen, and 1 piece of sausage, all moistened with a bit of the broth. Serve Red Sauce and Green Sauce on the side.

Makes 4 servings, plus enough to:
- **Reserve 4 pieces sausage for Chicken Cassoulet.**
- **Reserve 4 pieces Cornish hen for Chicken Cassoulet.**
- **Reserve remaining brisket for Enchilada Grande.**
- **Reserve 2 pieces veal shank for Twelve-Minute Pasta Bolognese.**
- **Reserve 4 pieces carrot, 4 pieces celery, and ½ cup onion for Chicken Cassoulet.**
- **Reserve 3 pieces carrot and 4 pieces celery for Twelve-Minute Pasta Bolognese.**
- **Reserve 4 cups potatoes for Pungent Tuna Potato Salad.**
- **Reserve 1½ cups vegetables for Enchilada Grande.**
- **Reserve 1 cup broth for Twelve-Minute Pasta Bolognese.**
- **Reserve 1 cup broth for Chicken Cassoulet.**
- **Reserve ½ cup broth for Enchilada Grande.**

Red Sauce

2 large red bell peppers, stemmed, seeded,
    and quartered
1 hot chili, stemmed, seeded, and minced
1 small onion, chopped
1 clove garlic

2 tablespoons red wine vinegar
Juice of ½ lemon
2 tablespoons olive oil
Salt and pepper to taste

Combine all ingredients in a heavy saucepan, and cook, covered, over medium heat until the peppers are soft, about 15 minutes. Puree and serve warm. Serve ½ cup.

Makes 4 portions, plus enough to:
✪ **Reserve ½ cup for Enchilada Grande.**
✪ **Reserve 2 tablespoons for Twelve-Minute Pasta Bolognese.**

Green Sauce

½ cup finely chopped parsley
8 anchovy fillets, finely chopped
2 cloves garlic, minced
2 teaspoons spicy brown mustard

2 tablespoons red wine vinegar
6 tablespoons olive oil
Salt and pepper to taste

Combine all the ingredients in a small bowl and mix thoroughly. Serve ⅔ cup.

Makes 4 servings, plus enough to:
✪ **Reserve ¼ cup for Chicken Cassoulet.**
✪ **Reserve ¼ cup for Pungent Tuna Potato Salad.**

Tomato Rice Soup

✪ **6 cups broth from Bollito Misto**
½ cup long-grain rice

½ cup canned crushed tomatoes
2 tablespoons chopped parsley

Heat the broth to a boil. Add the rice and simmer for 15 minutes. Add the tomatoes and parsley and heat for 1 more minute. Serve as a first course, before the Bollito Misto.

Makes 4 servings.

Mixed Vegetables with Garlic Oil

4 cloves garlic, minced
7 tablespoons olive oil

Salt and pepper to taste
✪ **4 cups vegetables from Bollito Misto**

Combine the garlic, olive oil, salt, and pepper. Drizzle 2 tablespoons over the warm vegetables.

Makes 4 servings, plus enough to:
✪ **Reserve 2 tablespoons garlic oil for Chicken Cassoulet.**
✪ **Reserve 2 tablespoons garlic oil for Pungent Tuna Potato Salad.**
✪ **Reserve 1 tablespoon garlic oil for Twelve-Minute Pasta Bolognese.**
✪ **Reserve 2 teaspoons garlic oil for Enchilada Grande.**

Enchilada Grande

✪ ½ cup reserved red sauce
✪ ½ cup broth reserved from Bollito Misto
1 teaspoon ground cumin
2 teaspoons chili powder
8 (6-inch) flour tortillas
✪ Brisket reserved from Bollito Misto

✪ 1½ cups vegetables reserved from Bollito Misto
✪ 2 teaspoons garlic oil reserved from Mixed Vegetables with Garlic Oil
Salt and pepper to taste
4 ounces monterey jack cheese, crumbled

Preheat the oven to 375°F.

Combine the reserved sauce, reserved broth, cumin, and chili powder in a small saucepan and bring to a boil. Set aside.

Wrap the tortillas in foil and warm in the preheated oven for 8 minutes. Or wrap in plastic wrap and microwave at full power for 1 minute.

Chop the reserved brisket and reserved vegetables and combine with the reserved garlic oil, salt, pepper, and ¼ cup of the sauce mixture. Pour the remaining sauce mixture into a pie plate. Lay a tortilla in the sauce and place 2 tablespoons of the meat mixture down the center. Roll up the tortilla around the filling and place, seam side down, in a baking dish large enough to hold the rolls in a single layer. Roll up the rest of the enchiladas and place them side by side in the baking dish. Spread the remaining sauce mixture over the top. Cover the dish and bake for 10 minutes. Remove cover, scatter the cheese over the top, and bake for another 5 minutes, uncovered, until the cheese melts. Serve hot.

Makes 4 servings.

Chicken Cassoulet

- **4 pieces sausage reserved from Bollito Misto**
- **4 pieces carrot, 4 pieces celery, and ½ cup onion reserved from Bollito Misto**
- **2 tablespoons garlic oil reserved from Mixed Vegetables with Garlic Oil**
- *2 teaspoons ground coriander*
- *1 teaspoon ground cumin*
- *½ teaspoon ground ginger*
- *Salt to taste*
- *½ to 1 teaspoon ground black pepper*
- **1 cup broth reserved from Bollito Misto**
- **¼ cup reserved Green Sauce**
- *2 cans (about 1 pound each) small white beans, drained and rinsed*
- **4 pieces Cornish hen reserved from Bollito Misto**

Cook the reserved sausage and reserved vegetables in the reserved garlic oil in a large skillet over medium heat for 1 minute. Add the coriander, cumin, ginger, salt to taste, and pepper and cook for another 30 seconds. Add the reserved broth and reserved sauce and stir to blend. Bring to a simmer, add the beans, and adjust the seasoning. Place the reserved hen pieces on top, cover, and simmer until the hen pieces are heated through, about 10 minutes. Serve.

Makes 4 servings.

Twelve-Minute Pasta Bolognese

✪ **2 pieces veal shank reserved from Bollito Misto**

✪ **3 pieces carrot and 4 pieces celery reserved from Bollito Misto**

1 pound pasta, such as ziti or penne

✪ **1 tablespoon garlic oil reserved from Mixed Vegetables with Garlic Oil**

½ cup milk

1 ½ cups canned crushed tomatoes

✪ **1 cup broth reserved from Bollito Misto**

✪ **2 tablespoons reserved Red Sauce**

Cut the meat from the reserved veal shanks and finely chop it. Finely chop the reserved carrot and celery and combine with the meat.

Bring a large pot of salted water to a boil, add the pasta, and boil vigorously until pasta is al dente, about 10 minutes. Drain.

Meanwhile, sauté the meat and vegetables in the reserved garlic oil in a large saucepan until heated through, stirring constantly, about 2 minutes. Add the milk and boil until all of it has been absorbed. Add the tomatoes and the broth and simmer gently for 5 minutes. Stir in the reserved sauce and keep warm. Toss the pasta with the sauce and serve right away.

Makes 4 servings.

Pungent Tuna Potato Salad

✪ **4 cups potatoes reserved from Bollito Misto**

✪ **¼ cup reserved Green Sauce**

✪ **2 tablespoons garlic oil reserved from Mixed Vegetables with Garlic Oil**

Juice of 1 lemon

1 can (about 6 ounces) tuna, drained and crumbled

Dice the reserved potatoes. Combine the reserved sauce, reserved garlic oil, lemon juice, and tuna in a bowl. Toss in the potatoes. Let stand for 10 minutes before serving.

Makes 4 servings.

Menu 39

Cheese need not mean fat. Two high-moisture lowfat cheeses—part-skim mozzarella and ricotta—are the secret ingredients behind this Sunday's nutritionally friendly Cheese Lasagna. Fat is reduced further with the use of egg white, rather than whole egg, to bind the ricotta and with a lowfat homemade tomato sauce. It is accompanied by two salads that complement its mild creaminess with a spark of lemon juice and a wallop of sundried tomato. One is a simple green salad with a dressing that's so easy and delicious it will become a standard in your kitchen. The other is a bean salad of chick peas that radiates garlic, hot pepper sauce, and the concentrated tomato flavor of sundried fruit.

The cheese mixture becomes a coating for Monday's Turkey Saltimbocca, which gets its punch from a paste of sundried tomatoes and garlic concocted for Sunday's Chick Pea and Sundried Tomato Salad. And the lasagna's tomato sauce makes Thursday's Lamb Chops Oreganata a snap. On Wednesday, a roasted Cornish hen is glazed in the dressing from Sunday's dinner salad, and on Tuesday, shrimp gazpacho is made effortlessly by combining the marinated salad with poached shrimp, vegetable juice, and a shot of hot sauce. Not only is this gazpacho easy to make, the salad dressing and croutons season and thicken the soup as it is pureed.

THE SUNDAY DINNER

Cheese Lasagna

Mixed Green Salad with
Lemon Vinaigrette

Chick Pea and Sundried Tomato Salad

THE WEEKNIGHT ENTREES

Turkey Saltimbocca

Shrimp Gazpacho with Hummus on Pita

Lemon Hoisin Hens

Lamb Chops Oreganata

Cheese Lasagna

NOODLES

1 tablespoon olive oil
16 lasagna noodles (about 1 pound)

SAUCE

2 tablespoons olive oil
1 medium onion, chopped
3 stalks fresh fennel, diced
2 sprigs fresh oregano, leaves only
2 sprigs fresh rosemary, leaves only
2 sprigs fresh thyme, leaves only
¼ cup basil leaves
2 cloves garlic, finely chopped
1 cup white wine
2 cans (28 ounces each) crushed tomatoes
Salt and pepper to taste

CHEESE

2 cups part-skim ricotta cheese
2 tablespoons freshly grated romano cheese
5 tablespoons freshly grated parmesan cheese
1 teaspoon freshly ground pepper
3 egg whites

FOR ASSEMBLING

1 pound part-skim mozzarella, grated
3 tablespoons freshly grated parmesan cheese

Heat a large pot of water until boiling. Add 1 tablespoon oil and the noodles. Do not crowd the pot; if necessary, cook in batches. Boil until tender, about 10 minutes. Remove the noodles, drain, and wash well under cold running water. Layer noodles on a sheet pan.

Heat 2 tablespoons olive oil in a large heavy saucepan. Add the onion and fennel and cook over medium-high heat, stirring frequently, until the vegetables have softened, about 2 minutes. Add the oregano, rosemary, thyme, basil leaves, and garlic and stir to combine. Add the wine and bring to a boil. Boil vigorously for 1 minute. Add the tomatoes, salt, and pepper and simmer for 15 minutes. Reserve 3 cups.

Combine the ricotta, romano, and parmesan cheeses with the pepper and eggs. Blend thoroughly. Reserve ½ cup.

Preheat the oven to 375°F.

To assemble, spread ½ cup of the sauce over the bottom of a large rectangular baking dish. Arrange 4 lasagna noodles over the bottom of the dish, slightly overlapping in a single layer. Top with another ½ cup of sauce. Spread 9 tablespoons (a little more than ½ cup) of the ricotta mixture over the noodles and top with about ¾ cup of the mozzarella. Top with 4 noodles, 1 cup sauce, 9 tablespoons ricotta mixture, and ¾ cup mozzarella. Repeat with the same quantities of noodles, sauce, ricotta, and mozzarella. Finish with the rest of the noodles, 2 cups sauce, and ¾ cup mozzarella. Sprinkle the top with parmesan cheese. You should have some mozzarella left over. Bake for 40 minutes. Let stand for 5 minutes before serving.

Makes 4 servings, plus enough to:
- ✪ Reserve 2 cups tomato sauce for Lamb Chops Oreganata.
- ✪ Reserve I cup tomato sauce for Shrimp Gazpacho with Hummus on Pita.
- ✪ Reserve ¾ cup mozzarella cheese for Turkey Saltimbocca.
- ✪ Reserve ½ cup ricotta mixture for Turkey Saltimbocca.

Mixed Green Salad with Lemon Vinaigrette

Juice of 2 large lemons
3 cloves garlic, minced
½ cup olive oil
Pinch of sugar
Salt and pepper to taste
1 head romaine lettuce leaves, washed and
  dried

1 head red-leaf lettuce leaves, washed and
  dried
1 head escarole leaves, washed and dried
4 scallions, white parts only, sliced
1 large cucumber, peeled, seeded, and diced
3 cups croutons

Make a vinaigrette by combining the lemon juice, garlic, olive oil, sugar, salt, and pepper and set aside. Tear the greens into bite-size pieces and toss with the scallions, cucumber, and ½ cup of the dressing. Mix in the croutons. Serve right away.

Makes 4 servings, plus enough to:
- ✪ Reserve 1½ cups salad for Shrimp Gazpacho with Hummus on Pita.
- ✪ Reserve ¼ cup vinaigrette for Shrimp Gazpacho with Hummus on Pita.
- ✪ Reserve 2 tablespoons vinaigrette for Lemon Hoisin Hens.

Chick Pea and Sundried Tomato Salad

12 oil-cured sundried tomatoes, chopped
2 tablespoons oil from sundried tomatoes
2 cloves garlic, minced
1 teaspoon hot pepper sauce
2 cans (15 ounces each) chick peas, drained and rinsed

6 scallions, white parts only, thinly sliced
1 tablespoon red wine vinegar
Juice of 1 lemon
Salt and pepper to taste

Combine the sundried tomatoes, oil, garlic, and hot sauce. Toss ¼ cup of this mixture with the chick peas, scallions, vinegar, lemon juice, salt, and pepper. Serve 2 cups.

Makes 4 servings, plus enough to:
✪ **Reserve 8 teaspoons sundried tomato mixture for Turkey Saltimbocca.**
✪ **Reserve 4 teaspoons sundried tomato mixture for Shrimp Gazpacho with Hummus on Pita.**
✪ **Reserve 1½ cups salad for Shrimp Gazpacho with Hummus on Pita.**

Turkey Saltimbocca

8 small turkey cutlets (2 to 3 ounces each)
✪ **¾ cup mozzarella reserved from Cheese Lasagna**
✪ **8 teaspoons sundried tomato mixture reserved from Chick Pea and Sundried Tomato Salad**

✪ **½ cup ricotta mixture reserved from Cheese Lasagna**
2 tablespoons milk
1 cup Italian-style bread crumbs
2 tablespoons olive oil
1 lemon, cut into 8 wedges

Place turkey cutlets between sheets of plastic wrap and pound the meat ⅛ inch thick. Scatter the reserved cheese and reserved sundried tomato mixture evenly over four of the turkey slices and top with remaining slices.

Combine the reserved ricotta mixture and the milk in a pie plate, and put the bread crumbs on a plate or a sheet of wax paper. Coat the sandwiched turkey cutlets in the ricotta mixture and dredge thoroughly with bread crumbs. Set aside for 5 minutes.

Heat the olive oil in a large nonstick skillet over medium-high heat. Add the breaded turkey and cook for 4 minutes per side, or until firm in the center. Serve with lemon wedges.

Makes 4 servings.

Shrimp Gazpacho with Hummus on Pita

GAZPACHO

1 cup water

1 tablespoon red or white wine vinegar

1 pound shrimp, peeled, deveined, and thickly sliced

✪ **1½ cups reserved Mixed Green Salad with Lemon Vinaigrette**

2 cups canned salt-free vegetable juice, chilled

✪ **2 tablespoons vinaigrette reserved from Mixed Green Salad with Lemon Vinaigrette**

✪ **1 cup tomato sauce reserved from Cheese Lasagna**

½ teaspoon hot pepper sauce

✪ **4 teaspoons sundried tomato mixture reserved from Chick Pea and Sundried Tomato Salad**

Salt and pepper to taste

HUMMUS

✪ **1½ cups reserved Chick Pea and Sundried Tomato Salad**

✪ **2 tablespoons vinaigrette reserved from Mixed Green Salad with Lemon Vinaigrette**

½ teaspoon hot pepper sauce

4 pita breads

Bring the water and the vinegar to a boil in a skillet. Add the shrimp slices, stir, and cook for 1 minute. Remove shrimp with a slotted spoon and chill.

Process the reserved salad in a food processor or blender until finely chopped. Add the vegetable juice and the reserved vinaigrette and process to incorporate. Transfer to a bowl and mix in the reserved tomato sauce, hot pepper sauce, reserved sundried tomato mixture, and chilled shrimp. Season with salt and pepper. Refrigerate.

Wash the workbowl of the processor and combine reserved chick pea salad, reserved vinaigrette, and hot pepper sauce. Process until finely chopped. Scoop into a serving bowl.

Just before serving, warm pitas in a 375°F. preheated oven or in a toaster oven for 5 minutes. Cut each pita into 4 wedges. Serve the gazpacho in chilled bowls accompanied by warm pita triangles for scooping up the hummus.

Makes 4 servings.

Lemon Hoisin Hens

2 Cornish hens, split in half lengthwise with
*   backbones removed (page 251)*
2 tablespoons hoisin sauce

✪ **2 tablespoons vinaigrette reserved**
from Mixed Green Salad with Lemon
Vinaigrette
2 tablespoons water

Preheat the oven to 400°F.

Place the hen halves, bone side up, in a shallow roasting pan, and roast for 10 minutes. Meanwhile, combine the hoisin sauce, reserved vinaigrette, and water. Brush the bone side of the hen halves with the hoisin mixture and roast another 10 minutes. Turn pieces and roast 10 more minutes. Brush with the hoisin mixture and roast another 10 minutes. Brush with remaining sauce and roast 10 more minutes, or until crisp and brown.

Makes 4 servings.

Lamb Chops Oreganata

8 rib or loin lamb chops, each ¾ inch thick
Salt and pepper to taste
1 tablespoon olive oil
1 tablespoon fresh oregano leaves or
*   1 teaspoon dried oregano*

✪ **2 cups tomato sauce reserved from**
Cheese Lasagna

Rub the chops on both sides with salt and pepper. Heat the oil in a large skillet over medium-high heat and thoroughly brown the chops on both sides. Pour off excess oil. Reduce heat to medium. Add the oregano and the reserved tomato sauce. Lift chops to distribute sauce evenly. Cover and simmer for 2 minutes. Serve 2 chops per person, topped with sauce.

Makes 4 servings.

Menu 40

This week's menu starts with one of this country's first farm-raised fish. Time was when catfish were denigrated for the muddy waters from which they were fished and the strong-tasting fatty meat lying just beneath the skin, but thanks to hydroculture (fish farming), catfish have slowly gained acceptance along with their increased availability and improved consistent meat quality.

This week's Sunday dinner calls for frying the fish in a crust of cornmeal and serving it with cilantro butter. The fish is accompanied by spicy stewed tomatoes laced with habanero peppers and a mélange of grilled vegetables.

On Monday, these vegetables are paired with turkey in a variation on a Native American succotash stew. Originally, succotash was made of meat fat, fresh corn, and beans. I'm expanding on that tradition with a version that combines corn, bell pepper, squash, turkey, chilied tomatoes, and beans in a hearty, spicy one-pot meal. It is interesting to note that all ingredients in this recipe are staples of the Native American larder. The catfish and tomatoes are combined on Tuesday in Cajun Catfish Benedict, and the tomatoes lend their heat to a fiery marinade for Tex-Mex Grilled Flank Steak on Wednesday. Thursday finds the cilantro butter and tomatoes blended with rice-shaped pasta and cheddar cheese for a unique spin on a traditional macaroni and cheese.

THE SUNDAY DINNER

White Corn Catfish with Cilantro Butter

Grilled Corn, Peppers, and Zucchini

Habanero Stewed Tomatoes

THE WEEKNIGHT ENTREES

Turkey Succotash

Cajun Catfish Benedict

Tex-Mex Grilled Flank Steak

Herbed Orzo and Cheese

White Corn Catfish with Cilantro Butter

FISH

½ cup buttermilk
2 cloves garlic, crushed
Salt and pepper to taste
1 teaspoon hot pepper sauce
1 teaspoon ground coriander
6 catfish fillets, trimmed (about 2½ pounds)
1½ cups white cornmeal
Pinch of cayenne

CILANTRO BUTTER

⅓ cup cilantro leaves, finely chopped
2 tablespoons olive oil
½ teaspoon ground coriander
1 large clove garlic, minced
6 tablespoons butter, softened

FOR COOKING AND SERVING

¼ cup corn oil
1 lime, cut into 8 wedges (optional)

Combine the buttermilk, garlic, salt, pepper, hot pepper sauce, and the 1 teaspoon of ground coriander in a nonmetallic pan large enough to hold the fish in a single layer. Place the fish in this mixture and turn to moisten. Cover and refrigerate for at least 1 hour.

Meanwhile, make the cilantro butter. In a small skillet, cook the cilantro leaves in the olive oil with the ½ teaspoon ground coriander for 3 minutes, or until the leaves wilt and turn bright green. Remove from the heat and mix in the garlic. Beat into the butter and set aside.

Mix the cornmeal, cayenne, and salt to taste in a large pie pan. Dredge the coated fish in the cornmeal mixture, turning the fillets until they are well coated. Place on a rack on a sheet pan to dry for 10 minutes.

Heat the corn oil in a large skillet and cook the fish in 2 batches until browned and cooked through, about 3 to 4 minutes per side. Drain the fish on paper towels. Serve four of the fillets, each topped with 2 teaspoons of the butter. Garnish each with 2 lime wedges, if desired.

Makes 4 servings, plus enough to:
✪ **Reserve 2 catfish fillets for Cajun Catfish Benedict.**
✪ **Reserve 2 tablespoons cilantro butter for Cajun Catfish Benedict.**
✪ **Reserve 3 tablespoons cilantro butter for Herbed Orzo and Cheese.**

DEFATTING CATFISH

Catfish are sold already skinned and filleted, but commercial skinning often leaves behind a layer of strong-tasting darker meat. To remove this layer, place the fillet, dark side down, near the edge of your cutting surface. Starting at the narrower and thinner tail end, insert the edge of a sharp thin boning knife just above the dark layer of meat, angling the knife so the blade is exactly parallel to the cutting surface. Cut gently back and forth until you've disengaged a small flap of fish. With your other hand, grasp this flap and pull back while sliding your knife toward the thicker end of the fillet.

Grilled Corn, Peppers, and Zucchini

4 ears of corn, unhusked
4 large red, yellow, and/or green bell peppers,
*   stemmed, seeded, and quartered*
2 tablespoons extra-virgin olive oil

3 medium zucchini, halved lengthwise
*   (about 1⅓ pounds)*
Salt and pepper to taste

Grill or broil the unhusked corn 4 inches from a hot fire for 12 to 15 minutes, turning every 3 minutes. Rub the pepper quarters with 2 teaspoons of the oil. Rub the zucchini with 1 teaspoon of the oil. When the corn has cooked for 3 minutes, place the pepper pieces on the grill. After 3 minutes, add the zucchini. Grill until everything is browned and softened. Set aside for 2 to 3 minutes.

Remove the husk from the corn and cut each ear into 4 sections. Cut the zucchini pieces in half. Arrange 8 pieces of each vegetable on a large platter, drizzle with the remaining olive oil, and season with salt and pepper.

Makes 4 servings, plus enough to:
✪ **Reserve 8 corn pieces for Turkey Succotash.**
✪ **Reserve 4 zucchini quarters for Turkey Succotash.**
✪ **Reserve 8 pepper quarters for Turkey Succotash.**

Habanero Stewed Tomatoes

3 tablespoons olive oil
1 large yellow onion, chopped
*1 habanero chili, stemmed, seeded, and
    halved*
*10 ripe tomatoes, cored and coarsely chopped
    (about 5 pounds)*

2 tablespoons ground cumin
½ teaspoon dried oregano
Salt and pepper to taste

Heat the olive oil in a large heavy saucepan over medium heat for 20 seconds. Add the onion and chili halves and cook for 1 to 2 minutes, or until the onion is soft. Add the tomatoes, cumin, oregano, salt, and pepper. Heat until simmering, stirring frequently, and simmer for 3 minutes. Remove the solid pieces of tomato with a slotted spoon. Boil the juice with the pepper halves until reduced by half. Remove and discard the pepper halves and return the tomato pieces to the pan. Serve 1 cup per person.

Makes 4 servings, plus enough to:
✪ **Reserve 1½ cups for Turkey Succotash.**
✪ **Reserve 2 cups for Cajun Catfish Benedict.**
✪ **Reserve 1½ cups for Tex-Mex Grilled Flank Steak.**
✪ **Reserve 1 cup for Herbed Orzo and Cheese.**

Turkey Succotash

- ✪ **8 pieces corn reserved from Grilled Corn, Peppers, and Zucchini**
- ✪ **4 zucchini quarters reserved from Grilled Corn, Peppers, and Zucchini**
- ✪ **8 pepper quarters reserved from Grilled Corn, Peppers, and Zucchini**
- *2 tablespoons vegetable oil*
- *1 medium onion, chopped*

- *1 pound skinless and boneless turkey breast, cut into 1-inch cubes*
- ✪ **1½ cups reserved Habanero Stewed Tomatoes**
- *1 can (16 to 19 ounces) lima beans, cannellini beans, or chick peas, drained and rinsed*
- *Salt and pepper to taste*

Cut the kernels from the corn cobs. Set aside. Cut the zucchini and peppers into 1-inch pieces. Set aside.

Heat the oil in a large skillet. Add the onion and cook, stirring frequently, until softened, about 1 minute. Add the turkey breast and brown the cubes on all sides, stirring occasionally. This should take about 5 minutes. Add the stewed tomatoes and heat to a simmer. Simmer 3 minutes. Stir in the beans and simmer 2 more minutes. Season with salt and pepper and serve.

Makes 4 servings.

Cajun Catfish Benedict

- ✪ **2 catfish fillets reserved from White Corn Catfish with Cilantro Butter**
- *1 tablespoon corn oil*
- ✪ **2 cups reserved Habanero Stewed Tomatoes**

- *8 eggs*
- ✪ **2 tablespoons cilantro butter reserved from White Corn Catfish with Cilantro Butter**

Cut the reserved fillets in half. Heat the oil in a large nonstick skillet, add the pieces of fish, cover, and cook for 2 minutes per side. Remove to a platter, and keep warm in a 200°F. oven.

Add the reserved stewed tomatoes to the pan and heat to a simmer. Crack the eggs onto the simmering tomato sauce. Turn the heat to low, cover the pan, and cook until the egg whites set, about 3 to 4 minutes. Lift the eggs from the pan with a slotted spatula, and place 2 eggs on each fish fillet. *continued*

Bring the tomatoes to a boil. Remove from the heat, whisk in the cilantro butter, and pour some of the sauce over each egg. Serve immediately.

Makes 4 servings.

Tex-Mex Grilled Flank Steak

1½ pounds flank steak, trimmed of fat
Salt and pepper to taste

○ **1½ cups reserved Habanero Stewed Tomatoes**
2 tablespoons cider vinegar

Poke the steak with a fork all over. Rub salt and pepper into both sides of the steak and set aside. Mix the tomatoes with the vinegar in a glass or ceramic container large enough to hold the steak flat. Place the steak in this mixture and turn to coat completely. Marinate for at least 1 hour, turning once.

Grill or broil 4 inches from a hot fire for 6 to 8 minutes per side, depending on desired doneness. Cut the meat against the grain into very thin slices and serve.

Makes 4 to 6 servings.

Herbed Orzo and Cheese

1 pound orzo
○ **3 tablespoons cilantro butter reserved from White Corn Catfish with Cilantro Butter**

○ **1 cup reserved Habanero Stewed Tomatoes**
8 ounces mild or sharp cheddar cheese, shredded (2 cups)

Preheat oven to 350°F.

Bring a large pot of salted water to a boil. Add the orzo and cook until tender, about 10 minutes. Drain thoroughly. Mix with the reserved cilantro butter, reserved tomatoes, and cheddar cheese, and turn into a 2½- or 3-quart casserole. Bake for 25 minutes and serve.

Makes 4 servings.

Everyone knows that chili peppers are what makes a bowl of chili hot, but the dish is also perfumed with cumin and sweetened with tomato. Hot peppers aren't enough, for fiery food will fail unless its heat is balanced with equally strong sensations.

This week's menu uses chilies in many guises. In the main course of the Sunday dinner, lamb shoulder chops are braised with ancho and pasilla chilies, aniseed, and tomato, and the sauce is thickened with a smoky puree of roasted eggplant. The lamb is served over rice with fresh tomatillo salsa; there is a side dish of black beans spiked with a habanero chili and tempered with lemon juice.

The green vegetable in the menu may be unfamiliar. Nopales (pronounced no-PAH-layz) are the fleshy oval-shaped pads of the Opuntia cactus. Nopales are often found fresh and canned in markets catering to a Mexican clientele. Select the smallest, thinnest fresh nopales you can find, rejecting any that are very dark green (an indication of coarseness) or split or shriveled. If you cannot find canned or fresh nopales, this recipe can be made with frozen green beans.

On Wednesday, the sauce from the lamb is transformed with lime juice and balsamic vinegar into a pungent dip for sea scallops, which have been seared in olive oil with coriander. On Tuesday, the lamb is shredded and stuffed into a Mediterranean pita bread. Monday's vegetarian dinner requires only fifteen minutes to transform Sunday's black-bean side dish into quesadillas topped with green salsa. The tomatillo salsa is also a key ingredient in Thursday's rice salad, in which the tomatillo rice is combined with some of the nopales and black beans and a grilled chicken breast.

THE SUNDAY DINNER

Red Chili Lamb Chops with Warm Tortillas

Savory Black Beans

Rice with Tomatillo Salsa

Sautéed Nopales

THE WEEKNIGHT ENTREES

Bean and Cheddar Quesadillas
with Green Salsa

Shredded Braised Lamb in a Pita

Seared Sea Scallops with Pungent
Dipping Sauce

Grilled Chicken and Rice Salad

Red Chili Lamb Chops with Warm Tortillas

4 diced ancho chilies, stemmed and seeded	*1 teaspoon ground aniseed*
1 dried pasilla chili, stemmed and seeded	*¼ teaspoon dried oregano*
2 cups hot water	*4 cloves garlic, finely chopped*
10 shoulder lamb chops (about 6 pounds)	*4 plum tomatoes, peeled and chopped*
Salt and pepper to taste	*1½ teaspoons sugar*
1 medium onion, chopped	*1 tablespoon cider vinegar*
1 bulb fennel, diced	*½ cup chicken broth, canned or homemade*
2 tablespoons olive oil	*1 medium eggplant (1½ pounds)*
1 teaspoon ground cumin	*8 (6-inch) corn tortillas*

Break the ancho and pasilla chilies into small pieces and soak in the hot water until softened, about 10 minutes. Remove the chilies and finely chop them. Set aside the chilies and the soaking liquid separately.

Liberally season the lamb chops with salt and pepper and brown under a high broiler or over a hot grill. Transfer to a large baking dish and set aside.

Preheat the oven to 350°F.

Sauté the onion and fennel in the olive oil until softened. Add the cumin, aniseed, oregano, and garlic and cook for another minute. Add the tomatoes, sugar, vinegar, chili soaking liquid, and chicken broth. Bring to a boil and adjust the seasoning with salt. Pour over the lamb, cover and bake for 1 hour. Bake the eggplant at the same time.

Remove the lamb and eggplant from the oven. Cut the stem from the eggplant and split in half lengthwise. Scoop out the flesh and mash it with a fork.

Transfer 5 or 6 chops, depending on their size, to a platter, and skim the fat from the surface of the roasting juices. Thicken the lamb sauce by mixing in the mashed eggplant. Serve 1½ cups of the thickened sauce on the side with the lamb.

Place the tortillas on a microwavesafe plate, cover loosely with plastic wrap, and microwave at full power for 1 minute. Or warm the tortillas in the oven. Wrap them in foil and heat in the oven with the lamb and eggplant for about 6 minutes. Serve the tortillas with the lamb.

Makes 4 servings, plus enough to:
✪ **Reserve 4 or 5 chops for Shredded Braised Lamb in a Pita.**
✪ **Reserve ⅔ cup sauce for Shredded Braised Lamb in a Pita.**
✪ **Reserve ½ cup sauce for Seared Sea Scallops with Pungent Dipping Sauce.**

Savory Black Beans

1 pound dried black beans	3 medium carrots, finely diced
2 ribs celery, halved	1 small onion, finely chopped
1 medium carrot, quartered	3 tablespoons olive oil
1 habenero chili	3 cloves garlic, minced
2 whole cloves	1 teaspoon ground coriander
1 small onion, halved	Juice of 1 large lemon
2 bay leaves	Salt and pepper to taste
3 ribs celery, finely diced	

Soak the beans overnight in 8 cups water. Or bring 8 cups of water and the beans to a boil, boil for 2 minutes, remove from the heat, cover, and set aside to soak for 1 hour. Drain.

Combine the beans, halved celery ribs, quartered carrot, and habenero chili in a heavy soup pot. Stick a clove into each onion half and add to the pot along with the bay leaves. Cover with water and bring to a boil. Simmer for 1 hour, or until the beans are tender, adding more water as necessary. Drain. Remove and discard the celery, carrot, onion, cloves, and chili. Or cook the beans in a pressure cooker at high pressure for 3 minutes. Release pressure valve and drain. Remove and discard the celery, carrot, onion, cloves, and chili.

Sauté the diced celery, diced carrots, and chopped onion in the olive oil until tender. Add the garlic and coriander and cook for another 30 seconds. Add 4 cups of the beans to the sautéed vegetables and reserve the remaining beans. Toss the vegetables to combine. Heat through, stir in the lemon juice, salt, and pepper, and serve half.

Makes 4 servings, plus enough to:
- ✪ **Reserve 2 cups plain beans for Bean and Cheddar Quesadillas with Green Salsa.**
- ✪ **Reserve 2 cups beans with sautéed vegetables for Grilled Chicken and Rice Salad.**

Rice with Tomatillo Salsa

3¾ cups water
Salt
¼ teaspoon freshly ground black pepper
2 cups long-grain rice (12 ounces)
8 large tomatillos, shucked, with 5 or 6 husks
   reserved for cooking the nopales
   (recipe follows)

¼ medium onion, finely chopped
1 clove garlic, minced
Pinch of crushed red pepper flakes

Bring the water to a boil with 1 teaspoon salt and the black pepper in a large heavy saucepan. Add the rice and stir to separate the grains. Reduce the heat, cover, and simmer for 15 to 20 minutes, or until the liquid has all been absorbed and the rice is tender.

    Meanwhile, make the salsa: Put the tomatillos in a small pot and cover with water. Bring to a boil, reduce the heat, and simmer until tender, about 5 minutes. Remove the tomatillos and mash with a fork. Stir in the onion, garlic, pepper flakes, and salt to taste. Add enough of the cooking liquid to make the mixture saucelike.

    When the rice is done, mix in 1 cup of the salsa and serve.

Makes 4 servings, plus enough to:
✪ **Reserve 3 cups rice for Grilled Chicken and Rice Salad.**
✪ **Reserve 1½ cups salsa for Bean and Cheddar Quesadillas with Green Salsa.**

Sautéed Nopales

1 pound fresh nopales, trimmed of spines, or
   12 ounces canned nopales, drained (see
   Note) or 1 pound frozen cut green beans
1 tablespoon vegetable oil
6 scallions, trimmed and thinly sliced
2 cloves garlic, finely chopped

Pinch of crushed red pepper flakes
Salt to taste
5 or 6 tomatillo husks, reserved from Tomatillo
   Salsa (above)
1 tablespoon chopped cilantro

Scrape off the spines from the edges and face of fresh nopales and trim away the hard end from each section. Cut the trimmed sections into small cubes. Set aside.

    Heat the oil in a large skillet until hot. Add the fresh or frozen nopales or frozen green beans, scallions, garlic, pepper flakes, and salt. Mix together and cover. Cook over low heat until the nopales are tender, about 5 minutes, stirring occasionally. They will become quite juicy.

If using canned nopales or frozen green beans, stop the cooking at this point. Add the cilantro and serve. If using fresh nopales, uncover and add the tomatillo skins and the cilantro. Cook over moderate heat until the vegetable is almost dry and the sticky liquid disappears, about 12 minutes. Adjust seasoning and serve.

Makes 4 servings, plus enough to:
✪ **Reserve 1 cup for Grilled Chicken and Rice Salad.**

PREPARING FRESH NOPALES

Using a small knife, scrape off the tiny spines protruding from the rounded edges and across the face of the nopales and cut the sections into ½-inch squares. Many recipes direct you to boil the nopales at this point to wash away the glutinous substance that exudes as the vegetable cooks, much like okra, but this step also diminishes the lemony fragrance. To keep the flavor but get rid of the slipperiness, sauté diced nopales with some tomatillo husks. They absorb the juices, leaving the nopales clean and fully flavored.

Bean and Cheddar Quesadillas with Green Salsa

2 tablespoons finely chopped onion
2 tablespoons olive oil
✪ **2 cups plain beans reserved from**
  Savory Black Beans
1 cup chicken broth, canned or homemade
Salt to taste
Pinch of crushed red pepper flakes

2 cloves garlic
16 (6-inch) corn tortillas
¾ cup shredded cheddar cheese
2 tablespoons corn oil
✪ **1½ cups salsa reserved from Rice with**
  Tomatillo Salsa

Sauté the onion in the olive oil in a large heavy skillet for 10 seconds. Add the beans, broth, salt, and pepper flakes. Stir and coarsely mash the beans with a fork until all the stock has been absorbed. Mix in the garlic. Transfer to a bowl and rinse out the skillet. Dry well.

Place 2 tablespoons of the bean mixture in the center of 8 tortillas. Top each with 1½ tablespoons shredded cheese and cover each with one of the remaining tortillas. Pat them so that the beans and cheese spread out evenly.

Add half the corn oil to the skillet, and heat until the oil smokes. Brown quesadillas in the oil, about 1 minute per side, a few at a time. Keep warm in a low oven while you brown the remaining quesadillas, adding more oil as necessary.

Serve 2 quesadillas to each person with the reserved salsa.

Makes 4 servings.

Shredded Braised Lamb in a Pita

✪ **4 or 5 chops reserved from Red Chili Lamb Chops with Warm Tortillas**
4 large pita breads
1 small onion, finely chopped
1 tablespoon olive oil

✪ **⅔ cup sauce reserved from Red Chili Lamb Chops with Warm Tortillas**
⅓ cup tomato puree
⅓ cup ketchup
2 teaspoons cider vinegar
Salt and pepper to taste

Preheat the oven to 300°F.

Remove the bones and most of the fat from the reserved lamb. You should have about ¾ pound of meat. Finely chop any large pieces. Set aside. Warm the pitas in the oven for 8 minutes.

Sauté the onion in the olive oil in a heavy saucepan over high heat until golden brown, about 3 minutes. Add the meat and toss to coat. Add the reserved sauce, tomato puree, ketchup, cider vinegar, salt, and pepper. Heat, stirring constantly, until boiling, about 4 minutes. Open a pocket in each pita, fill with a portion of the lamb mixture, and serve.

Makes 4 servings.

Seared Sea Scallops with Pungent Dipping Sauce

✪ **½ cup sauce reserved from Red Chili Lamb Chops with Warm Tortillas**
1 tablespoon balsamic vinegar
Juice of ½ lemon
1½ pounds sea scallops

1 tablespoon plus 1 teaspoon olive oil
1 teaspoon ground coriander
Salt and pepper to taste
Steamed rice or warmed tortillas, for serving

Puree the reserved sauce, vinegar, and lemon juice in a food processor or blender. Transfer to a small pan and bring to a boil. Remove from heat and keep warm.

Remove any hard parts from the sides of the scallops. Slice the scallops in half horizontally. Toss the scallops with 1 teaspoon of the olive oil and sprinkle with coriander, salt, and pepper.

Heat 1 tablespoon of olive oil in a large heavy skillet over high heat. Brown the scallops on both sides, about 1 minute per side. Transfer to a platter. Allow to rest for 1 minute. Pour any juices that collect on the platter into the sauce. Stir to combine. Serve the scallops with the sauce in a bowl for dipping. Serve with rice or warm tortillas.

Makes 4 servings.

Grilled Chicken and Rice Salad

1 skinless and boneless chicken breast or
  2 halves
1 teaspoon corn oil
✪ **3 cups rice reserved from Rice with Tomatillo Salsa, at room temperature**
✪ **2 cups beans with sautéed vegetables reserved from Savory Black Beans, at room temperature**

✪ **1 cup reserved Sautéed Nopales**
1 tomato, diced
2 tablespoons olive oil
1 tablespoon apple cider vinegar
Salt and pepper to taste
¼ cup chopped cilantro

Brush the chicken breast with the oil and grill or broil 4 to 5 inches from a hot fire until browned and firm, 6 to 7 minutes per side. Cut into chunks.

Toss the chicken with the reserved rice, reserved beans, reserved nopales, and the tomato. Mix the olive oil with the vinegar, salt, and pepper and toss with the rice mixture. Add the cilantro and toss. Adjust seasoning.

Makes 4 servings.

Menu 42

It's a fact of cooking that shellfish must be brought into the kitchen alive. Shellfish, therefore, has to be checked for signs of life before being cooked. For crustaceans, such as crabs and lobsters, this means movement. If the animal doesn't twitch or wiggle, don't cook it. Mollusks (mussels, clams, and oysters) do not have mobile parts. Their wholesomeness is judged instead by a tightly closed shell. An open shell should shut when you rap it on a hard surface; otherwise discard it. Clams and mussels are typically cooked by steaming them. Remove them from the pot as soon as they open. Every additional second of heat increases toughness.

Clams and mussels are steamed for this Sunday's dinner and are served with mint kefir. Kefir is a fermented milk product from high in the Caucasus mountains. It resembles a liquid yogurt and is sold in many American health-food stores, usually flavored with fruit. The kefir in this menu is made by thinning plain yogurt with lemon juice and inundating it with fresh mint leaves. Three salads accompany the shellfish—a mix of the endive-family vegetables escarole, radicchio, and Belgian endive, whose crisp texture and bitter flavor complement the sweet-and-sour dressing that coats them and slightly softens the leaves; Tomato Slaw, strips of tomato seasoned with chili powder and lime; and Pesto Tabbouleh, bulgur wheat untraditionally dressed with basil pesto and roasted red peppers.

During the week, the mussels are warmed with tomatoes and Chinese black bean sauce and served over pasta. Tuesday features braised lamb shoulder chops with clams and pesto, and on Wednesday, chicken breast is simmered with a tangy mix of yogurt and some of Sunday's greens. The tabbouleh is used as a stuffing for baked salmon steaks on Thursday.

THE SUNDAY DINNER	THE WEEKNIGHT ENTREES
Steamed Clams and Mussels with Mint Kefir	Conchiglie with Mussels and Black Bean Sauce
Warm Endive Salad	Lamb Braised with Clams
Tomato Slaw	Chicken Breast Sautéed with Radicchio and Yogurt Sauce
Pesto Tabbouleh	Salmon Stuffed with Bulgur

Steamed Clams and Mussels with Mint Kefir

CLAMS AND MUSSELS
½ medium onion, chopped
2 tablespoons peanut oil
Pinch of crushed red pepper flakes
2 cups white wine
3 cloves garlic, finely chopped
1 lemon, halved
3 dozen littleneck clams, cleaned
4 dozen mussels, cleaned

KEFIR
¼ cup mint leaves, finely chopped
1 cup plain yogurt
Juice of ½ lemon
Salt and pepper to taste

Cook the onion in the oil in a large saucepan over medium heat until softened, about 2 minutes. Add the pepper flakes and the wine. Bring to a boil and boil for 2 minutes. Add the garlic and squeeze the lemon juice into the boiling broth. Place the lemon halves in the liquid and turn down to a simmer. Add the clams and stir briefly. Cover the pan and simmer for 4 minutes. Uncover the pan and use tongs to remove any open clams. Keep warm. Continue cooking, covered, until all the clams have opened, removing them as soon as they have. Keep warm. Discard any clams that have not opened after 8 minutes of cooking. Add the mussels and stir briefly. Cover and cook for 2 minutes. Remove mussels as they open and keep warm. Continue to cook for 2 more minutes, discarding any mussels that have not opened in that time. Strain the cooking broth through a double thickness of moistened paper towels or a dampened coffee filter set in a strainer and set aside.

For the kefir, simmer the mint leaves in ¾ cup of the strained broth for 2 minutes. Let cool slightly and mix into the yogurt, along with the lemon juice, salt, and pepper, stirring until smooth.

Serve 6 clams and 8 mussels per person, accompanied by ¼ cup of the kefir for dipping. Store remaining clams and mussels in sealed containers. Refrigerate immediately.

Makes 4 servings, plus enough to:
- ✪ **Reserve 12 shelled clams for Lamb Braised with Clams.**
- ✪ **Reserve 16 shelled mussels for Conchiglie with Mussels and Black Bean Sauce.**
- ✪ **Reserve 1 cup broth for Lamb Braised with Clams.**
- ✪ **Reserve ¼ cup broth for Conchiglie with Mussels and Black Bean Sauce.**
- ✪ **Reserve ¾ cup kefir for Chicken Breast Sautéed with Radicchio and Yogurt Sauce.**

MOLLUSK MAINTENANCE

Before mussels and clams are cooked, the shells must be scrubbed in cold water with a stiff brush to remove any barnacles and sand. Reduce the amount of interior sand by soaking them in cold water mixed with a few handfuls of cornmeal for 30 to 60 minutes. Wild mussels (mussels are also farmed) require an additional cleaning step—debearding. Protruding between its shells is a small bristle or beard, by which the mussel attaches itself to rocks or pilings. Shortly before cooking, remove the beard by tightly grasping the hairs near their base and giving a sharp tug. The beard should snap off along with a tiny bit of mussel flesh.

Warm Endive Salad

1 head escarole leaves, washed and dried
1 large head radicchio leaves, washed and dried
2 heads belgian endive, leaves washed and dried
¼ cup olive oil
½ red onion, chopped

1 clove garlic, minced
2 tablespoons sugar
¼ cup apple cider vinegar
2 tablespoons ketchup
1 teaspoon hot pepper sauce
Salt and pepper to taste

Tear the escarole, radicchio, and endive leaves into smaller pieces and toss together in a large salad bowl.

Heat the olive oil in a saucepan over a medium-high heat, add the onion, and cook until softened, about 2 minutes. Add the garlic, sugar, vinegar, ketchup, hot pepper sauce, salt, and pepper. Stir to combine and bring to a boil. Pour over the greens, toss well, and serve.

Makes 4 servings, plus enough to:
✪ **Reserve 1½ cups for Chicken Breast Sautéed with Radicchio and Yogurt Sauce.**

Tomato Slaw

3 large tomatoes, cored and sliced
1 small onion, finely chopped
Juice of 1 lime
2 teaspoons chili powder

1 teaspoon ground cumin
1 tablespoon vegetable oil
Salt and pepper to taste

Cut the tomato slices into thin strips and toss with the remaining ingredients.

Makes 4 servings, plus enough to:
✪ **Reserve ½ cup for Conchiglie with Mussels and Black Bean Sauce.**
✪ **Reserve 1 cup for Lamb Braised with Clams.**

Pesto Tabbouleh

2 cups bulgur or tabbouleh
2 cups water
4 cups basil leaves
4 cloves garlic

½ cup olive oil
2 roasted peppers, homemade or jarred,
    stemmed, seeded, and diced
Salt and pepper to taste

Combine the bulgur and water in a large bowl. Set aside until all the water has been absorbed, about 30 minutes.

Meanwhile, finely chop the basil leaves and the garlic in a food processor. Add 6 tablespoons of the olive oil and process until the mixture forms a loose paste. When the bulgur is ready, stir in ½ cup of the basil mixture, the remaining 2 tablespoons of olive oil, the roasted peppers, salt, and pepper. Stir to combine. Serve 2½ cups.

Makes 4 servings, plus enough to:
✪ **Reserve 2 tablespoons pesto for Lamb Braised with Clams.**
✪ **Reserve 2 cups tabbouleh for Salmon Stuffed with Bulgur.**

Conchiglie with Mussels and Black Bean Sauce

2 tablespoons garlic black bean sauce
2 cloves garlic, minced
✪ ¼ cup broth reserved from Steamed Clams and Mussels with Mint Kefir
✪ ½ cup reserved Tomato Slaw
1 tablespoon vegetable oil

½ medium onion, chopped
2 teaspoons sugar
✪ 16 shelled mussels reserved from Steamed Clams and Mussels with Mint Kefir
12 ounces conchiglie (medium pasta shells)

Combine the black bean sauce, half the garlic, the reserved broth, and the reserved slaw. Heat the oil in a small saucepan, add the onion, and cook until softened, about 2 minutes. Add the remaining garlic, the sauce mixture, and the sugar. Heat until simmering and stir in the reserved mussels. Remove from the heat.

Meanwhile, bring a large pot of lightly salted water to a boil. Add the pasta and boil for 10 minutes, or until tender. Drain, shaking off any excess water. Toss pasta with sauce and serve immediately.

Makes 4 servings.

Lamb Braised with Clams

4 shoulder lamb chops (about 8 ounces each)
⅓ cup flour seasoned with salt and pepper to taste
2 tablespoons olive oil
½ medium onion, chopped
1 clove garlic, minced
✪ 1 cup reserved Tomato Slaw

✪ 1 cup broth reserved from Steamed Clams and Mussels with Mint Kefir
✪ 12 shelled clams reserved from Steamed Clams and Mussels with Mint Kefir
✪ 2 tablespoons pesto reserved from Pesto Tabbouleh

Coat the lamb with the seasoned flour. Heat the olive oil in a large skillet and brown the lamb on both sides. Transfer lamb to a plate. Add the onion to the pan and cook for 30 seconds, stirring constantly. Add the garlic, reserved slaw, and reserved broth. Return lamb to the liquid in the pan, cover, and simmer for 15 minutes. Transfer lamb to a warm platter. Boil pan juices over high heat for 2 minutes. Stir in the reserved clams and reserved pesto. Pour over lamb and serve.

Makes 4 servings.

Chicken Breast Sautéed with Radicchio and Yogurt Sauce

2 skinless and boneless chicken breasts, split
Salt and pepper to taste
1 tablespoon olive oil

✪ **1½ cups reserved Warm Endive Salad**
✪ **¾ cup kefir reserved from Steamed Clams and Mussels with Mint Kefir**

Place the chicken breasts between sheets of plastic wrap and pound gently until flattened to a uniform ½-inch thickness. Remove from the plastic and season with salt and pepper. Heat the olive oil in a large skillet until smoking. Sauté the chicken breasts until browned on both sides and firm, about 8 minutes. Remove to a platter and keep warm. Add the reserved endive salad to the pan and heat until bubbling. Remove from the heat, add the kefir, pour over the chicken, and serve.

Makes 4 servings.

Salmon Stuffed with Bulgur

4 salmon steaks (about 6 ounces each)
1 tablespoon olive oil
Salt and pepper to taste

✪ **2 cups reserved Pesto Tabbouleh**
Juice of 1 lemon

Preheat the oven to 400°F. Cut a sheet of foil into four 4 x 6-inch rectangles.

Rub the salmon with half the oil and season with salt and pepper. Place each salmon steak on a piece of foil and place on a baking sheet. Mound ½ cup of the reserved tabbouleh in the opening of each salmon steak. Sprinkle the remaining olive oil over the top. Bake for 10 to 15 minutes, or until the salmon flakes to gentle pressure. Sprinkle lemon juice over each salmon steak. Slide each salmon steak with tabbouleh stuffing from the foil onto a dinner plate and serve.

Makes 4 servings.

Stew takes time. Time to trim and cut the ingredients, time to brown the meat, but mostly time to just sit there and, well, stew. It is through long, gentle cooking that the toughness of stew meat yields and the flavor of the broth takes on body and depth. But before simmering comes an equally important step—browning. The only trick to browning is to keep the oil hot and avoid crowding the pan. Once the meat is browned, vegetables are added and they too are browned lightly. Then the meat goes back in, liquid is added, and the wait begins.

Stew is done when its ingredients are fork-tender, usually at least an hour, depending on the type of meat. Then it's time to thicken the gravy. Some recipes call for stirring in a bit of moistened starch or flour, but I prefer to mash a cup or two of the stewed vegetables and mix them back into the pot.

Sunday's stew is loaded with vegetables. All that's needed to complete the meal is a green vegetable, in this case a gratin of spinach, and bread. Here, traditional buttermilk biscuits are peppered with fresh rosemary leaves.

The biscuit dough becomes the top crust for Tuesday's Beef Pot Pie with Herb Crust, and the spinach mixture becomes a stuffing for portobello mushrooms on Monday. These meaty mushrooms are so large that one is enough for a single serving, and because they are a cultivated, rather than a wild, mushroom, they're available all year long. Spinach returns Wednesday to season a tuna pilaf that's vegetable, starch, and protein simmered in a single pot. And on Thursday, the beef sauce from Sunday's stew combines with red wine and toasted pine nuts for a most unusual salmon preparation.

THE SUNDAY DINNER

Beef Stew with Winter Vegetables

Spinach Gratin

Rosemary Biscuits

THE WEEKNIGHT ENTREES

Stuffed Portobello Mushrooms

Beef Pot Pie with Herb Crust

Tuna Pilaf Florentine

Salmon in Red Wine Sauce

Beef Stew with Winter Vegetables

3 pounds boneless beef stew meat, trimmed
1½ cups flour seasoned with salt and pepper
    to taste
2 to 3 tablespoons vegetable oil
2 medium onions, chopped
½ pound carrots, cut into large chunks
½ pound parsnips, cut into chunks
3 ribs celery, cut into large chunks
½ pound turnips, cut into chunks
1 large sprig rosemary

8 sprigs thyme
2 cups red wine
2 cups beef broth, canned or homemade
2 teaspoons tomato paste
6 cups water
4 large long white potatoes, peeled and cut
    into large chunks
1 butternut squash, peeled, seeded, and cut
    into large chunks
2 sweet potatoes, peeled and cut into chunks

Dredge the beef in the seasoned flour. Pat off any excess. Heat 2 tablespoons of the oil in a large skillet over medium-high heat until very hot. Add the beef in batches and brown on all sides, about 3 minutes per side, adding more oil if needed. Do not crowd the pan. Transfer to a large soup pot when finished.

When all the beef is browned, add the onions, carrots, parsnips, celery, and turnips to the oil remaining in the skillet. Cook until the vegetables soften slightly, about 5 minutes, stirring occasionally. While the vegetables are cooking, tie the rosemary and thyme sprigs into a bouquet with a piece of string. Add to the vegetables for the last minute of cooking.

Add the red wine and boil for 1 minute. Add the beef broth and transfer the contents of the skillet to the soup pot. Dissolve the tomato paste in the water and add. Cover and cook over medium heat until simmering. Reduce the heat and simmer for 1½ hours. Add the potatoes, squash, and sweet potatoes. Cover and simmer 1 more hour, testing for doneness after 45 minutes. Skim fat.

Remove 2 cups of the vegetables, particularly the squash, and mash with a food processor, fork, or potato masher into a puree. Return mashed vegetables to the stew and stir to thicken. Serve 8 cups.

Makes 4 servings, plus enough to:
✪ **Reserve 3 cups meat and vegetables for Beef Pot Pie with Herb Crust.**
✪ **Reserve 2 cups sauce for Salmon in Red Wine Sauce.**

Spinach Gratin

4 packages (10 ounces each) frozen chopped
    spinach, defrosted
1½ pounds white mushrooms, stems trimmed,
    cleaned and sliced
3 cloves garlic, minced
4 tablespoons butter

Pinch of freshly grated nutmeg
1½ cups ricotta cheese
¾ cup freshly grated parmesan cheese
2 eggs, beaten
Salt and pepper to taste

Preheat the oven to 375°F.

    Place the defrosted spinach in a strainer and squeeze out as much of its water as possible. Cook the mushrooms and garlic in the butter in a large skillet over medium heat until softened, stirring occasionally, about 5 minutes. Remove 1 cup of the cooked mushrooms and reserve.

    Add the spinach and nutmeg to the mushrooms remaining in the pan and toss to combine. Transfer to a mixing bowl and beat in the ricotta cheese, ½ cup of the parmesan, the eggs, salt, and pepper until well combined. Remove 1 cup of this mixture and reserve. Pack the rest into a 1½-quart baking dish and smooth the top. Sprinkle the remaining parmesan over the top and bake for 35 minutes, until brown and bubbly.

Makes 4 servings, plus enough to:
- ✪ **Reserve 1 cup mushrooms for Beef Pot Pie with Herb Crust.**
- ✪ **Reserve 1 cup spinach mixture for Stuffed Portobello Mushrooms.**
- ✪ **Reserve 1 cup gratin for Tuna Pilaf Florentine.**

IN PRAISE OF FROZEN SPINACH

Frozen spinach is often superior to what you'll find in the produce bins. It's prewashed, chopped, and blanched. The only hitch is defrosting.

    To defrost frozen spinach in a microwave, place the spinach, still in its box, on a plate and microwave at full power for 3 minutes. To defrost frozen spinach on the stove, remove the brick of frozen spinach from the box and place it in a skillet or a saucepan with a small amount of water. Cover and heat over medium heat for 8 to 10 minutes, turning and breaking up the block every few minutes.

    Fresh spinach is easily cooked in a large pot, but the microwave affords an even easier solution for cooking bagged spinach. Check that the spinach is prewashed and free of wilting leaves, pierce the bag once, place in a microwave, and cook at full power for 2 minutes.

Rosemary Biscuits

3 cups flour
1 teaspoon salt
4 teaspoons baking powder
1 teaspoon baking soda
3 tablespoons finely chopped fresh rosemary
    leaves

¼ cup cold vegetable shortening or butter
2 eggs, lightly beaten
1½ cups buttermilk

Preheat the oven to 400°F.

Combine the flour, salt, baking powder, baking soda, and rosemary in a large bowl. Add the shortening and, working quickly with your fingertips, pinch the fat into smaller and smaller pieces until it is fully dispersed into the dry ingredients and the mixture resembles coarse meal.

In a separate bowl, combine the eggs and the buttermilk and stir all but ¼ cup of the liquid mixture into the dry mixture, mixing just enough to form a uniformly moistened dough.

Turn the dough out onto a floured board. Sprinkle the top of the dough with flour and, with floured hands, gently push the dough into a circle about ½ inch thick. Cut with a 2- or 3-inch biscuit cutter into 12 biscuits and place the biscuits no more than ½ inch apart on a dry baking sheet. Brush the tops of the biscuits with the remaining buttermilk-egg mixture. Gather the remaining dough, wrap in plastic, and refrigerate.

Bake the biscuits until puffed and brown, about 15 minutes. Cool for a few minutes before serving.

Makes 12 biscuits, plus enough to:
✪ **Reserve remaining dough for Beef Pot Pie with Herb Crust.**

Stuffed Portobello Mushrooms

4 portobello mushrooms, stems removed,
  wiped clean
¼ cup olive oil
✪ 1 cup spinach mixture reserved from
  Spinach Gratin

¼ pound smoked turkey, finely diced (¾ cup)
1 cup shredded cheddar cheese (4 ounces)
Salt and pepper to taste
3 tablespoons freshly grated parmesan cheese

Preheat the oven to 375°F.

Rub the mushrooms with 3 tablespoons of the oil. Place, smooth side down, on a sheet pan and bake for 10 minutes. Meanwhile, combine the reserved spinach mixture, the smoked turkey, and the cheddar in a bowl. Season with salt and pepper.

When the mushrooms are done, heap ½ cup of the spinach mixture on each mushroom cap. Drizzle on the remaining oil. Smooth the tops and dust with parmesan cheese. Return to the oven and bake for 15 minutes, or until the filling is set and the tops are golden brown.

Serve 1 stuffed portobello per person.

Makes 4 servings.

Beef Pot Pie with Herb Crust

✪ 3 cups meat and vegetables reserved
  from Beef Stew with Winter Vegetables
✪ 1 cup mushrooms reserved from
  Spinach Gratin

✪ Dough reserved from Rosemary
  Biscuits
2 tablespoons milk

Preheat the oven to 400°F.

Warm the reserved meat and vegetables and the reserved mushrooms in a saucepan over medium heat until simmering, stirring occasionally, and turn into a 1- to 1½-quart casserole. Or heat in a covered glass casserole in a microwave at full power for 4 minutes.

While the meat and vegetables are warming, unwrap the reserved biscuit dough, leaving the sheet of plastic wrap under the disk of dough. With floured hands, flatten the dough into a rough circle just big enough to rest inside the rim of the casserole. Lift the dough, still on its plastic, and flip over on top of the meat and vegetables in the casserole. Brush the top of the dough with the milk.

Bake for 20 minutes, or until the crust is puffed and brown. Serve immediately.

Makes 4 servings.

Tuna Pilaf Florentine

2 tablespoons olive oil
1 medium onion, finely chopped
1½ cups long-grain rice
3 cups hot chicken broth, canned or
    homemade

✪ 1 cup reserved **Spinach Gratin**
1 can (about 6 ounces) water-packed white
    tuna
Salt and pepper to taste

Heat the olive oil in a large saucepan over medium-high heat, add the onion, and cook until softened, about 2 minutes. Add the rice, and toss until coated with oil. Add the chicken broth and stir to combine. Heat to a simmer, cover, and simmer for 10 minutes.

Chop the reserved spinach. Scatter the spinach and tuna over the surface of the rice, cover, and simmer about 5 minutes more, or until all the broth has been absorbed. Season with salt and pepper. Serve immediately.

Makes 4 servings.

Salmon in Red Wine Sauce

1 tablespoon olive oil
¼ cup pine nuts
1¼ pounds salmon fillet, cut into 4 equal
    portions
Salt and pepper to taste
⅓ cup red wine

2 cloves garlic, minced
✪ 2 cups sauce reserved from **Beef Stew
    with Winter Vegetables**
1 tablespoon chopped parsley
Juice of 1 lemon

Heat the oil in a large skillet over medium-high heat. Remove from the heat, add the pine nuts, and stir briskly for 30 to 60 seconds, or until the nuts color lightly. Remove with a slotted spoon and set aside.

Season the salmon with salt and pepper and return the skillet to the heat. When the oil is hot, add the salmon pieces, skin side up. Brown on both sides, flipping once, about 3 minutes per side. Reduce heat to medium-low. Add the wine and bring to a boil. Add the garlic and reserved broth. Cover and simmer gently for 2 to 4 minutes, or until the fish flakes to gentle pressure. Stir in the parsley and lemon juice. Adjust seasoning with salt and pepper.

Serve fish in the sauce, sprinkling the toasted pine nuts over the top.

Makes 4 servings.

Made from cross-cuts of veal shank, the subtle flavors and rich texture of Osso Buco make it the quintessential example of a stew made from shanks. Shanks must be cooked in liquid, and as they simmer, they release their full meaty flavor, roasted aroma, and a silken, almost syrup-like texture to their broth. The flavors of Osso Buco are subtle and rich—onion, carrot, celery, an undercurrent of basil and garlic, a glimmer of lemon and white wine—but its panache comes at the end from the blend of finely chopped raw garlic, parsley, and lemon zest that is swirled into the stew just before serving. This mixture, called gremolata, picks three distinct, previously unrelated flavors from the recipe and forces them to the forefront, creating a separate layer of sensation that sends one's taste-buds topsy-turvy.

Traditionally, Osso Buco is served with a golden risotto. I've steamlined the preparation of this Sunday dinner by retaining the original flavorings but using basmati rice, a grain that cooks in half the time as risotto. The meal is completed with peas and carrots and a glaze of caper butter.

On Monday night, the gravy from the Osso Buco is transformed into a sauce base for braised tuna, and on Thursday it adds depth of flavor to a quick microwaved stew of spareribs. The saffron-infused rice is used in Golden Shrimp Fried Rice on Wednesday, while Sunday's Peas and Carrots in Caper Butter form the groundwork for Tuesday's Tortellini Primavera.

THE SUNDAY DINNER	THE WEEKNIGHT ENTREES
Osso Buco	Braised Tuna Lombardy
Basmati Rice Milanese	Tortellini Primavera
Peas and Carrots in Caper Butter	Golden Shrimp Fried Rice
	Quick Ribs

Osso Buco

4 pieces veal shank, each about 2 inches thick
  (3 ¼ pounds)
½ cup flour seasoned with salt and pepper to
  taste
2 tablespoons butter
2 tablespoons olive oil
2 large onions, finely chopped
3 carrots, finely chopped
2 ribs celery, finely chopped
4 cloves garlic, minced

Zest of 1 lemon, cut into strips or large pieces
1 ½ cups white wine
3 cups chicken broth, canned or homemade
2 cups canned plum tomatoes, coarsely
  chopped
1 ½ teaspoons dried thyme
1 bay leaf
1 tablespoon chopped basil leaves
Salt and pepper to taste
1 tablespoon finely chopped parsley

Tie a piece of string around the perimeter of each piece of veal shank. Dust both sides with the seasoned flour. Heat the butter and oil in a large deep heavy skillet until foaming. Brown the shanks on both sides and set aside. Add the onions, carrots, celery, and three fourths of the garlic and toss in the hot fat in the pan. Return meat to pan. Scatter half the lemon zest over the meat. Add the wine and simmer until the alcohol evaporates. Add the broth, tomatoes, thyme, bay leaf, and basil. Heat to a simmer and season with salt and pepper. Cover and cook over low heat for 1½ hours, or until the meat is tender.

Finely chop the remaining lemon zest and combine with the remaining garlic and the chopped parsley. Set aside.

When the shanks are fork-tender, use tongs to transfer them to a platter. Remove and discard the strings. Skim the fat from the surface of the sauce left in the pan. Remove and reserve 3½ cups of the sauce. Stir the parsley mixture into the remaining sauce and spoon it over the shanks.

Makes 4 servings, plus enough to:
✪ **Reserve 1 cup sauce for Braised Tuna Lombardy.**
✪ **Reserve 2½ cups sauce for Quick Ribs.**

Basmati Rice Milanese

⅛ teaspoon ground saffron
¼ cup white wine
2 cups basmati rice
2 tablespoons olive oil
4 scallions, white parts only, finely chopped

1 clove garlic, minced
3½ cups water
1 teaspoon salt
¼ teaspoon freshly ground pepper

Mix the saffron and wine in a small bowl and set aside.

Place the rice in a medium mixing bowl. Cover with cold tap water and mix until the water becomes cloudy. Drain through a strainer, return rice to the bowl, and wash 2 or 3 more times, or until the rinsing water comes almost clear. Drain.

Heat the olive oil in a 3-quart saucepan over moderate heat and cook the scallions and garlic for 30 seconds. Add the water, salt, and pepper and bring to a boil. Add the saffron-wine mixture and the rice. Stir to combine and heat until simmering. Cover and simmer for 15 minutes, or until the water has been absorbed. Fluff with a fork, and serve half of the rice (about 3 cups).

Makes 4 servings, plus enough to:
✪ **Reserve 3 cups rice for Golden Shrimp Fried Rice.**

Peas and Carrots in Caper Butter

6 medium carrots, cut into small chunks
1¼ cups water
1½ pounds frozen tiny peas

3 tablespoons capers, drained
3 tablespoons butter
Salt and pepper to taste

Cook the carrots in the water in a 10- to 12-inch skillet over medium heat until all the water evaporates. Add the peas and stir until they defrost. Add the capers, butter, salt, and pepper and simmer 1 more minute.

Makes 4 servings, plus enough to:
✪ **Reserve 1 cup for Tortellini Primavera.**
✪ **Reserve 1½ cups for Golden Shrimp Fried Rice.**

Braised Tuna Lombardy

1 ½ pounds tuna steak, 1 inch thick
Salt and pepper to taste
2 tablespoons olive oil
½ cup white wine

✪ **I cup sauce reserved from Osso Buco**
2 whole peeled tomatoes, canned or fresh,
    coarsely chopped
Juice of ½ lemon

Cut the tuna into 4 pieces, and season liberally with salt and pepper. Heat the oil in a 10-inch nonstick skillet until smoking. Add the tuna, and brown on both sides. Add the wine, reserved sauce, and tomatoes. Cover and simmer for 8 minutes, turning the tuna twice. Add the lemon juice and simmer 1 to 2 minutes more. Serve the tuna with the sauce.

Makes 4 servings.

Tortellini Primavera

1 medium onion, chopped
2 tablespoons olive oil
5 large ripe plum tomatoes, fresh or canned,
    chopped
2 cloves garlic, minced
½ cup chopped roasted red bell peppers, fresh
    or jarred

3 ounces (½ jar) marinated artichoke hearts
    with liquid, coarsely chopped
✪ **I cup reserved Peas and Carrots in
    Caper Butter**
Salt and pepper to taste
12 ounces cheese tortellini, refrigerated
¼ cup freshly grated parmesan cheese

Sauté the onion in the olive oil in a large saucepan until softened, about 2 minutes. Add the tomatoes and garlic and cook for 1 minute. Add the bell pepper, artichoke hearts, and the reserved peas and carrots and heat through. Season with salt and pepper.

Meanwhile, bring a large pot of salted water to a boil. Add the tortellini and boil until tender, about 6 to 7 minutes. Drain the tortellini and toss in the sauce. Turn into a serving bowl and toss with the parmesan cheese.

Makes 4 servings.

Golden Shrimp Fried Rice

✪ **3 cups reserved Basmati Rice Milanese**
3 tablespoons vegetable oil
¾ pound medium or large shrimp, peeled,
   deveined, and finely chopped
2 teaspoons minced fresh gingerroot
3 eggs, beaten
2 teaspoons low-sodium soy sauce

✪ **1½ cups reserved Peas and Carrots in
   Caper Butter**
3 scallions, finely chopped
1 clove garlic, minced
1 teaspoon sesame oil
2 tablespoons sesame seeds

Spoon the rice onto a large rimmed sheet pan. Wet your hands, and rub the rice with your fingers, separating it into individual grains. Set aside.

Heat 2 tablespoons of the oil in a large wok over high heat until smoking. Add the shrimp and gingerroot and stir-fry until the shrimp lose their raw look, about 30 seconds. Add the eggs and 1 teaspoon of the soy sauce. Using a metal spatula, scrape the egg off the bottom of the wok as soon as it sets, continuing until all the egg is scrambled. Transfer the contents of the wok to a plate and wipe out the wok with a damp towel.

Return the wok to high heat. Add the remaining tablespoon of oil and heat until smoking. Add the rice and stir-fry until it is heated through and some of it is lightly crisped. Add the shrimp-egg mixture, the reserved peas and carrots, scallions, garlic, and remaining soy sauce and stir-fry for 1 more minute. Turn mixture into a large serving bowl.

Return the wok to high heat, add the sesame oil and the sesame seeds, and stir until the seeds begin to pop, about 10 seconds. Pour over the top of the rice and serve.

Makes 4 servings.

Quick Ribs

1 rack pork spareribs (about 4 pounds)
Salt and pepper to taste

✪ **2½ cups sauce reserved from Osso Buco**

Rub the rack of ribs liberally with the salt and pepper. Place 5 inches from the high flame of a broiler or grill, and cook until browned, about 2 to 3 minutes per side. Transfer the rack to a cutting board and cut into individual ribs. Arrange the ribs in a single layer in a large rectangular microwavesafe dish. Pour the reserved sauce over the ribs and cover with plastic wrap.

Cook in a microwave oven at full power for 10 minutes. Carefully remove plastic wrap and turn ribs over. Cover with fresh plastic wrap and microwave 10 more minutes, or until the ribs are completely tender. Carefully remove plastic and serve.

Or place the individual ribs and reserved sauce in a large deep skillet with a tight-fitting cover. Add ½ cup water, heat to a simmer, cover, and simmer until the meat is tender, about 30 minutes, stirring every 5 minutes. Add more water if the sauce reduces too much.

Makes 4 servings.

Menu 45

ooking is at heart a folk art, and the quality of a dish lies not in the purity of its recipe or the authenticity of its ingredients but in how it fits the taste, lifestyle, and habits of the people who cook it and eat it. That conviction has led me to this week's Sunday dinner. Paella is the signature dish of the coastal villages of Spain, and like all folk foods, there are countless recipes for it, all including rice, saffron, shellfish, and *sofrito*, a mixture of onion, sweet peppers, and tomato.

Sofrito is to Spanish cooking what the combination of carrot, onion, and celery is to ours. This Sunday's paella has all the basic elements, but the shellfish is replaced with grilled vegetables, which are less expensive yet bring their own smoky redolence to the classic. The paella is served with braised artichokes and a quick olive bread.

The rice from the paella becomes the base for Monday's quick Sofrito Shrimp and Rice. On Tuesday, some olive spread from Sunday's bread rubbed under the skin of boned chicken breast provides an instant flavor punch, while Sunday's artichoke is combined with more olive paste to fill a frittata on Wednesday. A frittata is an Italian open-face omelette that starts out in a skillet over medium heat but finishes under a broiler or in a hot oven. Broiling yields a frittata that's browner and more moist, while baked frittatas are more thoroughly cooked through. I prefer broiling, but if you balk at placing your favorite skillet directly under the broiler, an oven will give perfectly fine results. The paella's grilled vegetables return on Thursday as a topping for individual pizzas.

THE SUNDAY DINNER	THE WEEKNIGHT ENTREES
Roasted Vegetable Paella	Sofrito Shrimp and Rice
Artichokes Braised with Fennel	Grilled Black Chicken
Warm Tapenade Bread	Frittata Carciofi
	Grilled Vegetable and Chèvre Pizza

Roasted Vegetable Paella

1 large Spanish or other sweet onion, cut into
   6 thick slices
2 small heads of garlic
3 red or yellow bell peppers, stemmed, seeded,
   and halved
8 medium white mushrooms, stems trimmed
   and cleaned
2 sweet potatoes, scrubbed and cut into 6
   slices each
1 medium eggplant, stemmed and cut into 8
   thick slices
1 yellow squash, stemmed and cut lengthwise
   into 4 ¼-inch-thick slices

1 zucchini, stemmed and cut lengthwise into
   4 ¼-inch-thick slices
8 plum tomatoes
Olive oil spray
¼ teaspoon saffron threads
1 cup white wine
2½ cups long-grain rice
2 tablespoons olive oil
2¼ cups vegetable or chicken broth, canned or
   homemade
1 tablespoon chopped parsley
1 lime, cut into wedges

Coat the onion, garlic, mushrooms, sweet potatoes, bell peppers, eggplant, squash, zucchini, and tomatoes with olive oil spray. Grill the onion, garlic, mushrooms, and sweet potatoes on an oiled rack set 4 inches from a hot fire for 6 minutes, turning once. Add the peppers, eggplant, squash, zucchini, and tomatoes to the rack and grill all for 8 minutes more, turning as necessary, until all the vegetables are softened and well browned.

Finely chop and combine the grilled onion, bell peppers, and tomatoes. Cut the garlic in half crosswise and squeeze the flesh from each half. Mix into the chopped vegetables. You should have 4 cups of sofrito. Reserve 1 cup. Chop the eggplant, squash, zucchini, and mushrooms into large cubes. Reserve 1½ cups. Cut the sweet potatoes into large cubes and add them to the rest of the eggplant mixture.

Meanwhile, crumble the saffron into the wine and set aside. Cook the rice in the olive oil in a large skillet over medium heat for 1 minute, stirring constantly. Add the 3 cups of sofrito and stir into the rice. Add the saffron-wine mixture and the broth. Stir and heat to a simmer. Reduce the heat, cover, and cook for 12 minutes, or until the rice is tender and all the liquid has been absorbed. Remove and reserve 3½ cups of the rice mixture. Stir the eggplant-sweet potato mixture into the rest of the rice and heat through. Turn onto a platter and serve, garnished with parsley and lime.

Makes 4 servings, plus enough to:
✪ **Reserve 1 cup sofrito for Grilled Vegetable and Chèvre Pizza.**
✪ **Reserve 1½ cups eggplant mixture for Grilled Vegetable and Chèvre Pizza.**
✪ **Reserve 3½ cups rice mixture for Sofrito Shrimp and Rice.**

Artichokes Braised with Fennel

8 small artichokes
Juice of 1 lemon
1 medium onion, chopped
¼ cup olive oil
4 cloves garlic, minced
Pinch of crushed red pepper flakes

1 tablespoon fennel seed, ground
1 cup white wine
Salt and pepper to taste
1 large tomato, cored, peeled, and chopped
1 cup water
¼ cup basil leaves, coarsely chopped

Peel the tough outer leaves from the artichokes down to the point where the leaves become pale and tender. Slice off the thorny top of each artichoke and trim the stems. Cut the artichokes in half lengthwise, scoop out the hairy choke from the center, thinly slice the artichokes, and place the pieces in a bowl with the lemon juice.

Cook the onion in the olive oil in a skillet over medium heat until the onion has softened, about 2 minutes. Add the garlic, pepper flakes, and fennel seed. Stir for 30 seconds. Add the artichokes and any lemon juice in the bowl and toss to coat with oil. Add the wine, salt, pepper, tomato, and water. Toss well, cover, and simmer for 35 to 40 minutes, or until the artichoke slices are tender and most of the liquid has evaporated. Stir in the basil leaves and add salt and pepper. Reserve 1 cup and serve the rest.

Makes 4 servings, plus enough to:
✪ **Reserve I cup for Frittata Carciofi.**

Warm Tapenade Bread

30 oil-cured black olives, pitted
4 cloves garlic, minced
⅔ cup extra-virgin olive oil

Salt and pepper to taste
Pinch of cayenne
1 sourdough baguette, about 18 inches long

Preheat the oven to 400°F.

Using a food processor or a mortar and pestle, make a paste of the olives, garlic, olive oil, salt, pepper, and cayenne. Reserve ½ cup of the olive mixture. Slice the loaf 1 inch thick without cutting all the way through. With a pastry brush, brush 1 side of each slice of bread with the remaining olive mixture. Wrap the bread in foil and bake for 15 minutes, or until heated through.

Makes 4 servings, plus enough to:
✪ **Reserve ¼ cup olive mixture for Grilled Black Chicken.**
✪ **Reserve ¼ cup olive mixture for Frittata Carciofi.**

Sofrito Shrimp and Rice

1 tablespoon olive oil
24 large shrimp, peeled and deveined
2 small dried chilies
½ teaspoon ground cumin
1 teaspoon ground coriander
Salt and pepper to taste

✪ **3½ cups reserved rice mixture from Roasted Vegetable Paella**
1 package (10 ounces) frozen peas, defrosted
½ cup water
1 tablespoon chopped cilantro or parsley

Heat the oil in a large skillet until hot. Add the shrimp and the chilies and toss until the shrimp lose their raw look, about 1 minute. Add the cumin, coriander, salt, and pepper and cook for 1 more minute, stirring constantly. Add the reserved rice mixture, peas, and water and cook, stirring frequently, until everything is heated through, about 4 minutes. Stir in the cilantro and serve.

Makes 4 servings.

Grilled Black Chicken

2 large chicken breasts, boned
Salt and pepper to taste
✪ **¼ cup olive mixture reserved from Warm Tapenade Bread**

2 teaspoons olive oil
1 lime, cut into 4 wedges

Lift the skin from the chicken breasts by sliding your fingers underneath; keep the skin attached at 1 end. Fold the skin back to expose the meat and rub it with salt and pepper. Spoon 2 tablespoons of the reserved olive mixture over the surface of each breast and fold the skin back over the meat. Rub the chicken breasts with olive oil.

Grill or broil about 4 inches from a hot fire for 8 to 9 minutes per side, turning the chicken every 4 to 5 minutes, or until firm and thoroughly browned on both sides. To serve, remove the skin and split each chicken breast in half lengthwise. Garnish with lime wedges.

Makes 4 servings.

Frittata Carciofi

✪ ¼ cup olive mixture reserved from
   Warm Tapenade Bread
8 eggs
2 tablespoons water
1 teaspoon hot pepper sauce

Salt and pepper to taste
✪ **1 cup reserved Artichokes Braised with**
   Fennel, chopped
1 tablespoon olive oil
3 tablespoons freshly grated parmesan cheese

Turn the broiler to high or preheat the oven to 450°F. Bring the reserved olive mixture to room temperature. Beat the eggs in a mixing bowl with the water, hot pepper sauce, salt, and pepper. Set aside. Chop the reserved artichokes.

Heat the olive oil in a large ovensafe skillet, preferably nonstick, over high heat for 30 seconds. Add the artichokes and toss for 1 minute. Add the egg mixture and reduce the heat to medium. Using a fork, arrange the artichoke pieces evenly. Cook until the egg has set around the edges of the pan, about ½ inch in. Scatter the parmesan over the surface of the egg. Place the skillet under the broiler or in the oven. Broil for 2 minutes or bake for 7 minutes, or until the egg is puffed and golden brown. Cut into 4 wedges and serve each wedge with 1 tablespoon of the reserved olive mixture.

Makes 4 servings.

Grilled Vegetable and Chèvre Pizza

2 teaspoons olive oil
4 serving-size prebaked pizza crusts or large
   pita breads
✪ **1½ cups eggplant mixture reserved**
   from Roasted Vegetable Paella

✪ **1 cup sofrito reserved from Roasted**
   Vegetable Paella
8 ounces fresh chèvre cheese or feta cheese,
   coarsely chopped

Place a pizza stone, if you have one, in the oven and preheat to 450°F.

Drizzle ½ teaspoon of olive oil over each pizza crust. Mound a portion of the reserved eggplant mixture on each one. Scatter a portion of the reserved sofrito over the vegetables. Scatter the chèvre over all. Place on a sheet pan or slide onto the pizza stone and bake for 15 minutes, or until the cheese is soft and lightly browned and the vegetables are steaming.

Makes 4 servings.

Menu 46

P reserving ingredients through pickling is among the most ancient of culinary endeavors. Long before ice and refrigeration helped retain the natural qualities of fresh food, preserved meats and vegetables were the norm, especially in winter and spring, when hunting and harvesting had become distant memories. Now, such preserved foods as sauerkraut, dill pickles, pickled beets, and the like are served for their flavor rather than out of necessity.

This week's Sunday main course of Sausages Braised with Sauerkraut in Beer is accompanied in Teutonic style with boiled potatoes, pickled beets, and sautéed apples. Together, they lay the groundwork for a week of diversity. On Monday, the rosemary apples are transformed into a sauce for sautéed veal scallops. The sausage and kraut are redesigned on Tuesday into a robust mixture of cabbage and pasta. On Wednesday, we go Russian with a hearty salad of beets, potatoes, pickled herring, and walnuts. The week ends with Sunday's potatoes simmered with bits of smoked salmon for the most sophisticated rendition of potato soup ever devised.

THE SUNDAY DINNER

Sausages Braised with Sauerkraut in Beer

Sautéed Cinnamon Apples

Boiled New Potatoes with Sage and Caraway

Pickled Baked Beets

THE WEEKNIGHT ENTREES

Veal Sautéed with Apples

Sausage with Two Krauts

Russian Herring Salad

Potato and Smoked Salmon Soup

Sausages Braised with Sauerkraut in Beer

1 medium onion, finely chopped
2 tablespoons vegetable oil
2 tablespoons brown sugar
1 teaspoon caraway seeds, crushed
1 teaspoon dried thyme
2 bay leaves

2 bottles (12 ounces each) beer
2 pounds sauerkraut, rinsed thoroughly and
   drained
6 bratwurst (about 1½ pounds)
12 garlic sausages (about 1½ pounds)

Sauté the onion in the oil in a large saucepan over medium heat until softened, about 2 minutes. Add the brown sugar, caraway seeds, thyme, and bay leaves and cook for 1 minute, stirring constantly. Add the beer and bring to a boil. Add the sauerkraut. Place the bratwurst and garlic sausages on top of the sauerkraut, cover the pan, and simmer for 30 minutes.

Using tongs, remove the sausages. Reserve 2 bratwurst and 4 garlic sausages. Stack the rest in the center of a platter. Lift out the sauerkraut with a slotted spoon. Reserve 1 cup. Arrange the remainder in a ring around the sausages on the platter. Moisten the top with some of the cooking liquid and serve.

Makes 4 servings, plus enough to:
✪ **Reserve 2 bratwurst and 4 garlic sausages for Sausage with Two Krauts.**
✪ **Reserve 1 cup sauerkraut for Sausage with Two Krauts.**

Sautéed Cinnamon Apples

2 tablespoons vegetable oil
¼ medium onion, thinly sliced
½ teaspoon dried thyme, crumbled
4 large Granny Smith apples, peeled, halved,
    cored, and thinly sliced

1 tablespoon sugar
⅛ teaspoon ground cinnamon
Salt and pepper to taste

Heat the oil in a large skillet over medium heat, add the onion, and cook until softened, about 2 minutes. Add the thyme and cook for 1 more minute, stirring constantly. Add the apple slices, sugar, and cinnamon. Cook until the apples soften and brown lightly. Season with salt and pepper. Reserve 1½ cups and serve the rest.

Makes 4 servings, plus enough to:
✪ **Reserve 1½ cups for Veal Sautéed with Apples.**

Boiled New Potatoes with Sage and Caraway

18 large new potatoes, scrubbed and
    quartered (about 4 pounds)
4 tablespoons butter

10 fresh sage leaves, stemmed and chopped
½ teaspoon caraway seed, crushed
Salt and pepper to taste

Bring a large pot of water to a boil, and cook the potatoes for 25 to 30 minutes, or until tender. Drain. Melt the butter in a pan with the sage and caraway seed. Set aside.

Reserve 18 pieces of potatoes. Toss the remainder with the melted butter mixture. Reserve 24 buttered pieces. Add salt and pepper. Serve the remainder.

Makes 4 servings, plus enough to:
✪ **Reserve 18 unbuttered potato pieces for Russian Herring Salad.**
✪ **Reserve 24 buttered and seasoned potato pieces for Potato and Smoked Salmon Soup.**

Pickled Baked Beets

2 pounds medium beets
½ cup water
⅓ cup sugar

¼ cup cider vinegar
Salt to taste

Preheat the oven to 350°F.

Trim and scrub the beets. Do not cut or peel them. Place in a baking pan large enough to hold the beets in a single layer without touching. Add the water, cover tightly with foil or a lid, and bake for 2 hours, or until easily pierced with a fork.

Or wrap each beet in plastic wrap, place on a microwavesafe dish, and microwave at full power for 25 minutes, turning the plate 3 times if your microwave does not have a carousel. Let cool for several minutes, then remove the plastic.

Cut off both ends of each beet and slip off the skins with your fingers. Cut each beet into quarters and each quarter into thin slices. Combine the sugar and cider vinegar in a small pan and bring to a simmer, stirring once or twice. Pour over the sliced beets, toss, add salt, and serve.

Makes 4 servings, plus enough to:
✪ **Reserve 1 cup beets for Russian Herring Salad.**

Veal Sautéed with Apples

8 large veal scallops, pounded thin (about 1½ pounds)

½ cup flour seasoned with salt and pepper to taste

2 tablespoons olive oil

✪ 1½ cups reserved Sautéed Cinnamon Apples

2 tablespoons butter

Juice of 1 lemon

Dredge the veal in the seasoned flour, tossing it from hand to hand to shake off any excess flour. Heat half the olive oil in a large nonstick skillet until smoking. Sauté half the veal until browned on both sides, about 1 minute per side. Transfer to a platter and sauté the remaining veal in the remaining olive oil. Transfer to the platter and reduce heat to medium. Add the reserved apples to the pan and heat through. Add the butter and lemon juice and stir until the butter is melted. Pour the apples over the veal and serve.

Makes 4 servings.

Sausage with Two Krauts

½ pound pasta, such as small shells or small bowties

✪ 2 bratwurst and 4 garlic sausages reserved from Sausages Braised with Sauerkraut in Beer

2 tablespoons olive oil

½ medium onion, finely chopped

½ small head cabbage, trimmed, cored, and thinly sliced

✪ 1 cup sauerkraut reserved from Sausages Braised with Sauerkraut in Beer

Salt and ground black pepper to taste

Bring a large pot of salted water to a boil. Add the pasta and boil until tender, about 10 minutes. Drain. Meanwhile, slice the reserved bratwurst and sausage. Heat the oil in a large deep skillet, add the onion, and cook over medium heat until softened, about 2 minutes. Add the sausages and cook 2 minutes more, stirring frequently. Add the cabbage and cook until tender, about 7 minutes. Stir in the reserved sauerkraut and season with salt and pepper. Heat through. Stir in the pasta, adjust the seasoning, and serve.

Makes 4 servings.

Russian Herring Salad

○ **18 unbuttered potato pieces reserved
from Boiled New Potatoes with Sage
and Caraway**
1 jar (8 ounces) pickled herring

½ cucumber, peeled, seeded, and diced
○ **1 cup reserved Pickled Baked Beets**
¼ cup mayonnaise
⅓ cup coarsely chopped walnut pieces

Cut the reserved potatoes into bite-size pieces. Cut the pickled herring into bite-size
pieces and set aside the liquid from the jar. Toss the potatoes, herring, cucumber, and reserved beets in a serving bowl. In a separate bowl, mix the mayonnaise with 2 tablespoons of the liquid from the pickled herring. Add to the herring mixture and toss to
combine. Chill for at least 30 minutes. Just before serving, toss in the walnuts.

Makes 4 servings.

Potato and Smoked Salmon Soup

1 medium onion, chopped
1 tablespoon olive oil
3 cloves garlic, minced
¼ cup chopped dill
4 lox wings (see Note)
6 cups water

Pepper to taste
○ **24 buttered and seasoned potato pieces
reserved from Boiled New Potatoes
with Sage and Caraway**
*½ cup light cream, half-and-half, yogurt, or
sour cream*

Cook the onion in the olive oil in a large heavy saucepan until softened, about 2 minutes. Add the garlic and dill and cook for 1 more minute. Add the lox wings, water, and
pepper and heat until the liquid simmers. Simmer for 15 minutes. Remove lox wings.
Cut the reserved potatoes into small pieces, add to the soup, and simmer for 5 more
minutes. Remove meat from bones and skin of lox wings and add to soup. Add the
cream, adjust the seasoning, and serve.

Makes 4 servings.

*Note: The meat that clings to the fins and collarbones of smoked salmon is sold separately as lox wings. It is
available in delis that slice their own lox and Nova Scotia salmon.*

Menu 47

Change is the only thing stable in American cooking. Propelled by the influxes of immigrants, Americans have tinkered relentlessly with the cooking of their ancestors and have developed a unique tradition of culinary experimentation. Italian and Chinese ingredients, techniques, and flavors, for example, have become part of the mainstream of American cooking. Now the foods of Southeast Asia are redefining our cooking and eating styles.

As eating habits change, so do our marketplaces. Most supermarkets, recognizing their communities' ethnic expansion, both demographic and culinary, have responded with larger and better stocked ethnic food sections. All of the Asian ingredients used in this week's menu should be available at any major grocery. A broad selection of Thai ingredients is imported under the Taste of Thai label. Asian produce, like shiitake mushrooms, coriander, snowpea pods, and gingerroot, are now commonplace to produce buyers, and Chinese and Japanese condiments, like rice-wine vinegar and dark sesame oil, share shelf space with soy sauce and other more familiar Asian ingredients.

In keeping with this fine American tradition, this week's Sunday dinner begins with a Thai Curried Shrimp, a straightforward stir-fry, flavored with red curry paste, fish sauce, and coconut milk instead of ginger and soy. The Thai curry is combined with hot pepper sauce on Tuesday to coat Fiery Barbecued Bluefish. The taste of Thailand dominates the week. On Monday it is in a variation on paht thai, the classic Thai noodle dish, this one made with cellophane noodles, ground turkey, and Sunday's Asian vegetables. It is garnished with tangerine, fennel, almonds, and cilantro. The fish sauce and curry paste are the flavor punch behind Wednesday's braised chicken thighs. The peanut dressing from Sunday's cucumber salad underlies Thursday's peanut soup and practically prepares itself.

THE SUNDAY DINNER

Thai Curried Shrimp

Brown Rice with Asian Vegetables

Cucumbers with Ginger Peanut Sauce

THE WEEKNIGHT ENTREES

Thai Turkey Stir-Fry

Fiery Barbecued Bluefish

Braised Sweet-and-Sour Chicken Thighs

Chili Peanut Soup

Thai Curried Shrimp

2½ tablespoons Thai red curry paste
1 tablespoon dark sesame oil
1 tablespoon water
6 tablespoons sugar
7 tablespoons ketchup
¼ cup Thai fish sauce
Juice of 1 large lemon

1 tablespoon peanut oil
1½ pounds medium shrimp, peeled and
   deveined
3 cloves garlic, minced
½ teaspoon crushed red pepper flakes
1½ cups coconut milk
6 scallions, thinly sliced

Mix the curry paste, sesame oil, water, and 1 tablespoon of the sugar until smooth in a small bowl. Set aside. In a separate bowl, combine the ketchup, fish sauce, lemon juice, and 3 tablespoons of the sugar. Set aside.

Heat the peanut oil in a large wok until smoking. Add the shrimp and stir-fry until they start to lose their raw look, about 30 seconds. Add the garlic, pepper flakes, and 1 tablespoon of the curry paste mixture. Stir to combine. Add ¼ cup of the fish sauce mixture and the remaining 2 tablespoons of sugar. Bring to a boil and stir in the coconut milk. Heat through. Stir in the scallions and serve.

Makes 4 servings, plus enough to:
- ✪ **Reserve 1 tablespoon curry paste mixture for Braised Sweet-and-Sour Chicken Thighs.**
- ✪ **Reserve 2½ tablespoons curry paste mixture for Fiery Barbecued Bluefish.**
- ✪ **Reserve ¼ cup fish sauce mixture for Thai Turkey Stir-Fry.**
- ✪ **Reserve ¼ cup fish sauce mixture for Chili Peanut Soup.**
- ✪ **Reserve ¼ cup fish sauce mixture for Braised Sweet-and-Sour Chicken Thighs.**

Brown Rice with Asian Vegetables

2 cups long-grain brown rice
1 tablespoon plus 1 teaspoon vegetable oil
4½ cups water
2 medium carrots, peeled and sliced diagonally
1 red bell pepper, stemmed, seeded, and cut into chunks
2 cloves garlic, minced
2 teaspoons minced gingerroot
Salt and pepper to taste

10 stalks asparagus, trimmed and cut into 1-inch pieces
12 shiitake mushrooms, stems discarded, sliced
18 snowpeas, stemmed
½ cup bean sprouts
6 scallions, thinly sliced
1 tablespoon soy sauce
1 teaspoon dark sesame oil

Cook the rice in 1 teaspoon of the oil in a large saucepan over medium heat for 10 seconds. Add 4 cups of the water and stir once. Bring to a boil. Reduce heat, cover, and simmer for 40 minutes, or until all the liquid has been absorbed and the rice is tender. Set aside.

Meanwhile, sauté the carrots and bell pepper in the remaining vegetable oil in a large skillet over medium heat until softened, about 3 minutes. Add the garlic, ginger, salt, and pepper and stir thoroughly. Add the asparagus and mushrooms and cook for 1 minute. Add the remaining ½ cup water and simmer for 2 minutes. Add the snowpeas and bean sprouts and heat through. Remove and reserve 2 cups of vegetables.

Add 4 cups of the rice to the pan of vegetables, and mix well. Toss in the scallions, soy sauce, and sesame oil and serve.

Makes 4 servings, plus enough to:
✪ **Reserve 2 cups vegetables for Thai Turkey Stir-Fry.**
✪ **Reserve 2 cups rice for Chili Peanut Soup.**

Cucumbers with Ginger Peanut Sauce

2 cucumbers, peeled, seeded, and cut into
    2-inch-long sticks
½ teaspoon salt
1 tablespoon peanut oil
4 cloves garlic, minced
2 teaspoons finely chopped gingerroot
2 teaspoons garlic chili paste

2 tablespoons tomato paste
1 cup water
5 tablespoons peanut butter
3 tablespoons low-sodium soy sauce
2 tablespoons rice wine vinegar
2 teaspoons sugar

Toss the cucumbers with the salt. Set aside for 10 minutes.

Combine the oil, garlic, gingerroot, chili paste, and tomato paste in a small skillet over medium heat. Stir until the chili paste begins to soften, about 30 seconds. Add the water and bring to a boil. Remove from the heat and whisk in the peanut butter, soy sauce, vinegar, and sugar until sauce is smooth. Let cool.

Place the cucumbers in a clean dish towel and wring out any excess moisture. Toss with about ½ cup of the peanut sauce and serve.

Makes 4 servings, plus enough to:
✪ **Reserve 1 cup peanut sauce for Chili Peanut Soup.**

Thai Turkey Stir-Fry

1 package (3¾ ounces) cellophane noodles
2 tablespoons vegetable oil
½ pound ground turkey, broken up
3 cloves garlic, chopped
½ teaspoon crushed red pepper flakes
✪ **¼ cup fish sauce mixture reserved from Thai Curried Shrimp**
2 eggs, beaten

✪ **2 cups vegetables reserved from Brown Rice with Asian Vegetables**
¼ cup bean sprouts
¼ cup slivered almonds, toasted
2 fennel bulbs, thinly sliced
2 tablespoons chopped cilantro
2 tangerines, peeled and sectioned

Cover the cellophane noodles with hot water and soak for 15 minutes or until soft and pliable. Drain and set aside.

Heat the oil in a large wok until smoking. Add the turkey and stir-fry until it loses its raw look, about 1 minute. Add the garlic and pepper flakes and stir-fry another 10 seconds. Add the reserved fish sauce mixture and heat until boiling, about 10 seconds. Add the drained noodles and the eggs and stir-fry for 1 minute. Add the reserved vegetables and stir-fry for 1 more minute. Turn onto a plate, garnish with the bean sprouts, almonds, fennel, cilantro, and tangerine sections, and serve.

Makes 4 servings.

Fiery Barbecued Bluefish

✪ **2½ tablespoons curry paste reserved from Thai Curried Shrimp**
2 tablespoons vegetable oil
1 teaspoon hot pepper sauce

1½ pounds bluefish fillet, skinned, cut into 4 equal portions (see Note)
1 lime, cut into 8 wedges

Mix the reserved curry paste, oil, and hot pepper sauce in a small bowl. Brush all over the bluefish. Set aside for 5 minutes.

Grill the fish on an oiled rack 4 inches from a hot fire for 3 to 4 minutes per side, or until the outside is browned and the fish flakes to gentle pressure. Serve each portion of fish with 2 lime wedges.

Makes 4 servings.

Note: If some pieces are very thick, butterfly them. Slit horizontally but not all the way through. Open the sides up like a book and even out the thickness by pressing firmly in the middle with the palm of your hand.

Braised Sweet-and-Sour Chicken Thighs

8 chicken thighs, skinless and boneless, or
   bone-in
¼ cup flour
2 tablespoons olive oil
1 medium onion, chopped
2 cloves garlic, minced
✪ ¼ cup fish sauce mixture reserved from
   Thai Curried Shrimp

✪ 1 tablespoon curry paste reserved from
   Thai Curried Shrimp
2 tablespoons dark brown sugar
2 tablespoons rice wine vinegar
1 cup water

Dredge the chicken pieces in the flour and pat off any excess. Heat the oil in a large saucepan. Add the chicken in 2 batches and brown on both sides. Set aside.

Drain off all but 2 teaspoons of the oil in the pan. Add the onion and cook until softened, about 2 minutes. Add the garlic, reserved fish sauce mixture, reserved curry paste, brown sugar, vinegar, and water. Stir to combine and bring to a boil. Add the chicken and any juices that have collected on the plate and simmer until done, 30 minutes for bone-in thighs, 10 minutes for boneless thighs.

Makes 4 servings.

BONING CHICKEN THIGHS

Remove the skin from a chicken thigh and turn it over. Run a thin sharp knife down the center of the thigh, following the line of the bone. Using short scraping motions, cut around the bone, keeping the knife as close to the bone as possible. Insert the knife under the bone and scrape up the underside. Holding the thigh by the bone, cut around both ends of the bone to disengage the meat.

Chili Peanut Soup

1 medium onion, chopped
2 medium carrots, diced
1 tablespoon vegetable oil
4 cups chicken broth, canned or homemade
✪ **2 cups rice reserved from Brown Rice with Asian Vegetables**

✪ **I cup peanut sauce reserved from Cucumbers with Ginger Peanut Sauce**
✪ **¼ cup fish sauce mixture reserved from Thai Curried Shrimp**
1 tablespoon peanut butter

Cook the onion and carrots in the oil in a large heavy saucepan over medium heat until softened, about 3 minutes, stirring frequently. Add the broth and simmer for 5 minutes. Add the reserved rice, reserved peanut sauce, reserved fish sauce mixture, and peanut butter, stirring until the soup boils and the peanut butter melts, about 1 minute. Simmer until thickened, about 4 minutes more, and serve.

Makes 4 servings.

Cornish hens are plump, tender, mild, juicy, and diminutive; they are elegant yet affordable and they can be fried, stewed, roasted, or grilled. Cut in half lengthwise for grilling, they're on the table twenty minutes after the fire gets hot.

This week's Sunday dinner does just that. In the first recipe, hen halves are grilled after they've been infused with the flavors of olive oil, lemon, and rosemary. The oil helps the skin of the hen to crisp as it grills, and the lemon helps the birds absorb herbal flavors from the marinade. The hens are accompanied by brown rice enriched with walnut oil and pecans, green beans that are strikingly served with strips of red peppers, and carrots in a sheen of ginger and honey.

On Monday, Sunday's toasted pecans find a second home as a crispy coating for sautéed flounder that lends a rich roasted aroma to this wallflower of fish. Sunday's vegetables reunite Tuesday in a chicken stir-fry for which most of the ingredients need only to be rewarmed. Even the rice is ready. On Wednesday, pork is simmered with vegetables, capers, and sherry, and the flavor of the vinaigrette does double duty by lending its herbal perfume to grilled shrimp on Thursday.

THE SUNDAY DINNER

Grilled Cornish Hens with
Rosemary Vinaigrette

Brown Rice with Pecans and Garlic

Steamed Green Beans with
Stir-fried Red Peppers

Carrots Glazed with Ginger and Honey

THE WEEKNIGHT ENTREES

Pecan-crusted Flounder

Stir-fried Sweet-and-Sour Chicken
and Vegetables

Pork Chops with Capers, Carrots,
and Peppers

Herb-grilled Shrimp

Grilled Cornish Hens with Rosemary Vinaigrette

½ cup lemon juice
½ cup olive oil
1 tablespoon chopped fresh rosemary leaves
1 clove garlic, minced
Salt and pepper to taste

2 teaspoons red wine vinegar
3 Cornish hens, split in half lengthwise with
    backbones removed (page 251)
1 lemon, cut into 8 wedges

Combine the lemon juice, olive oil, rosemary, garlic, salt, pepper, and vinegar in a mixing bowl. Place the hen halves in a shallow dish and pour half the mixture over them. Turn to coat. Set aside for 10 minutes.

Remove the hens from the marinade and place, bone side up, on a rack. Grill or broil 6 inches from a hot fire for 10 minutes per side, turning once and basting with the remaining marinade. Serve 4 of the hen halves garnished with lemon wedges.

Makes 4 servings, plus enough to:
✪ **Reserve ½ cup vinaigrette for Herb-grilled Shrimp.**
✪ **Reserve 2 Cornish hen halves for Stir-fried Sweet-and-Sour Chicken and Vegetables.**

Brown Rice with Pecans and Garlic

4½ cups water
2 teaspoons soy sauce
2 cups long-grain brown rice
1 tablespoon walnut or olive oil

2 cups pecans, finely chopped
2 cloves garlic, minced
Salt and pepper to taste

Bring the water and soy sauce to a boil in a heavy saucepan over high heat. Add the rice and stir until water returns to a boil. Reduce heat to low, cover, and simmer for 45 minutes, or until all the water has been absorbed and the rice is puffed and tender.

While the rice is cooking, heat the walnut oil in a skillet over medium-high heat. Add the pecans and cook, stirring constantly, until the pecans are lightly toasted, about 3 minutes. Remove from heat and stir in the garlic, salt, and pepper.

When the rice is done, season liberally with salt and pepper. Mix half the nuts (1 cup) with half the rice (3 cups) and serve.

Makes 4 servings, plus enough to:
- ✪ **Reserve 3 cups rice for Stir-fried Sweet-and-Sour Chicken and Vegetables.**
- ✪ **Reserve 1 cup toasted garlic pecans for Pecan-crusted Flounder.**

Steamed Green Beans with Stir-fried Red Peppers

1 tablespoon vegetable oil
2 large red bell peppers, stemmed, seeded, and cut into thin strips
Salt and pepper to taste
1 clove garlic, minced

Pinch of sugar
2 pounds green beans, trimmed and cut in half
1 cup water

Heat the oil in a large wok or skillet over medium-high heat. Add the bell pepper strips and cook, stirring constantly, until barely tender, about 3 minutes. Add the salt, pepper, garlic, and sugar and remove from heat. Transfer to a bowl and set aside. Wipe out the pan.

Return the pan to the heat and add the green beans and water. Over high heat, cook until the beans are tender, about 3 minutes. Drain the beans and toss them with ¾ cup of the peppers. Serve half (about 3 cups).

Makes 4 servings, plus enough to:
- ✪ **Reserve 3 cups for Stir-fried Sweet-and-Sour Chicken and Vegetables.**
- ✪ **Reserve ¼ cup peppers for Pork Chops with Capers, Carrots, and Peppers.**

Carrots Glazed with Ginger and Honey

2 tablespoons vegetable oil
2 tablespoons finely chopped gingerroot
2 pounds carrots, cut into thin diagonal slices
3 cloves garlic, minced

1½ cups water
¼ cup honey
Salt and pepper to taste
2 teaspoons lemon juice

Heat the oil in a large skillet over medium-high heat. Add the gingerroot, carrots, and garlic and toss to coat with the oil. Add the water and bring to a boil. Add the honey, salt, and pepper and simmer until all but a thin film of the water has evaporated, stirring occasionally. Add the lemon juice, and serve half the carrots (about 2 cups).

Makes 4 servings, plus enough to:
✪ **Reserve 1 cup for Stir-fried Sweet-and-Sour Chicken and Vegetables.**
✪ **Reserve 1 cup for Pork Chops with Capers, Carrots, and Peppers.**

Pecan-crusted Flounder

○ **I cup toasted garlic pecans reserved from Brown Rice with Pecans and Garlic**
½ cup flour
Salt to taste

Cayenne to taste
4 skinless flounder fillets
  (about 4 ounces each)
2 tablespoons vegetable oil
1 orange, cut into 8 wedges

With a few quick pulses, process the reserved pecans in a food processor until they are coarsely chopped. Add the flour, salt, and cayenne and process until the pecans are very finely chopped. Thoroughly dust the fish with the pecan mixture.

Heat the oil in a large nonstick skillet until very hot. Cook the fish fillets, two at a time, until the fillets are golden brown on both sides, about 2 minutes. When done, the fish will flake when pushed gently with a fork. Blot quickly on paper towels and serve garnished with the orange wedges.

Makes 4 servings.

Stir-fried Sweet-and-Sour Chicken and Vegetables

- ✪ **3 cups rice reserved from Brown Rice with Pecans and Garlic**
- *1 tablespoon rice wine vinegar or apple cider vinegar*
- *1 tablespoon honey*
- *1 tablespoon soy sauce*
- *1 tablespoon dry sherry*
- *1 teaspoon dark sesame oil*
- ✪ **2 Cornish hen halves reserved from Grilled Cornish Hens with Rosemary Vinaigrette**

- *1 tablespoon vegetable oil*
- *1 medium onion, chopped*
- *Pinch of crushed red pepper flakes*
- ✪ **3 cups reserved Steamed Green Beans with Stir-fried Red Peppers**
- ✪ **1 cup reserved Carrots Glazed with Ginger and Honey**
- *1 teaspoon minced garlic*

Warm the reserved rice, either in a microwave oven at full power for 3 minutes or with 2 tablespoons of water in a small saucepan over low heat. Thoroughly mix the vinegar, honey, soy sauce, sherry, and sesame oil in a small bowl. Remove and discard the skin and bones from the reserved hen halves and cut the meat into small pieces. Set aside.

Heat the vegetable oil in a large wok or a large skillet until smoking. Add the onion and stir-fry for 10 seconds. Add the pepper flakes and the meat and stir for 30 seconds more. Add the reserved green beans and peppers and the reserved carrots and toss until heated through, about 1 minute. Add the garlic and the liquid ingredients and toss. Remove from heat and serve the stir-fried mixture with the rice.

Makes 4 servings.

Pork Chops with Capers, Carrots, and Peppers

4 boneless pork chops, ¾ inch thick
   (about 4 ounces each)
⅓ cup flour seasoned with salt and pepper to
   taste
1 tablespoon vegetable oil
1 small onion, chopped
2 tablespoons capers, drained

✪ **I cup reserved Carrots Glazed with
Ginger and Honey**
✪ **¼ cup peppers reserved from Steamed
Green Beans with Stir-fried Red
Peppers**
¼ cup dry sherry
Juice of ½ lemon

Dust the pork chops with the seasoned flour and pat off any excess. Heat the oil in a large nonstick skillet over medium-high heat. Add the chops and brown well on both sides, about 5 minutes. Reduce heat to medium and cook the chops another 3 to 5 minutes, turning them several times until they are firm and only slightly pink in the center. Remove and keep warm.

Pour off all but a thin film of fat from the pan. Add the onion, capers, reserved carrots, and reserved peppers and cook until heated through, about 1 minute. Add the sherry. It will boil up immediately. Remove from the heat, and add the lemon juice. Adjust seasoning with salt and pepper. Pour over the chops. Serve immediately.

Makes 4 servings.

Herb-grilled Shrimp

2 tablespoons chopped fresh herbs, such as
   parsley, dill, basil, or chives
✪ **½ cup vinaigrette reserved from Grilled
Cornish Hens with Rosemary
Vinaigrette**

24 large shrimp, shelled and deveined
   (about 1¼ pounds)

Combine the herbs and reserved vinaigrette. Toss the shrimp with ¼ cup of this mixture and set aside for 10 minutes. Arrange shrimp on an oiled mesh rack and grill or broil 4 inches from a hot fire for 1 to 2 minutes per side, or until opaque and firm. Serve the shrimp, drizzled with the remaining vinaigrette.

Makes 4 servings.

Menu **49**

In my kitchen, an ingredient may not rest until it gives its all. Obviously, no one wants to chomp on shrimp shells for supper, but much of shrimp's flavor is in the shell. All you have to do is cook the shells to extract it. Knowing that, you can prepare a creamy bisque bursting with full-bodied shrimp flavor.

This week's menu takes advantage of just such frugal principles. The tough ends from Sunday's asparagus side dish, instead of being discarded, enrich Monday's bisque, for which Sunday's Boiled Shrimp provides both the shrimp shells and broth. The broth also underlies a classic sauce that turns simple fish fillets into a sophisticated entree later in the week. Wednesday's Stir-fried Chicken Curry is thickened with Sunday's Fragrant Beans, and is served in a ring of Sweet Barley Pilaf with a jolt of Hot Pepper Chutney. The Fragrant Beans reappear as a base for Roasted Vegetable Chili—a dish that's made in minutes by combining freshly grilled vegetables with the already seasoned bean mixture.

THE SUNDAY DINNER

Boiled Shrimp with Hot Pepper Chutney

Sweet Barley Pilaf

Grilled Lemon Asparagus

Fragrant Beans

THE WEEKNIGHT ENTREES

Shrimp and Asparagus Bisque

Roasted Vegetable Chili

Stir-fried Chicken Curry

Sautéed Flounder with Sauce Cardinal

Boiled Shrimp

3 cups white wine
3 cups water
1 carrot, finely chopped
1 rib celery, finely chopped
1 medium onion, finely chopped
½ teaspoon salt
1 teaspoon black peppercorns

3 sprigs fresh dill
1 whole clove
½ lemon
2½ pounds medium shrimp
2 cups ice water
Hot Pepper Chutney (recipe follows)

Combine the wine, water, carrot, celery, onion, salt, peppercorns, dill, and clove in a 4-quart saucepan. Bring to a boil, reduce the heat, and simmer for 5 minutes. Squeeze the lemon into the liquid and add the lemon half. Return to a boil, add the shrimp, and stir until shrimp become firm and pink, about 2 minutes. Remove the saucepan from the heat and, using tongs, transfer the shrimp to a bowl. Pour the 2 cups of ice water over the shrimp and toss until the water becomes warm. Drain this water back into the saucepan. Strain and reserve.

Shell and devein the shrimp. Serve 12 shrimp per person with the chutney.

Makes 4 servings, plus enough to:
✪ **Reserve shrimp shells for Shrimp and Asparagus Bisque.**
✪ **Reserve 12 shrimp for Shrimp and Asparagus Bisque.**
✪ **Reserve 8 shrimp for Sautéed Flounder with Sauce Cardinal.**
✪ **Reserve 6 cups broth for Shrimp and Asparagus Bisque.**
✪ **Reserve 2 cups broth for Sautéed Flounder with Sauce Cardinal.**

Hot Pepper Chutney

1 poblano chili, roasted

2 red, 1 yellow, and 1 green bell pepper,
roasted

1 small dried chili

1 teaspoon coriander seeds

2 whole cloves

1 tablespoon grated gingerroot

1 medium onion, finely chopped

2 cloves garlic, minced

1 serrano chili, minced

2 tablespoons vegetable oil

¼ cup cider vinegar

¼ cup sugar

¼ cup water

¼ cup chopped cilantro

Remove the stems and as many of the seeds as possible from the roasted chili and bell peppers. Reserve one of the red peppers. Dice the others.

Combine the dried chili pepper, coriander seeds, cloves, and gingerroot in a heavy skillet. Place over high heat and cook, stirring constantly, until the spices become aromatic, about 1 minute. Remove from heat. Grind to a fine powder in a spice grinder. Set aside.

Cook the onion, garlic, and serrano chili in the oil in a heavy saucepan until soft. Add the spices and peppers and cook for 3 minutes, stirring frequently. Stir in the cider vinegar, sugar, and water. Cover and simmer for 20 minutes, or until the flavors have blended and the excess liquid has boiled away. Stir in the cilantro. Let cool to room temperature. Serve half and refrigerate the rest.

Makes about 3 cups, plus enough to:
- ✪ **Reserve 1 roasted bell pepper for Roasted Vegetable Chili.**
- ✪ **Reserve 1½ cups chutney for Stir-fried Chicken Curry.**

ROASTING PEPPERS

To roast chilies or peppers, place them directly over the high flame of a gas burner, under a broiler, or on a grill until they char. Give the peppers a quarter turn and char again. Continue until the peppers have blackened all over. Place in a paper bag, loosely close it, and allow the peppers to cool for 10 minutes. Peel by rubbing the blackened skins with your fingers. Do not wash the peppers as this would wash away their flavorful oils. Good-quality roasted red peppers are available in jars.

Sweet Barley Pilaf

½ medium onion, chopped
1 1–inch cinnamon stick
1 teaspoon grated gingerroot
2 tablespoons butter
2 cups medium pearled barley
4 cups chicken broth, canned or homemade

4 cups water
Salt and pepper to taste
¼ cup chopped dried fruit, any kind
¼ cup chopped nuts, any kind
1 tablespoon vegetable oil
2 tablespoons sugar

Cook the onion with the cinnamon stick and gingerroot in the butter in a heavy saucepan over medium heat until softened, about 2 minutes. Add the barley and toss with the butter. Add the chicken broth, water, salt, and pepper. Bring to a boil, reduce the heat, and simmer for about 40 minutes or until all the liquid has been absorbed and the barley is tender.

Meanwhile, cook the dried fruit and nuts in the oil until toasted. Stir in the sugar. When the barley is done, stir in the fruit and nuts. Fluff with a fork and serve half.

Makes 4 servings, plus enough to:
✪ **Reserve about 3 cups for Stir-fried Chicken Curry.**

Grilled Lemon Asparagus

16 medium thick asparagus
⅓ cup extra-virgin olive oil
⅓ cup lemon juice

1 clove garlic, minced
Salt and pepper to taste

Snap the tough ends from the asparagus. Reserve the ends. Blanch the asparagus in a skillet of simmering water until barely tender, about 3 minutes. Drain well and set aside.

Mix the oil, lemon juice, garlic, salt, and pepper in a wide bowl. Set aside.
Preheat the broiler.
About 5 minutes before serving, dip the asparagus in the oil mixture and broil for 2 minutes per side, or just until the surface of each asparagus stalk is lightly browned. Return asparagus to the dressing and serve.

Makes 4 servings, plus enough to:
✪ **Reserve asparagus ends for Shrimp and Asparagus Bisque.**

Fragrant Beans

1 tablespoon ground cumin
2 teaspoons ground coriander
2 teaspoons chili powder
Salt and pepper to taste
1 medium onion, chopped
½ bell pepper, diced
¼ pound smoked ham or smoked turkey
   breast, diced

1 tablespoon vegetable oil
1 clove garlic, minced
⅓ cup canned crushed tomatoes
1 cup chicken broth, canned or homemade
1 package (10 ounces) frozen lima beans,
   thawed
1 can (19 ounces) cannellini beans
2 teaspoons chopped cilantro

Combine the cumin, coriander, chili powder, salt, and pepper in a small bowl. Cook the onion, bell pepper, and ham in the oil in a heavy skillet until the vegetables have softened. Add the garlic and spice mixture and cook another 30 seconds. Stir in the crushed tomatoes and broth and bring to a boil. Add the lima beans and cannellini beans and simmer for 5 minutes. Stir in the cilantro. Serve half.

Makes 4 servings, plus enough to:
✪ **Reserve 2 cups beans for Roasted Vegetable Chili.**
✪ **Reserve ⅓ cup beans for Stir-fried Chicken Curry.**

Shrimp and Asparagus Bisque

- ✪ **Shrimp shells reserved from Boiled Shrimp**
- 2 tablespoons butter
- 2 tablespoons olive oil
- 1 medium onion, finely chopped
- 2 ribs celery, finely chopped
- ✪ **Asparagus ends reserved from Grilled Lemon Asparagus**
- ⅛ teaspoon dried oregano
- ½ teaspooon dried basil

- Pinch of crushed red pepper flakes
- Pinch of freshly grated nutmeg
- 3 cloves garlic, minced
- 3 tablespoons flour
- ✪ **6 cups broth reserved from Boiled Shrimp**
- ½ cup canned crushed tomatoes
- 1 bay leaf
- Salt and pepper to taste
- ✪ **12 shrimp reserved from Boiled Shrimp**

Coarsely chop the reserved shrimp shells in a food processor. Melt the butter in the olive oil in a large heavy saucepan, add the shrimp shells, onion, celery, and reserved asparagus ends, and cook until the vegetables have softened and the shrimp shells are brightly colored, about 3 minutes. Add the oregano, basil, pepper flakes, nutmeg, and garlic and cook 1 more minute, stirring constantly. Add the flour and stir briskly for 1 minute. Stir in half the reserved broth and bring to a boil, stirring in any bits of flour stuck to the bottom of the pan. Add the remaining broth, the tomatoes, bay leaf, salt, and pepper. Heat to a simmer, cover, and cook for 20 minutes.

Strain into another pot. Discard the remaining solids. Slice the reserved shrimp, reheat the soup, add the shrimp, and serve.

Makes 4 servings.

Roasted Vegetable Chili

- ¼ cup olive oil
- ¼ teaspoon salt
- ¼ teaspoon ground black pepper
- 1 large zucchini, sliced 1 inch thick
- 6 large white mushrooms, stems trimmed and cleaned
- 1 small eggplant, peeled and cut lengthwise into ½-inch slices

- 2 large beefsteak tomatoes, cored and thickly sliced
- 2 ears corn, husked
- ✪ **1 roasted red bell pepper reserved from Hot Pepper Chutney**
- ✪ **2 cups reserved Fragrant Beans**
- ½ cup water or canned vegetable juice

continued

Combine the oil, salt, and pepper. Brush the zucchini, mushrooms, eggplant, tomatoes, and corn with the oil and grill or broil over a hot fire until browned and tender, about 5 minutes per side. Cut the zucchini, mushrooms, eggplant, and tomatoes into ½-inch dice. Remove the corn kernels from the cobs with a small knife. Dice the reserved bell pepper.

In a medium saucepan, heat the reserved beans. Add the diced roasted pepper and the grilled vegetables, along with any accumulated juices. If the mixture is too thick, thin with some water or canned vegetable juice. Heat through and serve.

Makes 4 to 5 servings.

Stir-fried Chicken Curry

1 boneless and skinless chicken breast
½ cup flour
1 teaspoon dry mustard
Salt and pepper to taste
3 tablespoons vegetable oil
1 teaspoon minced gingerroot
½ teaspoon sugar
½ medium onion, chopped
8 white mushrooms, stems trimmed, cleaned,
    and sliced

1 carrot, diced
2 teaspoons curry powder
✪ **⅓ cup reserved Fragrant Beans**
1¼ cups chicken broth, canned or homemade
2 tablespoons ketchup
1 clove garlic, minced
6 scallions, white parts only, sliced
✪ **About 3 cups reserved Sweet Barley Pilaf**
✪ **1½ cups reserved Hot Pepper Chutney**

Trim the chicken breast and cut into 1-inch chunks. Combine the flour, dry mustard, salt, and pepper and dredge the chicken in this mixture.

Heat a wok until smoking. Add the oil and heat for 30 seconds. Add the chicken and cook until crisp on all sides, about 1 minute. Push the chicken up the sides of the wok. Add the gingerroot, sugar, onion, mushrooms, carrot, curry powder, and reserved beans to the oil in the center of the wok and stir-fry for 30 seconds. Toss in the chicken to combine. Add the chicken broth and ketchup and simmer for 3 minutes, or until the chicken is cooked through. Add the garlic and scallions. Turn off heat.

Arrange the reserved barley pilaf in a ring on a serving dish and spoon the chicken curry into the middle of the ring. Serve with the reserved chutney on the side.

Makes 4 servings.

Sautéed Flounder with Sauce Cardinal

½ cup flour
½ teaspoon paprika
½ teaspoon salt
½ teaspoon ground black pepper
4 flounder fillets (about 5 ounces each)
✪ 8 shrimp reserved from Boiled Shrimp
¼ cup olive oil
1 medium onion, finely chopped

✪ 2 cups broth reserved from Boiled Shrimp
2 teaspoons tomato paste
Juice of ½ lemon
Salt and pepper to taste
1 teaspoon chopped dill
2 teaspoons chopped parsley
1 large clove garlic, minced

Mix the flour, paprika, salt, and pepper in a small pie pan. Dredge flounder fillets in this mixture and set aside. Reserve 1 tablespoon of the seasoned flour. Slice the reserved shrimp and set aside.

Sauté the flounder in the olive oil in a large skillet over medium-high heat for about 2 minutes per side. When the fish is golden brown and flakes when gently pressed with a fork, remove to a warm platter. Keep warm. Add the onion to the oil remaining in the pan and cook until onion has softened, about 2 minutes. Add the reserved tablespoon of seasoned flour and stir for 1 minute. Add the reserved broth, tomato paste, lemon juice, salt, and pepper. Simmer until lightly thickened. Add the dill, parsley, garlic, and shrimp. Adjust seasoning with salt and pepper and heat through. Pour over fish and serve.

Makes 4 servings.

Roasting is foolproof—almost. Be sure the roast is placed on a rack (be it made of metal, bones, or vegetables) and set in a low-sided, heavy metal or ceramic pan. These steps ensure that air circulates around the roast and that moisture doesn't touch the meat, for if the meat sits in hot liquid, it will steam instead of roast, and you'll be left with something that's pale, dry, and tough. Avoid foil tents for the same reason. Two other tips: Always roast fat side up, and when rubbing seasonings into the meat, go easy on the salt. Too much will draw juices out of the meat.

Sunday's roast lamb is infused with mustard, garlic, and thyme, an intense mixture that works beautifully with the gamey flavor of lamb while standing up to the assertive side dishes. Anchovies add just the right saltiness to the potato pancakes without becoming fishy, and broccoli rabe, usually steamed or braised, is perfect for stir-frying.

Monday's Braised Anise Lamb explodes with flavor. Its fragrance comes from star anise, a dried pod found in Chinese groceries. Asian cuisine influences Tuesday's dinner, too, with the combination of Sunday's ginger-scented broccoli rabe, a boneless chicken breast, and two classic Japanese ingredients— wasabi (powdered horseradish) and pickled ginger. They may be familiar as sushi garnishes, but here they bring a cool, spicy note to an exotic but simple preparation. Wednesday's Scottish Lemon Lamb Soup is thickened with oatmeal, a versatile grain trapped in the stereotype of a breakfast cereal. Thursday's sauté of fish is served on a bed of hashed potatoes, aromatic with basil, roasted peppers, and anchovy.

THE SUNDAY DINNER	THE WEEKNIGHT ENTREES
Roasted Leg of Lamb Dijonnaise	Braised Anise Lamb
Potato Anchovy Pancakes	Chicken Steamed with Greens and Pickled Ginger
Stir-fried Broccoli Rabe	Scottish Lemon Lamb Soup
	Sautéed Shad on Hashed Basil Potatoes

Roasted Leg of Lamb Dijonnaise

¼ cup Dijon mustard
4 cloves garlic, minced
3 tablespoons olive oil
1 teaspoon dried thyme

Salt and freshly ground pepper to taste
5 pounds boneless leg of lamb, rolled and tied,
    with the bones, if possible

Combine the mustard, garlic, oil, thyme, salt, and pepper and set aside.

Preheat the oven to 400°F.

If you have the bones from the leg, place them in the bottom of a roasting pan, and use them as a rack. If not, set a metal rack in the pan. Rub half the mustard mixture all over the lamb, and place the meat on the rack or the bones. Roast for 1 hour. Reduce the temperature to 375°F. and roast for 1 more hour, brushing more of the mustard mixture on the meat from time to time, until done. For medium, a meat thermometer inserted in the thickest section of the lamb should register 135°F.

Transfer the lamb to a cutting board and allow it to rest for 10 minutes before slicing. Cut half of the lamb, against the grain, into thin slices and serve.

Makes 4 servings, plus enough to:
✪ **Reserve 1 pound lamb for Braised Anise Lamb.**
✪ **Reserve 1 pound lamb for Scottish Lemon Lamb Soup.**
✪ **Reserve ½ cup drippings for Braised Anise Lamb.**
✪ **Reserve ½ cup drippings for Scottish Lemon Lamb Soup.**

Potato Anchovy Pancakes

4 large russet potatoes, scrubbed or peeled
5 eggs, lightly beaten
¼ cup flour
1½ teaspoons salt
¼ teaspoon ground black pepper

2 tablespoons finely chopped onion
2 cloves garlic, minced
12 anchovy fillets, finely chopped
Olive oil, for frying

continued

Grate the potatoes into a large bowl filled with cold water. Swish the potato around in the water. When the water is cloudy with potato starch, drain the potatoes and place them in the middle of a towel. Wring out any moisture.

Combine the potato, eggs, flour, salt, pepper, onion, garlic, and anchovy in a medium bowl. Mix until well blended. Pour a thin film of oil into a skillet. Place heaping soupspoonfuls of the potato mixture in the hot oil and flatten to form pancakes ¼ inch thick and 3 inches in diameter. Brown well on one side, flip, and brown on the other. Drain on paper towels. Serve hot.

Makes 4 servings of 2 pancakes each, plus enough to:
✪ **Reserve 8 pancakes for Sautéed Shad on Hashed Basil Potatoes.**

Stir-fried Broccoli Rabe

broccoli rabe (2½ bunches)　　　　*1 clove garlic, finely minced*
1 medium onion, chopped　　　　*1 teaspoon finely chopped fresh gingerroot*
¼ cup olive oil　　　　*Salt and pepper to taste*
Pinch of crushed red pepper flakes

Trim the broccoli rabe of the stems and any wilted leaves. Cut into 1- to 2-inch pieces. Fill a clean sink with cold water and add the rabe. Swish back and forth to clean off any grit clinging to the greens. Lift the broccoli rabe from the water and shake off excess but do not dry it.

Cook the onion in the olive oil in a large heavy skillet or wok until softened, about 2 minutes. Add the pepper flakes and the broccoli rabe (it will shrink considerably). Toss well to coat the greens with oil. Cover, reduce the heat to medium-low, and cook for 10 to 15 minutes, or until the rabe has wilted and the moisture has evaporated. Stir in the garlic and ginger and season with salt and pepper. Serve ⅔ cup per person.

Makes 4 servings, plus enough to:
✪ **Reserve 1 cup broccoli rabe for Chicken Steamed with Greens and Pickled Ginger.**

Braised Anise Lamb

½ ounce dried wild mushrooms, any type

1 cup hot water

3 tablespoons soy sauce

¼ cup dry sherry

3 tablespoons honey

Pinch of crushed red pepper flakes

6 star anise

1 tablespoon cornstarch

½ cup chicken or beef broth, canned or homemade

✪ ½ cup reserved drippings from Roasted Leg of Lamb Dijonnaise

1 teaspoon tomato paste

✪ I pound reserved Roasted Leg of Lamb Dijonnaise

2 tablespoons peanut oil

1 large leek, white part only, cleaned and sliced

1 tablespoon minced gingerroot

2 teaspoons minced garlic

8 medium to large white mushrooms, stems trimmed, cleaned and sliced

1 red bell pepper, stemmed, seeded, and diced

1 teaspoon dark sesame oil

4 scallions, sliced

Soak the dried mushrooms in the hot water in a small bowl until softened, about 20 minutes. Squeeze excess water from mushrooms and chop coarsely. Strain soaking liquid through a coffee filter or paper towel set in a strainer. Set both aside. Combine the soy sauce, sherry, honey, pepper flakes, and star anise in a small bowl. Stir or whisk until the honey dissolves. Set aside. In a separate bowl, combine the cornstarch, broth, reserved drippings, and tomato paste. Set aside.

Cut the lamb into 4 thick slices, then cut across to cube it. You should have about 2 cups. Set aside.

Heat the oil in a large wok or deep skillet until smoking. Add the leek, gingerroot, garlic, white mushrooms, and bell pepper. Toss until the leek softens and the mushrooms brown lightly, about 2 minutes. Add the soy mixture, the soaked wild mushrooms, and the mushroom soaking liquid. Bring to a boil and add the lamb. Simmer for 4 minutes. Stir the broth to redistribute the cornstarch and add to the pan. Stir until the liquid thickens lightly. Turn onto a large platter and drizzle the sesame oil over all. Scatter the scallions over the top and serve.

Makes 4 servings.

Chicken Steamed with Greens and Pickled Ginger

2 skinless and boneless chicken breasts, split
    and trimmed
2 teaspoons dark sesame oil
½ teaspoon wasabi (see Note)

Salt to taste
✪ **1 cup reserved Stir-fried Broccoli Rabe**
⅓ cup Japanese pickled ginger
    (about 2 ounces) (see Note)

Rub the chicken breasts with the sesame oil. Place the chicken breasts between sheets of plastic wrap and pound until about ¼ inch thick and at least 5 inches wide at the widest point. Rub each piece with a pinch of wasabi powder and salt. Finely chop the broccoli rabe, scatter about ¼ cup of it over each piece of chicken breast, and roll up jellyroll-style, starting from one of the longer sides.

Line up a few pieces of pickled ginger in the center of a piece of plastic wrap. Put a chicken roll on the ginger and top with more ginger. Roll the plastic wrap tightly around the chicken. Repeat with remaining chicken rolls.

Set a steaming basket over a pan of water, place over high heat, and bring to a boil. Place the chicken rolls in the basket, cover the pan, and steam for 15 minutes, or until the chicken is firm.

Remove the rolls from the steamer and let cool for a few minutes. Snip an end of the plastic from each roll and drain any liquid from the wrapper into a small bowl or cup. Unwrap the rolls, using scissors to cut open the plastic and slice each roll in half on a diagonal. Serve moistened with a bit of the juices.

Makes 4 servings.

Note: Wasabi, powdered dried Japanese horseradish, and Japanese pickled ginger, or sushi ginger, are available in specialty grocery stores and some supermarkets.

Scottish Lemon Lamb Soup

2 tablespoons oil
2 medium carrots, sliced
2 ribs celery, sliced
1 medium onion, diced
1 tablespoon finely minced lemon zest
3 cloves garlic, minced
1 teaspoon ground coriander
½ teaspoon rubbed sage
1 teaspoon dried thyme
Pinch of crushed red pepper flakes

1 can (about 14 ounces) beef broth
✪ **½ cup reserved drippings from Roasted
Leg of Lamb Dijonnaise**
⅓ cup old-fashioned or quick oatmeal
(not instant)
✪ **1 pound reserved Roasted Leg of Lamb
Dijonnaise**
Salt and pepper to taste
Juice of 1 lemon
¼ cup chopped parsley

Heat the oil in a large heavy saucepan. Add the carrots, celery, and onion and cook until the vegetables have barely softened, about 3 minutes. Add the lemon zest, garlic, coriander, sage, thyme, and pepper flakes. Cook for 1 minute, stirring frequently. Add the broth and the drippings and bring to a boil. Add the oatmeal, reduce the heat, and simmer for 15 minutes. Cut the lamb into 4 thick slices, then cut across to cube it. You should have about 2 cups. Add the lamb to the soup, season with salt, pepper, lemon juice, and parsley, and heat through, about 4 minutes.

Makes 4 servings.

Sautéed Shad on Hashed Basil Potatoes

HASHED POTATOES
✪ **8 reserved Potato Anchovy Pancakes**
1 tablespoon olive oil
1 medium onion, finely chopped
1 roasted bell pepper, jarred or homemade, stemmed, seeded, and diced
Salt and pepper to taste
2 cloves garlic, minced
About ¼ cup chopped basil

SHAD
1 tablespoon olive oil
1½ pounds shad fillets (see Note)
2 cloves garlic, minced
Juice of 1 lemon

For the potatoes, finely chop the reserved potato pancakes. Heat the oil in a large non-stick skillet, add the onion, and stir for 30 seconds. Add the chopped pancakes and the roasted pepper, and cook over medium-high heat until the mixture browns lightly, about 4 minutes, stirring frequently. Season liberally with salt and pepper. Add the garlic and basil and stir until the basil softens, about 1 minute. Transfer to a platter and keep warm.

For the shad, add the olive oil to the skillet and heat until smoking. Add the shad, skin side down, and cook over high heat for 3 minutes, or until the skin is very brown and crisp. Turn the fish and cook about 2 minutes more or until browned and crisp. Transfer the fish, flesh side up, onto the potato hash.

Remove the pan from the heat and stir in the garlic and lemon juice. Pour over the fish.

Makes 4 servings.

Note: Substitute thin fillets of salmon, mackerel, or rainbow trout if shad is not available.

t is a quirk of food financing that the tastiest meat is frequently the cheapest. So if you want to save money, it makes sense to seek out the less popular cuts like shanks, brisket, breast, and ribs. The only problem is how to tenderize them.

The solution is as old as cooking itself—just add water. The traditional techniques of stewing, braising, and boiling not only tenderize tough fibers but by gently cooking the meat in liquid, they release the meat's juices into a broth that enhances the natural flavors of the meat by simmering it with aromatic vegetables, herbs, and spices.

Sunday's dinner does just that to a breast of veal. In this preparation, the breast is stuffed with basil, rosemary, thyme, walnuts, and Italian fontina cheese, and is simmered in chicken stock and white wine. Be sure you get the right fontina. Italian fontina has a beige rind embossed with its name, and the cheese is creamy and emits a nutty aroma as it melts. Its Danish namesake, which has a red wax coating, is more rubbery, less aromatic, and less interesting. The veal has two accompaniments—ripe tomatoes stewed with black and green olives, and a brown-rice pilaf made sweet and pungent by dried currants and capers.

The tomatoes become both an instant pasta sauce to serve over penne and tuna on Monday as well as a broth for veal stew on Tuesday; the broth cooks in less than 10 minutes because its intense flavors and fork-tender morsels of meat are ready. The herb filling from the veal becomes a walnut pesto that bastes and sauces Wednesday's grilled chicken. On Thursday, you'll turn Sunday's pilaf into an opulent salad with roasted peppers, capers, and beans.

THE SUNDAY DINNER

Breast of Veal Braised with
Cheese and Herbs

Tomatoes Stewed with Olives

Mixed Rice Pilaf with Currants
and Capers

THE WEEKNIGHT ENTREES

Penne with Tuna and Olives

Veal Stew with Artichokes and Lime

Grilled Chicken Breast Stuffed
with Walnut Pesto

Salad of Brown Rice, White Beans,
and Roasted Red Peppers

Breast of Veal Braised with Cheese and Herbs

3 cups basil leaves
2 sprigs fresh rosemary, leaves only
6 sprigs fresh thyme, leaves only
¾ cup walnut pieces
3 cloves garlic
3 tablespoons extra-virgin olive oil

¼ teaspoon salt
5 tablespoons grated parmesan cheese
6-pound breast of veal, with a pocket
4 ounces Italian fontina cheese, cut into strips
2 cups chicken broth, canned or homemade
½ cup white wine

Preheat the oven to 400°F.

Coarsely chop the basil, rosemary, and thyme leaves in the workbowl of a food processor, using several quick pulses and scraping down the sides of the bowl as necessary. Add the walnuts and garlic and pulse until finely chopped. Transfer to a bowl and work 2 tablespoons of the olive oil into the mixture. Mix in the salt and parmesan cheese.

Reserve ¼ cup of the herb paste. Coat the pocket in the veal breast with the remaining herb paste. Make a layer of the fontina cheese in the pocket and secure the openings of the pocket with metal skewers. Rub the outside of the veal with the remaining olive oil.

Place the meat in the bottom of a covered roasting pan, bone side down, and roast for 20 minutes. Lower the oven temperature to 350°F. Pour the broth and wine over the meat and cover the pan. Roast for 2 hours, basting the meat with the liquid in the pan every half hour.

Slice half the breast of veal into 8 thin or 4 thick slices and serve. Skim cooking liquid and moisten meat with some of it.

Makes 4 servings, plus enough to:
- ✪ **Reserve ¼ cup herb paste for Grilled Chicken Breast Stuffed with Walnut Pesto.**
- ✪ **Reserve remaining breast of veal for Veal Stew with Artichokes and Lime.**
- ✪ **Reserve about 2½ cups cooking liquid for Veal Stew with Artichokes and Lime.**

PICKING POCKETS

Because breast of veal is traditionally stuffed, it is often sold with a pocket cut between the meat and the bone. If not, just ask to have a pocket cut. You can also request that chicken breasts have pockets cut.

To cut the pockets yourself, insert a long thin knife into the meaty part of the breast right above and parallel to the bone. Move the knife parallel to the bone with a small sawing motion, opening up as wide and deep a pocket as possible without completely disengaging the meat from the bone. Before stuffing, remove as much visible fat as possible from the pocket and surrounding meat as you can without destroying the shape of the meat.

Tomatoes Stewed with Olives

2 medium onions, chopped
¼ cup olive oil
8 large tomatoes, peeled, cored, and cut into
    1-inch chunks (about 6 pounds)
3 large cloves garlic, minced

¾ cup chopped pitted oil-cured black olives
    (about 20)
½ cup chopped pitted green olives (about 14)
½ cup chopped basil leaves
Salt and pepper to taste

Cook the onions in the oil in a large heavy saucepan over medium heat until softened, about 2 minutes. Add the tomatoes and the garlic and cook over high heat for 4 to 5 minutes, or until the tomatoes release their juice but are still more or less intact. With a slotted spoon, transfer the tomatoes to a bowl and set aside.

Simmer the liquid in the pot for 5 minutes, or until it thickens slightly. Return the tomatoes to the pot along with the black olives, green olives, and basil. Heat through. Season with salt and pepper. Serve ¾ cup to each person.

Makes 4 servings, plus enough to:
✪ **Reserve 3 cups for Penne with Tuna and Olives.**
✪ **Reserve 1 cup for Veal Stew with Artichokes and Lime.**

Mixed Rice Pilaf with Currants and Capers

5 cups water
2½ cups brown rice blend (see Note)
½ cup boiling water
½ cup dried currants

1 tablespoon vegetable oil
½ medium onion, finely chopped
2 tablespoons capers, drained
Salt and pepper to taste

Bring the water to a boil in a large heavy saucepan. Add the rice, reduce the heat, cover, and cook for 45 to 50 minutes, or until all the water has been absorbed and the rice is tender. Remove from heat and set aside for 5 minutes. Fluff with a fork.

While the rice is cooking, pour the boiling water over the currants and soak for at least 30 minutes. Drain.

When the rice is done, heat the oil in a large skillet. Add the onion, and cook over medium-high heat until the onion has softened, about 1 minute. Add the capers and the drained currants. Add 4 cups of the rice, season with the salt and pepper, and toss to combine thoroughly.

Makes 4 servings, plus enough to:

✪ **Reserve 3½ cups cooked rice for Salad of Brown Rice, White Beans, and Roasted Red Peppers.**

Note: Check the package directions of the rice to confirm that a 2-to-1 ratio of water to rice is recommended. If a different amount is called for, follow the package directions rather than the directions in this recipe.

Penne with Tuna and Olives

1 pound penne
- ✪ **3 cups reserved Tomatoes Stewed with Olives**

1 can (about 6 ounces) water-packed white tuna, drained

Bring a large pot of lightly salted water to a boil. Add the penne, and boil vigorously for 10 minutes until tender. Drain. Meanwhile, heat the reserved tomatoes to a simmer. Place the drained pasta in a large serving bowl and crumble the tuna over the top. Pour the tomatoes over the tuna and toss thoroughly. Serve immediately.

Makes 4 servings.

Veal Stew with Artichokes and Lime

- ✪ **Reserved Breast of Veal Braised with Cheese and Herbs**
- ✪ **About 2½ cups cooking liquid reserved from Breast of Veal Braised with Cheese and Herbs**
1 medium onion, chopped

2 tablespoons flour
Finely grated zest and juice of 1 large lime
- ✪ **1 cup reserved Tomatoes Stewed with Olives**
1 can (14 ounces) artichoke hearts, drained and quartered

Trim the fat from the reserved veal and cut the meat into 1-inch chunks. Set aside.

Place 1 tablespoon of fat from the surface of the reserved cooking liquid in a large heavy saucepan. Carefully skim off and discard the remaining fat. Cook the onion in the fat in the pan until lightly browned. Add the flour, and cook for another 2 minutes, stirring constantly. Add the lime zest and the veal chunks and toss to coat. Add the remaining cooking liquid and heat to a simmer. Simmer for 5 minutes, stirring occasionally. Add the reserved stewed tomatoes and the artichoke hearts and simmer another 3 minutes. Stir in the lime juice and serve.

Makes 4 servings.

Grilled Chicken Breast Stuffed with Walnut Pesto

✪ ¼ cup herb paste reserved from **Breast of Veal Braised with Cheese and Herbs**

2 chicken breasts, split, with pockets cut (page 341)
2 teaspoons olive oil

Place 2 teaspoons of the reserved herb paste in each breast pocket and rub the remaining paste on the meat under the skin of each breast. Rub the outsides of the breasts with the olive oil. Grill or broil 4 inches from a medium-high fire for 5 to 8 minutes per side, turning frequently, until the chicken is no longer pink near the bone.

Makes 4 servings.

Salad of Brown Rice, White Beans, and Roasted Red Peppers

1 large clove garlic, minced
¼ cup extra-virgin olive oil
¼ cup red wine vinegar
Juice of 1 lime
4 large roasted red bell peppers, jarred or homemade

✪ **3½ cups rice reserved from Mixed Rice Pilaf with Currants and Capers**
1 can (14 ounces) small white beans, drained and rinsed
Salt and pepper to taste
¼ cup chopped parsley

Combine the garlic, olive oil, vinegar, and lime juice in a large salad bowl. Set aside. Core and seed the roasted peppers and cut into ½-inch dice. Toss with the dressing. Add the reserved rice and the beans and toss. Season liberally with salt and pepper and toss in the parsley. Serve at room temperature.

Makes 4 servings.

Menu 52

What gives food soul? The people who cook it? The ingredients they use? In America, soul food almost always refers to the home cooking of southern blacks—greens, beans, sweet potatoes, and pork. Whether stuffed into a sausage, country-cured, or hickory-smoked, pork is the preferred soul-food meat.

This week's menu starts with a meal of soul food (liberally interpreted) surrounding a baked ham. Extravagant? Not really. Sunday's ham finds economy by multiplying its uses during the week. On Monday, it adds a smoky nuance to a creamy carbonara sauce with squiggly pasta. On Tuesday, it plays off the tang of cheddar cheese in a Grits Soufflé with Sunday's greens. It is essential for Wednesday's Hoppin' John Soup, which incorporates the rest of Sunday's succotash. On Thursday, the last of the ham is finely diced and tossed with capers in a piquant garnish for sautéed trout.

Soul food is traditionally identified with long, slow cooking. I have accelerated the schedule by starting with a prebaked ham and greens that can be cooked quite quickly. The black-eyed peas in the succotash can be speeded up by doing them in a pressure cooker or substituting canned beans for the dried.

THE SUNDAY DINNER

Honey Baked Ham

Spicy Corn and Black-eyed
Peas Succotash

Braised Greens

THE WEEKNIGHT ENTREES

Radiatore Carbonara

Grits Soufflé

Hoppin' John Soup

Pan-fried Trout with Ham and Capers

Honey Baked Ham

2 tablespoons spicy brown mustard   3 pounds boneless baked ham (see Note)
¼ cup honey

Preheat the oven to 375°F.

    Combine the mustard and honey and brush the mixture all over the surface of the ham. Place on a rack set in a shallow roasting pan and roast for 45 minutes. Remove from the oven and slice. Serve 2 slices per person, about half the ham.

Makes 4 servings, plus enough to:
- ✪ **Reserve 3 slices for Hoppin' John Soup.**
- ✪ **Reserve 2 slices for Radiatore Carbonara.**
- ✪ **Reserve 1 slice for Grits Soufflé.**
- ✪ **Reserve 1 slice for Pan-fried Trout with Ham and Capers.**

Note: Boneless smoked turkey breast may be substituted.

Spicy Corn and Black-eyed Peas Succotash

1 cup dried black-eyed peas (see Note)   1 teaspoon ground cumin
4 cups cold water   Pinch of crushed red pepper flakes
½ medium onion, finely chopped   Pinch of sugar
½ red bell pepper, finely diced   Salt and black pepper to taste
2 teaspoons corn oil   2 cans (7 ounces each) corn kernels, drained
2 teaspoons chili powder

Combine the black-eyed peas with the water in a heavy saucepan and bring to a boil. Boil for 2 minutes, remove from the heat, cover, and set aside for 1 hour. Drain well and wash out the saucepan. Rinse peas and return to the saucepan and cover with 4 more cups of water. Bring to a boil, reduce the heat, cover, and simmer for about 1 hour, or until the peas are soft. Drain and set aside.

    Meanwhile, cook the onion and bell pepper in the corn oil in a large skillet over medium heat until softened. Add the chili powder, cumin, pepper flakes, and sugar. Stir and cook for 1 minute. Season with salt and black pepper.

When the peas are done, add them to the onion mixture. Stir in the corn, and heat through. Reserve 2 cups and serve the rest.

Makes 4 servings, plus enough to:
✪ **Reserve 2 cups for Hoppin' John Soup.**

Note: You may use a pressure cooker for the black-eyed peas. After soaking, drain off the liquid, rinse the peas, cover them with fresh water in a pressure cooker, seal the pot, and cook at full pressure until tender, 2 to 3 minutes. Two cans black-eyed peas (14 ounces each) may be substituted for the cooked dried black-eyed peas. Drain and rinse the canned black-eyed peas and add them with the corn.

KNOW YOUR BEANS

Bean aficionados may insist that canned beans are a poor substitute for homecooked dried beans, but the canned version is so convenient that the slightly softer texture seems a fair tradeoff. If you prefer starting with the dried, there are several routes to go.

Dried beans must be rehydrated before they are cooked. Soak them overnight in 4 times as much cold water as beans. Or combine the beans and water in a pot and bring to a boil. Boil for 2 minutes, remove from the heat, cover, and let stand for an hour.

Drain the soaked beans, cover with 4 times their volume of water, and simmer until tender. This can take as little as 45 minutes for tender beans like peas or up to several hours for very hard beans like soy beans.

Cooking time can be cut down to a few minutes by using a pressure cooker. After soaking, drain the beans, cover with fresh water in a pressure cooker, seal the pot, and cook at full pressure for 2 to 10 minutes, depending on hardness. Unseal the pressure cooker and drain.

Braised Greens

4 pounds greens, such as chard, escarole,
    kale, collards, mustard, rabe, dandelion,
    or a combination
1 medium onion, chopped

¼ cup olive oil
Pinch of crushed red pepper flakes
Salt and pepper to taste

Trim greens of thick stems and wilted leaves. Place the greens in a clean sink filled with cold water and swish them back and forth to clean them. Lift the greens from the water and shake off the excess water but do not dry.

Cook the onion in the oil in a large heavy pot until softened, about 2 minutes. Add the pepper flakes and the greens. Toss well to coat the greens with oil. Cover the pot and cook for 3 to 4 minutes, stirring once, until the greens have wilted. Uncover and continue cooking until all the water has evaporated, stirring occasionally, about 10 to 12 minutes. Season with salt and pepper. Reserve 1 cup and serve the rest.

Makes 4 servings, plus enough to:
✪ **Reserve ½ cup for Pan-fried Trout with Ham and Capers.**
✪ **Reserve ½ cup for Grits Soufflé.**

Radiatore Carbonara

1 pound radiatore
3 eggs, at room temperature
¼ cup buttermilk, half-and-half, or sour
    cream
¼ cup freshly grated parmesan cheese

2 tablespoons grated romano cheese
✪ **2 slices reserved Honey Baked Ham**
2 teaspoons olive oil
3 tablespoons chopped parsley

Bring a large pot of salted water to a boil and add the radiatore. Cook until tender, about 10 minutes.

Meanwhile, set a large serving bowl in a larger bowl of warm water. Add the eggs and beat lightly. Beat in the buttermilk, parmesan, and romano cheese. Set aside. Dice the reserved ham and cook in the olive oil until lightly crisped and very hot. Keep warm.

When the pasta is done, drain and immediately add it to the egg mixture. Toss well until the pasta is completely coated. Add the meat and parsley and toss. Serve immediately.

Makes 4 servings.

Note: The hot pasta only partially cooks the egg yolks.

Grits Soufflé

3 cups water
Salt and pepper to taste
¾ cup quick grits
¾ cup shredded cheddar cheese (3 ounces)
3 tablespoons butter
✪ **I slice reserved Honey Baked Ham**
✪ **½ cup reserved Braised Greens**

1 cup diced green bell pepper
3 scallions, sliced
3 egg yolks
Dash of hot pepper sauce
2 to 3 tablespoons cornmeal
5 egg whites

Bring the water to a boil and season liberally with salt and pepper. Add the grits in a thin stream, stirring constantly. Simmer for 10 minutes until thick and light. Remove from the heat and stir in the cheddar cheese and 1 tablespoon of the butter.

Meanwhile, chop the reserved ham and reserved greens. Set aside. Cook the bell pepper in 1 tablespoon of the remaining butter over medium-high heat for 1 minute.

continued

Add the scallions and ham and cook for another 2 minutes. Beat this mixture into the cooked grits along with the greens, egg yolks, and hot pepper sauce. Set aside to cool. Grease a 2-quart soufflé dish with the remaining butter and dust the dish with the cornmeal.

Preheat the oven to 400°F.

Beat the egg whites until they form soft peaks. Mix a third of the beaten whites into the cooled grits. Fold in the remaining whites in 2 additions. Pour the batter gently into the soufflé dish. Bake for 30 minutes, or until well browned, fully puffed, and barely jiggling in the center when moved gently. Serve right away.

Makes 4 servings.

Hoppin' John Soup

Dice the reserved ham medium fine. Heat the oil in a large heavy saucepan, add the

✪ **3 slices reserved Honey Baked Ham**
2 teaspoons corn oil
1 medium onion, finely chopped
Pinch of crushed red pepper flakes
½ cup long-grain rice
6 cups chicken broth, canned or homemade

✪ **2 cups reserved Spicy Corn and**
   Black-eyed Peas Succotash
Salt and pepper to taste
1 teaspoon cider vinegar
2 tablespoons chopped parsley

ham, onion, and pepper flakes, and cook over medium heat until the onion has softened, about 2 minutes. Add the rice and toss to coat with oil. Add the chicken broth and simmer for 12 minutes until the rice is barely tender. Add the reserved succotash, salt, and pepper and simmer for 5 more minutes. Stir in the vinegar and parsley and serve.

Makes 4 servings.

Pan-fried Trout with Ham and Capers

○ **1 slice reserved Honey Baked Ham**

○ **½ cup reserved Braised Greens**

2 tablespoons olive oil

4 brook or rainbow trout, boned
(6 to 8 ounces each)

3 tablespoons capers, drained

Juice of 2 lemons

Finely dice the reserved ham and set aside. Coarsely chop the reserved greens and set aside.

Heat 1 tablespoon of the oil in a nonstick skillet. Add the ham and cook for 1 minute. Add the greens and stir until heated through. Transfer to a platter and keep warm. Add the remaining oil to the pan and heat until smoking. Add the trout, and cook over medium-high heat for 3 minutes per side. Add the capers and cook 1 more minute. Remove from the heat, add the lemon juice, and deglaze the pan. Serve the trout on the greens with the liquid in the pan poured over the top.

Makes 4 servings.